For Such a Time as This: Let My People Go, You End-Times Doomsday Sayers!

FOR SUCH A TIME AS THIS: LET MY PEOPLE GO, YOU END-TIMES DOOMSDAY SAYERS!

ERNEST REAGAN CLARK, II
Xulon Press

Xulon Press
2301 Lucien Way #415
Maitland, FL 32751
407.339.4217
www.xulonpress.com

ISBN-13: 9781545610442

Contents

Notes. ix
Acknowledgments xv
Preface xvii
Introduction. xxvii

What is Your Standard? 1
   Should Every Christian of Every Generation Never Sleep? 3
   Who Were the Prophets Speaking To? 6
   What Is Your Standard? 14
   Imminence versus Relevance 22

Prophecy and Prophets. 37
   Measure of a Prophet 39
   Prophetic Timing. 57

Who is "This Generation"? 65

Consummation: End of the World or End of the Age? 98
   Words for World 85
   End of the World, End of a Nation, or End of an Empire? 98
   Consummation of the Old Testament Covenant 106

Coming: What is It and When is It? 121
   Thy Kingdom Come 123
   Coming on Clouds 137

The End Days are Not the Last Days 155
   New Testament Scriptures Designating the End of an Era 157
   Day of the Lord. 168
   Day of Wrath. 177
   The End of the World or End of an Age? 184
   The Last Days/A Little While. 193

Death and Resurrection **203**
    Death under the Old Covenant and the New Covenant. 205
    Resurrection: Past or Future 223

The Thousand-Year Reign **238**
A New Heaven and a New Earth **258**
Not One Jot or Tittle. **271**
The Beast and Other Characters of the Last Days **289**
Conclusion **327**
Recommended Reading Material **343**

Notes

The source that I use when I am studying and comparing biblical versions is the online Blue Letter Bible at https://www.blueletter-bible.org. It has written commentaries, as well as audio and video helps within the tools section. Commentaries are nothing more than man's opinion. I use commentaries just to see if man's interpretation aligns with what the scriptures state, along with extra-biblical historical facts. I will be using many different versions of the Bible to prove that some are better than others. None are perfect, and some are worse than others. Below is a list of abbreviations that I will be using to denote the Bible version being used. I also use my own version a few times just to show that, based on our current language, there is room for improvement.

ASV—American Standard Version	**NIV**—New International Version
DBY—Darby Translation	**NKJV**—New King James Version
ESV—English Standard Version	**NLT**—New Living Translation
HCSB—Holman Christian Standard Bible	**RSV**—Revised Standard Version
HNV—Hebrew Names Version	**TR**—Textus Receptus (Greek Language)
KJV—King James Version	**WEB**—Webster's Bible
NASB—New American Standard Bible	**YLT**—Young's Literal Translation
NET—New English Translation	**ERC**—My Translation

Other Abbreviations

BLB—Blue Letter Bible

NT—New Testament

NTC—New Testament Covenant

NC New Covenant

OT—Old Testament

OTC—Old Testament Covenant

OC—Old Covenant

Suggestions

I suggest that you keep a notebook and a pen handy when reading this material. Make notes of scriptures to read, as well as notations of people, events, nations, and so forth so that you can do your own research, using the Internet. When one acquires their own knowledge from their own efforts, it seems to stick in the mind better. I encourage you to do your own research. There are many things mentioned within the covers of this book that will tweak your interest. Please, follow your instincts and research it for yourself. Do not let the teachings of man be your standard.

Acknowledgments

*T*his study and evolutionary process has taken about thirteen years. As a child, I noticed that what was coming from the pulpit did not match up with what the scriptures stated. When I graduated from high school, I fled from God for many years and was not associated with the church in any way. Looking back, I believe it was to my advantage and not my demise. I believe that if I had stayed affiliated over all of those years, listening to the false teachings, I probably would have become obstinate, unwilling to hear the truth that I have discovered since God kindled a fire within my heart to educate myself to the truth of His word and not the false teachings of man. This has been a process. When I began hearing other views and doing the studies myself, I realized that the standard that most men use in the pulpit is the latest hot-selling book that is attributed to a self-professed prophet. This will be addressed within these pages. There are no prophets today, so says Paul, the greatest of the apostles. What we need today are discerning individuals who use the word of God as their standard and not the teachings of man. If it contradicts the word of God, it is a false teaching that is probably the figment of a very obstinate imagination.

I want to acknowledge my crew at Mars Hill, Inc. I am not a degreed scholar, but I am more than capable to teach and preach a correct theology and eschatology. I have been blessed with the freedom and time to do missionary work in other nations. I have also been blessed with the time to study the word of God and extra-biblical history that spans the timeframe beginning with the Assyrian captivity to the consummation of the Old Covenant with the Jews that ended with the destruction of the temple in AD 70. My CEO and best friend, Marshall Wood, has been a God-send for a time such as this. If not for him, this work would have taken many more years. He made it possible for me to live in another culture for eight months that spoke a different language. This has helped me to truly comprehend the differences in language and idioms that cultures use that can really confuse the foreigner. It can also really confuse the interpreter. This has happened with much of the symbolic language in the scriptures.

I would also like to acknowledge my secretary, Doll Swindle, and salesmen, Wayne Carlisle, Marshall Wood, Jr., Charlie Britton, and Terry Lane. Without them, this endeavor would probably have taken at least another decade. It takes time and due diligence to truly research and study all the avenues that leads one to the real Truth. I pray that this endeavor will begin a process in the world that leads to the healing of the nations.

Preface

"*I*'m not what I once was, but I am not yet what I shall be." That statement can be positive or negative, depending on where you are headed. I know that when I was a youngster, I had a relationship with my Father who is in heaven, but I turned my back on Him when I approached my teen years. I rebelled because I wanted to live my life on my terms. I walked that path for about twenty-two to twenty-five years. If I had made that statement when I was sixteen, it would not have had the same meaning as it does today. I was heading in the wrong direction when I was sixteen. By the time I was thirty-five, I realized that this world has nothing in it that could fill the void in my heart. So, I repented and came back to my Father who is in heaven. Today I seek Him daily. When I make that statement today, it has a totally different meaning.

I have become a very passionate person. I have a firm belief in my Lord and Savior, Jesus Christ. There are times when I am expressing my faith to others, and it may appear that I am angry, when I am in fact anything but angry. Passion can come across as anger at times, so I must be careful when expressing myself. I study the Bible more than anyone I know. I also read extra-biblical sources with an open mind. I even read stuff that I know I will disagree with just to get a clear picture of what others are teaching and preaching. That is the only way that one can refute false teachings. It also affirms my faith when I see false teaching that is so obviously so, but I would have fallen for years ago.

I have heard radio commentators and preachers state that your eschatological (end-times) view is not essential for salvation. I believe that God would take issue with this statement. Here is a better way to look at this view. Is vision (eyesight) essential for life? Are arms and legs essential for life? All men of all beliefs know that an individual who does not have sight is handicapped, or limited in life. Those who are without arms or legs are classified, with the blind, as disabled. If you have a false view of scripture you are also limited. A false end-time view is very damaging. It is critical that one has a proper understanding of the "end" that the Bible prophecies. A proper view of the scriptures takes down barriers that have hindered intellectuals from coming to a saving knowledge of Jesus. If you are a thinker and a student of the Bible, then you have either realized that there are either errors in the scriptures or there are errors in the understanding of the teachings of the Bible. If you are ignorant of what I am stating here, then you are not discerning what you are reading in the Bible or you are not reading the Bible. I am not refuting the Bible in this work. I am refuting false teaching that is prevalent in the world today, not just in the United States.

Sadly, the average Christian is not aware that there are several end-times views (eschatology), but the majority of preachers are preaching one based on dispensationalism. I have spent much time researching dispensationalism. It is where the "rapture theory" has its roots. Yes, rapture is a theory, not a fact, kind of like evolution, maybe worse. It was introduced around 1830 by John Nelson Darby. If the average person were to hear the eschatological views laid out by a knowledgeable person, they would change their beliefs. I will address the scripture where rapture theory was derived from and will expand upon it with other scripture from the same author, Paul, where he is more descriptive within this work.

When I was a child I thought as a child. Today I am a man, and I think nothing like I used to think. I am not a defeatist. Rapture theology is defeatism. I believe that the word of God will be victorious in this world, and though that is not what is being preached in the overwhelming majority of churches, it is what the Bible says. I have an open mind but a discerning mind. When I hear a lie about the word of God, I know it immediately. It took many years of biblical study to come to this point. That is why man is admonished in the Scriptures to teach his children the word of God every day and in every way, but you must be knowledgeable or you will be a false teacher.

The average professing Christian today has made their standard the teachings of man, even when it contradicts the scriptures and the facts of history. These believe the beliefs of a radio, television, popular mega-selling authors, or local church preachers. If most were discerning, they would notice that many of these contradict themselves regularly, sometimes even within the same sermon. They also contradict each other, but mostly they contradict the scriptures. God's people are to be of one mind. This is a sign of true believers. There is so much false teaching out there today that most people do not even realize all of the issues.

Where are the Bereans today? Are there any out there that have made the word of God their standard? This is the standard that God has provided to all of humanity as the stalwart way to live a life beholden to Him. If one is ignorant of the scriptures, then he is bound to be beholden to the beliefs of others. Only one who is ignorant of the scriptures has a false belief that there are prophets today. No, there are no prophets today. Prophecy was sealed when the temple was destroyed in AD 70, so says the scripture, as will be revealed. What we have today are profiteers, those seeking to profit from a lie, whether they realize it to be a lie or not. Regardless, whether out of ignorance or out of evil, the results are the same—failure. We will address this in a huge way with scriptural, as well as historical proof.

I have noticed today that the average churchgoer is not a student of the Bible. I know people who have been attending church for fifty-plus years, yet they claim they do not know what the Bible says. Several come to mind whom I have asked personally what they think the Bible says about a particular issue. They tell me that they do not know what the Bible says on that issue. They stated that they do not understand the Bible. Well, one of the gifts of the Spirit is discernment. If you read the Bible every single day for years, yet you do not comprehend what you are reading, then why waste your time? I have a theory about this; actually, I believe it is more fact than theory. If you read the word of God regularly and you believe what you are reading, yet the preacher in the pulpit, on television, or on radio, contradicts what you have read, well, after a while you will lose all confidence in your discernment. Actually, you may be far more discerning than the teacher.

Is ignorance an excuse for violating the law? My understanding is that it is not an excuse. "Well, officer, I did not know that I was in a 35 mph zone." "Sorry, that is no excuse," says the officer. It will not fly in court, either. The judge will not allow ignorance to be a defense.

There is scripture that I really used to struggle with because it seemed to go against the nature of God. During his kingship, David was enticed by Satan to take a census. This was done out of a sense of pride. It would give David a sense of security that was of man and not of God. It was a sign of distrust toward God and trust in the numbers that would be David's military. When the census had been taken, God gave David some choices as to the punishment. What would ensue would be the death of over seventy thousand men. They died of pestilence, a fatal epidemic, which may have been the bubonic plague.

I really had a difficult time with this. Over seventy thousand men were killed because of the sin of David? I do not question the sovereignty of God, but I really had a hard time with this. Well, the law states that when a census is taken, a tax must be paid by the ones numbered. Nothing is mentioned about a tax being collected during this census. Guess what the biblical mandate was for violating this law? Pestilence. Maybe these men did not pay the tax, and the others did. Either way, David lost a great many fighting forces. There is no mention of the tax in this instance, but the penalty that was carried out was the penalty for violation of this law.

Ignorance of the law is no excuse with God. Write it on your heart. Jesus stated that He did not come to do away with or annul the law but to fulfill it. What does this mean? Well, the wages of sin was death for all before the New Testament Covenant, saint and pagan alike. The saint had only the hope of a future resurrection. Guess what the wages for sin are today? Tis still death. The repentant sinner is saved by grace. He shall not experience death. He will rise when he takes his last breath on planet Earth. The unrepentant sinner shall experience death and shall descend to perdition.

> When thou takest the sum of the children of Israel after their number, then shall they give every man a ransom for his soul unto the LORD, when thou numberest them; that there be no plague among them, when thou numberest them. This they shall give, every one who passeth among them that are numbered, half a shekel after the shekel of the sanctuary: (a shekel is twenty gerahs) an half shekel shall be the offering of the LORD. Every one who passeth among them that are numbered, from twenty years old and above, shall give an offering unto the LORD. (Exodus 30:12–14, KJV)

> So Gad came to David, and told him, and said unto him, Shall seven years of famine come unto thee in thy land? Or wilt thou flee three months before thine enemies, while they pursue thee? Or that there be three days' pestilence in thy land? Now advise, and see what answer I shall return to him that sent me. (2 Samuel 24:13, KJV)

The law to Moses was applicable through all generations of the Jewish nation until its destruction in AD 70. The penalty for violation was a plague, or equivalent term is *pestilence*. Nowhere does it say that David ordered his men to collect the ransom, nor does it say that one was turned in. It seems mighty peculiar that the penalty for violation of the Mosaic Law was the very one that was rendered. Now, this is an argument from silence, but it sure seems to put the onus back on man and not on God. Man failed to pay what God had required; therefore man paid the price for failure.

My intention with this point is to make a point that is so important. Ignorance of the law is no excuse. Ignorance of His word shall be no excuse, either. Men have twisted the scriptures to fit their preconceived notions, as do evolutionary scientists. I recommend a book, *Icons of Evolution*, if you want to consider that your children and grandchildren in grade school and college alike are being fed lies that have been proven to be hoaxes as far back as the 1950s, yet they are still in the textbooks today as if they are facts. Make note and do an online search.

There are people in the church today who have been fed with unscriptural heresies that were derived from a rich 1800s heretical environment from which Mormonism and the Jehovah's Witnesses were born. Both of these sects were born out of a false end-times understanding. It has filtered into all denominations of the church today, and some are worse than others, but even the best are getting progressively worse in their views on the "latter days." I pray that this will incite the truly discerning individual to become alert and aware that there is a price to be paid for truth. It takes much time and a passion for the Truth that is the Father, Son, and Holy Spirit. The scriptures say what they mean and mean what they say, in spite of what you have heard over the radio, television, or pulpit.

I pray that after you have parsed through this book that you will have developed a hunger for truth and a more discerning heart and mind, so you can begin your evolution as a human being and become a friend of God. There is no species evolution among mankind. There is evolution among humanity. God desires that no man remain a babe in Christ all of his days. His desire is that newborn Christians evolve to the point where they can walk on water for Him. The greater and more mature the number of men walking on water, the lesser the waves of destruction in this life will be. Ignorance shall be no excuse on that day when you take your last breath in this life. You shall either rise or fall. If you are ignorant of God and His ways in this day and time, it is because the things of this world have become your god. A passion for God will create a burning desire within the true believer to educate himself to the nth degree for the glory of God, the edification of the church, and the growth of the kingdom.

I will be addressing many issues that are imminent for the times we live in and relevant for all times. The standard that you choose to derive your decisions on will determine the quality of life you experience and the quantity of life. Your worldview comes from your standard. A faulty standard can compromise your life. Your standard, the Bible, may be perfection, but a wrong translation or interpretation can destroy lives. I hope to correct some errors that have been around for many years.

We will be looking at the concept of prophecy and the timing of prophecy. We will also reveal that when all prophecy has been fulfilled, there will be no more prophets. Is this in our past or future? Reality is not what we think it to be. It is what it is—reality. Many think today that we are the last generation to experience life on this earth. I have heard many say that we are living in the last or latter days. The generation that experiences the wrath of God is not the last generation to experience life on this earth, and we will allow the standard of scripture and historical fact to confirm this.

What was the *end* that the Old Testament prophets prophesied? Was it the *end* of the *world*? If you have a faulty translation of the Bible or have been taught by someone who has used this as their standard, then you have been deceived about the end-times. I was deceived for many years until I began my own journey that God put me on. I was deceived as a child, and insomnia that persisted for well over a decade set in. I fell away in my early teen years, probably because of false teachers. I dare say it was to my benefit and not my demise, looking back on it. With all of the end-times garbage out there today, mostly coming from "Christian" sources, I have risen to the challenge to ferret out heresy and point it out. If you were not affected by it like I was as a child, there is no way that you could have the passion about it that I do today. It is time to end the lies and for men to man up and admit they were had. Those who continue to cause little ones, not just children but babes in Christ, to stumble shall have sheol as a price to pay one day.

What if we get to heaven and are asked by Jesus if we believed in His word? What would your response be? Most would state, "Of course I believed Your word." At that point, He will state to most "No, you did not believe my word. You did not believe that the generation that walked the earth with me experienced everything I told them they would experience. I told them that the temple would fall and not one stone would be left unturned. I told them that they would not have gone through all the streets of Israel before I came back. Well, I came back and did all that I promised. Not one jot or tittle was left unfulfilled. While you were waiting on me, I was waiting on you. The believers are the leaves on the tree of life, and they are for the healing of the nations. I am the Tree of Life. You need to go yonder because that is where all the ones who did not believe my word shall be. You shall be with the "least" group in heaven. You chose to believe the traditions of man over the word of God."

If Jesus were to ask you what eschatological (end-times) view you had, what would be your response? There are many views. I recommend that you do your own research on this. Most have been brought up on Dispensationalism. Dispensationalists believe that most of the end-time prophecies are yet to be fulfilled. Full preterists believe that all prophecy has been fulfilled and partial preterists believe that most prophecy has been fulfilled. There are variants within the Dispensationalist view. The average churchgoer is not even aware of these views. Please do your own research on this.

Jesus stated that "this generation shall not pass" until all these things take place. He stated to His apostles that they would not have even gone through the streets of Israel before He comes back. He also stated that not one jot or tittle would be left unfulfilled. If Jesus asks me what my beliefs are when I get to heaven, I will have to state to Him that I am a jot and tittle man. At this point He will likely ask "Why did you take that view, seeing that it is a rarity?" I will state "Well, I pray that I was correct, but I just believed what your word stated." At this point I believe that I will hear, "Well done, My good and faithful servant. You are a rarity. Most do not believe what my Bible states. Most believe the traditions of man and not the teachings of My word."

Jesus asked His disciples to pray "Thy kingdom come." We will define His kingdom. We will show where His kingdom is, what His kingdom is, and when His kingdom is. All are very important. Most are very confused on each of these aspects of the kingdom. We are going to shine a light on it. I also hope to enlighten all to the symbolism that is used in the scriptures. Many take what is not meant to be taken literally and try to beat it to death. Keep heading in that direction, and you just may arrive there. Death is not in my future. I seek to enlighten this world and not to blind it by lighting my own fires.

Many today are awaiting the day that Jesus comes floating overhead in the clouds. This would be the prophesied day of His coming. Well, was it to be a day of pleasure, a joyous and wonderful day? We will enlighten you to the reality of the coming day of the Lord. There are many days in the scriptures that man has a faulty view on. Were they literal twenty-four-hour days? Is Resurrection day in our future? What is the new heaven and earth that the scripture speaks of? If the old was to pass away and the new was to come, then what happens to this old earth? You will be enlightened beyond your imagination if you have been a victim of the current end-times doomsday hype.

I recommend for the truly hungry and astute readers to get a notepad and pen to take notes. I mention several names that you need to do an online search to see it for yourself. There are many scriptural references that you will want to check out for yourself and I highly encourage this. I also encourage you to go to the Blue Letter Bible online and do the word searches for yourself. Always look at the Textus Receptus version and see what the word it uses for the English word, such as "world." The Textus Receptus will use any of the following:

1. *kosmos*
2. *aion*
3. *oikoumenē*

The key with this word is to look up the Greek definition and see what the writer was actually communicating and not what the translators are communicating. *Kosmos, aion,* and *oikoumenē,* in no way have the same definition. Yet, many Bible versions insert *world* where each of these Greek terms are used. To know what God has said, you need to know what the ones who documented the scriptures were communicating to their contemporaries. It is also paramount to see how each word is used in other places to get a true sense and definition of the word. The documented definitions are not sufficient to reveal the true meaning of each word. The key at this point is to use the Textus Receptus version and search for that particular word and then look at the other versions to see which actually gives the best translation. You will be shocked at what you discover. The key, however, is that you discover this for yourself. What the astute will discover will be enough to truly set a person free. I will state this as fact. The end is nowhere in our sight. If you do the work for yourself, you will see what I am referring to. It is a real eye-opener.

There are many scriptures, as well as statements of mine, that are relevant to several subject matters within these covers. Therefore, do not be alarmed when you see the repetitive nature of this study. It is all relevant and very important to drive the point home. If you are a regular church attender, you are probably used to this. You hear the same message pretty much each week. Hmmm—what is one to do after salvation? The weightier issues are the ones that will step on the toes of many. Therefore those weightier issues are left unaddressed. Much is repeated in this study to make a point. I just wanted to make mention of it because I noticed it.

There is much talk today in the public square about the times we are living in. Most involved in any denomination of the church today have a false view of the end-times. Social media and YouTube videos abound with end-times stories and hype. We will address some of the end-times characters mentioned in the scriptures that will be truth. There is a lot of finger pointing going on out there out of sheer ignorance. I will go through a list of many of the end-times characters or events, and describe them based on scripture and extra-biblical sources that were contemporary with the times the events took place. Has any of Daniel's prophecy been fulfilled? What about Jesus' prophecies, as well as John the Revelator's? It is my desire to shine a floodlight on this subject that will continue to shine long after I am alive and gone.

False teachings seem to flourish, and truth is always killed. That is a strange thing, but it is scriptural. People love to have their ears tickled. The false prophets tickled their ears and found favor with the people and the kings. The true prophets told truth and were killed. People do not like truth because it does not tickle the ears. Actually, what is within the covers of this compilation should tickle your heart. Truth sets a man free, and man needs to be set free from all the end-times lies out there today. The end is past. I hope this is the beginning for many and that it brightens the paths for the many who are stumbling. I have come along for such a time as this. Let my people go, you end-times doomsday sayers!

Introduction

*O*ver my lifetime, I have heard many preachers. I attended three churches, all of different denominations, before I graduated high school. One was a Presbyterian, another was Southern Methodist, and the other was a Baptist church. Since I came back into the church in 1998, I have only been affiliated with one denomination, but I have watched a lot of televangelists up until 2006 or 2007. I heard Pat Robertson prophesy that there would be an attack on American soil that year affiliated with Islam. I quit watching TBN that day. By the way, there was no attack.

I travel quite a bit and listen to many radio preachers. I am not sure how many times I have heard preachers speak on the event recorded in Second Kings where Elijah is taken up to heaven in a fiery chariot, but I have heard it many times over the span of my life. For someone who is not a Bible scholar, it would seem that this is truth. I imagine it is also taught in many seminaries because I have never heard a preacher contradict the teaching. Well, I am going to contradict it.

The first mention of Elijah in the Bible is in First Kings 17 when he confronts King Ahab. Ahab's reign was either 874–869 BC or 853–850 BC, according to the source you use. There is inconsistency in man's work, but there is none in the word of God. The king who reigned when Elijah turned his prophetic responsibilities over to Elisha was Jehu. His reign was from about 841–814 BC. Again, there is inconsistency in man's research. So, Jehu was king when Elijah left in the chariot, and Elisha took over.

The following scripture verses are during the reign of King Jehoram, king of Judah:

> And a letter came to him from Elijah the prophet, saying,
> "Thus says the LORD, the God of David your father,
> 'Because you have not walked in the ways of Jehoshaphat

your father, or in the ways of Asa king of Judah, but have
walked in the way of the kings of Israel and have enticed
Judah and the inhabitants of Jerusalem into whoredom,
as the house of Ahab led Israel into whoredom, and also
you have killed your brothers, of your father's house,
who were better than you, behold, the LORD will bring
a great plague on your people, your children, your wives,
and all your possessions, and you yourself will have a
severe sickness with a disease of your bowels, until your
bowels come out because of the disease, day by day."
(2 Chronicles 21:12–15, ESV)

This letter was written a few years after Elijah had his "fiery chariot"
experience. We know that letters are not hand delivered from heaven to
earth. God used His prophets to speak to man. This hand-delivered letter
was written on earth by Elijah. Most preachers do not read ahead to see
this verse, or they think that it was just another account in a different
book of the Bible that obviously is not chronological with Kings. Well,
the chronology that matters is the order of the kings. Jehoram of Judah
follows his father, Jehoshaphat, as king, and this would have been after
the kingship of Ahab and Ahaziah in the Northern Kingdom, whose rule
paralleled Jehoshaphat, Jehoram's father. The hand-delivered letter was
obviously delivered after the time that Elijah was supposedly taken up
to heaven. Elijah was obviously not taken to heaven, since about nine
hundred years later, Jesus states that no man has ever gone up to heaven.
John penned his gospel, according to the majority of scholars, at least
twenty years after Jesus' ascension. If the thief had gone to be with Jesus
on crucifixion day, then John surely would have stated that Jesus statement was prior to the introduction of the new and better covenant, but
there is no mention of it. The state of things when John penned his gospel
account was still as it was when Jesus was on this earth, or he would have
stated otherwise. The Old Testament Covenant was still in effect but was
waxing old. Elijah was taken to another place on this earth where he likely
would have experienced peace. He had been put through the wringer as
a prophet of God. Scripture does not contradict itself. This is why it is
crucial to develop a true understanding of the Old Testament and the New
Testament. One does not conflict with or contradict the other. If it appears
to do so, then what is wrong is either our perception of the scripture, the
translation of the scripture is faulty, we are not knowledgeable about the
entire Bible, or all three. I believe that by the time you are finished with

this material, you will see the truth in this statement. Yes, there are faulty translations out there, as well as false perceptions and false teachings. What is your standard? Is it the word of God, or is it the teachings of man? I know of no one who would admit that their standard is the teachings of man, but issues addressed in this book will reveal that this is the case.

The main point here is that no man had ever gone up to heaven at the time that John penned his Gospel account, which was twenty-plus years after Jesus' ascension, according to the overwhelming majority of theologians and scholars. This would also be about 900 years after Elijah turned his responsibilities as prophet over to Elisha. The proof is in the scriptures. It has to be parsed out with an open mind. *"And no man hath ascended up to heaven, but he that came down from heaven, even the Son of man which is in heaven"* (John 3:13, KJV). This is Jesus speaking here, not John. John penned this two decades after Jesus ascended to heaven. Something else had to happen before man entering into heaven would become a reality. That which was new had not yet come. God is patient and longsuffering. He gave the generation that killed Messiah forty years to repent and then the end would come—the end of the era in AD 70. The scriptures do not contradict each other. If there appears to be a contradiction, man needs to give serious attention to the interpretation of the passages in question. What you will find is that man has misinterpreted the scriptures. Actually, what I see as being the biggest problem is that scripture is no longer the standard to many preachers, teachers, and others.

"And all the prophets who have spoken, from Samuel and those who came after him, also proclaimed these days" (Acts 3:24, ESV). The current standard that most preachers use is the teaching of other men. I will give an example here. I recently pointed out to a preacher that Acts 3:24 is the answer to the timing of biblical prophecy. He kind of shrugged me off. He stated that he believed what so and so (radio or television preacher) believed. Well, I thought to myself, why would any preacher allow the teaching of other men to become their standard? If scripture seems to conflict or contradict itself, think about the interpretation and where you got the interpretation. It very well may be that you have been given a false interpretation. Also, we must look at other verses in the scriptures that concern the same issue. What do these verses state? In addition, timing changes everything. Since when did the wisdom of Solomon become foolishness? In times of crisis, things that are the norm become foolishness that could get you killed, but would be considered sin in times of peace. Is it not wise to store up a generous inheritance for your children's children? Proverbs states just this, yet prophecy in the

New Testament seems to contradict this. Times of turmoil change every-thing. The first-century church was about to experience the wrath of God in AD 70 for rejecting Messiah. The wisdom of Solomon is wisdom and not foolishness. However, when all hell breaks out on this earth, survival becomes paramount over storing up treasures. Your treasures could get you killed in such tumultuous times.

If you were a young male who was single and knew that war was about to break out in your nation within the next few years, and that you would either have to battle or flee, it would be foolish to get married and have a few babies. It would also be foolish to build a house. It would all be lost. It would be given to others if it were not destroyed. Solomon's wisdom is still wisdom today. Chaotic times change things. If you truly believe that the end is near, why aren't you selling your goods? Why aren't you sharing all that you have with others? Why are you buying new automobiles and upgrading your home? It appears to me that people who believe this end-times garbage are not being true to their beliefs. I see none in my area fleeing to the mountains. What I see is them fleeing to vacation destinations and pleasures of this world, yet they believe that the end is near. I have a true belief about the times that we live in, and the end is not near. The end of your life may be near, but this world will continue on. Eventually there will be a generation that sees the light, and the leaves on the Tree of Life shall be for the healing of the nations. God will honor that generation because that will be a wise generation that has overcome rapture theory, as well as the theory of evolution. Both are ignorant and deadly. Woe be unto those who propagate such heresies.

When I was a child I can remember an experience that I had in church one morning. I was between nine and twelve years old. I never discussed this with anyone as a child, as I was very shy, and maybe because of that "man thing." Men like to keep things to themselves that they do not understand. The church had invited a preacher from somewhere else to preach a "revival" service. This would have been between 1974 and 1976. Recently I began to contemplate the message that was preached. I certainly cannot remember everything that was preached, but I certainly remember the things that will haunt a little fellow. Now, maybe forty or forty-two years later, all of the hype going on right now about "end time" events has brought all of those memories back.

It was a Sunday morning, and my mother, two sisters, and I were about midway back in the church pews. This preacher was telling us of an event that was about to happen in the next few years. I do not recall the exact year, but I knew that the time was at hand by the language he used. What I remember vividly is that he spoke about Russia. At that time in America, real history that matters was taught in our schools. I very well knew what Russia was. Our nation had fought against communistic socialism tooth and nail in the twentieth century, and at the time, we were in the Cold War. The preacher spoke about how convenient it was for the Russian army that our community was just eighty to ninety miles from Mobile Bay. He spoke of how they would roll into Mobile Bay in their warships. They would then disembark the ships and begin a long march up Highway 45 to my hometown. When they got here, he talked about how they would kill opposition, take hostages, driving stakes through their ears to deafen them and putting their eyes out. When they had destroyed this area and conquered and enslaved the people, they would then march us back to their ships and take us back to Russia to be put into gulags (forced labor camps).

I recollect that on that very night I lay awake in my bed all night imagining the soldiers killing my family and friends. I could see pictures in my mind of soldiers driving stakes through my mother and dad's ears and blinding them. I even sat up and cried out to God. I remember making a statement to God that night that I have never forgotten, but I do believe there have been times when I misinterpreted the meaning. I remember as if it was yesterday stating to God "No! Not me! I am too bashful and shy. That is not what I want to do with my life." I will wait until I get to heaven to ask Him, but I do believe that I am doing His will for my life now. I have gotten off on some wild goose chases in the past.

I was terrified with what I had heard that day in church. Beginning that night, I developed insomnia that would take me into my late twenties. It seems that after that sermon, I was never able to go to bed and go to sleep quickly. I used to go to bed before I had heard that sermon and never remembered my head hitting the pillow. I was usually out in ten to fifteen minutes of turning out the lights. However, beginning with that sermon, I never went to bed again and experienced rest and relaxation until several hours went by. For fourteen to sixteen years, I would go to bed and toss and turn many hours before I would eventually pass out. It is not as though I thought about that sermon for all those years. I probably thought about it for a few months after I heard it and then it passed into the recesses of my memory; however, the damage had been done.

I suppose that I went around thirty-eight years without even remembering or thinking about that sermon until recently. I can recollect my first memory of going to bed after hearing that sermon back in the mid-1970s and actually sleeping through the night and not even remember my head hitting the pillow. This occurred in 1990 when I had moved to Fort Walton Beach, Florida, to work for a family business. I have slept well ever since, other than the normal disturbances that go on in life. I do not know what triggered the end of the sleepless night syndrome, whether it was a change in environment or the sound of the waves on the beachfront. All I knew was that I liked it!

I am not sure what year I fell away from the church, but it was shortly after I graduated from high school in 1981. In 1998, a prodigal son returned to his Father who is in heaven. Ever since then I have had an insatiable desire to know the word of God. I watch virtually no television now. I read the Bible and study books, such as the writings of Eusebius, Josephus, C. S. Lewis, and the like, as well as books on creation/evolution. I see people compromising their lives today as false teachings of end times events prevail in our culture.

As I recently began to contemplate my very negative experience with the same teachings back in the mid '70s, I realized that there was highly likely something that triggered that preacher into preaching what he preached that day, as there are preachers in the church doing today. They are motivated by something, and it is not the Holy Spirit, but listening to these end-times preachers today and reading their books. This is just a theory of mine, but I dare say there is more evidence to back it up than there is for evolution. I would say that this preacher that freaked me out in that service and affected my sleeping habits over the next decade and a half highly likely read the book by Hal Lindsey, *The Late Great Planet Earth*. I know that he mentions in the book a specific year that the rapture would take place.

If you do any research on Jim Jones and the notorious "Kool-Aid" drinkers of the Guyana incidence of 1978 that resulted in the death of 918 people, you will quickly see that he was subject to "end-times" preaching and influences. I did a bit of Internet research on him and found that he was looking for a safe haven from a nuclear attack. Originally, he had heard that Belo Horizonte, Brazil, was a safe place in case of a nuclear war. When he went to Brazil to check out the place, he also visited Guyana, which is where the infamous Jonestown Kool-Aid killing would take place. By the way, do your research. It is very interesting that this man even had influence over people in high places. If these people had biblical wisdom, they would have separated themselves from him. He was a communist and a community organizer. My point, though, is that due to the timing of the Jim Jones "Kool-Aid" incidence and the timing of the events prophesied by Hal Lindsey's book, it definitely appears that he read this book and was influenced by it.

Harold Camping, a radio speaker in California, prophesied that the rapture would take place in 1994. Many people sold their homes and gave up their life savings in preparation for this event. Well, time always bears out a false prophet. His dates came and went, and nothing happened. Lives were destroyed, and people were broke due to listening to the false teachings of an ignorant man. At least these people were true to their convictions. What I find amazing is that seventeen years later, he pulled the same stunt again. He prophesied the rapture would take place in 2011, I believe in May, but it did not happen, so he revised it to October of 2011. Well, we are all still here. I dare say that if he is even in heaven today, he will be considered least for all eternity.

Men fall for this garbage because they do not understand the scriptures. Nowhere in the Bible does it talk about a rapture. It speaks of the resurrection of the dead and the living being transformed on that day. Resurrection Day (R-Day) and Judgment Day (J-Day) are associated with the same end-time event. The consummation of the Old Testament covenant was the culmination of the judgment of Israel and the Day of Resurrection. This occurred in AD 70. That is another chapter, but this was a good place to introduce it since most people are familiar with these "doomsday sayers" that continue to prophesy the end of the world. Scriptures prophesy the end of the Old Testament covenant era, not the end of the world.

There are young children today being subjected to the same end-times garbage that took place in the 1970s. You can see it in the countenances of some of these young ones. There are those who have no comprehension of historical reality about what the prophets prophesied, yet are in pulpits today preaching lies about reality. They may have a "sheol" of a price to pay one day also. Now, this price could be to be considered the least in the kingdom of God for all eternity, or it could be something else. Men that are not aware of historic reality of fulfilled prophecy are not men that God has put behind pulpits. These are men who chose the pulpit for themselves. False teachings in the church have driven many away from the church. Many have fled the church over the last generation due to an ignorance of the men in the pulpit, spouting out that we are living in the latter days. If Jesus and the apostles told their contemporaries that they were living in the last days and the last days are still going on about 2000 years later, then where is the end? No, Jesus and His apostles were not ignorant of the times they were living in. They were also not ignorant enough to believe that the events prophesied would end this world. What they knew was that they were about to go through "sheol" on this earth for the betterment of the coming age that was on the horizon.

The law was still in affect when Jesus left this world, contrary to what most believe. What is your standard, the word of God, or the teachings of man? This is my standard: *"And no man hath ascended up to heaven, but he that came down from heaven, even the Son of man which is in heaven"* (John 3:13, KJV). Again, this is Jesus speaking here. He was speaking to Nicodemus, the Pharisee, a ruler of the Jews. Notice that John did not state "except the thief on the cross." Scripture is truth, and all versions of the scripture attest, as does the KJV, that no man had ever gone to heaven at that time. If the New and Better Covenant had already taken effect, surely John would have stated that "Since Jesus made this statement, things have changed. Man is now allowed into heaven, but not until Jesus' death." Well, it was not until Jesus' death that the Old Testament Covenant would reign. It would reign until the waning days of that generation and the time for the fulfillment of Gods timing. The Old Covenant had to be consummated, and it was still in the apostles' future. Jesus did not tell the thief that he would be with Him in heaven on that day. There are no punctuation marks in the ancient Greek or Hebrew languages. The translators of the scriptures added the punctuation marks. I will make a remark here. "I tell you today, you will die." Will you die today? I doubt it. Now, if I state "I tell you, today you will die" and you do not die today, then I am a false prophet. Actually, there are no prophets today. Prophecy has been sealed. I did not state previously that you would die this day. I am stating that you will die eventually, but I am stating it today.

Jesus did not go to heaven on that day. He went to perdition. The wages for sin was not heaven. The wages for sin was death, and it still is for the unrepentant. Jesus paid the price. He even stated after His resurrection to Mary, *"Do not touch me. I have not yet ascended to My Father"* (paraphrase John 20:17). I have heard many preachers over the years state that the thief went to heaven with Jesus on that day. Well, they are wrong. They have allowed the teachings of men that they respect to be their authority and not the word of God. There are many instances where such as this has occurred. There are no discrepancies in the scriptures. The scriptures do not contradict themselves. If you believe that they do, then you need to adjust your views. One must have knowledge of all scripture to truly comprehend what any of it states. Anyone who believes that the thief on the cross went to heaven that day has a wrong understanding of that verse due to John's written account of Jesus' words to Nicodemus penned by John about twenty years later in John 3:13. If you are wrong on this very small matter, how much more scripture have you misinterpreted? This is serious stuff that will have everlasting consequences.

I am shocked at all the false views in the church today about the end times that are prophesied in the Bible. Our current generation is not the first to experience such lies and twisting of scripture. The 1800s experienced such falsehood as this. The difference in the issue today is the many forms of media that spread information rapidly, including the Internet, books, social media, television, and so on. In the 1800s, the Jehovah's Witnesses and the Mormon religions were born out of this heretical teaching. In the 1800s, information traveled slowly. Generally, these false religions were off-shoots of a conservative Protestant denomination. Back then, you would be dismissed from a church for teaching such heresy that went against the reality of the scriptures. Individuals would be run off from a church, and likely a few members would go with them. Therefore, they would go out and begin their own denomination, sect, or cult. Because of the schism in the body of Christ, this is the result. When there is no unity, you will get all kinds of off-shoots, and many will be propagators of lies and heresy. If the church was united, this would not be possible.

Today there are many out there who are posting stuff on the Internet that is being accepted by at least half of the professing Christians, if not the majority. I see stuff getting posted on social media by people who I am at least acquainted with that really does not surprise me. This end-times garbage is rampant today. This kind of garbage wreaks havoc on one's life in ways that he or she is not even aware. It can really have an adverse effect on young males. I know. I was a victim.

In the past eighteen years, I have really evolved as a Christian. There have been weeks that I have spent well over twenty hours reading the Bible. Chunk in all the other research that I do with extra-biblical sources, and that number goes to well above thirty hours. God has blessed me with time, and I am no leech. I am a business owner who has been blessed to have a crew that I can count on to take care of business, so I can take care of what I feel God has apportioned to me.

I have always noticed that there are men in the pulpit who state a thing about a particular verse in the Bible that just does not make sense. There are many, many verses in the Bible that get twisted by man to fit a preconceived end-times view, yet that is not what the scripture states. We will look at many verses throughout this endeavor that will make this point.

In 2003, I bought a new vehicle and had an after-market satellite system installed. At that time not many, if any, came with factory-installed satellite radio. I began listening to Hank Hanegraaff, president of the Christian Research Institute. His radio program, *Bible Answer Man*, came on at 5 o'clock pm central time. Today it is on Sirius Satellite Radio channel 131. I noticed that what he was stating made the scriptures come to life. He was not contradicting the scriptures, as do many in the pulpit. Over the years, I have come to do my own studies. I do not allow any man to be my standard.

Hank Hanegraaff contradicts false teachers and calls them out. I even heard a preacher state something negative about his radio program because of his willingness to call a lie a lie and false teachers false teachers. Well, that is what Jesus, John the Baptist, Paul, Peter, and the Old Testament prophets did. It got them killed. Iron sharpens iron. Iron will not sharpen banana pudding or paper.

My standard is the word of God. If the word of God is your standard, you will surpass your teachers in knowledge. The Holy Spirit is the best Teacher. He will make Himself known to those who seek Him in Spirit and in Truth. The Truth is His word. If the teachings of man are your standard, then you are bound to be misled. At the end of this book, I will list some resources that have helped me to evolve as a Christian. Odds are that I do not agree with every statement in any of them, but they will make you think and begin your own process of evolving from a babe in Christ to a fully functional light-bearing believer.

There are denominations and seminaries that quote the teachings of certain men as though they were quoting scripture. They attribute certain men as being the "early Church fathers." Well, Jesus is the Foundation of the church, and His apostles were the "early Church fathers." I am sorry, but Irenaeus and Hippolytus do not qualify as Church fathers. Their teachings contradict the scriptures, as do some of Augustine's teachings. Anyone who contradicts the teachings of the scripture is a false teacher. You can be spot on with the issue of a particular scripture, but if there is a time issue with the scripture and you are wrong about the timing, then God Almighty will consider you a false teacher. To teach that a past event is in our future is heresy and a sure mark of a false teacher. I will assure you that Hitler did not deem himself to be an evil man. He was just living out his true beliefs. He believed in Darwinian evolution. He truly believed that his was a superior race over others. His ignorance led to the destruction of millions. He lived out his beliefs. Most false teachers are in the same situation today as they were in the time of the apostles.

These people lived out their false beliefs. Regardless of whether out of ignorance or out of evil, the results are the same, and the judgment just well may be the same. Most evil men are just living out their beliefs. Most ignorant men are just living out their beliefs. Regardless of intentions, the results are the same, and likely, the judgment will be the same.

All believers that believe this false end times teaching today just may be asked one day by Jesus "Why did you not believe My word? Why did you allow the superimpositions of man to become your standard? You have caused many to stumble. You shall be declared least in the kingdom of God forevermore." The scriptures are my standard and not the teachings of man, but we also need to consider the original language above any interpretations. Let's get it on!

WHAT IS YOUR STANDARD?

Should All Christians of Every Generation Never Sleep?

But of the times and the seasons, brethren, ye have no need that I write unto you. For yourselves know perfectly that the day of the Lord so cometh as a thief in the night. For when they shall say, peace and safety; then sudden destruction cometh upon them, as travail upon a woman with child; and they shall not escape. But ye, brethren, are not in darkness, that that day should overtake you as a thief. Ye are all the children of light, and the children of the day: we are not of the night, nor of darkness. Therefore let us not sleep, as do others; but let uzs watch and be sober. (1 Thessalonians 5:1–6, KJV)

Watch ye therefore: for ye know not when the master of the house cometh, at even, or at midnight, or at the cockcrowing, or in the morning: Lest coming suddenly he find you sleeping. And what I say unto you I say unto all, watch. (Mark 13:35–37, KJV)

These are just a few of the verses that the preacher used in that sermon of the end-times that I was unfortunate enough to have been present to hear when I was a child. It was not as though I had thought of what that preacher had said that morning for all of those years or for even many months. I suppose after a few months that I began to think of other things when I went to bed, but the damage had been done. Is this what God has in store for all children that come to Him? Maybe some children sit in church and feign paying attention. When I was a child, I was drawn to my Father who art in heaven. I wanted to know all

3

that I could about Him. I was very attentive in church. Children are like blank computers when they are born into this world. It is up to the owner as to what he chooses for an operating system, search engine, email provider, security software, and so forth. All of these are decisions that must be made by the owner or by the one who sells the computer to the owner. More often than not, the computer owner will accept whatever the seller has chosen. The one selling the goods may not necessarily have any better knowledge than the one buying the goods, but because he is in the position selling the goods, it is assumed that he is an expert. Well, that just isn't always the case.

It is not mandatory for a pastor of a church to have a seminary degree, thank God. However, odds are that those who do not have seminary degrees have been influenced by those who do. Seminaries across this nation are putting out much of this false end-times garbage that is being force-fed to the children sitting in the pews across this nation. Many of these children will drop out of church upon high-school graduation, and some will drop out after they have been convinced in college that there is no God. Sadly, the ones who are left in church, the few, will be brain-washed to the point that it will not matter, even if they are truly living in the end-times. They will just sit back and wait. They will also perpetuate this lie to the point that it may even turn family members against them. I hope the information that is packed within the covers of this book will open the eyes of those who have been victims of such. *"But whoever causes one of these little ones who believe in Me to stumble, it would be better for him if a millstone were hung around his neck, and he were thrown into the sea"* (Mark 9:42, ESV).

It appears from the content of this verse that one who caused a first-generation child who believed in Jesus, a Christian, to stumble, well—it sounded like he did not make it to heaven. Of course, Jesus was speaking to His contemporaries when He made this statement. Does it apply to our generation today? Paul did state in First Corinthians 13:8 that knowledge would vanish after the prophesied events had taken place, and boy, was he right about that. We have many in positions today that are preaching/teaching this end-times doomsday stuff who are causing many to stumble today, and the effects in future years will be that many will fall away because of false teachings. If the events that Jesus stated would happen to "this generation," the evil, perverse, wicked generation that crucified Him did not happen within that generation, then He is a false prophet. Likewise, if the events that John the Revelator stated were" near," "at the door," "shortly," and "at hand," did not occur shortly, then he also is a false prophet. Now, I believe by this time that all reading this material would have come to the conclusion that I do not believe that Jesus and John were false prophets. I do, however, believe that we have many preachers/teachers today that have very little or no knowledge of the events prophesied by the Old Testament prophets, as well as the New Testament prophets, as well as the Prophet, Priest, and King, Jesus.

I can remember very well not sleeping that night after hearing the sermon about the Russians marching up Highway 45. If I slept that night, it was in the wee hours. I can remember picturing in my mind being captured by the soldiers and them deafening and blinding my mother and dad. Tears poured out that night. It began a ritual that would last several months before the nightmares would fade into the recesses of my memory. However, once the memories had lapsed, the damage had been done. I could not go to bed and go to sleep. I would lay there and toss and turn for hours. After quite some time, it just became the norm, yet, this is not normal at all. This is not at all what God intended for rest and sleep to be about. This is not at all the effects He desires for children of all generations to go through for all time, waiting on the Lord to return. No, this was for the specified generation that crucified the very Son of God.

I would like to think that I am the only individual in the world who suffered through this false end-times sleepless night syndrome, but I am sure that I am not. It is a good thing that most innocent children who are Christians would never file a lawsuit in court because we understood that part of scripture correctly. Otherwise, there could be a lot of broke end-times doomsday sayers out there. Actually, I know some kids today who are going through this, except it is being foisted upon them by their false end-times-believing parents. You can see the torment in their demeanor. Their whole countenance appears bedeviled. Thoughts and ideas have consequences, and they can be very negative. Wrong ideologies probably play a larger role in physical health than the American Health Association is even aware of. To place a burden on children that is a total fabrication in any sense is an abomination to God, and to mankind. This is done in the church concerning which generation will experience the wrath of God, and in the classrooms of American schools and colleges concerning creation. I am sorry, but time and chance has always only produced chaos and entropy. Wake up "scientist." You aren't any better than the bullies in the pulpit. At least they know who Messiah is—or pretend to anyway. An event that happened about 2,000 years ago should never be taught as yet future, nor should evolution and global warming be taught as fact, when all three are in fact figments of a very obstinate imagination. To take a stance like "How dare you! I am too intelligent to have been fooled for all these years. You do not know what you are talking about. You are a demon possessed godless man," is the norm for those who have false beliefs about the prophecies of the Bible. I had a guy say to me that he was pretty much settled on his views. Well, his views are not the views of the Bible. They are the views of men with little knowledge, as Paul stated. I believe that obstinacy is also an issue with lots of people. I am wise enough to know that if I have not done the research myself and come to my own conclusions, then I really have nothing to go to battle for. You may argue with man and win, but you shall never win against God. He wins every time. I think this is a good point to take a look at a saying from Oswald Chamber's writings. This one comes from *Baffled to Fight Better*:

> Like a theological buzzard, he (Eliphaz) sits on the perch of massive tradition and preens his ruffled feathers and croaks his eloquent platitudes. There is no trace of the fraud in Eliphaz; he vigorously believes his beliefs, but he is at a total loss to know God. Eliphaz represents the kind of humbug that results from remaining true to conviction instead of to facts which dispute the conviction. The difference between an obstinate man and a strong-minded man lies just here: an obstinate man refuses to use his intelligence when a matter is in dispute, while a strong-minded man makes his decision after having deliberately looked at it from all standpoints, and when opposed, he is willing to give reasons for his decision.

Eliphaz is one of the men that were dealing with Job when he was under so much torment from Satan. Below are two verses that highlight how God feels about those who give wrong information about Him to others.

> After the LORD had spoken these words to Job, the LORD said to Eliphaz the Temanite: "My anger burns against you and against your two friends, for you have not spoken of me what is right, as my servant Job has. Now therefore take seven bulls and seven rams and go to my servant Job and offer up a burnt offering for yourselves. And my servant Job shall pray for you, for I will accept his prayer not to deal with you according to your folly. For you have not spoken of me what is right, as my servant Job has." (Job 42:7–8, ESV)

The nature of God is brought to light in this situation, well, a small aspect of it. It is obvious that God cares about how He is represented. He let Eliphaz know that He would not even listen to his prayers. His ways are to be made known to man, but woe unto them that make a false accusation against the ways of God. It would be interesting to know what God would have done to Eliphaz and his friends had Job not prayed for them. This also shows that children of God are to pray for the enlightenment of others about true history and the manifestations of the prophecies as they were played out almost two thousand years ago. A true understanding will set one free from the chains of a lie. Just think about this for a few seconds. What if your college professor told you that the American Revolution, the Civil War, World Wars I and II, the Korean Conflict, Vietnam, and so on were events that were yet to happen in the world? I believe that man would lose his job. He would be considered to be deranged, ignorant, and not qualified to be a professor of history. Hmmm. That's just food for thought.

I am a student of His story. Sometimes you have to get outside of the box to study His story. There are extra-biblical sources that confirm fulfilled prophecy, such as the writings of Flavius Josephus. He will be mentioned several times within this book as Josephus. John wrote Revelation prior to AD 70, contrary to what many liberal scholars claim. Otherwise, he surely would have mentioned the destruction of Jerusalem and the temple in AD 70 as being fulfilled prophecy from Jesus the Messiah. That generation had no need for anyone to inform them of the catastrophic events that had occurred. They had just lived through it, and I am sure that their children and grandchildren were made well aware of it. It is a shame that we have no documentation on how the Indians arrived in North and South America. Evidently no one documented it. If no one would have documented the American Revolution, no one in America or the world would even know that it occurred.

The destruction of Jerusalem is documented. Josephus is the historian of that epoch of time. He was a contemporary of Peter, Paul, and John. Most people are not even aware that his writings exist. The documentation is out there to be had, but it takes a hungry and willing soul to parse through all the resources that are available. Most people today are too consumed with the everyday concerns of this world to spend any time studying history from 2,000 years ago. Not me. I watch television only when I am eating dinner in the afternoons, and then I go out on the porch and read and research. I occasionally watch a portion of a college football game, generally less than an hour of the game. I find true history of things concerning eternity to be far more relative to my life than the things of this world. However, I do love to get out into nature and experience the awesome wonder of Gods' creation. I am in awe of Him, and I love admiring His creative genius in the wild. I think that most professing Christians would agree that to know Him is to be set free, but if you do not understand that the "end" has already come, then you are still in chains. A true understanding of the *end times* that the Bible foretells will truly set you free. It is not in your future. It is in your past. Get out there and live life to the fullest. Glorify Him in all you do and do not put stumbling blocks up in the paths of others. It appears from Job that one may well be held accountable for being a stumbling block to others. If it is not the truth then it is a lie. It matters not whether the outcome is the result of ignorance or evil. The results are the same. There is no excuse for either.

God would not have all children for all generations to suffer sleepless nights awaiting Jesus' return. If adults literally followed through with the mandates that Jesus and Paul made, listed at the beginning of this section, about not sleeping, this would be an even more dangerous world than what it is. There would be people falling to sleep every day at the steering wheel and falling out at work from exhaustion. What Jesus and Paul stated to the people was for that generation and not for all generations for all of time. Little children take such admonitions as these from Paul and Jesus seriously, at least the ones who are not feigning attention in church.

If one cries "The sky is falling. The sky is falling," and it never occurs, then the one who keeps crying it does not deserve the ears of the people, nor access to their wallets. No society should be responsible to keep one such as this in a state of well-being at the cost of others. Children should not have to listen to such lies. Many will never realize that it is a lie and will live compromised lives that do not glorify the Father who art in heaven. Some that do realize it is a lie will fall away from the church and become atheists. I hope by the time you have reached the end of this book that you will have a better understanding of the scriptures, and that you will understand who was being spoken to, what was being spoken, and comprehend the symbolic language that is used in the word of God.

I have heard radio talk show hosts state that a person's end-time view is not an essential to salvation. Well, I suppose not, but that is a state that a baby is in. All come into this life ignorant. God does not intend for His flock to remain babes in Christ forever. Racism is tied to one of the end-times views. We are to treat the ancestors of Abraham as dogs. Sorry, but that is what the dispensational system promotes. Jesus said to do unto others as you would have them do unto you. He did not put any exceptions in there. Wisdom of His word and history are a part of the maturation process. As stated earlier, being blind or without arms or legs does not prevent life, but it sure does hinder success and achievement in life. A false view of facts can greatly hinder your life. A person that is waiting on the rapture is like a baby in the crib, waiting on mama to change its diapers and to feed it. I believe that God is tired of us waiting on Jesus to return. He is waiting on us to come alive as the leaves on the Tree of Life that bring healing to the nations. Wake up and wise up. It is time to walk on water for our Father who art in heaven.

Who Were the Prophets Speaking To?

very critical issue about reading the Bible is understanding who God was addressing at the particular time. Remember, the Bible did not exist as we know it today back then. The Bible is the revelation to man of God speaking to prophets, and it was documented after the encounter.

The Bible is comprised of many different documents where God was speaking to a specific person or group of people. All of these compositions were later reviewed and compiled into what we have now, known as the Bible. The prophets of the Old Testament were speaking to the Jews. The prophets were God's messengers to the Jews, not the citizens of the United States. Jesus and the apostles spoke to their contemporaries about events that would take place within their generation and not our generation. Much of what God spoke to either the individual or the group is certainly not applicable to us today, but much of it is very relevant. I see no one building arks today, but there sure are many running around yelling "The sky is falling! The sky is falling!" Well, the flood was in Noah's day, and the sky fell in AD 70. Understanding who the audience is that God was speaking to is paramount to scriptural comprehension. We currently live in the new heaven and earth. By the time we get to the end I believe that the light will have been turned on. Only the obstinate will not be moved. Oh, by the way, the "end" here is the end of this book. You may guffaw at this point, but when you get a bit deeper into this study you will see the point that I am making in "this" paragraph, and not "that" paragraph.

I imagine that there were quite a few people hearing John's prophecy that had also heard Jesus' warnings. These warnings were for their generation and not our generation. When Jesus was warning His contemporaries of impending judgment as calamity on the nation of Israel, He was speaking to that generation, His contemporaries, not our generation. Of course He uses "this generation" to ensure that they understood without a doubt that He was speaking about their lives and times. John prophesied of the same events in Revelation, and he was speaking to his contemporaries when he wrote Revelation. Daniel and some of the other prophets had prophesied of this same end event. This event was the consummation of the Old Testament Covenant.

I notice that people today, because of false teachers/preachers, believe that these words are for our generation. That is a lie. What befuddles me is that I see no arks being built today or men walking around with rods, attempting to part the seas. Why is it that it is so obvious that those commandments were for a particular person of a particular time concerning current events of their times: Noah and Moses. Yet, why are the end-times doomsday warnings assumed to be for our time? It is because we are not aware of historical events beyond the end of the sealing of the word of God that ended prior to the destruction of Jerusalem and the temple in AD 70. I know that this may sound heretical to some, but the canon of scriptures was put together by man, not God. I do not know why those who put the canon of scripture together left out the historical event of AD 70, which was the fulfilling of Jesus prophecy about the destruction of the temple. Not a stone was left unturned. Josephus speaks of how terrible this event was in his writings. He even likens Nero, caesar of the Roman Empire from 54 AD to 68 AD, to a beast. Here is scripture from Paul that it appears is highly likely describing the death of the "lawless one," Nero, the beast; Second Thessalonians 2:8, (ASV) says, *"And then shall be revealed the lawless one, whom the Lord Jesus shall slay with the breath of his mouth, and bring to nought by the manifestation of his coming."* Nero committed suicide after a three-and-one-half-year full assault on the Christians that began in AD 64. Paul was prophesying the death of Nero here, and it occurred in AD 68. The Bible that Protestants have today was canonized around AD 363. I believe that if I had been alive at that time, I would have insisted that Jesus' and John's fulfilled prophecies be included. When John wrote his Revelation that was for the seven churches of the province of Asia, when he got to the end he wrote the following:

> For I testify unto every man that heareth the words of the prophecy of this book, If any man shall add unto these things, God shall add unto him the plagues that are written in this book: And if any man shall take away from the words of the book of this prophecy, God shall take

away his part out of the book of life, and out of the holy
city, and from the things which are written in this book.
(Revelation 22:18–19, KJV)

The Bible was not canonized at that time. Revelation was a letter to
the seven churches in Asia Minor. This admonition that John made at that
time was for his contemporaries. If anyone had changed it, added to it, or
deleted from it, it could have literally caused life-and-death issues. One
who was willing to twist the words of John's Revelation to the demise
of others had no right to everlasting life. The event that was prophesied
was to take place "shortly"; the time was "at hand." We have men today
that are bowing, warping, and twisting the scriptures to paint a picture
that has already occurred. I ponder if God's admonition through John to
the people of that generation would apply to man today. Anyone who
teaches that this event is in the future is doing just that. You can say what
you will, but ignorance shall be no excuse when dealing with issues that
affect the lives of others. This shall apply to men in pulpits, as well as to
politicians in Washington. If your actions are compromising the lives of
others, woe be unto you.

When the canon of scripture was put together, I would like to think
that they had knowledge of the destruction that took place in AD 70. The
historical events that Josephus had recorded were certainly known. Oral
tradition would have also been a huge factor in historical knowledge. The
destruction of Jerusalem and the temple in AD 70 would probably have
been as well known a fact in the first several centuries AD as World War
I and World War II are to us. Actually they probably would have had
a better knowledge of it because they did not have such as television,
sports, radio, and so forth to consume their time. Today there is a huge
chasm of ignorance about the events of AD 70. I cannot attest as fact that
I have ever heard a preacher even mention it in church. It was *the event
that was prophesied from the beginning*, yet it is neglected today in the
church as well as in our schools. It is the third most important event to
ever take place. Number one is creation. Number two is the coming of
Messiah and His death and resurrection, and number three was all the
fulfilled prophecy that occurred with the destruction of Jerusalem and the
temple in AD 70. Not a stone was left unturned. I do not believe that God
would take your name out of the Book of Life today if another chapter
was added to the Bible after Revelation that described the events of AD
70, and described to the best of our knowledge the characters and nations
that carried out God's will on the rebellious harlot, the nation of Israel. It

would also be a chapter that would acknowledge that Jesus was Messiah, and the evidence is fulfilled prophecy that took place within forty years of His crucifixion. It is critical that people know of this event. This history is more important to the entire world than all the rest of the world's history combined. If you do not know history you will keep repeating the errors that kill nations. If you do not have a firm grip on *His story*, you just may be killing yourself for all of eternity. Ignorance is no excuse for the law. Well, this applies a thousand times more with God.

Timing of prophecy is crucial. If I tell you that I am coming to see you next week on Wednesday morning at 9 a.m., and I never show up, ever, and you never hear from me again, I dare say that you may consider me a liar. I have heard or garnered from the writings of many preachers, biblical scholars, Christian radio talk show hosts, and others that understanding the timing of biblical prophecy is difficult. Well, I think that most would agree with that. There is lots of Old Testament prophecy that took place before Jesus was born. There was much prophecy that centered on the Assyrian captivity and the Babylonian exile. Daniel prophesied of events from the Babylonian exile, the Medes and Persians, Alexander the Great, and all the way up to the Roman Empire takeover of Judah in 63 BC, and then the end of the OTC, the consummation that occurred in AD 70.

It would be very difficult, probably impossible, to tie all Old Testament prophesy to particular events that transpired during the Old Testament era because there is no written record today and most of the nations, cities, and people groups are long gone from the face of this world. But I tell you this: the answer to that question is found in the book of Acts. This statement from Peter would include all prophecy that had not been fulfilled at the time he was speaking. The fact that Jesus and John prophesied of the same event that Daniel prophesied about some 550–570 years earlier would also make Peter's statement include their prophecy. After all, Jesus was Prophet, Priest, and King.

Well, what did all the prophets prophecy? They prophesied that there would come a day that God would pour out His wrath on the nation of Israel. Contrary to what many say today, the Old Testament Covenant was conditional. If you do not believe me just go read all of the Old Testament and document all the times there is a condition applied to it. There are times when it appears that there are no conditions, but most times, there are conditions tied to it. What was salvation about in the first-generation church? It was about salvation from the wrath of God. Those who heeded Jesus' warnings fled to other areas and were spared.

9

Afterward, they experienced peace like they had never known in their lifetime. I imagine that every one of them, along with those who denied Christ, bowed their knees and confessed that Jesus was Lord after the destruction of the temple and the Jewish nation. This would have been the greatest evidence that Jesus was sitting at the right hand of His Father who is in heaven. He had begun His reign forty years prior to this event. It was His rulership that led to the destruction and judgment that had been prophesied in past centuries. This was His thousand-year reign. The thousand years is not a literal number, but a symbol that denotes completeness. Does God just own the cattle of a thousand hills? What about the 1001th and 1002th hills? Does He not own them, too? Let's take a look at another verse where "thousand" is used. *"Know therefore that the LORD thy God, He is God, the faithful God, which keepeth covenant and mercy with them that love him and keep his commandments to a thousand generations"* (Deuteronomy 7:9 KJV).

Does God just show mercy through the thousandth generation? I dare say that He shows mercy to those who love Him and keep His commandments for all eternity. For the literalist, one who takes all scripture literally, this verse would mean that there are those who kept His commandments that shall be cut off after a thousand generations. Well, since no one lives beyond his own generation, this would mean that there is the possibility that some in heaven will be cast out after 40 thousand years. I think not. Or from a different standpoint, the earth will be here at least 40 thousand years. That would mean that we have about 34 thousand years to go before the world ends. I dare say that this world could go on into infinity. Scriptures do state that it will go on forever, but that is another issue and another study.

> And all the prophets who have spoken, from Samuel and those who came after him, also proclaimed these days. You are the sons of the prophets and of the covenant that God made with your fathers, saying to Abraham, "And in your offspring shall all the families of the earth be blessed." God, having raised up his servant, sent him to you first, to bless you by turning every one of you from your wickedness." (Acts 3:24–26, ESV)

"These days" are the days that Peter and his listeners are living in, not our days. Also, you will see in this verse that it says nothing of the Jewish nation blessing anyone. The "Seed of Abraham" was and is Jesus, and through this Seed, the world would be blessed. Jesus came to bless the Jew first, those who would accept Him, and then the Gentiles afterward. In the above verse, Peter even states that Jesus came to bless the Jews by turning them from their wicked ways, yet that was the generation that hung Messiah on the cross. Today there are many in the pulpits preaching that the nation of Israel has blessed the world. That is not what the scriptures state. The Seed of Abraham was and is Jesus Christ. He came to bless the Jew first because that was His culture and lineage. Time and again the prophets speak of the nation of Israel as being a reproach to other nations and peoples. This was not because of their spiritual superiority but because of their wickedness.

Sadly, there are many in the church today that are racist because of misunderstanding God's word. It is obvious to me that God is not a racist. *"There is neither Jew nor Greek. There is neither bond nor free, there is neither male nor female: for ye are all one in Christ Jesus"* (Galatians 3:28, KJV). This verse states that God does not play favorites to persons or nations. It is obvious that there was an issue during the times that Paul was speaking to the Galatians about the favored status of the Jewish people. It seems that there was confusion among the Galatians, who were Gentiles, about a particular verse in the Bible concerning the Seed of Abraham. There is still a misunderstanding about this issue even today. *"And I will bless them that bless thee, and curse him that curseth thee: and in thee shall all families of the earth be blessed"* (Genesis 12:3, KJV).

This verse is one of the most misquoted verses in the Bible. How many times have you heard someone state about the nation of Israel, "I will bless those who bless Israel and curse those who curse Israel"? This verse in not found anywhere in the Bible. People have taken the promise that was to Abraham and his Seed (Jesus) and applied it to the nation of Israel. "Thee" is singular and not plural. "Thee" was Abraham and not the nation of Israel. Evidently the people of Galatia were aware of the status of the Jewish people with God. I am sure that they had heard all of the legends surrounding the God of these people. It has been stated that every culture in the world today has a legend of the flood. If people over 4,000 years removed from the advent of the flood are familiar with it, surely people 2,000 years closer to the event would have been familiar with it. I am sure that they had also heard of the parting of the Red Sea. The Galatians evidently thought more of the Jews than they should have. Paul was just setting the record straight.

Abraham was blessed because of his faith and his Seed, Jesus, would be a blessing to those Jews that accepted him in His generation, and the proclamation of God would be taken from them and given to another nation, actually peoples: the Gentiles. It was never about the land. It was about God. The locus (center or focus) of the kingdom is Messiah. The locus was never the nation of Israel. Israel lost their focus on the locus long before Jesus entered the world. That generation was an elect people alright. They were the generation that God chose to bring in His plan for redemption, Jesus, as well as to pour out His wrath. I imagine that when His wrath was being poured out that He became the locus of the people. Every knee bowed and every tongue confessed that Jesus was Lord in AD 70.

"He shall come and destroy these husbandmen, and shall give the vineyard to others. And when they heard it, they said, God forbid" (Luke 20:16, KJV). Jesus was telling them that the end was near. The Old Testament Covenant that God had with them was about to be null and void. God had been patient for many years with the harlot, Israel. The killing of His Son would be the straw that broke the camel's back. Still, God gave the nation of Israel forty years to repent. In AD 70 He poured out His wrath on the nation of Israel. What God has put asunder, let no man put back together.

The thing that I want to reiterate here is that today we must understand that the scriptures document the past, such as the creation, the fall of man, and the flood. We have the Psalms and the book of wisdom, Proverbs, the account of Abraham being separated from his brethren in present-day Iraq, and the beginning of the lineage that God determined to bring in the Messiah. We have the historical account of the Exodus out of Egypt and the rebellious and whoring nature of the Jews. All of this history is relevant to us today. What was an abomination to God back then is still an abomination today. All the books of prophecy were very imminent for and relative to the ones they were written to, but they are not imminent to us today. The prophetic judgments that were revealed in those specific prophecies have all been carried out. Many were carried out centuries before Jesus came on the scene. The balance was carried out with Jesus' birth and with the destruction of the temple in AD 70. Not one jot or tittle has been left unfulfilled. Anyone who states otherwise is calling Jesus a liar and a false prophet.

This composition covers much territory, and all that has been stated above will be proven with none other than God's word. Many have some knowledge of the scriptures, but most have very little, if any knowledge of the events that took place in AD 70. This was the generation that John the Revelator and Jesus were prophesying to. It was imminent to them. If they did not heed the warnings, it could cost them eternity, but also much misery in their present lives even if they were believers. The warnings of impending destruction had to be heeded if one wanted to spare oneself and loved ones from such atrocities that were about to be poured out on "this generation," the "Mother of Harlots," which was the southern kingdom of Judah. They rejected Messiah. Now He was rejecting them. This was the same penalty that was carried out on the northern kingdom of Israel about eight hundred years earlier. If God issued the northern kingdom a divorce decree for their rebellion against Him, would you not think that the crucifixion of His Son would be considered an even greater atrocity? It is one thing to disrespect a person, but it is a crime to murder that person. To deny God's existence is one thing, but to kill His Son is another — yet it had to be done. I just thank God that ours is not the "elect" generation that He chose to bring salvation to the world. The very "elect" of God went through hell on earth, yet if someone even glances our way today, we are offended, when in fact they are probably looking beyond us. Well, God is not looking beyond you. I pray that this composition will help all, the sinner and the saint, to rise up and be what God would have man to be. He would have all to choose eternal life, which only comes through Jesus. The leaves on the Tree of Life are for the healing of the nations. If you are a racist, you are not attached to the Tree of Life. Ignorance is no excuse for the law. Now open your heart and mind to the truth of His story and history. It will change your life, and sleepless nights will be over with, once you are steeped in truth.

What Is Your Standard?

he standard that you choose to view the world from forms your opinions and shall determine the quality of your life and your eternal destination. Your worldview is formed by your standard. If you choose the wrong standard, you will have a tainted view of reality. We have people in the world today who want to call sin a disease rather than what it is. If you quit drinking alcohol or reduce the amount you consume to a low or moderate level, you will experience a difference in the way you look and feel. If you begin to drink and eat for the health of it and not as a habit, then you have taken control over your body. Self-control is a fruit of the Spirit. Let no man convince you that something is sin that God has not called sin. If you can't control your desires, then you are lacking in self-control, a fruit of the Spirit.

There are many worldviews in this present world. Determining factors for one's worldview are things such as religion, family history, education, personal experience, and so on. There is only one worldview that will lead to everlasting life. That is a true, biblical worldview. We all have different experiences in this life, but the word of God has answers for all situations. When we are young, we may take issue with certain commands in the Bible, but with age we look back and see that God was right and we were wrong. The more the merrier can be true, but it can also be a lie. It is all according to what the subject matter is. I have found as I have gotten older that all of those "thou shalt nots" in the Bible were for my benefit and not for my demise. They are there to give you a much higher quality of life. Sadly, most have to experience this from a rebellious standpoint to actually come to this truth. This can lead to many regrets and many broken hearts. It can also lead to death and destruction. The more obstinate a person, the more pain he shall experience in this life. God's way is the right way, the light way, and the bright way. His way is Jesus. He will lighten your load and give insight that will brighten the paths of this life.

We have choices to make in this life. A discerning soul will seek out truth and will know truth when he hears it if he has chosen the correct standard. The word of God is the correct standard. Self is never a right standard. If we only use ourselves as our standard, we will always deem ourselves to be superior to all others, when in fact that very opinion makes one less than all others. Jesus said that we are to esteem others more highly than ourselves. Now, that is wise to do in most circumstances, but would you allow a pedophile to babysit your child? Would you allow an intoxicated person to drive your aging parents 200 miles to see a medical professional? Discernment is always key. Every nation that has had God as the locus has been a great nation. Every nation that has rejected God has been removed from the place of a respected nation and becomes a nation of reproach. They also slide from the top spot to just another has been. History proves this to be fact.

America is changing right before our very eyes. Our anti-Christ government officials shall have a sheol of a price to pay one day for allowing atheism to be promoted in our classrooms, from pre-school through college. There is no neutrality in education. Either God is Creator, which is biblical and scientific, or Mother Nature is the creator, and that is evolution. Man runs wisdom out of the education process and then sits back baffled at why there appears to be so many fools in the world today. The innocent, hard workers are penalized for their success to pay for the obstinate self-centered criminals three square meals a day, and heating and air-conditioning. Success is penalized, and failure is rewarded. This is what happens when atheism and the ways of man become your standard. Your standard will determine quality of life and quantity of life. Some will experience high quality in the here and now, but it will last only about eighty years, which is low quantity. Some will experience low quality in the here and now, but high quantity after the here and now is over. Eternal life will take over at the last breath for the repentant sinner. Some will experience high quality and high quantity in this life and in the next.

The right standard will affect your choices forevermore. The word of God is the standard to base your decisions on. First, though, we must be sure that it is the word of God that we are basing our decisions on and not the teachings of man. If the teachings of man conflict with the word of God, then we have a problem. Now, the problem may be in the interpretation of the scripture or the translation of the text. Either one could be in error as we will show shortly.

You may have chosen the word of God as your standard, but if the one teaching you the word of God has chosen the word of man as his standard, then you are at a great loss. There are many "great men" of God that have allowed the teachings of other men to become their standard. This is a great place to introduce a heresy that has caused much confusion and consternation, yet I will state this. The one who began this false teaching is not a great man of God. He may be to some, but to God he has just sold out to another vain imagination that has wreaked havoc on little ones, the undiscerning, and the babes in Christ. Woe be unto him and the likes of him.

Hal Lindsey, in his book, *The Late Great Planet Earth*, referred to Jesus' warning to His apostles about the timing of the consummation of the Old Testament Covenant, where He used a fig tree and its leaves as his example of Israel becoming a nation again in 1948. He may have been taught this in seminary. From my studies, all biblical commentaries that I have viewed dated prior to 1970, none interpret Mark 13:28 this way. *"From the fig tree learn its lesson: as soon as its branch becomes tender and puts out its leaves, you know that summer is near"* (ESV). I recommend that you go to the Bible and read the whole chapter to get it into context. It is obvious that Jesus was using the leaves on the fig tree as a signal of an event that He and Daniel had prophesied. It was not the event. When you see the leaves turning color in October, it is a sign that fall is here and that winter is on the horizon. Jesus gave His apostles some signs that would confirm that the end was near. When you see these things, know that the end is near. It is as the leaves coming out on the fig trees. It was a sign that spring is here and that summer is on the horizon. I recommend that you do this yourself, so you can state this as fact upon your own efforts, rather than allowing another man to be your standard. I use the Blue Letter Bible online as my research tool. There are others out there, but it is akin to the Canon/Nikon issue. Which is better? You probably would say the one which you were used to. You can go to any verse in the Bible and pull up commentaries. There are text commentaries as well as audio/video ones. I prefer text. According to the particular verse you pull up, you may get as few as six commentaries or as many as eighteen. I suppose there could be more or less, according to the verse you pull up. The key is to never allow the commentator to contradict the word of God. Soon has always meant soon, and near has always meant near, unless you have allowed the teachings of man to become your standard.

One day while I was studying the scriptures, I got an idea to check and see what other commentators thought of Mark 13:28. Sure nuff! It appears that the majority of modern commentators after the 1970s have followed suit with Hal Lindsey's interpretation. He planted the seed, and what we have today with all of this end-times garbage is the result of that seed. Of course, all of these commentators had gotten their view from Hal Lindsey, whether they realize it or not, or they had gotten it from the same seminary that Lindsey went to. He may not be the first to make this interpretation, but he is the one who popularized it. He could have gotten this teaching from seminary. I hear many radio preachers today that got their teachings from Dallas Theological Seminary, and they all speak pretty much the same heresies. The teachings of man have become their standard and not the word of God. I encourage you to check commentaries that were written prior to 1970. I believe that you will discover that Lindsey may have been the first to interpret the leaves on the fig tree as Israel becoming a nation again prior to 1970. After he popularized the false teaching, it has become the standard for most commentaries since the heresy began. Well, after one thousand nine hundred and forty years after Jesus' death, someone finally got this wrong. This is a violation of Second Peter 1:20 (KJV): *"Knowing this first, that no prophecy of the scripture is of any private interpretation."* At this point I decided to see what Matthew Henry's thoughts were about this verse. He lived from 1662 to 1714; therefore his mind would not be tainted with Lindsey's false private interpretation of this verse. Using the Blue Letter Bible, I went to the Matthew Henry commentary, and sure enough, Matthew Henry stated just what I get out of this verse and basically what all other commentators before the twentieth century have stated. None stated that this had anything to do with Israel becoming a nation again. It was just a sign that all the events that Jesus had prophesied were about to take place.

I decided I would check to see what Matthew Henry thought about "antichrist." Sure nuff! He stated that antichrist was just a spiritual pandemic that was going on during the time that John was living. People were rejecting Jesus as Messiah. This was the spirit of the age. It was not a demonic spirit. We all know people who have "holier than thou" attitudes, or spirits, but this doesn't mean demonic spiritual possession. It was the spirit of the age for those who did not accept that Jesus was the prophesied Messiah. It is prevalent today all over the world, but it is not an individual. That is what Matthew Henry thought about antichrist. Many, if not most, modern commentators want to attach antichrist to a future or even present individual. Well, I thought to myself, let's check and see what Matthew Henry thought of the beast. Sure not! Matthew Henry got this one wrong, as have many since the sixteenth century.

Matthew Henry's mind had not been tainted with Hal Lindsey's false doctrine on the fig tree and the leaves because he was not subjected to this teaching. He was long dead and gone. His view on the beast, however, chimed in right along with what John Calvin and Martin Luther had taught about the beast, that it was the papacy. I shall study this more in the future, but I imagine that this teaching had begun prior to Martin Luther. John Calvin was likely a fan of Martin Luther, as he was just a bit younger, but his view on the beast could have come from other sources, too. I shall go into some detail in a later chapter with the characters of the end times that will put the identity that God placed on the beast into your mind forevermore. I will assure you that the beast is not the papacy. The papacy is just another biblically illiterate entity that has influence over far too many people who profess Christ. Well, if Jesus is your Messiah, you need to trash the papacy.

The Bible is a historical text that is written in many forms. Parts are written in poetic fashion and some in just a basic historical informative prose. There is much symbolic language used, as in our own everyday conversations. Sometimes full comprehension is blurred by cultural idioms and such. The only way that you can fully comprehend what I have just stated is to have experienced some time in a foreign culture with an unknown language. Idioms that we use are incomprehensible to them as are theirs to us. I am learning as I go. The more I begin to understand the symbolic language in the Bible, the more I comprehend the intended message that was being conveyed to the intended contemporary audience of that time.

The point to be made here is that the word of God should be the standard of the world. If man's teaching contradicts the word of God, then what needs to be questioned is man and not God. Do not esteem any man above the word of God. If man does not fully comprehend something, he is not likely to state such. More often than not, he will give you his opinion but will state it as fact. I know that there are certain characters in the end times as defined by the Bible that I am at a loss to assign an identity to, but there are many that I am sure about, and I can assure you that Barak Obama is not the antichrist. I am sure that President Trump will be declared the antichrist by many over the next four years. John had something else in mind, and we will look at the biblical definition of antichrist later in a section on the characters of the end-times. The reason I do not capitalize antichrist is because it is not capitalized in the scriptures either. Actually, there were no uppercase or lowercase letters in the Greek and Hebrew. John was not using antichrist as a noun but as an adjective describing a type of behavior that was prevalent of those first-century Jews who rejected Jesus as Messiah.

Sadly, man has made teachings of man the standard that he uses when reading the scriptures. Today, on a weekly basis, the word of God is being distorted in the pulpits across this world due to man esteeming man above the word of God. If the scripture states something and man contradicts it, then what you have is a non-discerning teacher. It happens to the best of men, sadly. Most modern commentators have used the most recent distortion of a passage of scripture from another man that turned out to be a bestseller. Not a single commentator that I am aware of ever interpreted the leaves sprouting on the fig tree as being Israel becoming a nation again prior to 1970. As stated previously, this false teaching could have come out of false seminary teachings. Once Hal Lindsey promoted it with his best-selling book, it became the norm, even in seminaries today. The fact that Matthew Henry has a correct view on antichrist, but a false view on the beast was surprising to me. Even he fell for false teachings that preceded him that were propagated by John Calvin and Martin Luther. I have a feeling that someone else likely started this heresy, possibly even a few centuries before Luther and Calvin lived. If all of these men allowed the scripture to be their standard, they would not have made errors that have bedeviled the world ever since. We very likely may never know whom all the characters were in the end-times mentioned by Daniel and John. One thing we can be assured of, and that will be proven by the end of this book, is that those events are in our distant past. The believers today are the leaves on the Tree of Life, and we are for the healing of the nations, not the destruction of the nations. This scripture is in Revelation. God is right, and man is wrong. If you are for the destruction of nations, then you are not a true believer. Healing of the nations will not come about with two sides warring against each other. *"Blessed are the peacemakers: for they shall be called the children of God"* (Matthew 5:9, KJV). Those who are war-mongers are not the children of God.

> There is neither Jew nor Greek, there is neither bond nor free, there is neither male nor female: for ye are all one in Christ Jesus. (Galatians 3:28, KJV)

> For there is no difference between the Jew and the Greek:
> for the same Lord over all is rich unto all that call upon
> him. (Romans 10:12, KJV)

Any man today who preaches racism in the church is an evil man. First, there is only one race, the human race. God favors no people group today. Those who promote such, as well as those who finance those who promote such, shall one day, when they take their last breath on this earth, be either found lacking or will be considered least in the kingdom of God for all eternity. Anyone who teaches other than this is teaching a gospel other than what Jesus and the apostles taught. Hmmm. I believe the scriptures state that these are accursed. *"But even if we, or an angel from heaven, should preach to you a gospel contrary to what we have preached to you, he is to be accursed"* (Galatians 1:8,NASB).

The gospel message that is being taught in many nations today is a false gospel of racism and division. Such as this is an abomination to God. Woe be unto those who profess such as this. We need more Bereans today. If you are being taught a gospel contrary to one of all nations and peoples being equal with God, you are being fed a lie. Paul addressed the Ephesians with the following statement that reveals what a central part of the gospel was about—peace:

> Wherefore take unto you the whole armour of God, that
> ye may be able to withstand in the evil day, and having
> done all, to stand.

> Stand therefore, having your loins girt about with truth,
> and having on the breastplate of righteousness; And your
> feet shod with the preparation of the gospel of peace;
> Above all, taking the shield of faith, wherewith ye shall
> be able to quench all the fiery darts of the wicked. And
> take the helmet of salvation, and the sword of the Spirit,
> which is the word of God: (Ephesians 6:13–17, KJV)

The gospel is a message of peace and not a message of superiority of one group over another. Another message that is central to the gospel message is the following: *"In the midst of the street of it, and on either side of the river, was there the tree of life, which bare twelve manner of fruits, and yielded her fruit every month: and the leaves of the tree were for the healing of the nations"* (Revelation 22:2, KJV).

Jesus spoke of the leaves on the fig tree as symbolism, so the last generation of Old Covenant Jews would heed the signs of the times and flee to the mountains for safety. It is ironic that in Jesus' Revelation to John that He also uses leaves as symbolism. Hal Lindsey took a warning that was for the last generation of Old Covenant believers and applied it to his generation. His dates from *The Late Great Planet Earth* failed, which is a sure sign of a false prophet and teacher, yet he is still professing his lies before the world today on TBN. According to the standard, *the Bible*, this man should not be heeded by anyone, nor should they heed anything from a network that allows such to be aired before the sheep. The symbolic leaves of the fig tree are not imminent, nor relevant to our generation. The leaves on the tree of life are very relevant to our generation and also imminent. Jesus is the Tree of Life. The believers are the leaves. We are for the healing of the nations. Now, is it heretical to think that God would have His followers to be peacemakers, which would also be healers of the nations? I think not. Allow Jesus to be your standard: *"Blessed are the peacemakers, for they shall be called sons of God"* (Matthew 5:9, HNV).

Is it heretical to think that God would have His followers to lie in a baby's crib, awaiting Jesus to come back and change their diapers? I think so. While man is waiting on Jesus, He is waiting on man to bring about the healing of the nations.

This book will touch on many issues that are of utmost importance as viewed by the scriptures. I hope that you have realized this early in this composition that the standard that we will be using will be the word of God. We will also use true history to convey His story that transpired shortly after John's Revelation, which was the same event that Daniel and Jesus prophesied. Put on your seat belt. This will be a bumpy ride.

Imminence versus Relevance

We will be looking at verses of scripture in this section that were very imminent to the first-century Christians. Imminent means likely to occur at any moment; close in time; about to occur. It certainly has relevance for us today, but it is certainly not imminent. Certainly God could pour out His judgment on this world today for the sinful state that man has become once again because of our ignorance of true history. History, "His story," is so much more important to the world today than American History, South American History, or the history of Spain, Great Britain, Asia, and so forth. We see in America today how the designers of school curriculums have made great attempts to revise American history, as well as to promote evolution as fact and Creation as a myth. They have attempted to deny and hide the Christian influence on this nation. I am sorry, but the pilgrims were here approximately 110 years before George Washington's birthday and 120 years before Thomas Jefferson was born. Attempts to revise history will likely keep the world in a constant state of turmoil until someone stands up and quits giving in to those who do not want truth.

I imagine that most Americans have no knowledge of this, but Thomas Jefferson edited the Bible to have his own version. He believed in the teachings of Jesus, but his thoughts were that Jesus was just a great teacher or prophet. He did not believe in the deity of Jesus. He edited the New Testament to reflect his beliefs. Any verse that gave a description of Jesus as deity, he either revised or omitted. He believed that Jesus was a superior teacher but not the Son of God. This is very telling on his part. Some men are not as great as you think they are. I would rather be considered a faithful and good servant of God than a great man of the people.

> Know ye not that the unrighteous shall not inherit the
> kingdom of God? Be not deceived: neither fornicators,

> nor idolaters, nor adulterers, nor effeminate, nor abusers
> of themselves with mankind, nor thieves, nor covetous,
> nor drunkards, nor revilers, nor extortioners, shall inherit
> the kingdom of God. (1 Corinthians 6:9–10, KJV)

Where this verse states "effeminate," it is not speaking of a man practicing homosexuality. That is the next category. It is speaking of men that do not have the heart of a man. A real man will man-up when he hears and sees error. Many will turn their head because they do not want to deal with confrontation. They would rather be hush-hush around the one committing the offense than to deal with the issue in a manly way. Iron sharpens iron. Banana pudding will not sharpen paper or iron.

We will not attempt to cover every verse in the New Testament that has imminence at its heart. That would take a whole book itself, probably the size of Josephus's complete work. I am going to begin with the *aion* verses and progress from there to *kosmos*, and then *oikoumenē*. We will look at other versions from the Blue Letter Bible. Generally, the improper interpretation is in the KJV, but it is not the only one in error.

Aion Verses of Imminence:

> The enemy that sowed them is the devil; the harvest
> is the end of the world; and the reapers are the angels.
> As therefore the tares are gathered and burned in the
> fire; so shall it be in the end of this world. (Matthew
> 13:39–40, KJV)

> The enemy who sowed them is the devil, the harvest
> is the end of the age, and the reapers are the angels.
> Therefore as the tares are gathered and burned in the fire,
> so it will be at the end of this age. (NKJV)

The "end of this age" was in their near future. At that time they had no hint of what lay ahead for them. They were a prosperous nation and had been mightily blessed of God. The end was approximately forty years away. Due to discrepancies in the Hebrew calendar and the Roman calendar, there are disputes about the time Jesus was born. Was it 3, 4, 5, or 1 BC or AD 1? 3 BC is the most agreed-upon date among scholars. Regardless, forty years after Jesus' crucifixion, burial, and resurrection AD 70 occurred and the wrath of God was poured out on the Jewish nation and the temple was destroyed. This may not seem like such an imminent issue to many today and certainly any event 1946 years in one's past or future is not going to put a sense of urgency into the people. If I was sixty years old and knew that the world was going to end in forty years, it would not be as big of an issue to me as it would be to a twenty-year-old. I would be highly concerned for my much-younger relatives, however. I would make sure that I did all in my power to warn them of the impending destruction. The key here, though, is that Jesus was not prophesying the end of the world. He was forth telling the destruction of Jerusalem and the temple. This was of major imminence to that generation. It is certainly relevant to us today, but the Old Testament and New Testament prophets did not prophecy the destruction of America. Now, Jesus certainly could allow the current state of hate, racism, double standards, political correctness over the right way, and so on, to cause much death and destruction in the world. Until man realizes that God does not have double standards, there is neither Jew, nor Greek, nor Gentile, nor red, yellow, black, or white, there will be turmoil in this world. Nations will rise, and nations will fall. The main issue here is that this was not prophecy about the end of the world. The KJV states just that, as well as four other English versions in the BLB. Fortunately, ten versions get it right. *Aion* is age, or time. *Kosmos* is world. The nation of Israel, God's chosen, had run out of time. The age was ending, that is, the OC era.

> So shall it be at the end of the world: the angels shall come forth, and sever the wicked from among the just.
> (Matthew 13:49 KJV)

> So it will be at the close of the age. The angels will come out and separate the evil from the righteous. (RSV)

Josephus stated that among all the dead bodies in the streets of Jerusalem, and there were many more thousands than we can imagine, there was not a known Christian among the dead. It is obvious that he found this astounding. They heeded the warnings of the prophets, apostles, and Jesus. They fled the city and were spared. This is how the Gospel was spread. The Christians were dispersed across the continent. If the world had ended at that time, we would not be here today, and the word of God would be irrelevant to us.

And as he sat upon the mount of Olives, the disciples
came unto him privately, saying, Tell us, when shall
these things be? And what shall be the sign of thy
coming, and of the end of the world?
(Matthew 24:3, KJV)

As he sat on the Mount of Olives, the disciples came to
him privately, saying, "Tell us, when will these things
be, and what will be the sign of your coming and of the
end of the age?" (ESV)

Four versions get it wrong and ten translate *aion* correctly as "age."
If Jesus would have told them that it was going to be some 2,000 years
into the future, it would have had no relevance to them and certainly no
imminence. However, it was just over the horizon, if you can call forty
years just over the horizon. I can tell you from experience. Forty years
flies by when you look back on your life. The apostles were highly concerned because they knew it would affect them. It would actually affect
them more than they could possibly have imagined. At this time they did
not know that it would cost them their lives, but their reward was everlasting life—just over the horizon.

Howbeit we speak wisdom among them that are perfect:
yet not the wisdom of this world, nor of the princes of
this world, that come to nought:
(1 Corinthians 2:6, KJV)

Now we do speak wisdom among the mature, but not a
wisdom of this age or of the rulers of this age, who are
perishing. (NET)

This verse would not be imminent to the apostles, but it would be
for the rulers of that age. This would apply to the Jewish rulers, as well
as the caesars. There was that year of four caesars in AD 69. Nero committed suicide in June, AD 68. Galba succeeded him and reigned for
seven months, ending in January 69. Galba died in battle. Otho succeeded
Galba and reigned for three months before committing suicide. Vitellius
succeeded Galba and reigned for eight months before being assassinated.
Vespasian succeeded Vitellius and reigned for ten years until AD 79, when
he died of illness at the age of sixty-nine. There would be many more

caesars after AD 70. The Jewish nation came into the Roman Empire under Julius, the first caesar, in 63 BC. The consummation of the OTC era and destruction of the Jewish nation took place under the tenth caesar in AD 70—Vespasian. Some say that these were caesars and not kings. What about "We have no king but Caesar"? If you research the caesar subject, you will find that some scholars did not even consider Julius to be a caesar. They state that Augustus was the first. The ancient historians, as well as the Jews, certainly viewed Julius in the same light as Augustus and the rest. There had been only five caesars up to Nero over a period of 117 years. Julius was assassinated. Augustus' death was questionable whether it was suicide, assassination, or natural. Tiberius possibly died of old age, but there is evidence that he could have been assassinated. Nero ascended the throne in AD 54. After his suicidal death in AD 68, the three deaths, and the ascension of Vespasian in AD 69, there was five caesars. This was a period of just fifteen years, with a year and a half timeframe witnessing the fall of four caesars and the rise of five. I dare say that this was certainly a time for the perishing of caesars.

> Now all these things happened unto them for ensamples: and they are written for our admonition, upon whom the ends of the world are come.
>
> (1 Corinthians 10:11, KJV)

> These things happened to them as examples for us. They were written down to warn us who live at the end of the age. (NLT)

The Greek word used in the TR version is αἰώνων, and its root form is αἰών, where the English word *aion* comes from, which is age. I will not do this for each verse used within this book, but this is the difference for this section. *Aion* is age and not world, which is *kosmos*. Of the fourteen English versions in the BLB, twelve get it right and two get it wrong, the KJV and WEB. Paul was warning his contemporaries that the promised destruction was on the horizon. As that generation that came out of Egypt refused to be obedient to God and enter in, so would "this generation" deny the Messiahship of Jesus and would forevermore be banished from heaven and eternal life. This generation was the "elect" that God chose to bring the Messiah into.This was the "elect" of God. He chose "this generation" for whatever reason to end the Old Testament Covenant Era.

They were a chosen generation, as Peter states in First Peter 2:9 (NKJV)," *But you are a chosen generation, a royal priesthood, a holy nation, His own special people, that you may proclaim the praises of Him who called you out of darkness into His marvelous light."* John Calvin started the predestination heresy in the 1500s because of the "elect" verses in the scriptures. Jesus died once for all and not once for some. *"By his will we have been made holy through the offering of the body of Jesus Christ once for all"* (Hebrews 10:10, NET).

I thank God that I was not one of the elect of that first generation of Christians. I strongly advise all readers of this material to get a modern version of Josephus's writings and read through all of it, but *Wars of the Jews* will reveal to you that you did not want to be there. It was a literal hell on earth.

> Who gave himself for our sins, that he might deliver us
> from this present evil world, according to the will of God
> and our Father: (Galatians 1:4, KJV)

> who gave himself for our sins to deliver us from the
> present evil age, according to the will of our God and
> Father, (ESV)

Nine versions translate *aion* correctly, and five get it wrong. Of course, God knew that the lives of the majority of Jesus' apostles would be required during the seditious time preceding Nero's persecution, and through the following persecution as well. Paul and Peter were put to death under the authority of Nero. Those who were in the crowds that Jesus warned about the signs of the times and heeded His warnings were spared a martyr's death. If all Christians had died, the Gospel would not have spread. As a matter of fact, it would not have been the Gospel. It was the death of some, but it has been life everlasting for far more than ever died during the times of those seditions and tribulations.

> Teaching us that, denying ungodliness and worldly lusts,
> we should live soberly, righteously, and godly, in this
> present world; (Titus 2:12, KJV)

teaching us, that denying the impiety and the worldly
desires, soberly and righteously and piously we may live
in the present age, (YLT)

Now, this is a verse that has as much imminence for our generation
as it did for "this generation." There is a school of thought out there today
that thinks we can live any way we desire and that we will be allowed
into heaven. This is due to a false understanding of grace versus the
law. Under the law, all died and suffered "soul sleep." Under grace, the
repentant believer, those who have bowed the knee to Messiah, will never
experience "soul sleep." Everlasting life begins when we take our last
breath in this life. It is not the end. It is the beginning of eternity for both
the saved and unsaved. The only difference will be your eternal destination. This is an issue that will always have imminence and relevance to
all generations. No one is perfect, but Jesus did state to the woman that
the scribes and Pharisees brought to Him that had been caught in the act
of adultery to "go, and sin no more." I have always wondered why they
did not bring the man.

Kosmos Verses of Imminence

There really are no verses where the Greek word *kosmos* is used
where the intended meaning is really compromised. I will, however, post
a few verses to show that the translators could have done a better job. Yes,
all scripture is inspired by God, but not all translators throughout the ages
are inspired of God. The original was to the Jew, not to us. Therefore,
they were imminent to them but relevant to us.

If ye were of the world, the world would love his own:
but because ye are not of the world, but I have chosen
you out of the world, therefore the world hateth you.
(John 15:19, KJV)

If you were of the world, the world would love you
as its own; but because you are not of the world, but I
chose you out of the world, therefore the world hates
you. (ESV)

Most people, by using deductive reasoning, can read this and comprehend what the meaning is, but if you are not familiar with the language,

you might think that the dirt of the earth actually hated you. I will make my own interpretation using English and the Greek words that are used for "world," even though it is obvious that one Greek word, κόσμος, is always associated with people. A more proper way of stating this would be as follows: *"If you were of the culture, the people would love you. However, because you are not of the culture, but I have chosen you out of the culture, the people will hate you"* (ERC).

The above "ERC" is my translation. Just think about what has become the norm over the past generation. Today if you speak out against sins that will condemn one to eternal perdition, the people of this ever-changing culture will hate you. They will mock and scoff at you and attempt to silence you. They will attempt to do it through the liberal media and the bought "injustice" system. The only judge in heaven will be the Righteous Judge. There will be no need for any other. Woe be unto you that attempt to silence truth!

> Behold, what manner of love the Father hath bestowed
> upon us, that we should be called the sons of God: there-
> fore the world knoweth us not, because it knew him not.
> (1 John 3:1, KJV)

> See ye what love the Father hath given to us, that chil-
> dren of God we may be called; because of this the world
> doth not know us, because it did not know Him; (YLT)

A better rendering of the above verse would be as follows: Know what love the Father has given us, that children of God we may be called, therefore the people know us not because they did not know Him. (ERC)

> They are of the world: therefore speak they of the world,
> and the world heareth them. (1 John 4:5, KJV)

> They are from the world. Therefore what they say is
> from the world, and the world listens to them. (HCSB)

A more understandable interpretation if you were speaking to a Martian would be as follows: *"They are from this world, therefore they speak worldly things and the people listen to them"* (ERC). No, there are no Martians out there, and the world has no ears. But if I dropped the average American into the city of Ita, Santa Catarina, Brazil, he may as well be on Mars. Actually, Brazil is spelled Brasil in South America. If you weren't familiar with the language, you would think it was a typo. The only reason I used the word *kosmos* was to show that man can do a better job of interpreting when he is thinking of a precise group of people who will be reading the material. As I stated earlier, the scriptures were written to the Jews originally, but it is certainly relevant to us today.

> And we know that we are of God, and the whole world lieth in wickedness. (1 John 5:19, KJV)

> We know that we are of God, and all the people are surrounded by wickedness. (ERC)

Note that my interpretation is more accurate. The planet earth is neutral. It is neither good nor evil. Actually, I would lean toward the fact that it is very good. Without the fall of man, it would be Paradise. It is still a very good thing. Without a planet to live on, we would all perish immediately.

We just took a few verses where the Greek word *kosmos* is used to show that it is pretty much translated properly in all instances. Perfect? No, but at least comprehensible in the English language. The next section will be far different than this one, as the original Greek word will be mistranslated where it has a totally different meaning with possible dire consequences for the earnest seeker.

Oikoumenē Verses (Greek Root Form)

When this word is used, it is not speaking of the whole world or earth. It is speaking of a particular area, such as the Roman Empire, or it could even be used to describe the Jewish nation or the Greek Empire. The United States could even be described using this word, or areas in the United States, such as the Southeast. South America could also be described using this term, the Amazon Rain Basin, as could Central America, or Mexico, as well as Canada. Oikoumenē does not mean "world" in any way. It is always used as a defined geological location in the scriptures in the Middle East. It appears that in the context it is used within the books of the New Testament, it almost always means the land occupied by the Jews, the southern kingdom of Judah, and sometimes as the Roman Empire. We will now look at some verses where imminence is the key to the ones being spoken to in the scriptures.

> And there stood up one of them named Agabus, and
> signified by the Spirit that there should be great dearth
> throughout all the world: which came to pass in the days
> of Claudius caesar. (Acts 11:28, KJV)

> One of them named Agabus stood up in one of the meet-
> ings and predicted by the Spirit that a great famine was
> coming upon the entire Roman world. (This was ful-
> filled during the reign of Claudius.) (NLT)

Of the fourteen English versions in the BLB, eleven make the error of not distinguishing between world and the Roman Empire. Three get it right. Claudius was the fifth caesar of the Roman Empire. He was the uncle of Nero, the greatest of the Roman tyrants against the Jews. Nero was as a beast, as recorded by Josephus, as well as Revelation. This famine was not a worldwide catastrophe. It was within the Roman Empire. It is possible that it did not even affect all of the empire. You would have had to have lived during that time to know the true effects of the famine, but it is a certainty that it did not affect South America, Central America, Mexico, North America, all of Europe, or Asia. Looking back on this event some 1,950 years in our past, it is of no relevance or imminence to anyone today. Claudius ruled from AD 41 to AD 54, so it happened within that timeframe. It was imminent to those who heard Agabus' prophecy. Those who heard sent food to the area in Judaea to relieve their brethren. Now, let's go onto some much more imminent verses for the first century believers.

> Because he hath appointed a day, in the which he will
> judge the world in righteousness by that man whom he
> hath ordained; whereof he hath given assurance unto all
> men, in that he hath raised him from the dead.
> (Acts 17:31, KJV)

> because he has set a day in which he is going to judge
> the habitable earth in righteousness by the man whom
> he has appointed, giving the proof of it to all in having
> raised him from among the dead. (DBY)

This verse was of great imminence to the first-century believer. The whereabouts would have tremendous effects on the believers. From our experience with the Greek *oikoumenē* it is obvious that this was not to have immediate impact on the whole world, but on the Roman Empire and the Jews in particular. The One doing the judging here was the One who had been hung on the cross and raised from the grave on the third day, the Messiah. This was of no imminence to the Americas about 1,940 years ago, or to India, Asia, the island nations, and so forth. Certainly today it is of great relevance to all people in the entire world today, whether the people realize it or not. We all have a decision to make concerning Jesus the Christ. If He is Lord of your life, your actions (fruit) will reflect your heart's desires. When you take your last breath in this life, your eternal future will either be sheol (hades) or heaven. Most, if not all people, choose heaven. The key, though, is Jesus. If you do not have the key, you will not enter in. Jesus is the only key that will open the door to heaven and everlasting life. There are those who say that there are many ways, or "keys" to heaven. *"Jesus saith unto him, I am the way, the truth, and the life: no man cometh unto the Father, but by me"* (John 14:6, KJV). The Father is in heaven. No man comes unto the Father except through the Son, Jesus. That is not my opinion. That's God's word.

> Because thou hast kept the word of my patience, I also will keep thee from the hour of temptation, which shall come upon all the world, to try them that dwell upon the earth. (Revelation 3:10, KJV)

> Because thou hast kept the word of my patience, I also will keep thee out of the hour of trial, which is about to come upon the whole habitable world, to try them that dwell upon the earth. (DBY)

Not only is this imminent, but the area it concerns is also of utmost importance. The only translation that varied from world, or whole world, is the DBY version. One other version, the NASB, notes literally "inhabited earth." The root form of this word is the same one used to describe the area that was to be taxed for caesar Augustus. It is obvious that John was warning his contemporaries of a soon-to-come catastrophic event. This event is the same event that all the Old Testament prophets, as well as Jesus, prophesied. Peter stated the following: *"Yes, and all the prophets from Shemu'el (Samuel) and those who followed after, as many as have spoken, they also told of these days"* (Acts 3:24, HNV). "These days" were the days they were living in. Peter was warning them that this was "the generation" that God would pour out His wrath on. Why did God pour out His wrath on the children of Israel? This gives us a great clue. *"Unto you first God, having raised up his Son Jesus, sent him to bless you, in turning away every one of you from his iniquities"* (Acts 3:26, KJV). I thought the Jews were to be a blessing to the whole world. Yet, Peter is telling them here that Jesus came to bless them first since they were the people descended from Abraham and the prophets. The "Seed" had come to bless the Jews first.

"Now to Abraham and his Seed were the promises made. He does not say, "And to seeds," as of many, but as of one, "And to your Seed," who is Christ" (Galatians 3:16, NKJV). The false belief about the "Seed" is most often preached by the Zionists. They even state "Those who bless my people I will bless and those who curse my people I will curse" as a word spoken by God. This was actually spoken to Abraham, and it had nothing to do with the Jews. It was directly to Abraham and to his "Seed," Jesus. God is not a racist. Some say that He is, though, those who are ignorant of the true word. Sadly, many of these men are in the pulpits of America. Paul knocks Zionism out the door with the following words just a few seconds later when he states in Galatians 3:28 (NKJV) *"There is neither Jew nor Greek, there is neither slave nor free, there is neither male nor female; for you are all one in Christ Jesus."* There are those today that preach ignorantly how the Jews are of favored status with God. Well, if there is neither Jew, nor Greek, nor slave nor free, nor male nor female, for you are all one in Christ Jesus, then where do they get that? Probably from a false understanding of the timing of prophecy. Regardless, whether out of ignorance or evil, the consequences will probably be the same; therefore, the punishment could likely be related. Also, if they were so special to Him, why did He allow the Romans to destroy the temple (not a stone was left unturned), and the land to be handed over to others? What God has put asunder, let no man put back together. Some may think this is twisting scripture. Well, God is not a God of double standards. If man is not to put asunder what God has joined together (Mathew 19:6), then surely He takes issue when man goes against what He has brought about. *"False weights and unequal measures-the Lord detests double standards of every kind"* (Proverbs 20:10, NLT).

> For they are the spirits of devils, working miracles, which go forth unto the kings of the earth and of the whole world, to gather them to the battle of that great day of God Almighty. (Revelation 16:14, KJV)

> for they are the spirits of demons, doing signs; which go
> out to the kings of the whole habitable world to gather
> them together to the war of that great day of God the
> Almighty. (DBY)

Most of the other translations state "whole world" or "world," and two or three state "earth." Still, the Greek root form is the same as for the Roman Empire. Now, we know that the temple was destroyed in AD 70, as well as the whole city of Jerusalem. I imagine since the Mayans, Incas, Aztecs, Eskimos, American Indians, and so on, had never heard of Jesus and had nothing to do with His crucifixion, then God would not have poured His wrath out on those nations and people groups. We know that Jesus died once for all, not once for some. Yet, a group that had never heard of Messiah would not likely have been the victim of the outpouring of God's wrath. God's wrath was for "this generation" that rejected Jesus, the very chosen people of God. Surely God can judge nations now. Today, condemnation for most will come at death. Quality of life is also imminent and very relevant to the individuals answer to who Jesus is. It will affect all of your decisions. You either have the key to heaven, Jesus the Christ, or you have the key to sheol. Actually, sheol can be entered without a key. There is no key to death. All will experience death of the flesh. Jesus is the key to life everlasting.

We have covered the New Testament verses in this section that use the Greek root form *oikoumenē* that show the imminence of the times of the first-century church. I hope that all can see that there is a great difference between imminence and relevance but also that there is a greater difference between the Roman Empire and the whole world. There is enough difference here to either make one compromise his life or to get it right. Live your whole life for Him uncompromised by a false "end of the world" theology that just leads to doom and gloom and is a mockery to the first-century church. They went through hell. Sorry, but during my lifetime, which dates back to 1963, we have had one president who was assassinated. Yes, there has been an attempt on another, but only one attempt was successful, and that was in 1963—JFK. Out of the first ten caesars, there is surety that eight of them either died in battle, committed suicide, or were assassinated. I would say that the world is a much better place today. We have become a bunch of pessimistic complainers. If someone looks at us the wrong way today, we feel so insulted, when in fact, odds are they were looking beyond us.

Imminent and relevant are two separate issues. We will list the definitions as found online at The Free Dictionary by Farlex:

Imminent
1.) likely to occur at any moment; impending
2.) projecting or leaning forward; overhanging

Relevant
1.) having a bearing on or connection with the matter at hand
2.) meaningful or purposeful in current society or culture

If you were to walk up upon a bear and her cubs and you saw the mother leaning forward, I believe you would really get a better understanding of what imminent really means. If you were to go ahead and take a few more steps, you would really understand. The best thing to do would be to slowly turn and walk away, as not to trigger the mother bear's protective instincts to charge. If you had really been attentive, you would have noticed the bear and her cubs long before you got that close, and you would not have been in such a situation. If you had spotted them a hundred yards off, the danger would not have been as imminent. When you are sharing this story with your friends later that day, it would likely not even be relevant to them and certainly not imminent.

The first-century Christians were in a den of wolves. They were in an imminently dangerous situation. If they heeded the warning signs that Jesus gave them, they would flee and their lives would be spared. It was appointed to the apostles to die for their faith, but Jesus had warned others of signs to be leery of and to flee when they saw them. They heeded the signs, sold their property, and fled. This is relevant to us today, but it was imminent to them. Their lives were on the line. Because of ignorance of what happened at that time, we have people today that appear to be ready to fall off of a cliff. If it is so imminent to the ones today who believe that it is the end-times, surely they would be selling their goods and fleeing. That is what Jesus told the first-century believers to do when they saw the signs. Jesus said absolutely nothing about a rapture. All of this is relevant to us today, but in no way should it be of greater imminence to our generation as it was to Jesus' generation. I hope that by the time you get to the end of this compilation, that this subject matter will have greater relevance to you. I also hope that it will enlighten those who have been fed lies about the times that we live in and that the imminence of the times we live in will be seen in a true light.

This world isn't about to end. Become a force for peace and healing and not a force of division, racism, and bigotry. Contrary to what liberals say, this is a two-way street. God despises double standards. Those who fiddle with the minds of others shall have a sheol of a price to pay one day. Open your eyes to true history and facts. The truth will set you free and then the Truth will truly set you free.

PROPHECY AND PROPHETS

Measure of a Prophet

here have been many that claimed to be prophets throughout time. There are those today that profess to be prophets, yet time and again they miss the mark. I can think of six or more right off the top of my head who prophesied an event to take place and it did not occur. Back in the OTC era, God destroyed false prophets on more than one occasion, but the event that included Elijah and the prophets of Baal is the one who comes to mind. God sent down fire from heaven to consume those false prophets. A man who prophesies events that do not come to fruition is a man that does not have a heart for God. Appearances are deceiving. Just because a man is behind a pulpit does not make him a man of God. As a matter of fact, if that man is making false prophesies, you need to abandon that church. God's word does not allow for error concerning this matter. I dare say that the ones who stay in a church like this and keep on funding a false prophet will be held accountable for such. This would be a sure-fire indicator of ignorance of God's word. The most appropriate thing to do today in such a situation would be to abandon that church. You may be ridiculed, but I would rather be able to look the One in the eyes that has power over the soul than the one who can tarnish my reputation. Please God, not man.

It is the Sovereign LORD who helps me. Who will condemn me? They will all wear out like a garment; the moths will eat them up.

Who among you fears the LORD and obeys the word of his servant? Let the one who walks in the dark, who has no light, trust in the name of the LORD and rely on their God. But now, all you who light fires and provide yourselves with flaming torches, go, walk in the light of

> your fires and of the torches you have set ablaze. This
> is what you shall receive from my hand: You will lie
> down in torment. (Isaiah 50:9–11, ESV)

It appears that the overwhelming majority claiming Christianity today have gone the route that Isaiah is speaking of here. Because of a lack of historical knowledge, particularly between the Assyrian captivity in the last half of the 700's BC and the destruction of the temple and city of Jerusalem in AD 70, there is much confusion about prophecy. This is the reason that prevalent thinking among the church today is that we are living in the *end times* and that we are the last generation. Well, I am sorry. We are not "this generation." You will be introduced to "this generation" in the next section. I hope it is a real eye opener for all.

Isaiah was a prophet of God in the OC era that lived about 700 years before Jesus was born into the world. Isaiah was connected to God. He spoke as God told him to speak. He revealed truths from God, but the men of that epoch of time, as always, did not want to hear what God had to say. God used prophets in those days. Today He uses His word, the written Bible. There are no prophets today, as prophecy has been sealed. Men of Isaiah's time lit their own fires rather than walking in the light that is God. We have far too many men today lighting their own torches, as well as the torches of their congregations. Sadly, these fires are blinding people to the true intent and purpose of God's word. I am not a prophet because God's word states that prophecy would be sealed after the events prophesied had taken place, which occurred in AD 70, and Paul even states that "tongues will cease and knowledge will decrease" after the prophesied destruction of Jerusalem in AD 70. I will make this statement, though. There will be many today who will lie down in torment because of the false fires they have kindled. To lie down here means death, the wages of sin, not the entry point into His kingdom. There will be a many a person who has taught a false message from the word of God that will be held accountable for all eternity. Now, that can mean eternal damnation, or your just rewards in heaven for all eternity, getting in by the hair of your chinny-chin-chin. Kindle the fires of God and not of man.

God gave His people in the OTC era a standard to use when measuring a prophet. He spoke this to His man, Moses.

But the prophet who presumes to speak a word in my name that I have not commanded him to speak, or who speaks in the name of other gods, that same prophet shall die. And if you say in your heart, "How may we know the word that the LORD has not spoken?"—when a prophet speaks in the name of the LORD, if the word does not come to pass or come true, that is a word that the LORD has not spoken; the prophet has spoken it presumptuously. You need not be afraid of him. (Deuteronomy 18:20–22, ESV)

Was this a mandate from God to put to death those who were false prophets? It does appear so. *"And if anyone again prophesies, his father and mother who bore him will say to him, You shall not live, for you speak lies in the name of the LORD. And his father and mother who bore him shall pierce him through when he prophesies"* (Zechariah 13:3, ESV). This verse from Zechariah affirms that death was the penalty and that it was even to be carried out by the prophet's family. Because of liberal progressives in the Jewish nation, it was a rare thing to put to death a false prophet. A true prophet, however, was very apt to be put to death because the people and the leaders did not want truth. A man who claims to speak a word from God and it does not come true does not deserve the respect of any God fearing Christian. He also does not deserve to be paid a salary from the church. There are many out there today in pulpits or radio preachers who have given false prophecies, yet they are still maintained by the same congregation or donors year after year. Last January 4, 2016, while I was traveling one morning, I heard a very popular radio preacher, James MacDonald, state that Jesus is coming in 2016. Well, I pulled over and set myself a reminder on my cell phone for December 31, 2016. That day has come and gone, but you are reading this now and the world is still here. Not a single living person has been raptured. His website claims that he has over 3 million daily listeners. Several years ago as I listened to this guy I was inspired, but as I matured in the word I began to notice questionable things he would say. To state that Jesus is coming in 2016 did it for me.

People flock to a lie and love to have their ears tickled, but this is no excuse for a media outlet to profit from the ignorance of the people. Those who allow such through their radio and television stations for profit will certainly be considered the least in the kingdom of God if they even make it there. Profit should not come at the expense of truth. Now, let's take a look at some prophecies that were made back in the OC era, and by the way, Jesus and John did live in the OTC era. It was consummated in AD 70.

> A period of seventy sets of seven has been decreed for your people and your holy city to finish their rebellion, to put an end to their sin, to atone for their guilt, to bring in everlasting righteousness, to confirm the prophetic vision, and to anoint the Most Holy Place. Now listen

and understand. Seven sets of seven plus sixty-two sets of seven will pass from the time the command is given to rebuild Jerusalem until a ruler—the Anointed One—comes. Jerusalem will be rebuilt with streets and strong defenses, despite the perilous times.

After this period of sixty-two sets of seven, the Anointed One will be killed, appearing to have accomplished nothing, and a ruler will arise whose armies will destroy the city and the Temple. The end will come with a flood, and war and its miseries are decreed from that time to the very end. The ruler will make a treaty with the people for a period of one set of seven, but after half this time, he will put an end to the sacrifices and offerings. And as a climax to all his terrible deeds, he will set up a sacrilegious object that causes desecration, until the fate decreed for this defiler is finally poured out on him.
(Daniel 9:24–27, NLT)

We see from this scripture that there are seventy sets of seven, seventy sevens, or seventy weeks, according to the version you are reading. This is where the "490 years" comes from that false teachers are saying that God put a gap between the sixty-ninth and seventieth weeks because they could not reconcile this verse with Jesus' and John's prophecy. We will shed some light on this faulty interpretation shortly. If you read ten different commentaries, you will get as many opinions about this subject. We are currently about 2,550 years from the beginning of the 490-year countdown. The 490th year would be *the end*. The end of what? It would be the end of the Old Testament Covenant era, which would signal the official beginning of the New Testament Covenant era. The OC had to be consummated, ended, before the NC could begin.

And he shall confirm the covenant with many for one week: and in the midst of the week he shall cause the sacrifice and the oblation to cease, and for the overspreading of abominations he shall make it desolate, even until the consummation, and that determined shall be poured upon the desolate. (Daniel 9:27, KJV)

After the Jews destroyed their Messiah, Jesus the Christ, God gave them forty years to repent. Now, this 490-year future event, was it the coming of the Messiah, or the literal destruction of Jerusalem in AD 70? I lean toward the AD 70 destruction, but remember, knowledge has decreased. The consummation of the Old Covenant signaled God's divorce decree with the Jewish nation. The parable about the wedding feast was a parable that signaled this forthcoming event. The wedding feast is preached as an event that all believers that there will ever be will be present, those who were under the Old Testament Covenant and those under the New — after the world ends. This is a faulty view. The wedding feast was symbolic of the Old Covenant believers being married into the New Covenant, which brings life for the repentant believer.

"And I saw, when for all the causes whereby backsliding Israel committed adultery I had put her away, and given her a bill of divorce; yet her treacherous sister Judah feared not, but went and played the harlot also" (Jeremiah 3:8 ,KJV). God divorced the northern kingdom of Israel in the 700s BC. Most sources give a date of 722 BC. There are Zionists today who state that God would never divorce Israel — what was left of her after God divorced the northern kingdom of Israel. This resulted in the lost tribes of Israel. What was left of the Covenant people was the southern kingdom of Judah. Well, what did all the Old Testament prophets prophecy? What did Jesus and John prophecy? It was not the destruction of the world. It was the destruction of the Jewish nation, which was the consummation of the OC era. God was very patient with the Jewish nation. Remember how He allowed the generation that refused to go into the Promised Land after liberating them from Egypt to wander in the wilderness for forty years? Well, he gave "this generation" forty years to repent after they had their Messiah, the very Son of God, crucified. One thing that causes confusion for many in the world today is the way the Bible is designed. No, Jesus did not live in the New Covenant era. He lived at the end of the OC era, the latter days, and His apostles experienced the events that brought about its consummation.

There are many differing opinions on Daniel's 490 years. When did the countdown begin? When did the 490th year end? Some say that the countdown on the last years, the seventieth week of sevens, has not yet begun. Well, the "Anointed One" came, and the temple and Jerusalem was destroyed. This was the prophecy of Daniel. It was fulfilled in AD 70. Because of man's ignorance, when he does not understand something, he just adds time to it unless you are an evolutionist. Then you add time and chance. Man created a gap theory because of ignorance of the events

43

that took place in AD 70 and of symbolic language used in the scriptures. Years ago when men were looking at the prophecy of Daniel, they realized that no significant event happened using the time frame that Daniel spoke of. So, they invented a gap between the sixty-ninth and seventieth weeks. I recently read that this may have been started with the Scofield Bible, which was the first commentary Bible. It appeared on the scene in the early 1900s. It is also credited with the popularization of the dispensationalist view that dominates the American Church and seminaries.

The timeframe is not what is important to us. What is important is that it occurred. If it had not occurred then Daniel, Jesus, John, and the other prophets were liars and false prophets. Many proclaim the time clock began again in 1948 with the restoration of Israel as a nation again. The reason this is an issue today is a long story that goes back to the Scofield Bible. Just take note and do an online search on "Scofield Bible, heresy." That is all I will say about this issue for now. I will say that it was the beginning of a great heresy. Now, if these end times doomsday sayers are correct in their thinking, then 2018 should be the end. Forty years didn't work out for them, so they will now attach it to seventy years. It is stupendous how they continue to attach time to future events using numbers from events that occurred over 2 millennia ago. The Babylonian exile was for seventy years. Forty didn't work out. Seventy is all that is left. I would not at all be surprised if all hell broke out in this world between now and 2018. If it does I believe it will be because of mans' racist tendencies (most will miss this). What God has put asunder let no man bring back together. Regardless of what happens, the world will still be here.

> And four great beasts came up from the sea, diverse one from another. The first was like a lion, and had eagle's wings: I beheld until the wings thereof were plucked, and it was lifted up from the earth, and made stand upon the feet as a man, and a man's heart was given to it.

> And behold another beast, a second, like to a bear, and it raised up itself on one side, and it had three ribs in the mouth of it between the teeth of it: and they said thus unto it, Arise, devour much flesh. After this I beheld, and lo another, like a leopard, which had upon the back of it four wings of a fowl; the beast had also four heads; and dominion was given to it.

After this I saw in the night visions, and behold a fourth beast, dreadful and terrible, and strong exceedingly; and it had great iron teeth: it devoured and brake in pieces, and stamped the residue with the feet of it: and it was diverse from all the beasts that were before it; and it had ten horns. (Daniel 7:3–7, KJV)

If you were to go through Daniel and get familiar with all of his prophecy, what would be your thoughts without reading any commentary? You would highly likely be at a loss for words, or even thoughts, unless you are familiar with historical events and characters that existed between the time Daniel made his prophecies and the destruction of the temple and city of Jerusalem in AD 70. I am not going to beleaguer this, but the first beast, or empire that Daniel speaks of is the one which he is living in, the Babylonian empire. The second one to come would be the Medo-Persian empire, which was on the horizon. The third beast would be the Alexandrian empire, which was about 250 years in Daniel's future when he made the prophecy, and the most hideous of the beasts, the fourth beast, was the Roman empire, which would overcome the Jewish nation in 63 BC, about 515 years from the time Daniel made his prophecy. It appears that many have not tied the beasts mentioned in Daniel to the beast mentioned in Revelation. This is the key to the identity of the beast and what the beast represents. If you are not familiar with this history, you are ripe for having your strings pulled by others that are also ignorant of these historical events and characters. Nebuchadnezzar was the leader of the first empire that the southern kingdom of Judah would be overtaken by. Cyrus was the first king over the Medo-Persian Empire that overtook the Babylonian Empire and most of its provinces, which included Judah. This was in the 530s BC. Alexander the Great would head up the Alexandrian Empire, which was a Grecian Empire. This came about in the 330s and 320s BC. After Alexander died in Babylon, at the age of thirty-three, his kingdom was divided among his four generals, Ptolemy, Seleucas, Lysimachus, and Cassander. Hmmm. It sounds like some of Daniel's prophecy.

I think that it is important that we look at a few verses here that will shed some light on matters. I have picked just a few verses for this purpose, but this could be the subject of a book that could exceed a thousand pages. I will list the verse and then comment on the meaning of the verse in relation to historical facts. John, when he was finishing up his apocalyptic prophetic revelation from God, stated the following: *"For I testify unto every man that heareth the words of the prophecy of this book, If any man shall add unto these things, God shall add unto him the plagues that are written in this book"* (Revelation 22:18, KJV). It may be that due to this warning that man has left off a very important event that took place in AD 70, the destruction of Jerusalem and the temple, that should have been part of the Bible. I have pondered this issue much, and I believe that I have come up with a more than sufficient answer. The people who John was writing to did not need to be made aware of the torment they had just gone through. Once the events had taken place, it would forever be etched into the minds of the ones who went through hell on earth and survived. They would need no written history of their history. When you are the generation that goes through the war, you need no history of it. Only future generations need a written account of past events. I dare say that the overwhelming majority of people in the church are not even aware of this event. I have never heard a sermon preached on it, and when mentioned, it is as if it were a very minor event. It is obvious to me that the first-century church, the ones who lived through hell on earth, were very well aware of the times they were living in. The greatest historian of that era, Josephus, states that there were well over one million Jews killed when the Romans and their cohorts stormed Israel. The church today is ignorant of that history. We will take a look at a verse in just a few seconds that will comply with this ignorance, but many commentators have even distorted the true meaning of that verse from Paul. As I said, it is still a few seconds away.

"Seventy 'sevens' are decreed for your people and your holy city to finish transgression, to put an end to sin, to atone for wickedness, to bring in everlasting righteousness, to seal up vision and prophecy and to anoint the Most Holy One" (Daniel 9:24, NIV). Daniel's prophecy is stating seventy sevens. Is this a literal 490 years? We will address this in just a bit. The countdown was not to begin until the word went out to restore and rebuild the temple and Jerusalem. The Babylonians had destroyed the city when they took the Jews into captivity. There is not 100 percent consensus among commentators, theologians, preachers, and others about who issued this decree and the timing of the decree. The Bible says that Cyrus would be the one to initiate the rebuilding of the temple. This is my standard. Josephus also notes that it was Cyrus. Darius and Artaxerxes are also mentioned as possibilities by theologians and scholars. There is no certainty about the exact date. There is also no consensus as to the genuine outcome of this prophecy. Was it just through Jesus' ministry, crucifixion, and resurrection, or was the timetable all the way to the destruction of the temple in AD 70? I lean more toward the falling of the temple and the destruction of Jerusalem. We do know that all these things occurred by the time AD 70 brought the destruction of the temple. I imagine that all the saints that fled to the mountains and were spared bowed the knee and confessed Jesus as Lord as soon as they heard about the fate of Jerusalem and the temple, as did the Jews who were antichrists.

I believe that this a good place to address the 490-year issue. If you go back to the date that Cyrus declared the rebuilding of the temple, which most scholar's state was 536 BC, then there is an issue with the 490 years. Daniel's prophecy states that the timeline is from the date the declaration is made. Well, Jesus would not even have been born at that time based on this faulty interpretation. His advent would still have been about a generation away. That is why other scholars and theologians list Darius and some list Artaxerxes as the reigning king when the declaration was made. Still, the numbers just do not add up. Daniel's prophecy goes to the end. He speaks of the consummation, as we listed the verse, Daniel 9:27, earlier in this section. We know that numbers are often used as symbols and not as quantities, such as the cattle on a thousand hills. The "thousand" here is used to show completeness, not literalism. He owns the cattle on all the hills. We will address this in a later chapter in much more detail, concerning the thousand-year reign.

Let's allow scripture to interpret scripture. Is there anywhere else in scripture where such numbers or mathematics is used? Think now—yes there is. It is used by the very Son of God, Jesus, in the following verses: *"Then came Peter to him, and said, Lord, how oft shall my brother sin against me, and I forgive him? Till seven times? Jesus saith unto him, I say not unto thee, until seven times: but, until seventy times seven"* (Matthew 18:21–22, KJV). I have heard this preached by many and ironically they are always spot on with the true meaning Jesus gave here. It is as a number of fullness, or completeness, but not an exact number. Jesus is saying here to forgive as many times as you are sinned against. Are we to stone the one who offends on the 491st offense? No. It is given in symbolic language of the Jewish nation. This language was obviously known throughout all epochs of time with the descendants of Abraham. Because of the seventh-day rest and Sabbath, the numeral 7 always had other meanings within the Jewish culture. Even the number 70 obviously had meaning, too. Seven seventies would be a number denoting completeness of time down to the nth degree, or fullness of time—the time was for the generation that walked the earth with Jesus. God had spent several hundred years aligning the powers that be in that area of the world for such a time as this. If you will, do a study on the number 490 in the scriptures. I encourage you to do it yourself. I have done it. You will see that 490 is not within the pages of the

47

Bible. If Daniel had meant 490 years, why didn't he just state it? There are many times in the Bible where numbers are used to show exactness, but here we have the symbolical use of numeration, which in all the instances that I am familiar with reference completeness or fullness of time, and not exactness. Do you need scriptural confirmation of this? Well, it is available. I am not my standard nor are the teachings of man. *"But when the fullness of the time was come, God sent forth his Son, made of a woman, made under the law, to redeem them that were under the law, that we might receive the adoption of sons"* (Galatians 4:4–5, KJV). The fullness, or completeness, of time had come. It was time to bring in the new and toss out the old. It would still take a generation to fulfill the completeness of the times, but it had to begin in God's timing. After this seventy-year epoch of time, man would have access to eternal life and the Throne of God for all eternity. The fullness of time had come, but it was not yet completed or consummated when Paul documented this scripture. The end was in sight, but not yet. AD 70 would bring about the completeness of the times prophesied by all the prophets that Peter spoke of in Acts 3:24.

Here is another way to look at this prophecy. This prophecy was to be handed down. I have not undertaken this task, but the Jews were very faithful to document the timing of events. With a prophesied destruction on the horizon, I imagine that the priests or prophets would have surely documented from one generation to the next as prophecy was handed down with a timeline. If they had a timeline, then why did Jesus give them signs to be aware of? Why did he not just state forty years from the time of his crucifixion? If Jesus did not know the day or hour, did Daniel at least know the day or the year? Because of the way the Jews documented their history and the nature of the priestly system, they would have had at least a year in mind from Daniel's prophecy, but they obviously didn't. I have never heard this as a resolution to the 490-year enigma, but I believe that it is more sound than any other proposed. I likes feeding the sheep with knowledge. God knows that we need it in this day and time. Four hundred and ninety years is never mentioned by Daniel. The "seventy sevens" was to show fullness of time and not a given year. If the people had a date, why would they need signs? They comprehended the numbers as fullness, or completeness, and not a literal timeframe because they were knowledgeable about the language of the culture.

"But you, Daniel, shut up the words and seal the book, until the time of the end. Many shall run to and fro, and knowledge shall increase" (Daniel 12:4, ESV). The above verse was written down about 600 years before John wrote Revelation. The time of this event was in the distant

future, about fourteen or fifteen biblical generations away. The "knowledge shall increase" statement has been particularly blown out of context. There are those today that say that this was prophesying of technology, the computer age, and so forth.

The knowledge Daniel was speaking of here was the knowledge of his prophecy. Daniel, I dare say, did not even understand fully all that he had prophesied. As the events began to unfold, the generation that experienced the prophetic events would begin to recognize the events as what Daniel had prophesied, but also what Jesus and John prophesied, as well as the other prophets.

Daniel does not give a timeframe for the completion of his prophetic events. He is not prophesying about the end of the world. He is prophesying of an event that other Old Testament prophets foretold. That event was the destruction of the Jewish nation in AD 70. It was also the fulfillment of Jesus prophecy about the temple: *"As for these things which ye behold, the days will come, in the which there shall not be left one stone upon another, that shall not be thrown down"* (Luke 21:6, KJV). This event is known as the destruction of Jerusalem, the temple, and the Jewish nation. It was the end of all things for the nation that had transgressed all the laws of God. This was the all-consuming event that all the prophets had prophesied. It was the end of the covenant with the Jewish nation. It was the consummation of the OTC. The definition that Dictionary by Farlex (online) gives for *consummation* is as follows:

1) The act of consummating; a fulfillment.
2) An ultimate goal or end.
3) A concluding action
4) A concluding or terminating

> And he shall confirm the covenant with many for one week: and in the midst of the week he shall cause the sacrifice and the oblation to cease, and for the overspreading of abominations he shall make it desolate, even until the consummation, and that determined shall be poured upon the desolate. (Daniel 9:27, KJV)

If you look at the 14 English versions in the BLB online you will see that they do not agree with each other on this verse. The difference is in how "desolate" is treated. The Hebrew word is שֹׁמֵם. Strong's Concordance gives the meaning as follows:

49

1. to be desolate, be appalled, stun, stupefy
2. to be desolated, be deflowered, be deserted
3. to devastate, ravage, make desolated

Some translations take the Hebrew root form and change it from an adjective to a noun, actually a person, the "desolator." What this verse is stating is that the temple will be desolate, or not in use from this time on up until the destruction of the temple in AD 70, which would also be the final sign of the end of the OC era. There was an image set up in the temple by Antiochus IV Epiphanes in 168 BC during the Maccabean revolt. There are many that say that this is the prophesied abomination of desolation. The issue I have with this being the prophesied abomination is that the entity, or person, that institutes the action, is present up to the consummation, which was the destruction of the temple, the city of Jerusalem, and the end of the OTC era. We know from Josephus that Galba set up an image of Nero in the temple after his suicide, which would have been about one and a half to two years from the destruction. The caesar system was still in power and the Beast was the Roman Empire, represented by 666, which was Nero. Were the temple sacrifice rituals halted from 168 BC to AD 70? I think not. Temple sacrifices are mentioned in the New Testament several times by Paul and the writer of Hebrews, as they were going on during their lifetime. The image of Nero better fits Daniel's prophecy of the abomination of desolation. It also appears that Daniel prophesied about two of these events taking place, which would cover Antiochus IV Epiphanes and Galba's abominations.

> That upon you may come all the righteous blood shed upon the earth, from the blood of righteous Abel unto the blood of Zacharias son of Barachias, whom ye slew between the temple and the altar. Verily I say unto you, all these things shall come upon this generation. O Jerusalem, Jerusalem, thou that killest the prophets, and stonest them which are sent unto thee, how often would I have gathered thy children together, even as a hen gathereth her chickens under her wings, and ye would not. Behold, your house is left unto you desolate.
>
> (Matthew 23:35–38, KJV)

Jesus was foretelling the great catastrophe that was to befall Jerusalem in about forty years. When Jesus stated "Behold, your house is left unto you desolate," He was using present tense. It was a done deal, even though it was forty years in their future. He knew that they would not repent. They had been rebellious since they left Egypt. He could have also been referring to the departure of the Holy Spirit from the temple after His crucifixion. Man did not realize that God had abandoned the temple at Christ's death. Man will not know all the facts until he arrives in heaven, but each believer under the NC will enter heaven upon their own death. It will not be a one-time event. Each will be caught up in his own order at his death. The repentant believer will be caught up, and the unrepentant will be caught down.

In Daniel 12:4, he is told to seal the book. Actually, Daniel would not be around when the end came. His timeframe was hundreds of years into the future. Is it not ironic that Daniel is told to seal up his prophecy, which is hundreds of years into the future, and John is told in Revelation not to seal up his prophecy because the time is at hand? "At hand" has always meant near, close by, about to happen. Daniel and John prophesied the same event. The difference in their prophetic timcline is about fifteen biblical generations. How many people can name their great-great-grandfather? I knew my great grandfather on my dad's side of the family, but I could not even tell you the name of either of my great grandfathers on my mother's side. By the way, my great grandfather nickname on my dad's side was "Dad." My point is that most people today can't even name all of their great grandfathers, much less have significant knowledge of events that took place 2,000 years ago. Daniel was told to seal his prophecy because it was far future, yet John was told not to seal his prophesy because the time was near. I am sorry, but 1950 years and going is not near.

> And he saith unto me, Seal not the sayings of the prophecy of this book: for the time is at hand.
> (Revelation 22:10, KJV)

> And he said to me, "Do not seal up the words of the prophecy of this book, for the time is near. (ESV)

Daniel and John prophesied the same event. It was far future to Daniel and was certainly not imminent or really relevant to Daniel, but it surely was to John. The time was "at hand," or "near." Jesus also prophesied of this same event. Let's look at some of his statements about this event and see if we can get a sense of the timing of the event.

51

From then on Jesus began to preach, "Repent of your sins and turn to God, for the Kingdom of heaven is near" (Matthew 4:17, NLT). There are many preachers today that state "No man knoweth the hour or the time that He cometh" as an excuse for Jesus making such statements as this. Well, he may not have known the hour or day, but He certainly knew it was "this generation," His contemporary generation, that would experience the times and events that all the prophets foretold.

> You will be hated by all because of My name, but it is the one who has endured to the end who will be saved. But whenever they persecute you in one city, flee to the next; for truly I say to you, you will not finish going through the cities of Israel until the Son of Man comes.
> (Matthew 10:22–23, NASB)

I am sorry, but Jesus is part of the triune God. He may not have known the exact hour, or day, while He was in the flesh, but He knew the generation that God would pour out His wrath on would be the one who rejected their Messiah and had Him crucified. The people had an opportunity to have Jesus released and spared from crucifixion, but instead, *"Then answered all the people, and said, "His blood be on us, and on our children"* (Matthew 27:25, KJV). You can be assured that God poured out His wrath on the ones who rejected Jesus. They had forty years to repent, but all would not.

> Who then is the faithful and wise servant, whom the master has put in charge of the servants in his household to give them their food at the proper time? It will be good for that servant whose master finds him doing so when he returns. Truly I tell you, he will put him in charge of all his possessions. But suppose that servant is wicked and says to himself, "My master is staying away a long time," and he then begins to beat his fellow servants and to eat and drink with drunkards. The master of that servant will come on a day when he does not expect him and at an hour he is not aware of. He will cut him to pieces and assign him a place with the hypocrites, where there will be weeping and gnashing of teeth.
> (Matthew 24:45–51, NIV)

The "Master" was Jesus. He charged His disciples, the apostles, with a task, and that was to take the Gospel throughout the area and to warn and prepare those who would become children of God. All of those apostles have gone on to be with Him. It is believed that all the apostles except John died martyrs' deaths. If Jesus was going to be coming back 2,000 years later He would not have been warning His apostles. The time was near in the scheme of things, but still, forty years away is quite a long way off. However, if you are sixty years old, it may as well be an eternity away because virtually no one would live to see it. Many followers of Christ would die before AD 70 and go through the resurrection.

"Now after John was put in prison, Jesus came to Galilee, preaching the gospel of the kingdom of God, and saying, 'The time is fulfilled, and the kingdom of God is at hand. Repent, and believe in the gospel" (Mark 1:14–15, NKJV). What time is fulfilled? Well, Messiah is on the scene, but He must be sacrificed first, and then Jesus's prophecies would have to be fulfilled as well as Johns' that had not yet been foretold. So, I suppose what has been fulfilled here are the prophecies that foretold of the Messiah, particularly Isaiah's. Being that Daniel, Jesus, and John prophesied the same event, and Jesus and John had not yet given their prophecies of this forthcoming event, then it becomes obvious that all prophecy was about to be completed.

"And Jesus was saying to them, "Truly I say to you, there are some of those who are standing here who will not taste death until they see the kingdom of God after it has come with power" (Mark9:1, NASB). Again, preachers and commentators state "No man knows the day or hour, so Jesus was wrong here in his prophetic statement." Jesus is not a liar. Only humans are liars. The problem here is that Jesus is the Creator, the Word that was there in the beginning, and nothing was made that was not made without Him, and the word became flesh. Jesus was not ignorant. He knew that the time for the wrath of God to be poured out was at hand and that "this generation" was the one who was to pay the price, the very generation that stated "His blood be on us, and on our children."

If we look at what Moses gave as the stalwart qualifications of a prophet, then based on current end times preaching and prophecy, Jesus, Daniel, and John would be disqualified. If the timing of prophecy did not come to fruition as foretold, then that fool was not a prophet and not to be feared. As mentioned earlier, Daniel was not giving a time indicator, but a completeness or fullness of time indicator. If you had the date why would you need signs? Jesus gave his converts signs to look for and to flee when they saw them. Jesus stated that "this generation" shall not pass away until the end. Jesus even stated that they would not even have gone through all the streets of Israel when He comes back. It is obvious that we have a false view of what His "coming back" was. Well, I used to, but not anymore. I used to be biblically illiterate, but not anymore.

"Love never ends; as for prophecies, they will pass away; as for tongues, they will cease; as for knowledge, it will pass away" (1 Corinthians 13:8, KJV). There are many different opinions in the commentaries about this verse Paul wrote, but I will untwist it here and allow it to become the light that God meant for it to be. I think we all understand the "love" part. "For God so loved the world that He sent His only begotten Son . . ." We are to be a reflection of His love to the world. The lost should see the love of God in the believer, but sadly that is a rarity. I shall say this, though; political correctness will not get you into heaven. Truth does not make you a racist or bigot. Truth convicts the soul and convinces man that he needs to be reformed. The destruction of Jerusalem in AD 70 was the fulfillment of Old Testament prophecy. This is not in our future, as the biblically and historically illiterate propagate today. We see the results of a flawed and illiterate view of the scriptures today in these end times books, as well as in most churches. No, the time is not near. The reason the world is in the shape it is today is because the church has failed. The believers are the leaves on the Tree of Life that are for the healing of the nations, yet the church has become so divisive. Oh, by the way, when AD 70 came and went, so did speaking in tongues. It has ceased with the Holy Spirit, but not with man. Remember Daniel's statement about knowledge increasing? Well, Paul states here that once the events have been fulfilled it will bring about a decrease in knowledge. We certainly are ignorant of most of the events that took place within the generation that crucified their Messiah.

Most churchgoers today are not even aware of the destruction of Jerusalem in AD 70. It is never mentioned in most churches. Men in any generation and in any nation today do not have a full historical understanding of the particular nation that they live in, probably beyond 50–100 years, much less 2,000 years. We must come to the realization that we will never understand every event prophesied in the Bible, but we can be assured that "this generation" experienced it to the full. Daniel spoke of an increase in knowledge as the events began to take place around Jerusalem, leading up to AD 70. Paul is stating here that once the prophetic events have taken place, then knowledge of the events will decrease. It is amazing that both the Old Testament prophecy, as well as Paul's prophecy, have been fulfilled. Knowledge has certainly decreased of those events. No, this was not a decrease of knowledge in heaven to spare us from the grief over lost loved ones.

Now back to the qualifications of a prophet from God. Obviously there are other prophets than prophets from God. A prophet from God never misses the intended timeframe of an event. If a man prophesied an event that did not take place back in the "Old Testament" (Jesus lived in the later days of the OTC era), he was supposed to be put to death. I dare say that this "evil generation" had taken on the effeminate behavior of political correctness that we see today in the world and was guilty of not carrying out this mandate. Woe be unto those who tell truth. If Jesus' and John's prophesies did not come to fruition during "this generation," then they would be disqualified as prophets and would deserve no less than stoning. They would have been killed because they told truth. The 490 years that Daniel did not prophecy has been a stumbling stone. The seven weeks of seventies was his prophecy, symbolic of fullness of time, not exactness. What Daniel prophesied has been a major obstacle to the simple, the theologian, preacher, teacher, and scholar alike. Regardless of how the 490 years has confused the issue, the prophesied event took place in AD 70.

Jesus was Prophet, Priest, and King. John was a disciple, an apostle, and a prophet. Daniel was a prophet. Prophecy has been fulfilled, and "Thy kingdom come" has come. Hmmm, do I need to do a section on that, too? Is this for now or later? I do not want to overload. The evolution of a tainted mind takes time, a bit here, a bit there. It has taken me years of study to see the Light that is Truth. His story is far more important than history. If we get His story right, then history will do a 180, and the leaves on the tree of life shall truly be used for the healing of the nations.

Jesus, Daniel, and John met the qualifications of a prophet from God. It is obvious that the generation that Daniel was living in would not have had any basis for even being affected in their lifetimes from the pouring out of God's wrath about a half a millennia away, but they would have to deal with the skirmishes going on at that time. Future generations would have to deal with battles and intra-Judah conflicts. The people of Jesus' day, "this generation," attempted to put Him to death, but He arose on the third day. He spent forty days in the area around Jerusalem after His resurrection. He either had limited contact with those who knew Him best at that time, or the events were not to be recorded. This time He left to our imaginations. He probably spent much of this time warning "this generation" of the coming wrath of God in AD 70. Few received His warnings, but many of those who did were spared because they heeded His warnings and recognized the signs. Still, many who did accept Jesus as Messiah died horrific deaths, but they had a wonderful reward awaiting them that would shortly be realized. Upon the consummation of the OTC would be the realization of a new and better covenant, where there would be no more death, nor sorrow, for the believer. From AD 70 forward, all who die in Christ shall immediately be in His presence in His kingdom. His kingdom has come. His disciples prayed for it, and God answered that prayer during "this generation."

It is early October 2016. I noticed many YouTube videos over the past several months that have touted "The end is near." Many gave dates of July 29 and July 30. Well, those guys failed the test of a prophet. There were several sights that gave August 29 and August 30 as the end of the world. It is now in the past, and nothing happened. Some even went into the fall and even winter. Regardless, time will prove all of these individuals to be false prophets. The world did not end in 2016, nor shall it end in this millennium. The rapture will not take place, ever. There are many that will state that I am a false prophet for making this statement. Well, as I have stated in other areas of this book, there are no prophets today. I am not a false prophet. I am no prophet, nor is anyone else today. I am just a hungry soul that has spent much time in the scriptures, as well as extra-biblical sources attempting to glean all the knowledge that I can about *His story*.

If the events that Jesus and John spoke of were not to take place during their generation, then they would have been considered false prophets. The Pharisees insisted that they were false prophets. They did not believe that John was a prophet and certainly didn't believe that Jesus was the prophesied Messiah, yet He performed many miracles among the people. He did not perform signs and wonders before the Pharisees. They were power hungry and greedy for the money that came through the system that they had corrupted. Even if Jesus had performed miracles in the presence of the Pharisees, they would not have accepted Him as Messiah. It was foreordained for this generation, the very elect of God, to be the one who would fulfill all the prophecy about the crucifixion of the Lamb that would take away the sins of the world (the repentant believer). All that Daniel prophesied that had not been fulfilled prior to Jesus was being fulfilled before their very eyes. All that John and Jesus prophesied would be fulfilled within "this generation," the one that consisted of the contemporaries of Jesus and John. Not one jot or tittle would be left unfulfilled. If you do not believe me, just ask when you get to heaven. Educate yourself and do not be a stumbling block. By the time that you get to the end of this book, I pray that an evolutionary process will have begun.

Prophetic Timing

he timing of prophecy is a very important issue. You can ask theologians, preachers, scholars, and laymen, and none seem to have all the answers. It is a difficult thing to pin down certain Old Testament prophecies and tie them to specific events that were the fulfillment. Many, if not most, of the Old Testament prophecies were fulfilled during the Old Testament Covenant era. Some were in the far future to the current hearers. To anyone with biblical discernment, it is obvious that Daniel, Jesus, and John the Revelator prophesied the same event. Daniel also prophesied of events that were fulfilled between the Babylonian exile and the birth of Jesus. Many of the other Old Testament prophets prophesied of the same event that these three prophets prophesied. If there is any doubt as to the timing of prophecy, there is one verse in the Bible that answers the question. This is *the answer* to the timing issue of prophecy. The verse is in the book of Acts, and it quotes Peter, stating the timing of all the Old Testament prophecies, which had not yet come to be fulfilled in his lifetime, but were on the horizon. The following scripture is the key to this question:

> For Moses truly said unto the fathers, A prophet shall the Lord your God raise up unto you of your brethren, like unto me; him shall ye hear in all things whatsoever he shall say unto you. And it shall come to pass, that every soul, which will not hear that prophet, shall be destroyed from among the people. Yea, and all the prophets from Samuel and those who follow after, as many as have spoken, have likewise foretold of these days. (Acts 3:22–24, KJV)

> Moses said "The Lord God will raise up for you a prophet like me from your brothers. You shall listen

> to him in whatever he tells you. And it shall be that
> every soul who does not listen to that prophet shall be
> destroyed from the people." And all the prophets who
> have spoken, from Samuel and those who came after
> him, also proclaimed these days. (ESV)

"And all the prophets who have spoken, from Samuel and those who came after him, also proclaimed these days." Peter was speaking to his contemporaries, not us. "These days" does not refer to our day and time. "These days" refers to the days that Peter and his contemporaries were living in. I hear many people today speaking of how America has changed in "these days." I know that they are not referring to days past or of a time in the future. They are speaking of the here and now, as was Peter of his here and now. This verse also states that this was about an event that all the prophets spoke of, *all* prophets that ever spoke, including the One who we know as Prophet, Priest, and King—Jesus. I believe that a major problem we have today in the world is ignorance of world history and particularly history of what happened to Israel in AD 70. Due to a possible calendar error, it is proposed that Jesus was actually crucified in AD 30, yet born in 3–5 BC (Yes, there is no consensus on Jesus' age among theologians and scholars.). Hmmm. Were they once again allowed to wander in the wilderness? This would go along quite well with what the average Christian knows about the biblical forty-year generation. It is a shame that the ones who canonized the Bible did not include a book after Revelation that showed the fulfillment of prophecy and the destruction of Jerusalem. Otherwise, there would be no question as to the accuracy and timing of prophecy. Men would treasure the Bible as if it were far more precious than gold.

I admonish all readers to go back and study the prophecies. It is difficult for us to understand the timetable of the prophecies because they were not meant for us. They were meant for the people of ancient Israel. This would include prophecies from Isaiah, Ezekiel, Jeremiah, and so on. This would also include the prophecies of the One who we know as Prophet, Priest, and King. Jesus prophesied of the events that took place in AD 70 in His sermon on the mount. He even stated that "this generation," His contemporaries, shall not pass until these things come to be. Due to what seems to be intentional, many in our culture today are ignorant of American history. If you are not aware of the past you are bound to repeat it. I have made mistakes in my past, but I am not bound to repeat them because I have a memory. Wicked men attempt to hide or deny the past. Heaven will be heaven because there will be no wicked men there.

I believe "this generation" is a subject that has gotten little to no attention in the modern church. I have never heard a sermon preached on it, yet "this generation" is mentioned sixteen times in the New Testament. It has really struck a chord with me. It is obvious that "this generation" is of extreme importance in the Bible. We will take a look at some of the verses now. I would also like to state my views on the "elect" of God at this time. It seems obvious to me that the "elect" of God was "this generation," the one whom He chose to bring salvation to the world to through Jesus, the Messiah. God elected "this generation" to bring in grace but also to pour out His wrath upon. "This generation" was the one that received what all the prophets had spoken about in times of old. I thank God that I was not of "the elect" generation that He chose to bring in salvation, but also to pour out His wrath. Regardless of what side you were on, it was a most miserable time to live in. The apostles, Jewish Christians, and Gentile Christians were persecuted and martyred. After forty years, time to repent and get right with your Maker, God poured out His wrath on "this generation," the one whom He elected. Now, let us take a look at some of the "this generation" verses. You can also do an online word search, using Blue Letter Bible. I encourage you to do your own research. Do as the people from Berea did. *These were more noble than those in Thessalonica, in that they received the word with all readiness of mind, and searched the scriptures daily, whether those things were so"* (Acts 17:11, KJV).

We do not live in the first century. Today you can become better educated than the theologians and scholars of the past with readily accessible online research sites, as well as access to purchase the writings of Josephus, Eusebius, and other ancient historians. When you become familiar with the Old Testament prophecies, you will begin to see historical events that took place within the pre-first-century geographical area of Israel, which would have included Greece that was accessible by land at approximately 1,700 miles away, and Rome, about 2,550 miles from Jerusalem. Persia, which is current day Iran, is approximately 1,450 miles from Jerusalem. Considering the Babylonian exile, which is current-day Iraq, is approximately 725 miles from Jerusalem. Today we can jump on an aircraft in Atlanta, and if there were no stops, we could be there within twenty hours. I imagine that to travel with a military force back in the centuries before Jesus came would have taken about a day to travel just forty miles. This is just to put far north and south into perspective in the days of the apostles. It did not take far to be long.

"The men of Nineveh will rise up at the judgment with this genera-tion and condemn it, for they repented at the preaching of Jonah, and behold, something greater than Jonah is here" (Matthew 12:41, ESV). It is obvious that the judgment was to happen within "this generation." Also, "here" is now, not 2,000 years in the future. Jesus was speaking to His contemporaries, not a generation 2,000 years into the future.

> You serpents, you brood of vipers, how are you to escape being sentenced to hell? Therefore I send you prophets and wise men and scribes, some of whom you will kill and crucify, and some you will flog in your synagogues and persecute from town to town, so that on you may come all the righteous blood shed on earth, from the blood of righteous Abel to the blood of Zechariah the son of Barachiah, whom you murdered between the sanctuary and the altar. Truly, I say to you, all these things will come upon this generation. (Matthew 23:33–36, ESV)

We know from biblical, as well as extra-biblical sources, that the apostles and other believers were martyred by "this generation." Certainly many professing Christ have been killed for their beliefs since the time of Jesus. Even today, it is going on in the world. However, no other gen-eration except the one who Jesus and the ones he sent could be called "this generation." This is also the same generation that was referred to by John the Baptist as the "generation of vipers" in the following: *"But when he saw many of the Pharisees and Sadducees come to his baptism, he said unto them, O generation of vipers, who hath warned you to flee from the wrath to come"* (Matthew 3:7, KJV)?

The wrath to come was upon "this generation" and it was about a gen-eration away. Jesus also used the viper phrase in Matthew 12:34 (KJV) that says, *"O generation of vipers, how can ye, being evil, speak good things? For out of the abundance of the heart the mouth speaketh."* He also used it in Matthew 23:33 (HNV), *"You serpents, you offspring of vipers, how will you escape the judgment of Gehinnom?"*

Mark 12:34 says, *"Truly, I say to you, this generation will not pass away until all these things take place."* Again, this is not our generation, or a future generation. This was the "generation of vipers" that Jesus and John the Baptist lived among.

"For as Jonah became a sign to the people of Nineveh, so will the Son of Man be to this generation" (Luke 11:30, ESV). Jonah was a sign to the generation that he was living in. Jonah spent three days and three nights in the belly of a whale. Because of his reluctant obedience to God, the Ninevites were spared God's judgment because they repented. Jesus spent three days and nights in the belly of the earth to pay for the wages of sin, which is death. The generation that crucified Jesus would also be the one that was still present in AD 70. Many had died, but many were still alive. Most in "this generation" did not repent, and God's judgment was poured out in AD 70.

> And the LORD said to me: "The prophets are prophesying lies in my name. I did not send them, nor did I command them or speak to them. They are prophesying to you a lying vision, worthless divination, and the deceit of their own minds." (Jeremiah 14:14, ESV)

God did not send those lying prophets in Jeremiahs day, nor did He send those who are prophesying lies today.

> And the LORD said to me: "The prophets are prophesying lies in my name. I did not send them, nor did I command them or speak to them. They are prophesying to you a lying vision, worthless divination, and the deceit of their own minds. For we know in part, and we prophesy in part, but when that which is perfect is come, then that which is in part shall be done away.
> (1 Corinthians 13:8–10, KJV)

The New Testament Covenant had not yet been brought in. "That which is perfect" in the above scripture is the New Covenant. God is patient and long-suffering. He was giving "this generation" forty years, a biblical generation, to repent and get it right. Jesus gave His contemporaries signs to look for. It was appointed to the apostles, except John, to give their lives for the gospel message, but Jesus told the other converts to flee to the mountains for safety and security. He never told them that they would be raptured out of tribulation. He told them the following: *"These things I have spoken unto you, that in me ye might have peace. In the world ye shall have tribulation: but be of good cheer; I have overcome the world"* (John 16:33, KJV). Jesus is telling them that tribulation is associated with this fallen world. We are to trust in Him. Those who hold on to Him to the end of their lives shall overcome this world. The repentant believer will take his last breath in this life and his next in His kingdom, heaven. Each believer will be taken up upon his death. The resurrection was for those under the law. Sinner and saint experienced death under the law, the Old Covenant. Under grace, the New Covenant, the unrepentant still shall experience the wages for sin, but the repentant believer shall never experience the wages of sin. That is what is superior about the New Covenant over the Old Covenant. That which is perfect has come. While many are sitting around waiting on the rapture, I am going to be experiencing some of my Father who art in heaven's glorious creation on Planet Earth.

There are many more verses that I could expound upon, but I hate to beat a live horse. Let the dead horse die. Again, I encourage you to do your own search. When you see it for yourself, you will be better able to understand and defend the truth if the need shall arise. I don't believe it because the preacher said it. I shall only believe if the scriptures state it. What is your standard, the traditions or teachings of man, or the word of God, the scriptures? The word of God is my standard. If there is a consistency issue with scripture, there is an interpretation issue that is highly likely wrong. Scripture does not contradict itself. Man contradicts scripture every day and particularly on Sundays. No scripture is of a private interpretation. It says what it means and means what it says, in spite of what many that are biblically and historically illiterate say. Near is near, at hand is at hand, and shortly is shortly. It always has been and always will be, unless you are an end-times doomsday sayer.

The first-generation believers went through great tribulation, but they were not spared. They hung in there. Let's look at a verse here that will give us an idea of how John felt. He knew that he would live through the consummation and into the New Covenant era. *"He which testifieth these things saith, surely I come quickly. Amen." " Even so, come, Lord Jesus"* (Revelation 22:20, KJV).

John had an idea of what to expect on that day. He understood what "coming on clouds" was all about. Jesus is the one who stated "surely I come quickly." John states "Even so, come, Lord Jesus." "Even so" is not a happy, happy, thing here. This is a statement of dread. John knew that it would literally be hell on earth, but he also knew that what was coming, the New Covenant, would be superior to the Old and that he would never have to experience what all the other apostles experienced. He knew that as bad as things were going to get in the coming years, it would all be worth it when all was said and done. "Even so, come" is a statement of dread but also of future hope for that which is perfect: the NTC.

Timing of prophecy and fulfillment of prophecy are the best indicators of whether the prophets were true prophets and prophets of God. Daniel foretold events that occurred from the Babylonian exile to the consummation of the Old Covenant. The fullness of time was the timeline and not 490 years. If 490 years was the time indicator, then they needed no signs. Because of the meticulous way the Jews documented lineage, we can trace Jesus' birth all the way back to Abraham and can do it with great numerical accuracy because of ages and reigns of kings. This is about forty-five biblical generations. The average human today cannot even trace his ancestry back even four or five generations. Actually, we can trace Jesus' lineage back to the beginning. The numbers were there to be had if Daniel had meant a literal 490 years, but that is not at all what he meant. The Jews knew the symbolism of their culture and language. They fully comprehended that it was all up to God's timing, which is fullness of time.

If I were to tell you that the American Revolution has not yet taken place, you would think that I am the most ignorant person in the world. Why would you think that? Because history documents it. Well, history also documents fulfilled prophecy. Not one jot or tittle has been left unfulfilled. Those who claim otherwise do not comprehend what the kingdom of God is, where the kingdom of God is, and when the kingdom of God arrived. They also do not understand what the new heaven and earth are. I am sure that they do not realize this, either, but they are calling Jesus and John false prophets. They stated that their generation would experience all the prophets had prophesied. Peter even confirmed this: *"And likewise, all the prophets who have spoken, from Samuel and his successors onward, also announced these days"* (Acts 3:24, NASB).

"These days" are their days, the days that the first generation of Christians was walking the earth. My standard is the word of God, but you also must be historically literate of the events that took place from the Assyrian captivity all the way to the destruction of the temple and city of Jerusalem in AD 70. The information is out there, but it takes much time and effort. Do not be deceived. The "end" is not in your future. It is in your past. Do not compromise your life with the teachings of false prophets and teachers. If you were affected the way I was as a child, it would burn within your heart to correct the errors that are tarnishing the minds of God's people. I see young ones today who are bedeviled with all of this false end-times garbage in the world today. This is my attempt to shine the light on the truth that is in our past and the truth on what is designated to the believer today.

> In the midst of the street of it, and on either side of
> the river, was there the tree of life, which bare twelve
> manner of fruits, and yielded her fruit every month: and
> the leaves of the tree were for the healing of the nations.
> (Revelation 22:2, KJV)

Because of a false end-times view, the current doom-and-gloom heresy, man has missed this mandate from God. This is not to take place in heaven. This is for the here and now. There will be no nations in heaven. It is the responsibility of the true Christians to promote the healing of the nations. National supremacy and racism are an abomination to God. Woe be unto you who promote such as this in the world. This is a two-way street and not a one-way street. Blessed are the peacemakers and cursed are the war-mongers.

Who Is "This Generation"?

$\mathscr{T}$he Bible is a book of history, prophecy, wisdom, instruction, admonition, and revelation. This list is not meant to be all inclusive, for it is so much more. It is the Book of Life. Particular parts of the Bible are revelations of historical events, such as the creation in the beginning, the fall of man, the flood, the Tower of Babel dispersion, the Exodus, and so forth. The prophetic portions were letters written to particular people in a particular time and place. These portions were very imminent to the people to whom they were written. Most had warnings with promised destruction, exile, and even death, but there was always an out if the people would heed the warnings and turn from their wicked ways. There is much wisdom throughout the Bible, but there is also the book of wisdom: Proverbs. Wisdom is wisdom, no matter the epoch of time or the place. We have a lack of wisdom today because there is a lack of historical knowledge. If one knows history, a rational person will not continue to do things that have caused harm, confusion, and poverty in past generations.

To whom was God speaking when He told that man to build the ark? To whom was God speaking when He told that fellow to hold up his staff and part the Red Sea? I believe any rational logical, thinking person would answer "Noah" and "Moses." When Jesus spoke many times about "this generation," to whom was He speaking? There are many today that would say that He was speaking to you and me. Why is it that a logical and rational thinking person would answer that question with "you and me," yet answer the other two questions with the obvious, "Noah and Moses?" Well, that is not a logical rational response.

Most people today are not aware of an earth-shattering event that took place in AD 70. The city of Jerusalem was overtaken by Roman forces, and the temple was destroyed. Jesus had stated that "not a stone will be left unturned." The temple had much gold in it. It was set on fire and the gold melted into the stones of the building. The Roman armies took hammers and chisels and literally turned every stone in the temple to recover the melted gold from it. There are many in the church awaiting this event today, as if it were in our future. Most have never heard a sermon that links the destruction of Revelation to the AD 70 event. I have heard preachers mention the event, but they gloss over it like it was a very small event at an obscure moment in time. Well, it was the consummation of the Old Covenant. That was a huge event for the Jewish nation, as well as for the Gentile nations of the Roman Empire. The nation of Israel was destroyed, and God gave the keys to the Gentiles. Actually, the land was literally given to the meek, the ones who didn't take up the sword against the Judaizers, Zealots, and Roman forces.

Entry into the Kingdom of God for all the peoples and nations forevermore was also part of the consummation. The consummation of the OTC era was the beginning of the Kingdom of God. His kingdom has come. Jesus told His disciples to pray "Our Father which art in heaven, hallowed be thy name. Thy kingdom come. Thy will be done . . ." "*Ask, and it shall be given you; seek, and ye shall find; knock, and it shall be opened unto you*" (Matthew 7:7, KJV). Jesus did not tell them to pray for something that was not expected or attainable in their lifetime, but fifty generations away, about 2,000 years. His kingdom has come. Now, it appears that man has been ignorant of this for some years now.

We will look at some scriptures now that should make it obvious to the discerning soul who Jesus was speaking to. It was not meant to be a great mystery. If it were it would serve no purpose for any generation. I am sorry, but God is not a cruel, hateful, and spiteful Being. He would not have all generations, from Jesus' time until now, and forevermore, to be schizophrenic about timing of prophecy. God would not have all generations of believers to compromise their lives awaiting the end of the world. Jesus meant for His generation to know beyond a shadow of a doubt that they were the chosen generation, the elect of God, and that He would consummate the OTC, destroy the enemies of Christ (those who actually killed Him), and make way for the Gentiles to enter into the kingdom of God once for all time. This was what the prophets had prophesied since the beginning of prophecy, which began in Genesis. It was about to take place during the generation that saw Jesus the Messiah perform miracles, die on the cross, rise again on the third day, and come in judgment in AD 70 on clouds.

The word *generation* is used thirty-seven times in thirty-five verses in the New Testament of the King James Bible. In most instances, it is referring directly to the generation and timeframe that Jesus lived in and walked in the flesh among the Jews.

I recently bought a used copy of Hal Lindsey's *The Late Great Planet Earth*. I was testing a theory that I had about the timing of the Jim Jones Kool-Aid drinking massacre back in 1978, as well as the sermon that I heard between 1974 and 1976, the one which gave me insomnia for between fourteen and sixteen years. I believe that this book, after reading it, was the catalyst behind both events. The preacher used the same entities in his sermon as Lindsey did in his fictitious end-times scenario. If my assumption is correct, then Hal Lindsey will have the blood of over 900 people on his hands. Lindsey states that the generation that sees Israel become a nation again is the one who will experience the end of Planet Earth. I believe by the time you get through this section, you will have a superior knowledge about prophecy than he did. Many are still preaching the heresies of Lindsey today.

The purpose of this endeavor is to educate people to what the Bible says and not to what man says. One of the main issues that Jesus had with the Jews was that their leaders had created their own traditions that were promoted as superior to God's ways. Many today have made the teachings of man their authority and not the word of God. "This generation" means the one who Jesus was living in, and not "that generation," the one which we are living in almost 2,000 years later. This end-times doomsday stuff has become so much a tradition of the church that it is not even paid much attention to by the members today. It has also had the side effect of making the church look ignorant and ridiculous. There may be much upheaval in the American culture today and across the world, but I will make a prediction, not a prophecy. There are no prophets today since prophecy has been sealed. My prediction is that this generation, the one which we currently live in (I shouldn't have to spell it out, but . . .) shall pass away, yet the world will go on and on.

It is obvious that "this generation" was being addressed by Jesus and John the Baptist. It would also be the same generation that the apostles would be dealing with after Jesus death, resurrection, and ascension. Once I noticed the frequency of the mention of "this generation", I began to do a word study using the BLB. The term generation occurs 37 times in 35 verses in the New Testament of the KJV. I will list below the noun and adjective used to describe "this generation" in the verses where "generation" is relevant to the subject matter. I will also list the one making the statement about "this generation."

Scripture Adjective and Noun Speaker

Scripture	Adjective and Noun	Speaker
Matthew 3:7	generation of vipers	John the Baptist
Matthew 11:16	this generation	Jesus
Matthew 12:34	generation of vipers	Jesus
Matthew 12:39	evil and adulterous generation	Jesus
Matthew 12:41	this generation	Jesus
Matthew 12:42	this generation	Jesus
Matthew 12:45	wicked generation	Jesus
Matthew 16:4	wicked and adulterous generation	Jesus
Matthew 17:17	faithless and perverse generation	Jesus
Matthew 23:33	generation of vipers	Jesus
Matthew 23:36	this generation	Jesus
Matthew 24:34	this generation	Jesus
Mark 8:12	this generation; this generation	Jesus
Mark 8:38	adulterous and sinful generation	Jesus
Mark 9:19	faithless generation	Jesus
Mark 13:30	this generation	Jesus
Luke 3:7	generation of vipers	Jesus
Luke 7:31	this generation	Jesus
Luke 9:41	faithless and perverse generation	Jesus
Luke 11:29	evil generation	Jesus
Luke 11:30	this generation	Jesus
Luke 11:31	this generation	Jesus
Luke 11:32	this generation	Jesus
Luke 11:50	this generation	Jesus
Luke 11: 51	this generation	Jesus
Luke 16:8	their generation	Jesus
Luke 17:25	this generation	Jesus
Luke 21:32	this generation	Jesus
Acts 2:40	untoward generation	Peter
1 Peter 2:9	chosen generation	Peter

Of the thirty-seven times that "generation" is used in the KJV New Testament, thirty-one of those are referring to the "this generation" that was going to be the one who experienced the wrath of God, the consummation of the OTC era, and the beginning of the promised better NTC era, where death would be abolished for the repentant sinner. "O death, where is thy sting? O grave, where is thy victory?" Death still had its sting when Paul made this statement. He knew that he would have to experience "soul sleep" and go through the resurrection, but he also knew that many of his hearers would survive the dreaded day of the Lord and would be the first generation to experience the superiority of the NC. *This generation* was a special elect group that God had chosen since the beginning to bring in the Savior of the world. From my studies in extra-biblical sources, I believe I can safely state that John is the only apostle of Jesus who got to experience "to be absent from the body is to be present with Christ." This was not a possibility until the consummation of the OC era had taken place.

I have often heard preachers say that when Jesus said "Verily, verily, I say unto you . . ." that the subject matter was to be of utmost importance to those Jesus was speaking to, as well as to us today. "This generation" was the one to whom his imminent statements were most important. Yes, it is relevant to us today, but it was of imminent importance to "this generation." It is obvious that "this generation," "generation of vipers," "wicked and adulterous generation," "faithless generation," and so on was *the generation* that was standing before Jesus. Each term obviously refers to the same generation. It would be the very generation that would kill the prophesied Messiah. "This generation" is the one who made the following statement to Pilate when they refused to have Jesus released and chose to release the murderer, Barabbas; *"Then answered all the people, and said, His blood be on us, and on our children"* (Matthew 27:25, KJV). Well, they asked for it, and they got what they asked for. God poured out His wrath on "this generation." Actually, Jesus was the One doing the judging, but He used the Roman Empire to judge the "generation of vipers." We will now parse through some of the most relevant verses about "this generation."

"But when he saw many of the Pharisees and Sadducees come to his baptism, he said unto them, O generation of vipers, who hath warned you to flee from the wrath to come" (Matthew 3:7, KJV)? John was the prophesied one whom Isaiah had stated would be the forerunner before Christ. He came onto the scene warning "this generation," which was the "generation of vipers." Why would John waste his time warning the "generation of vipers" about the coming wrath if it was not to come upon that generation? If it did not occur to that generation, then John the Baptist would have been just another false prophet. It is amazing that the people always heeded the false prophets but killed the true prophets. The wrath to come was for this very generation, the one who would kill the Son of

God, and given the opportunity to release Jesus or a murderer, they chose the murderer. That is a pretty defining moment for "this generation." It proves that they were a "generation of vipers." This is not the only generation that would have done this to the Son of God. There were previous generations that would have done it, as well as generations to come that are under the NC. I believe that this generation, our generation, would likely be as zealous as any to have Messiah slaughtered. We let murderers out of prison every day, abort babies, and want to crucify those who are righteous and speak out against such horrendous deeds. Woe be unto those who participate in such, as well as those who support such. Repent and get right with your Maker or suffer the pleasantries of perdition.

"O generation of vipers, how can ye, being evil, speak good things? For out of the abundance of the heart the mouth speaketh" (Matthew 12:34, KJV). Jesus was speaking to the Pharisees here. They were a Jewish sect that believed in God and the resurrection, but they were also progressives. They believed in taking what God had initiated and adding to it as they deemed to be appropriate. They also created many "traditions of man" that Jesus condemned. This is still going on in the church today. Man has added many things to the church, as well as left off many things that were mandated by God. This is what is wrong with the world today. The church is a mirror image of the world. There are many common sins that are just as prevalent among the church today as in the surrounding culture. Man has a tendency to want to take what God calls sin and call it a disease, mental illness, or related socioeconomically. I am sorry, but being poor does not create a thief and a murderer. I know many poor people who would never do such a thing. Character is the determining factor in how one will prevail in this life, and there is no better producer of character than Jesus the Christ.

Man has made a god out of Buddha, yet he was of such small character that he abandoned his newborn son and went into the wilderness. It appears to me that Buddha was not seeking enlightenment. What he was seeking was to lighten his load of responsibilities. Today he would be on welfare in America, likely feigning disability. I believe that his son was six or seven when they had their first encounter. A man who abandons his family is an abomination to the One and True God, Yahweh.

"He answered, a wicked and adulterous generation asks for a sign. But none will be given it except the sign of the prophet Jonah" (Matthew 12:39, NIV). Any generation that calls righteousness evil and evil righteous is a wicked generation. "This generation" had obviously reached a climax that if left unfettered, would have left a much more evil and

wicked world than even what we see today. We have people today who would love to see a sign, some miracles, from God. There are also those feigning miracles today in the church. Well, "this generation" was likewise. The signs were all around them. Creation is the most awesome spectacle of His miraculous powers. I can point to my life as a sign. I used to be washed in selfishness, greed, lust, and so forth. Today my only desire is to bring glory to my Father who is in heaven and to edify the church. Jesus gave "this generation" a sign when He arose from the grave. Multitudes saw Him afterward. He was here for about forty days after He was resurrected from the grave. He provided them with the greatest sign possible of whom He truly was upon His resurrection. Even after this sign, they still continued down the path that would lead them to the destruction of AD 70. He gave them what they wanted, and they were blinded by the lusts of their hearts and vain imaginations. Wake up, America! God may not literally destroy the United States, but it will slip away from the greatness she once was as we chase after the evil, wicked ways of this world.

"The men of Nineveh will arise at the judgment with this generation and condemn it; for they repented at the preaching of Jonah, and behold, something greater than Jonah is here" (Matthew 12:41, RSV). "This generation" is the one who Jesus is referring to here, not some future generation 2,000-plus years into the future. It is the generation that would experience all the prophets had prophesied from ages ago until John the apostle; then prophecy would be sealed, done, and over with forevermore after AD 70.

Another thing that arises from this verse that many miss is that "this generation" would also be the generation that all the dead in Christ would rise in. The destruction of AD 70 is the judgment event here that Jesus is referring to. This means that the resurrection is also in our past and not in our future. The resurrection was for the OTC era and not for the NTC era. They were under the law and had to be judged by the law. The wages of sin is death. We are under grace today. After you take your last breath in this life, if you are in Christ, you will be in His presence. If not, you will not arise but will be lowered into the grave and perdition.

I have a section devoted to the resurrection and Old Covenant death versus New Covenant death coming up in a few chapters. *"For the wages of sin is death; but the gift of God is eternal life through Jesus Christ our Lord"* (Romans 6:23, KJV). If you are in Christ you will live a changed life. Your life will bear fruit, one way or the other. You will be known by the fruit you bear. *"Either make the tree good, and his fruit good; or*

71

else make the tree corrupt, and his fruit corrupt: for the tree is known by his fruit" (Matthew 12:33, KJV). Heaven will be heaven because liars, thieves, cheats, murderers, adulterers, and fornicators won't be there. They would not feel at home in heaven.

"The Queen of the South will rise up with this generation at the judgment and will condemn it, because she came from the ends of the earth to hear the wisdom of Solomon; and behold, something greater than Solomon is here" (Matthew 12:42, NASB). The Queen of the South, or Sheba, had heard about the ways of the Jews and of the wisdom of King Solomon. She recognized the superiority of the ways and wisdom of this nation and culture. Notice, it does not say that she went to Greece seeking the knowledge of the Greeks. The Jews were ahead of the Greeks in knowledge and wisdom, contrary to what philosophers say. Greece came along after the nation of Jews. According to Josephus, the Greeks are a mixture of Egyptians and Syrians, which also means that their culture came afterward. The Queen of Sheba knew wisdom when she heard it. Obviously, this non-Jewish Queen of Sheba had accepted the God of true Israel as her God since Jesus stated that she would partake in the judgment. Actually, the Roman forces, those within the Roman Empire and possibly even some allies, were the ones who did the judging. The resurrection also took place during this time. We will look at this subject in much detail in another section.

Many today do not recognize wisdom because they do not want a standard to live by. They want to pick and choose their own standards. *"There is a way which seemeth right unto a man, but the end thereof are the ways of death"* (Proverbs 14:12, KJV). We have seen man's ways in government and how they lead to destruction. Facts are facts, not racism. Welfare has destroyed the black family and created much enmity between the races in America. I know of instances where African-American mothers have left their babies in the sun, withheld food and drink and such to promote dysfunction in the child so the mother could get what is called in my area, a "crazy check." This is a slow learning disability check. It is almost invariably done with the male child. If the punishment for this crime was decapitation, it would not exist or would be rare. Sadly, we shall never know how truly rampant this crime is, but I imagine the numbers would shock the sane person.

I also know for a fact that grandmothers and mothers of eleven to fifteen-year-old black children are encouraging them to get pregnant so that they can get another check for the home. Mothers and grandmothers are encouraging their children to fornicate to enrich the household? Yes, it is going on all over America. Woe be unto those who encourage such, as well as those who will not man up and speak out against such atrocious demands on little ones. I have also spoken to several men, young and old, that told me that they had been in relationships with black women on welfare and that they would not get married because it would disqualify them from getting a "free" welfare check and force them to work for a living. Yes, this is going on in Mississippi and all of America in the black community. Why? Because we have evil and ignorant ways of man ruling over the nation. You cannot take from one and give to the sluggard without some evil, heinous consequences. God will hold those who support such laws as responsible as if they had done the crime themselves. *"Anyone who isn't with me opposes me, and anyone who isn't working with me is actually working against me"* (Luke 11:23, NLT). Sorry, but it is biblical. Also, there are those in the pulpit and government jobs who see it happening, but will not speak out against it because they do not want to offend anyone. Well, they are offending God. The truth will set you free.

"An evil and adulterous generation seeks for a sign, but no sign will be given to it except the sign of Jonah. So he left them and departed" (Matthew 16:4, ESV). Jesus was speaking to the Pharisees here. They wanted Him to perform signs and wonders to prove that He was the Son of God. Even if He had complied with their wishes, they still would not have believed Him. He would give them a great sign and wonder when He was resurrected on the third day, as He stated to them, but I am sure that probably didn't register with them, either. The greatest sign and wonder would occur forty years in the future when the temple was destroyed, not a stone was left unturned, and Jerusalem was destroyed. Every knee bowed and every tongue confessed that Jesus was Lord. Yet, there are still those who do not believe today that He was the Son of God.

"Ye serpents, ye generation of vipers, how can ye escape the damnation of hell" (Matthew 23:33, KJV)? Jesus is speaking to the same generation that John the Baptist had warned about the coming wrath of God in the first verse of scripture used in this section. The coming wrath of God would be poured out on "this generation," otherwise why would they even be warned about a coming wrath? As the days of the OTC era began to wind down the environment in the Jewish nation began to deteriorate. Even though traditions of man had overtaken the Law of God, it was still a safe place to live at the time. The Roman Empire had overtaken the Jewish nation in 63 BC. The Jewish religion was recognized by the Roman Empire, and they greatly admired the magnificent temple building. The Roman Empire was a pagan empire and believed in freedom of religion. Hmmm. How did that work out for them in the long

run? The Roman Empire no longer exists. There will be no freedom of religion in heaven. Only those who profess Jesus the Christ as Messiah shall ever enter in. God recognizes the horrendous results of freedom of religion, and it is forbidden for all eternity in heaven.

Our forefathers did in no way intend to put Christianity at the same level with pagan religions in this country. What they intended to prevent was any denomination of the Christian religion colluding with the government to harass and force the people to comply with the wills of hate-filled men who claimed to be prophets, but are really seeking to profit from fleecing the people. This was the reason the pilgrims came to America. They were fleeing religious persecution in Europe that was brought on by the Catholic Church colluding with kings and queens, as well as the Reformed Church of England. There were no Buddhists, Hindus, Muslims, Mormons, Jehovah's Witnesses, or the like in America at that time. Mormonism and the Jehovah's Witnesses did not exist until the 1800s. There were also no professing atheists. None of the founding fathers declared that he was an atheist. Of course, the founding fathers did not found this nation. The American Indians were here long before George Washington, Thomas Jefferson, and James Adams. The pilgrims were here about 112 years before George Washington was even born. I believe that the generation that we live in today would be classified as a generation of vipers. Atheism is on the rise, and false teaching abounds in the church today. The truly hungry and repentant sinner will diligently seek out the truth, and the Truth will set you free.

"Truly, I say to you, all this will come upon this generation" (Matthew 23:36, RSV). "This generation" was the one who Jesus was speaking to. This was the generation that would crucify the Son of God, as well as torture and kill most of Jesus' apostles, except John. Jesus told them that upon "this generation" shall the wrath of God be poured out because of all the blood of previous saints that were slain, as well as the ones who would be persecuted, scourged, and slain in "this generation.". This was not a future generation some 2,000-plus years into the future. It was just a mere forty years away. This would be the tribulation that Jesus and the apostles spoke of.

> Now learn a parable of the fig-tree; When its branch is yet tender and putteth forth leaves, ye know that summer is nigh: So likewise ye, when ye shall see all these things, know that it is near, even at the doors. Verily I say to you, This generation shall not pass, until all these things shall be fulfilled. (Matthew 24:32–34, WEB)

Matthew 24:32 is the verse that Hal Lindsey used in his book, *The Late Great Planet Earth*, to show that the generation that saw the Jewish nation of Israel become a reality again was the beginning of a forty-year countdown. Since he believed in the false pretribulation rapture theory of John Nelson Darby (Google his name), then the rapture would take place in 1981 and the end of the late great Planet Earth would culminate in 1988. Well, 1981 is the year I graduated high school. It was just another sleepless year for me. Several decades have passed since then, and I am still here, as well as the church and the planet. Woe be unto the one who offends a little one or causes others to stumble. I believe that if Jesus, Peter, John, and Paul were here today, they would be looking for a millstone!

If you were driving on the Blue Ridge Parkway of Virginia and North Carolina and observed that the leaves were red, yellow, orange, and brown, and that some were falling to the ground, what would be your conclusion? Mine would be "Hallelujah. I have hit primetime for fall foliage." It would be a sign for a glorious event that takes place every year at about the same time. Some years are more colorful than others, but it is still a glorious sight to behold.

Jesus had given warnings about events that would take place before the destruction of Jerusalem in AD 70. He was stating to "this generation," the one who was listening to Him, that once they saw these events begin to happen, it would be time to flee to the mountains. Fall is a symbol that winter is on the horizon, but it is still a little way out. Fall foliage change begins in October in most of the Southern mountain states and runs over into November in the Ozarks. You know that winter is still a little way off. Cooler weather is a sign that winter is approaching, but winter is not official until December 21. I imagine that there were many people who heeded Jesus' warnings and fled years before the destruction. When the persecution began under Nero, there were probably some who began to flee to the mountains. Some may have even sensed earlier that the time was getting near and had fled even before this event. It was not about a literal day. It was about the whole period of time. Israel was fairly well at peace within the Roman Empire from 63 BC until the persecution began in AD 64 under Nero. The biggest obstacle the Christians faced was the Jewish persecution, which began with the death of Jesus. The Roman persecution began in earnest in AD 64 after the city of Rome burned and was blamed on the Jews. This is the supposed event that took place while Nero was fiddling. Nevertheless, there were probably some Christians who had fled some years before this event and some would even wait until the last minute. We all know human nature.

"I tell you the truth, this generation will not pass away until all these things take place" (Mark 13:30, NET). As Jesus and His apostles were leaving the temple, He told them that not a stone would be left unturned. He told them many things that would happen to them. They would be beaten in the synagogues, brought before kings and rulers, and they would be hated by all men for His name's sake. He also told them that they would see Daniel's abomination of desolation, and there would be wars and rumors of wars. He said that if the days were not shortened, no flesh would be saved. I recommend that you mark this chapter and come back and read it and meditate upon it. Take a look at this verse again. If Jesus was not telling the truth, then He was telling a lie. He was giving His generation the signs to be aware of, not our generation. He states "until all these things take place." He did not state "some of these things." Not one jot or tittle. If the warning was for our generation, I dare say that He would have said, "Write it down and seal it up. The signs are not for this generation, but for that generation 2,000 years into the future and fifty generations from this generation." If it had not occurred during His apostles' generation, then Jesus would have been just another false prophet, the likes of those we have today among the churches. Well, I guess if there are no prophets today, would there be false prophets? Yes. Gods' word states that prophecy has been sealed (No more prophecy = no more prophets), but if men continue to have a false belief, then, yes, there are false prophets among us today.

I have heard many state that "No one knows the day or hour that Jesus is coming back. Jesus did not even know." Well, He knew enough to state that it would happen during His apostles' generation and lifetime. He may not have known the day or hour, but He knew the generation. He knew enough not to tell a lie to His apostles. There are enough liars in the world today, as there was then. Surely Jesus was not the King of lies. He was King of kings.

> That the blood of all the prophets, which was shed from the foundation of the world, may be required of this generation; From the blood of Abel unto the blood of Zacharias, which perished between the altar and the temple: verily I say unto you, It shall be required of this generation. (Luke 11:50–51, KJV)

The prophets of Israel were always persecuted and killed by the Jews. The ones who were not killed experienced mocking, disrespect, and so forth. Back in their day, there was no Bible. The Bible we have today is composed of the revelations, visions, and spoken word of God to His appointed ones. They were expected to know the laws of God and not to violate them. God judged the nation of Israel many times for violating His ways and disrespecting His appointed leaders and messengers. God had spared them of the horrors of another great catastrophic flood but not the horrors of war. When the Jewish nation was right with God, they always won the war. When they were antagonistic toward God, He would judge them with the force of a more powerful nation. The nation of Israel had experienced a time of peace for over two generations since Roman General Pompey captured Jerusalem in 63 BC. They had experienced about a hundred years of peace within the Roman Empire since that defeat. Nations feared the power of the Roman Empire, and those within the empire were at relative peace. The Roman tormenting of the Christians began under the rule of Nero in AD 64 after the burning of Rome. He blamed the Christians for the fire, and the persecution began. In AD 66, the Jewish nation revolted against Rome. This would induce a war that would lead to the destruction of Jerusalem in AD 70. I will cover this in more detail in another section, but I will say that the book of Revelation is loaded with images that mirror the Roman Empire and her caesars.

It is ironic that Jesus stated this to His apostles and the Jews would, at the time right before Jesus crucifixion, say "His blood be on us, and our children." They did not realize that their end had already been determined. They had sealed their doom. You reap what you sow.

"But first He must suffer many things and be rejected by this generation" (Luke 17:25, NASB). "This generation" was His generation. He suffered many things during His life on this earth. Even after turning water into wine, calming the storm, making the blind to see and the lame to walk, healing lepers, resurrecting the dead, and even dying and rising again in three days, most did not believe He was who He claimed to be. I think that most people know what it is like to be rejected by another. We have all suffered humiliation, rejection, lies, and fabrications. Jesus suffered all of this and so much more. He was the very Son of God, the Word that was there in the beginning. Nothing was created that was not created by Him and for Him, yet "this generation" scourged Him, spat on Him, ridiculed Him, stripped Him, placed a crown of thorns on His head, and nailed Him to a cross. We get so bent out of shape if we even think that someone is looking at us in a wrong way, whether it be true or not. Who are we? I have heard

people state about others, "Did they not realize who they were talking to?" I have often wanted to ask, "Who were they talking to?" But, who am I to question the heart of another? Actually, we should attempt to right the error in these situations, but most have determined that it just ain't worth it! "This generation" was the one who crucified their prophesied Savior; therefore, it would be the very one that would experience the wrath of God on the Day of the Lord, Judgment Day.

"Truly I tell you, this generation will certainly not pass away until all these things have happened" (Luke 21:32, NIV). If "these things" did not happen to "this generation," the one Jesus lived among, then He is certainly a false prophet and a liar. He stated "this generation certainly will not pass." Well, it either certainly did or it certainly didn't. Jesus was speaking to His apostles here. He gave them many signs to look for that would take place prior to the judgment of the Jewish nation and the destruction of the temple. This is the same conversation where Jesus mentioned the destruction of the temple a few verses back. He also warns them that many would come in His name. The scriptures allude to at least a couple of seedy characters that claimed to be somebody. These men are mentioned in the latter verses in Acts 5. They are Theudas and Judas of Galilee. Josephus mentions a few men also who deceived the people as if they were somebody. There was one man who drew about four thousand into the desert, and all of them were overtaken by the Roman forces and killed. Such as this was what Jesus was forth telling. It happened in "this generation," the one which Jesus lived in. He also warned them of signs in the heavens, famines, pestilence, and earthquakes. Josephus speaks of a horrendous earthquake that shook the Israeli nation prior to AD 70. Jesus had warned them of wars and rumors of wars, which took place over the Roman Empire, which Israel was part of since 63 BC when the Roman general Pompey conquered the nation. He also warned His apostles that they would be captives, brought before synagogues, put into prisons, and brought before kings and rulers for His name sake. He even warned them that they would be betrayed by parents, siblings, relatives, and friends. He told them that some would be put to death on account of their testimony of Him. All of these things occurred during "this generation," the one who the apostles lived in. Now, sadly, we do occasionally have something like this that happens in our generation due to man's ignorance of true history. Do an online search of Jim Jones. His followers believed that they were living in the end times in the 1970s, and he led them to Guyana where he poisoned them as well as himself with poisoned Kool-Aid. I remember the newscasters on television reporting

this after it happened. This is where the term "Kool-Aid drinkers" comes from. There were over 900 deaths. Woe be unto those who plant such wicked, evil, and ignorant thoughts into the minds of others out of their own ignorance of His story that is true, and true history.

"And with many other words did he testify and exhort, saying, "Save yourselves from this untoward generation" (Acts 2:40, KJV). Peter was speaking to the crowds here. The term *untoward* is not a term that we use today. I had to look the definition up. I certainly knew that it would not be a positive thing. The online Dictionary by Farlex defines it as (1) improper; unseemly, (2) Unfavorable or adverse. As an adjective it describes character that is unseemly or improper, out of the ordinary, out of the way, and archaic refractory, perverse. Hmmm—maybe it is our generation.

This untoward generation was the one they were living in. This untoward generation was the one that God was going to pour His wrath on. Peter was not warning us today. It may appear that we live in an untoward generation, but that is nothing new. Political correctness is the number one factor contributing to this untoward generation's downfall. Not willing to call sin a sin is the issue of the day. If you are ignorant of truth, do not seek to lead the people into tyranny and upheaval. If the ways of the world are your standard, then you have a standard that leads to death. Jesus was the standard that "this generation" would be judged by. He is also the standard that will judge every generation from AD 70 into all eternity. The world needs to raise its standard.

> But ye are a chosen generation, a royal priesthood, an
> holy nation, a peculiar people; that ye should shew forth
> the praises of him who hath called you out of darkness
> into his marvelous light. (1 Peter 2:9, KJV)

Peter was highly likely speaking to a different crowd here. It is obvious that he is speaking to the generation that he was referring to: the chosen generation. This is the generation that would experience the consummation of the OTC and the beginning of that which is new and better. This chosen generation was the elect of God. These were the ones who would have to suffer through much trial and tribulation to consummate the OTC and ring in the new. There are those today who hold to a view that believers of all generations are predestined for salvation, that they are the "elect of God." This view comes from John Calvin. Beware of any teachings that have an "-ism" attached to them. Calvinism is the teachings of John Calvin and Lutheranism is the teaching of Martin Luther.

"This generation" was a special generation that was the one that God elected to experience the consummation process of the OTC. I thank God that I was not part of that group of His elect. It was truly hell on earth. Jesus died once for all is the correct teaching on this matter. *"And by that will we have been sanctified through the offering of the body of Jesus Christ once for all"* (Hebrews 10:10, ESV). Jesus died once for all, but not all will choose Him. Those who choose Him will endeavor to learn as much as they can by the reading of His word and becoming familiar with the facts surrounding the history of the generation that walked with Him. Those who choose Him will also place as utmost authority over their lives the ways of the scriptures. Sadly, there are those today that follow after the ways of the world, yet they claim to be one of His. If you are one of His, people will know it. It will show in your demeanor and all of your characteristics.

"Behold, I stand at the door, and knock: if any man hear my voice, and open the door, I will come in to him, and will sup with him, and he with me" (Revelation 3:20 KJV). He still knocks at the doors. It does not state that He forces Himself in. He knocks, and each individual can either open the door or just ignore it. I promise it will take a tremendous burden off of your life if you will make a positive response when He knocks. There will come a day when you realize that all of those "thou shalt nots" are not burdens but delights. Those "thou shalt nots" are for your benefit and not to hinder. When you violate those laws, you hinder your own life and image. Even a wicked, perverse generation will mock you behind your back. They know right from wrong but will put on a façade when it comes to moral issues, yet they will still gossip behind the backs of the violators of God's law.

Hal Lindsey states in *The Late Great Planet Earth* that the generation that saw Israel become a nation again in 1948 is the generation that will experience the rapture before the tribulation begins. Well, there is not a verse in the New Testament where generation is used in a future sense when it is referring to judgment or wrath. It is obvious that John the Baptist and Jesus were calling their contemporary generation a "generation of vipers" and yet had a future generation in mind when talking about the coming wrath? I think not. Actually, I do not even have to think about this issue. It is obvious to the discerning soul. The generation that was the "generation of vipers" experienced the wrath of the Almighty.

Yes, Jesus' and John's prophecy about the destruction of the temple and Jerusalem is relevant to our generation, but it is not imminent. I believe that a true understanding of this true history is very imminent today. We need to come together and become the leaves on the Tree of Life that are for the healing of the nations. Racism and bigotry are supposedly not acceptable in our culture, but it is fostered in the church. There is neither Jew nor Greek (Gentile), freeman nor bondservant, male nor female. The Jews were not a race of people. They were a covenant people. Abraham was from present-day Iraq. He is the father of the Jews, yet his mother, father, and siblings, were not considered Jewish. That is only because God covenantcd with Abraham. It was covenant and not race. It was about the Seed of Abraham and not "seeds."

This is all that we will cover in this section about "this generation." I hope and pray that you have discerned that "this generation" is not our generation some 1,985 years into Peter, John, Paul, and Jesus' future, and even into our future. This was the generation that would experience the judgment of God and the consummation of God's covenant with His chosen people, the ones whom He chose to be the lineage of the Messiah.

Uhhhh-ohhhhh! One more thing. There are those today who state that they believe that all that is left to occur is for Jesus to come back. That is not reality. His coming on clouds was His coming. The judgment of Israel was Jesus coming on clouds, symbolic language. Jesus also stated to His apostles the following: *"Yet a little while, and the world will see me no more, but you will see me; because I live, you will live also"* (John 14:19, RSV). Jesus also stated that He was going to prepare a place for His disciples, the apostles. His second coming that people are awaiting today was His coming on clouds, symbolic apocalyptic language, associated with the judgment of Israel in AD 70. Now, did Jesus contradict Himself? How can one reconcile His coming on clouds with "the world will see me no more"? This statement is literal. "Coming on clouds" is not literal, but Old Testament symbolic language. Sorry, all that is left is for man to believe that all was accomplished and let the healing of the nations begin. This is all that is left to be done. The believers are the leaves on the Tree of Life, which is Jesus. The mandate of the healing of the nations is on us. Hmmm. Never heard that from a pulpit.

CONSUMMATION:
END OF THE WORLD OR
END OF THE AGE?

Words for World

$\mathcal{T}$he meaning we apply to a word is very important. When speaking in a foreign language, one who is not from that culture may never truly master the language because of idioms and such. I have spent time in several South and Central American countries visiting with friends. I spent eight months in the Amazon Rain Basin in 2011 and 2012. I was in the state of Rondonia, a very rural agricultural state. I learned quickly that just because a Brazilian word sounds like an English word does not mean that they are the same word. The Brazilian language is Portuguese, but there can even be differences from region to region. Anyone here in the United States can communicate with others from all states even though certain idioms are used from region to region. Accents also change from region to region here in the United States and in Brazil, but those from the country still communicate with each other very easily. Sadly, because of the fallen state of man, when a telephone conversation between people from different geographic regions within a country ends, one side will mock the other for not speaking with the same accent. Accent is not a determining factor for IQ.

There are two towns in Rondonia that I am more familiar with than the others. I have used several online translators to translate messages I get from my friends in Brazil, Bolivia, and Peru. I noticed that when I typed in the name of the town that I was staying in, Pimenteiras, that it would translate to "pepper" in English. I have a missionary friend that lives outside of Cerejeiras. When you type that into the online translators, you will get "cherry tree." So, I lived in a pepper and my friend lived in a cherry tree? Hardly, but you see how in the right context, this could cause a major issue for the one not from that culture.

We are going to take a look at three words that obviously have different meanings, but for whatever reason, they are used as if they have the same meaning in the New Testament. Using the Blue Letter Bible, I began to do a word search. Since current and past end-times doomsday sayers spoke of the end of the world, I did a search on *world* in the KJV. This is only a New Testament search for this study. The search revealed that the word *world* shows up 241 times in 202 verses. I began to study these verses and also to compare the KJV with other versions. In the ESV there are 207 occurrences of *world* in 170 verses. The NIV gives an occurrence of 205 times in 173 verses, and the NLT gives 279 occurrences in 244 verses. When I did a search using the Greek version, the Textus Receptus, I immediately noticed a tremendous difference in the numbers. The differences in the other English versions also caught my attention, but not like the differences in the Textus Receptus because of the magnitude of the discrepancies. The Textus Receptus shows the Greek term for world, κόσμου, is used only 73 times in 62 verses in the KJV of the New Testament. This is when I began to notice that the discrepancies are due to the differences in the actual words used in each translation. In the English versions, I noticed that some versions would take the Greek word "αἰών" (*aiōn*) and insert the English word "world." This is the word that we get our term "eon" from. "Oh, that happened eons ago." It is obvious that we are talking about time here—ages or epochs and not the world. I have never heard anyone state "that happened worlds ago." I have heard people state "that is worlds away" when they were thinking of distance, but not in time. At this point I realized that I would need to go to the Greek translation to get a better understanding of the true sense of what the writers of the New Testament wanted to convey to their first-century audience. They are the audience, not us today. Yes, scripture is very relevant to us today, but it was of imminent importance to the inhabitants of the first-century Roman Empire. By the time we get through with this chapter, I believe that most will be enlightened and agree that there is a difference between imminence and relevance, as well as *kosmos* and *aion*.

As I read through the verses, I began to notice that in many instances there was an obvious contextual difference. I began to study the verses and found that there are at least three words in the Greek that are translated into the English as *world*. Some of the word differences are noticeably just past/present tense differences among the three words. I will list those words below, and I truly believe that most readers will notice which would make obvious differences in determining the meaning of a passage of scripture. I will use the Greek word in English (Arabic) alphabet and list the definition. Most people in all countries use idioms that are common to their culture that could cause a foreigner with a different language to interpret the meaning in a totally different way from what is intended. I learned early on when communicating to people in a foreign country, using an interpreter, that it is very difficult for them to understand idioms. If I state that the world is going crazy, it is very likely that the interpreter will stop and stare at me. He will then ask me to repeat myself. It is obvious that the world has no brain and cannot go crazy, unless you believe in Mother Nature. The world isn't going anywhere. This is an obvious point where the term *people* ought to be used. The most accurate way to state this sentence would be as follows; "The people in the world are going crazy." Actually, this is just an ignorant statement because no one is familiar enough or even aware of all cultures and nations in the world to be able to make this remark. It is highly likely more descriptive of the one making the remark. These differences can cause problems for foreigners who do not speak the same language.

The following definitions of *kosmos*, *aion*, and *oikoumenē* that I have made as it was meant to be used, or the way it is commonly used throughout the scriptures, since the translators appear to have changed the definition to mean something other than what most common sense people would comprehend. The King James Bible is the main one who confuses the terms *kosmos* and *aion*. It is not the only one, but as I recollect, nowhere is the Greek term *aion* translated as "age" in the KJV. It is always translated as "world." This is a mistake that delivers a false message to the reader as to what is actually at stake: the end of an age or the end of the world. Which is it?

The Ole Miss Rebels were the team of the decade back in the 1950s. They haven't been the team of any decade since. That era of time has come and gone. Now if we could just do something about that team of the twentieth and twenty-first centuries, Alabama. If only we could cause this world to end. Ooooppppssss—I meant the Alabama Age.

Kosmos—the world; the earth
Aion—age or epoch of time, such as eighteenth, nineteenth, or twentieth century, OC era, NC era, Industrial Age, Computer Age, and so forth
Oikoumenē—a localized area, such as state, or region; a country or county; Jewish Nation; Roman Empire, British Empire, Han Dynasty, Ming Dynasty, and so on

These Greek terms obviously have totally different meanings. The end of the British Empire was not the end of the world. The end of the Iron Age did not end the world. The only thing that will end the world will be when it ceases to exist. Yet there is much scripture that states that it will go on forever. Mistranslation of these above terms has caused much confusion and ignorance about what the scriptures actually state. I am about to shine a light on these errors. You may want to get your sun shades out and put them on. You are about to be blinded by the light of truth!

I will begin with *kosmos* and list a few verses for each word representing "world" where the meaning is the obvious intended meaning. I will just list one Bible translation, as each of the fourteen English versions in the BLB uses the proper translation of the Greek *kosmos* to world in these verses.

Kosmos:

> For what will it profit a man if he gains the whole world (*kosmos*) and forfeits his soul? Or what shall a man give in return for his soul? (Matthew 16:26, ESV)

> For what shall it profit a man, if he shall gain the whole world (*kosmos*), and lose his own soul?
> (Mark 8:36, KJV)

> Assuredly, I say to you, wherever this gospel is preached in the whole world (*kosmos*), what this woman has done will also be told as a memorial to her. (Mark 14:9, NKJV)

> The one who is the true light, who gives light to everyone, was coming into the world (*kosmos*). (John 1:9, NLT)

There are no translations that differ with these verses. They all translate *kosmos* as "world," which is correct. This is not an all-inclusive list of verses that do not conflict. There are many more. This is just to show that sometimes we all get it right, but it is a rare thing for all to get it right in any instance.

Aion:

I can't do it using the KJV. Every time "age" is used in the KJV of the New Testament, it is in the context of years of age only, and it is used ten times. Example: "Therefore said his parents, He is of age; ask him" (KJV) John 9:23.

The Greek word here, ἡλικία (*hēlikia*), means years of age, and not epoch of time.

Oikoumenē:

Using the localized area, such as state, or region, country, county, Jewish nation, or Roman Empire definition, there are no verses where it would be used in the true sense in the KJV. Sorry, but area is not world.

Now, keep in mind that we are using the King James Version only for this purpose. The reason is because it is the most used translation in the United States. Because of the way it is written, it is certainly easier to remember because of its poetic swang. Now, if you are not from the south you may not catch my swang. Swang can mean accent or in this essence, manner. The verses I list below will be in the KJV and other translations that reflect the true meaning of the verse due to a discrepancy of the English word used for the Greek word. This is the "world/age" dilemma that I have been leading up to. Up to this point I have used the ESV version more than any other, but that is because it is one of my preferred versions due to the correctness of this word dilemma. I will use as many versions as possible in this section to show the error. Now, I am not saying that the KJV is the only one who makes the "age/world" error.

Aion **Verses:**

The original word used in these verses in the Greek is *aion*. *Aion* is representative of time, an era, or epoch of time. In no way should it ever be confused with the literal world, the people of the world, or the literal earth. The King James takes the term *aion* in the verses that are most critical and mistranslates it to mean "world." This is one of the biggest flaws in the church today. The King James-only advocates are totally unaware of this error. I am inclined to say that it was not an error. An error would be to make the error once or twice in twenty-five attempts, but to get it wrong 100 percent of the time almost seems intentional. Now, was it out of ignorance or out of evil? Regardless, the results have been the same. The people of God have been misled by this error. The end is nowhere in sight. Let's get it right!

> And whosoever speaketh a word against the Son of man,
> it shall be forgiven him: but whosoever speaketh against

the Holy Ghost, it shall not be forgiven him, neither in this world, neither in the world to come.

(Matthew 12:32, KJV)

Anyone who speaks a word against the Son of Man, it will be forgiven him; but whoever speaks against the Holy Spirit, it will not be forgiven him, either in this age or in the age to come. (NKJV)

Of the *fourteen* English versions in the Blue Letter Bible, five of them use "world" as a translation of "*aion.*" What this verse is stating is that the sin of speaking against the Holy Spirit will not be forgiven during the OTC era, nor during the NTC era. This really meant while Jesus was walking the earth and after the consummation of the OTC in AD 70. As to the meaning of this verse, I am sure there are many different opinions. My view is that this is stating that anyone who rejects the calling of the Holy Spirit will be condemned eternally to sheol or hades. Quite frankly, I have never really heard anyone condemning, or putting down, the Holy Spirit. Now, I have heard many speak against God the Father and Jesus the Son. The main issue here, though, is that this is contrasting the era before the consummation of the OC and the NC era. Concerning the rejection of the Holy Spirit, there is no contrast, but world is world and age is age.

The enemy that sowed them is the devil; the harvest is the end of the world; and the reapers are the angels.

(Matthew 13:39, KJV)

and the enemy who sowed them is the devil; the harvest is the close of the age, and the reapers are angels. (RSV)

There are four translations that use "world" in this verse for *aion.* This is not the end of the world being defined here. It is the end of the OTC era. Many have used this verse to describe a future event, but this happened in the OC era. The harvest was the separating of the children of the kingdom from the tares, the children of the wicked one. The children of God heeded Jesus' warnings and fled to the mountains. The children of the wicked one are the ones in the OC era who rejected Jesus as Messiah. Of course, those who reject Him today are still considered tares and will be dealt with when they take their last breath. Again, this has nothing to do with the world ending. It is the passing from the old to the new, from the OC era to the

NC era. The New Testament section of the Bible actually takes place in the latter days of the Old Testament era. That is why the writers of the scriptures always referred to the "latter days" or "end days."

> So shall it be at the end of the world: the angels shall come forth, and sever the wicked from among the just,
> (Matthew 13:49, KJV)

> This is how it will be at the end of the age. The angels will come and separate the wicked from the righteous. (NIV)

There are five versions of the Bible that use "world" in this verse. This destruction took place in the streets of Jerusalem, as well as other cities in the Jewish nation. This was not a one-day event. It took place over several years, but the literal destruction of the city of Jerusalem and the temple occurred in AD 70. Josephus even reports that there was not a known Christian among all the dead bodies in the streets of Israel. Many sources state that there were over 1 million killed and thousands and thousands captured and enslaved. The ones who recognized Jesus as Messiah heeded his advice and fled to the mountains. One of the haven cities was a place called, in English, Pella. It is found in northwestern Jordan, about seventeen miles south of the Sea of Galilee, according to Wikipedia. Pella, Iowa gets its name from this city of Perea. The people had moved into that area seeking religious freedom and famine relief in 1847, according to "cityofpella.com/index.aspx?NID=235", the Pella, Iowa official website. Pella Windows gets its name from the city it is located in. I suppose that if Pella, in the Middle East, was a safe haven for the first-century Christians, then windows with a name Pella should provide a safe haven against the storms of weather. They are questionably the number-one quality window manufacturer in the world.

I encourage you to go online and do a search on the city of Pella in the Middle East. I have never heard it mentioned from a pulpit, but it was a safe haven for those who heeded Jesus' warnings. It is obvious that the people who founded Pella, Iowa, knew about this city in the Middle East. As we forget His story, we will continue to repeat the follies of man. Actually, to denigrate the Father and the Son is not folly. It has dire consequences. To deny His ways is to reap a cesspool of torment upon the peoples of the nations. Just look at America today. She has fast become a cesspool, thanks in large part to political correctness. One reason the Jews hated Jesus, the prophets, and the apostles so much was because they told truth even when it was not politically correct. Truth hurts, but those who are not willing to hear truth will not have to live for all eternity with the Truth. God has a special place for the believer and also one for the unbeliever: heaven and sheol.

> But he shall receive an hundredfold now in this time, houses, and brethren, and sisters, and mothers, and children, and lands, with persecutions; and in the world to come eternal life. (Mark 10:30, KJV)

> but that he will receive a hundred times as much now in the present age, houses and brothers and sisters and mothers and children and farms, along with persecutions; and in the age to come, eternal life. (NASB)

Four versions use *world* in this verse and ten use *age*. The age that was, the OC age, did not allow for eternal life. This would only be ushered in at the consummation (end) of the OC era. There was not going to be a new world, just a new age, but the old age had to be consummated first. We will look at another chapter that will explain the often misconstrued beginning of this new age, the NC era. I will say this, though. Eternal life begins here on this place called Earth. The believer passes from this life to eternal life into the place Jesus went to prepare for His saints when they take their last breath in this life. Then life really begins for all eternity.

> Now all these things happened unto them for ensamples: and they are written for our admonition, upon whom the ends of the world are come.
> (1 Corinthians 10:11, KJV)

> These things happened to them as examples for us. They were written down to warn us who live at the end of the age. (NLT)

There are only two versions that translate *aion* into world for this verse, the KJV and the WEB. Twelve actually get it right, but still there is much inconsistency among all the versions as to where they choose to use "world" for *aion* and "age" for *aion*. Paul is communicating to his contemporaries that the end of the OC era is coming to an end during their lifetime, the end of the age. This was communicated to them, not us, as a warning of what God was about to do. Those who believed in the Son of God would be spared, and those who chased after the lusts of the flesh and rejected Messiah would face eternal death, not life everlasting. Destruction was coming, but who knew the date and hour? None at that time, but history reveals unto us the exact timing of this event: AD 70. The world was not ending. The new heaven and earth was about to begin, an earth where death was abolished for the believer, and a heaven that allowed the believer to enter upon passing from this life unto eternal life. *"O Death, where is your sting? O Hades, where is your victory"* (NKJV) 1 Corinthians 15:55? For the believer death was abolished at the consummation and not before.

> Who gave himself for our sins, that he might deliver us from this present evil world, according to the will of God and our Father: (Galatians 1:4, KJV)

> who gave himself for our sins to rescue us from this present evil age according to the will of our God and Father, (NET)

Five versions mistranslate *aion* here to world. Paul would not be delivered from the current age, nor from the world into heaven until after his death and future resurrection. They did not arise to eternal life at the time of death, or experience "to be absent from the body is to be present with the Lord." That was still on the horizon.

You will notice here that they were still living in the present evil age when this statement was made by Paul. This is the "present evil age" that killed Messiah. Therefore, the OTC era was still alive, but not well. They were still in the age of Christ, which was at the end of the OC era or age. So, what are they waiting on? What is the NTC era waiting on? It is waiting on an event that has been prophesied since the beginning. The event that all the prophets spoke of was on the near horizon, but until that event occurred the OC era still persisted, along with its curse of death, being the wages of sin. The consummation would also entail the crushing of the serpents head. Yes, past, not future. Well, it was in their near future, but it is in our far past.

> For then must he often have suffered since the foundation of the world: but now once in the end of the world

> hath he appeared to put away sin by the sacrifice of him-
> self. (Hebrews 9:26, KJV)

> for then he would have had to suffer again and again
> since the foundation of the world. But now he has
> appeared once for all at the consummation of the ages
> to put away sin by his sacrifice. (NET)

The KJV uses "world" twice in this verse. The first use is appropriate since the Greek word is *kosmos*. The second use is where the error comes in. The Greek word used here is *aion*. Therefore, *age* should be the appropriate word. Out of the *fourteen* English translations, twelve get it right, and the KJV and WEB get it wrong. The time for a "once in an age" sacrifice for sin was in the "here and now" for that generation. Many millions of animals had died since the sacrificial laws of Moses were handed down about 1,300–1,400 years before. Jesus died once for all. If the world was about to end why would He need to be sacrificed for man? If the world was about to end, it would be an eternal judgment against man. No man would ever live on earth again, ever. But that is not what this verse is saying, unless you take the KJV and WEB translations as being correct. The world did not end. The OTC era was about to end. Believers from that day forward would never have to experience the wages of sin again. This also puts *grace* versus *law* into a new and proper perspective. Grace allows the repentant sinner to forego death. The law did not allow this. Death was for the children of God, as well as for the children of paganism. Their hope was in a future resurrection. The penalty for sin is still in force today, but only for the unrepentant sinner. Those who continue on living sinful lives under the blood are not really under the blood. Grace is for the repentant sinner only. The law is for all others, which carries the penalty now of an all-time separation from God into sheol, or hades.

Oikoumenē Verses:

The verses listed under this section are verses that speak of a definitive area, such as the Roman Empire or even the area that was inhabited by the Jews. The Roman Empire is not the world, nor is the southern kingdom of Judah. *Kosmos* is "world" in the Greek and *oikoumenē* is a distinct area. Never is it "world." The King James translators get it wrong about 100 percent of the time. The destruction of the Han Dynasty was not the end of the world. The destruction of the United States of America today would not end the world, either. The land mass would still be here. It does not end the world, nor is it representative of the whole world.

> And it came to pass in those days, that there went out a decree from Caesar Augustus, that all the world should be taxed. (Luke 2:1, KJV)

> At that time the Roman emperor, Augustus, decreed that a census should be taken throughout the Roman Empire. (NLT)

> But it came to pass in those days that a decree went out from Caesar Augustus, that a census should be made of all the habitable world. (DBY)

"World" is used in eight of the *fourteen* English versions of the BLB. Four versions either state empire, Roman Empire, or Roman world. Two versions state either "inhabited earth" or "habitable world." It is obvious that the Roman Empire did not contain the Americas, Australia, India, Asia, all of Europe, Russia, Africa, and others. As a matter of fact, Wikipedia shows it to be number twenty seven in size compared to other so-called empires, kingdoms, or dynasties that existed in years past. The Roman Empire is shown to have been 1.93 million square miles, as compared to the British Empires 13 million square miles. The continental United States, the lower 48, occupies 3,119,884.69 square miles, according to Wikipedia, and is 1.58 percent of the total surface area of the earth. Using Wikipedia's numbers shows that the Roman Empire comprised just a little under 1 percent of the surface area of the earth. The destruction of the whole Roman Empire would have been a nonevent if you lived in the Americas then. Certainly there were no bombs going off that could be heard from that far away. Yet, because of the significance of the event and who was involved, Jesus, time has been divided into BC and AD. The significance of the events between Jesus' birth, death, resurrection, and the destruction of Jerusalem in AD 70 has been felt around the world. AD 70 was the event the Old Testament prophets foretold. The Day of the Lord was the Day of Wrath, the day of God's judgment on apostate Israel.

The terms "inhabited earth" and "habitable world" are very erroneous. If you do a search for "empire" on the Internet, you will find that there were empires, dynasties, and kingdoms that existed from tens of years to thousands of years before the Roman Empire. Much of the world was inhabited by the mid-first-century BC. It is clear that the census for taxation was for a very specific area. The Greek word *oikoumenē* appears to always designate a very specific area and not the whole of anything. We will proceed from here to prove this point.

> And there stood up one of them named Agabus, and signified by the Spirit that there should be great dearth throughout all the world: which came to pass in the days of Claudius Caesar. (Acts 11:28, KJV)

> One of them, named Agabus, stood up and through the Spirit predicted that a severe famine would spread over the entire Roman world. (This happened during the reign of Claudius.) (NIV)

Nine versions give an erroneous translation of "all the world," two state "inhabited world," and three state "Roman world." Which of these is the obvious correct translation of the Greek word *oikoumenē*"? Three use "Roman world," which "Roman Empire" is a better interpretation of the intended meaning. There is no Roman world, Greek world, Egyptian world, or British world. There is the world which is comprised of various people groups, regions, and nations. Only God owns the world. Claudius was the caesar that preceded Nero. He reigned from AD 41–54. His reign began a little over a decade after Jesus' crucifixion. The Roman Empire was at peace with the southern kingdom of Judah at this time, which would carry over into AD 64, when the city of Rome burned and Nero blamed the Christians.

> For we have found this man a pestilent fellow, and a mover of sedition among all the Jews throughout the world, and a ringleader of the sect of the Nazarenes:
>
> (Acts 24:5, KJV)

> For we have found this man to be a plague, an agitator among all the Jews throughout the Roman world, and a ringleader of the sect of the Nazarenes. (HCSB)

The HCSB is the only version that interprets *oikoumenē* correctly in this verse, that is, one out of fourteen. I dare say that the term could have even been whittled down to even a more localized area than the whole Roman Empire. This is akin to stating that the whole world is going crazy, or that the whole world is sick. No, there are many sane and responsible people in the world. The whole world is not sick, literally or mentally, just those who incite that we are living in the end-times or last days.

I hope that my point is clear concerning the way the many translations of the Bible take the intended *aion* and misinterpret it into "world" instead of "age," and how *oikoumenē* is misinterpreted as "world" instead of "Roman Empire" or "Jewish nation." This is paramount to understanding what the original writers of the scriptures were communicating to their audience at the time it was documented. The end of the age is not the end of the world, nor is the destruction of the temple and the Jewish nation the destruction of the world. Sorry, but the end is nowhere in sight. Let's get busy with the healing of the nations.

I hope that the purpose of this session has brought to light that there are issues with scriptural translations. The KJV-only advocates come up as short as any translation when it comes to the critical time elements. It is also lacking when it comes to the geographical area that is being prophesied to. This is critical stuff for all times and peoples. What you have seen here is truth. If anyone wants to contend with the *kosmos* and *aion* issues brought up here, I recommend you just walk off or even leave the church that takes issue with this. They are not at issue with me. They are taking issue with the very word of God, the scriptures. Man can bow, warp, and twist all he wants, but the truth of God will always surface.

End of the World,
or End of a Nation or Empire?

*A*s I was researching the subject of the "end times," I really examined the words that represent "age" (*aion*), and "world" (*kosmos*). I noticed that there was another word that the KJV had misinterpreted as world. The Greek word οἰκουμένη was being used by the King James translators as just another word for world. The Greek root form of the word is *oikoumenē*. This is the form I will use throughout this section. When I noticed this, I began to research this word to see what context it was being used in and to see if there were reasons to believe any conflicts would render an improper interpretation of the scriptures. I was not surprised to find that it was just as big an obstacle as *kosmos* and *aion*. Actually, I consider it to be a bigger obstacle. With the other two words the KJV is the main version that is consistently wrong. For whatever reason, *oikoumenē* is consistently misinterpreted by most of the other versions of the Bible. Let's take a look at a few verses that will give us a much more accurate meaning of the word. I will include a third version when the situation requires it to give a better rendering of the true meaning of the word *oikoumenē*. I have noticed from my studies that men oftentimes attach definitions to a term that are not at all consistent with the way it is used in the scriptures. The use of *oikoumenē* is absolutely one of those occurrences. The key to the solution is to go to the original language, the Greek in the New Testament, and research the Greek term using the Textus Receptus version. Once you get all the verses together, read through them and get the context. "World" is not America, Canada, Cuba, Mexico, Europe, the Southeast, the Northwest, the Northeast, nor *the Roman Empire or Israel*

> And it came to pass in those days, that there went out a decree from Caesar Augustus, that all the world should be taxed. (Luke 2:1, KJV)

> In those days a decree went out from Caesar Augustus
> that all the world should be registered. (ESV)

> At that time the Roman emperor, Augustus, decreed
> that a census should be taken throughout the Roman
> Empire. (NLT)

It is obvious that Augustus did not decree a census of the whole world. It would have been impossible for them to reach the Americas and to take a census of all the native people groups at that time. It would also have been impossible to reach all of Asia, India, the island nations, the Eskimos, Mayans, and so forth. This was about a particular geographic region that was called the Roman Empire. The nation of Israel became a part of the Roman Empire about a generation and a half before Jesus was born. There are many in the seminaries and pulpits today that believe the prophesied events were prophecy about the destruction of the Roman Empire, but that is not at all what the prophets prophesied. Judgment begins at the house of God. *"For it is time for judgment to begin at the household of God; and if it begins with us, what will be the outcome for those who do not obey the gospel of God"* (1 Peter 4:17, ESV)? What the prophets prophesied was the AD 70 destruction of the Jewish nation. It happened as Daniel had said it would. Now let's look at some more relevant verses to this subject.

> And this gospel of the kingdom shall be preached in all
> the world for a witness unto all nations; and then shall
> the end come. (Matthew 24:14, KJV)

> And these glad tidings of the kingdom shall be preached
> in the whole habitable earth, for a witness to all the
> nations, and then shall come the end. (DBY)

The Darby interpretation renders the best of the fourteen English versions represented by the Blue Letter Bible. However, it leaves a lot to be desired. He was also the one who came up with the rapture theory. What was meant in this scripture by Jesus was not the whole world nor the Roman Empire, but the nation of Israel. *"And taking the twelve, he said to them, "See, we are going up to Jerusalem, and everything that is written about the Son of Man by the prophets will be accomplished"* (Luke 18:31, ESV). Notice that Jesus did not say in 2,000 years everything would be accomplished. He also did not state that part of what had been prophesied would be accomplished. It was about to be accomplished in that generation.

"When you are persecuted in one place, flee to another. Truly I tell you, you will not finish going through the towns of Israel before the Son of Man comes" (Matthew 10:23, NIV). Are Jesus' apostles still going through the towns of Israel? I think not. He was speaking to them and not to us. What is relevant to us is that this is fulfilled prophecy that Jesus foretold. These people had no hope for a rapture. They had the hope of dying for their Messiah. Jesus had told His disciples how they would die, but He also gave warnings to the crowds to flee when they saw certain events taking place. Some were to flee and be spared. Others were to make a stand for the Gospel and give their lives. We today need to be living our lives for Him. We should be salt and light in this world today rather than doom-and-gloomers.

> And the devil, taking him up into an high mountain, shewed unto him all the kingdoms of the world in a moment of time. (Luke 4:5, KJV)

> And the devil, leading him up into a high mountain, shewed him all the kingdoms of the habitable world in a moment of time. (DBY)

Again, all the English versions misinterpret *oikoumenē* as world, when it is obviously not speaking of the whole world. I have been on mountains in the Pacific Northwest, South America, Europe, and all over the Appalachian and Smoky Mountains. There are places where you can view several states from one vantage point, but you cannot view the whole world from any vantage point on this planet. Satan was not offering Jesus the world. He was offering Him the area that made up parts of the Roman Empire. Jesus, in the flesh, was limited at that time as all humans were. He was not omnipresent in the flesh. If He had been given the whole world by Satan, He never would have been able to travel and see all that He possessed. We have a different view today because of automobiles and jets. Regardless, this was not representative of the whole world.

> And there stood up one of them named Agabus, and signified by the Spirit that there should be great dearth throughout all the world: which came to pass in the days of Claudius Caesar. (Acts 11:28, KJV)

> One of them, named Agabus, got up and predicted by
> the Spirit that a severe famine was about to come over
> the whole inhabited world. (This took place during the
> reign of Claudius.) (NET)

Claudius Caesar ruled over the Roman Empire from AD 41 to AD
54. The writer of Acts would have zero knowledge about what was going
on in the Americas, India, Asia, Australia, the island nations, and so on.
Famines have never affected the whole world at one time. They affect
specific geographical areas and are generally weather related. This was a
localized event. I dare say that the Amazon Rain Basin and the rainforest
areas of Washington State were not affected by this event, whether men
lived in those areas at that time or not.

> Because he hath appointed a day, in the which he will
> judge the world in righteousness by that man whom he
> hath ordained; whereof he hath given assurance unto all
> men, in that he hath raised him from the dead.
> (Acts 17:31 KJV)

> because he has set a day in which he is going to judge
> the habitable earth in righteousness by the man whom
> he has appointed, giving the proof of it to all in having
> raised him from among the dead. (DBY)

This verse gives us a clue as to who will be doing the judging, as well
as to whom and where the judgment would take place. The Judge will
be the One they pierced. Many of those who pierced Him would live to
see J-Day. This was not going to be a worldwide judgment some 2,000
years in the future. This judgment was at hand, near, at the door. The
Greek word defining the place of judgment here is the word *oikoumenē*.
We know that this defines a specific area and not the whole world. The
judgment was a once forever event for the ones who pierced the Savior.

> Behold, he is coming with the clouds, and every eye will
> see him, even those who pierced him, and all tribes of
> the earth will wail on account of him. Even so. Amen.
> (Revelation 1:7, ESV)

> For the time is come that judgment must begin at the
> house of God: and if it first begin at us, what shall the
> end be of them that obey not the gospel of God?
>
> (1 Peter 4:17, KJV)

The house of God was the nation of Israel. This could also be viewed as the coming destruction of the temple. Both occurred in the same event, about forty years after Jesus' ascension.

Does Jesus still judge nations today? I suspect that He is awaiting those who profess Him as Savior to snap out of the daze we are in and be about His business.

> For we have found this man a pestilent fellow, and a
> mover of sedition among all the Jews throughout the
> world, and a ringleader of the sect of the Nazarenes:
>
> (Acts 24:5, KJV)

> For we have found this man to be a plague, an agitator
> among all the Jews throughout the Roman world, and a
> ringleader of the sect of the Nazarenes. (HCSB)

Paul is being accused here by the Jewish leaders. They are against Christ. They are exhibiting anti-Christ behavior. I am certainly not a historian of historians, but the Jews were not dispersed throughout the whole world at that time. The Holman Christian Standard version is the only one in the Blue Letter Bible that interprets *oikoumenē* correctly. There were no televisions, satellites, or Internet providers at that time. The Christian faith was heard of only in that region at that time. Jesus even stated that His apostles would not even have gone through all the towns of Israel before He came and judged the nation that had pierced Him.

> But I say, "Have they not heard?" Yes verily, their sound
> went into all the earth, and their words unto the ends of
> the world. (Romans 10:18, KJV)

> But I say, "Have they not heard?" Yea, surely, their voice
> has gone out into all the earth, and their words to the
> extremities of the habitable world. (DBY)

END OF THE WORLD, OR END OF A NATION OR EMPIRE?

I believe that there is no archeological information out there today that would definitively define when certain geographical areas became inhabited. When the scriptures state "inhabitable" or "habitable" world, this would be the areas inhabited by Jews. We know that Buddha was born about 563 years before Jesus and lived for about eighty years. Surely Nepal was inhabitable at that time, as were many parts of the world. If you research the Internet for the times of the Mayans, you will see that they were around about 2,000 years prior to Jesus' birth. There are likely many civilizations that pre-dated Christianity by hundreds and even a few thousand years. Again, the point here is that this scripture was not intended to mean the whole world.

> Because thou hast kept the word of my patience, I also will keep thee from the hour of temptation, which shall come upon all the world, to try them that dwell upon the earth. (Revelation 3:10, KJV)

> Because thou hast kept the word of my patience, I also will keep thee out of the hour of trial, which is about to come upon the whole habitable world, to try them that dwell upon the earth. (DBY)

Here we have another situation where the word *oikoumenē* is misinterpreted to mean the whole world and not the nation that pierced the Son of God. John was speaking to the church of Philadelphia in this verse. I do not believe that God or John would bother that generation about something that was 2,000 years in the future. This was critical for that generation. It has become critical to our generation because the majority of professing Christians today believe that this event is in our future. For the biggest part, they are rendered helpless and useless to the kingdom of God. They are still awaiting His kingdom, yet it is already in existence. It is not an earthly kingdom, as Jesus stated. His kingdom is not of this world, nor is it by observation. It is a spiritual kingdom in heaven.

> And the great dragon was cast out, that old serpent, called the Devil, and Satan, which deceiveth the whole world: he was cast out into the earth, and his angels were cast out with him. (Revelation 12:9 KJV)

> And the great dragon was cast out, the ancient serpent,
> he who is called Devil and Satan, he who deceives the
> whole habitable world, he was cast out into the earth,
> and his angels were cast out with him. (DBY)

Satan is not omnipresent. It is obvious from the definition of the Greek word *oikoumenē* that Satan was out to deceive those in the Jewish nation. He was not out to deceive the Mayans, the Eskimos, or any others. He was out to deceive those who were being ministered to by the apostles. Other people groups on other continents were in no way a threat to the plans of the enemy. It would be centuries before the Gospel message reached the farthest regions, such as the Americas, as well as other geographic areas. Several Internet sources reveal that the Christian faith did not reach Australia until 1788, Korea in the early 1600s, Brazil in the fifteenth century, and Russia in supposedly the late 900's AD. This has to be an eye-opener for most professing Christians. Why would Satan waste his time attempting to deceive those who would be centuries away from even hearing the Gospel message? It would be a tremendous waste of his time as well as of his servants' time. If they had attempted to deceive the far reaches of the world, they would actually have been introducing people to the Gospel. I believe that Satan would have been much smarter than that.

There are other verses that have taken the Greek word *oikoumenē* and translated it to mean the whole world. I have not listed them all. If I attempted to use every verse that concerns the issue of the end times, I would likely produce a series of books that contain over 900 pages each with a double column and eight-point font size. That type of book is generally very intimidating to the average reader. I am not out to intimidate. I am out to educate.

I hope that being exposed to the errors in the King James Version of the Bible, as well as other interpretations, will open the eyes of the world to the ways of man. Man has attempted many times to remake the Bible, but his purpose is profit. If your motivation is profit and not edification of the church, then you very well may not experience His kingdom. A discerning soul sees the errors of man and will attempt to point them out, even if it causes the mockers and scoffers to come out of the closet. Mockers and scoffers are never spoken of in a positive light in the word of God. If you see a man in error, point it out to him. Do not become a mocker and scoffer behind his back. If he will not see the light and correct himself, then it is time to move on. I have been guilty of such mocking and scoffing at times. It is easy to do in the times that we live in today.

Right has become wrong, and wrong has become right. Sin has become the norm, and righteous living has become rare. This is nothing new. The Jews hung the most righteous One who has ever walked this planet on a cross and pierced Him with a sword. That generation was also judged for their sin, and the Old Covenant was consummated and the New Covenant was ushered in for all of mankind. God is not a racist. He has a plan for all of mankind. Those who follow the plan shall experience eternal life in His kingdom when they take their last breath on this earth. Eternal life is to never experience death. The wages for sin is still death. The unrepentant shall suffer what all suffered prior to the advent of Christ.

Consummation of the Old Testament Covenant

Consummation: (The Free Dictionary By Farlex)
1.) The act of consummating; a fulfillment.
2.) An ultimate goal or an end.
3.) Completion
4.) Termination
5.) End

> And he shall confirm the covenant with many for one week: and in the midst of the week he shall cause the sacrifice and the oblation to cease, and for the overspreading of abominations he shall make it desolate, even until the consummation, and that determined shall be poured upon the desolate. (Daniel 9:27 KJV)

> Otherwise, He would have needed to suffer often since the foundation of the world; but now once at the consummation of the ages He has been manifested to put away sin by the sacrifice of Himself.
> (Hebrews 9:26 NASB)

*D*aniel and the one speaking in Hebrews are speaking of the same event: the consummation. What was about to be consummated, or ended? Of course, Daniel was prophesying a far future event. The one speaking in Hebrews was speaking of the same event. The terminology that Jesus had used alerted His contemporaries that they would be the generation that would experience the prophetic event prophesied by Daniel and all the other prophets. This far future prophecy of Daniel's was relevant to his contemporaries, but it would be imminent to Jesus contemporaries. It was the consummation of all things, as far as the southern kingdom of Judah was concerned. The *end* was near.

In order for there to be a consummation, there has to be something in mind that must be fulfilled, terminated, or ended. In the situation with the nation of Israel, it was all three. What had all the prophets from Samuel forward prophesied? They had foretold the coming destruction of the nation of Israel after she had played the harlot ever since leaving Egypt. Moses even speaks of the end times concerning Israel. Revelation was written prior to AD 70, and the main theme throughout Revelation is an "at hand-," "near-," "at-the-door," "shortly-" to-come destruction of the temple and city of Jerusalem and the consummation of the Old Covenant. AD 70 was the fulfillment of what all the prophets had foretold that had not as yet been fulfilled. It would also be the termination of the Old Covenant with the Jewish nation. Yes, the covenant was conditional. Go back and read the Old Testament. Yes, there are times when it is mentioned without conditions, but far more often than not it is tied to conditions. Obedience and loyalty are the two key ingredients. A child must obey his parents. A spouse must be loyal and faithful. God had taken the rod to Israel many times since leaving Egypt for being disobedient and untrusting. The Jews had also played the harlot on many occasions. The only biblical reason that divorce is allowed is for the sin of adultery. We know that in Revelation the term "great whore," "great harlot," or "great prostitute," according to what version, is used to describe what is obviously a great mystery to many today. Well, this was none other than the nation of Israel. The martyrs of Jesus and the blood of the saints had been shed in Jerusalem, not Rome. The Jews of that generation had the blood of Jesus on their hands. The Old Testament saints are never said to have had any connection with Rome. God was about to give her the divorce decree that she had so often deserved from years past. They rejected Jesus as Messiah, so God, being loving and patient, gave them forty years to get it right. This was the end of the Jews as God's chosen people.

Today there is neither Jew, nor Greek, male or female, free man, or slave, and so on with God. There are no exceptions in there. No, there is no favored nation today. If you believe that today, then you are considered in God's eyes as a racist. Now this is not mentioned as being an unforgivable sin, but it very well may be that it could put you in the position of being considered least in the kingdom of God forevermore because you will cause many to stumble and to look at others with tainted eyes.

"Nations will see your righteousness and all kings, your glory. You will be called by a new name that the LORD's mouth will announce"

(Isaiah 62:2, HCSB). The new name was for the children of God. In no way do any of the scriptures state that there will be two peoples of God. The one people will be given a new name. Not all who are of Israel are true Israel, so states Paul in the following: *"Not as though the word of God hath taken none effect. For they are not all Israel, which are of Israel:"* (Romans 9:6, KJV). God does not have two peoples today, nor has He ever. There are only one people of God today, and "Jew" is not their name. "Christian" is their name, which encompasses people from all nations. If you refute this, you are not refuting me. You are refuting the very word of God.

The Old Testament prophets foretold of an event in their far future that would lead to the wrath of God being poured out on the nation of Israel. By the time of Jesus, they had played the role of harlot far too long. All of the Old Testament prophecies were not about this particular event, but much of it was. Other prophecy had already been fulfilled earlier in the OTC era. As seen in the above definition of consummation, the events prophesied by the prophets were about to be fulfilled during the time of the apostles and after Jesus ascension, which would lead to the ultimate goal of the beginning of the never ending NC. It is obvious from the following words from Peter to the people at the temple (the Jews) that they were living in the times foretold and that prophetic fulfillment was on the horizon.

"And all the prophets who have spoken, from Samuel and those who came after him, also proclaimed these days" (Acts 3:24, ESV). If there is any doubt as to the timing of biblical prophecy, this is the crucial verse that gives the answer. I advise you to go back and read the whole chapter, so it will be obvious that I have not taken it out of its context as is so often done with scripture. Peter was speaking to his contemporaries about the events that they were seeing before their very eyes. I am sure that they had taken notice that something was brewing in the air. They had known peace for some time, but things were changing. Daniel had prophesied of this time. There was much derision in the nation of Israel. A schism was taking place. You were either for Christ, or you were against Christ. There was no middle ground—no fence straddlers. The Romans had been at peace with the Jewish nation ever since conquering her in 63 BC. All the nations that surrounded Israel at this time were part of the Roman Empire. There was safety within the Roman Empire because the pagan nations feared the might of the Roman Empire.

"But you, Daniel, shut up the words and seal the book, until the time of the end. Many shall run to and fro, and knowledge shall increase"

(Daniel 12:4, ESV). There are many today that take this prophecy out of context. Daniel did not state that there would be an increase in technology. What he meant was that there would be an increase in the knowledge of his prophecy as the events began to unfold. What he was stating was that as the events begin to unfold people will begin to see that the events they were living through were the events prophesied by the Old Testament prophets, including Daniel's prophecy. The Old Testament prophets did not prophecy the end of the world, but the end of an era, or age, which would culminate with the destruction of the temple and the nation of Israel. This consummation would be the beginning of the NC era. This would usher in the possibility of salvation for the world going forward, but until that event (and after) Jesus was the Way, the Truth, and the Life. Through Christ was one saved from the destruction of AD 70. Salvation was from the wrath of God. Today, the believer is saved from eternal damnation in sheol, or hades. The wages for sin is still in effect. The difference in the OC and the NC is that today the believer does not have to experience death, as does the unbeliever. Under the OC, all experienced death, and their only hope was in the future resurrection. Many today misunderstand God's grace. It is by His grace that the believer does not experience death. Under the OC, sinner and saint experienced death. Under the new and superior covenant, the believer is granted eternal life that was not available for the Old Testament saint. The law and blood of animals was not sufficient to cover the sins of man. It was all a foreshadowing of a superior Sacrificial Lamb who would be sufficient for all time and all of mankind that will bow the knee to Jesus as Messiah.

Now, let's take a look at a view that may open up our understanding of the "end-times" scriptures. The following verse is from Malachi, and he speaks of the treading down of the wicked. *"For behold, the day is coming, burning like an oven, when all the arrogant and all evildoers will be stubble. The day that is coming shall set them ablaze, says the LORD of hosts, so that it will leave them neither root nor branch"* (Malachi 4:1 ESV).

Isn't this the infamous "Wrath of God" being poured out? Notice that Malachi states "the day is coming," and "the day that is coming." This is the same day that all the other prophets, including the Prophet, Priest, and King, Jesus, would foretell. This is the Day of the Lord, or Judgment Day. Was this a literal one-day event? Nope. The persecution broke out against the Jews in AD 64 under the rule of Nero, the caesar of the Roman Empire. It sure is ironic that the persecution under his rule lasted three and one-half years. It began in the latter half of AD 64 and ended in June

AD 68. He is also the sixth king, or caesar. There is a section later in this book that will cover this.

> For the Father judgeth no man, but hath committed all judgment unto the Son: For as the Father has life in himself, so he has granted the Son also to have life in himself. And he has given him authority to execute judgment, because he is the Son of Man.
> (John 5:22, 26–27, KJV)

It should be obvious to us by now that the One who is to do the judging shall be Jesus himself. If He didn't know the day or the hour, He knew that it would be within the generation of His apostles, the very generation that He was manifest in the flesh and walked the earth in. I guess the Father had to alert Him when the hour and the day came. I can liken this to my life. I do not know the day, nor hour, but I know that I shall pass from this life to eternal life within my lifetime, my generation. I will be in His literal kingdom in heaven. It could be that even though Jesus saw from His throne all the events transpiring in the Roman Empire, particularly in Jerusalem, that He still had to wait for God to say "Chargeeeeeeeeeee!" Hmmm. Ask Him when you get there.

> Then will appear in heaven the sign of the Son of Man, and then all the tribes of the earth will mourn, and they will see the Son of Man coming on the clouds of heaven with power and great glory. (Matthew 24:30, ESV)

> Behold, he is coming with the clouds, and every eye will see him, even those who pierced him, and all tribes of the earth will wail on account of him. Even so. Amen.
> (Revelation 1:7, ESV)

There are those who claim to be literalists, but only when it fits in with their eschatology, or "end-time" views. The above verses were not meant to be taken literally. This is Old Testament apocalyptic language. Jesus was not stating that you would literally see Him sitting or standing on some clouds some day in the future. This was to reveal that Jesus was in heaven and that He was who He claimed to be, the Messiah. What He was stating was that when "They shall look on him whom they pierced," they would see the signs that He foretold and they would know that these were the events that He foretold. It amazes me when I hear someone in the pulpit preach this as literal and future. The only way that this could be literal would be for God to literally give the world four corners. All life would have to be on the top side, though, if all are to see His face, or His face will be so huge that the top side will see part of the face and the bottom side will see the other half of His face. People all around the world see a different view when looking up. East is west to some and south is north to some. Due to the circumference of the earth, it would take a reshaping of the planet for all to get the same view. This was not a literal statement, as literalists claim. Also, "those who pierced Him" was a literal statement. For those to see Him, they still had to have the breath of life in them. I am sorry, but I know of no one who is anywhere close to 2,000 years of age, unless of course he is hiding in a cave somewhere in the Middle East. Of those who pierced Him, many were still living in AD 70. I am sure God preserved particular individuals and groups so they would experience the judgment on "this generation."

The actual force that Jesus used to destroy the culture of the Jews was the Roman army, but the Roman Empire at that time was a compilation of nations that they had conquered, including the nation of Israel. There were actually many armies of the empire that came against Israel. It was the nature of the beast, if you catch my drift. An empire comprised of many different nations would entail many different armies. The kings of these nations are mentioned in Revelation, but not by name. We shall never know who they are by name because there is either no written record of it, or man has neglected this history.

One of the differences in the Old Covenant era and the New Covenant era was that the NC era would allow for man to inhabit heaven. The OC disallowed man's presence in heaven.

A New Heaven and a New Earth.

Let's take a look at a few verses and parse through them.

"No one has ascended into heaven except he who descended from heaven, the Son of Man" (John 3:13, ESV). According to scholars, the Gospel of John was written no earlier than the fifties AD. Well, we also know and understand the state of fallen man. Obviously, many had died in the past twenty years or so since Jesus' ascension who were professors of Christ before John wrote Revelation, his Gospel, and his epistles. Now, where were these individuals when John was putting the pen to his Gospel? I heard a preacher recently state from the pulpit that even the Old

Testament saints upon death experienced heaven. They were just waiting on their bodies. Sorry, that doesn't fly. The above verse denies that. Some may say that "Well, his soul, or spirit, went to heaven under the OTC." I must admit that I had never heard a preacher speak on this before, but it is obvious that the teaching is out there. Well, it is not biblical. The very essence of man is spirit. That is what the scripture says. These bodies are just tents that the spirit, or soul, occupies. There are verses that allude to the spirit of man rising, but it is obvious from this very definitive statement of Jesus documented in John's gospel that up until the very second that he wrote that statement that no man, that would be spirit or flesh, had ever ascended to heaven except for Messiah. If the current state of the fate of the dead had changed since Jesus made this statement, John surely would have made mention of it. The current dominion of the Old Covenant was still in effect. The resurrection was always the hope of the Old Testament saints, but future hope was not present reality at the time John penned all of his writings.

There is a verse that is often quoted out of context. It is as follows: "To be absent from the body is to be present with Christ." Well, that is not what the verse states. We will look at the KJV and ESV.

> We are confident, I say, and willing rather to be absent
> from the body, and to be present with the Lord.
> (2 Corinthians 5:8, KJV)

> Yes, we are of good courage, and we would rather be
> away from the body and at home with the Lord. (ESV)

Paul is not stating here that for a Christian "to be absent from the body is to be present with Christ." That was his present hope; it was future reality but not until Consummation Day/Judgment Day. What he is stating is that he would rather be in the presence of Jesus in heaven rather than to be facing the woes of this world, but that this was the plan of God. God uses the repentant sinner to accomplish His plan for redemption. When we look at this verse in context, it is obvious that at that time it was not "to be absent from the body is to be present with Christ." Before the OC was nullified, or consummated, all who experienced death experienced "soul sleep." Until the consummation of the OC in their very near future, all who died were still to suffer the OC biblical penalty for sin: "soul sleep." Yes, they would rather to be present with the Lord than to be in a body that would perish, and a soul that would

112

experience "soul sleep" apart from the consummation of the OTC era and the introduction of the NTC era.

If you look at the other twelve English versions of this verse, you will see that several of them are slanted toward the "to be absent from the body . . ." All the translations we have of this scripture today are, of course, post-AD 70. Our view today is literally "to be absent from the body is to be present with the Lord." That was not the view of the apostles. They all lived pre-AD 70. Yes, they would have rather have been in heaven with the Lord, but it was not yet a possibility. It was yet a few years off until they would actually experience the resurrection. Resurrection was for the dead in Christ prior to AD 70. The resurrection is not in our future, United Church of God (a denominational split off from the Worldwide Church of God). The United Church of God believes in a future resurrection, physically and spiritually, which denies the existence of the New and Better Covenant. According to their teaching, the world is still under the curse of the law and Old Covenant.

The resurrection occurred during the consummation. It is past, not future. That is the major difference between the OC and the NC. To be absent from the body is to be present in the dirt versus to be absent from the body is to be present with the Lord. Otherwise, there is no superiority of the NTC over the OTC.

Many today think that the thief on the cross went to be in heaven with Jesus on the day that they were crucified, but we have addressed that in another chapter. Let's parse through some scripture to get at the answer to this enigma.

"And if I go and prepare a place for you, I will come again and will take you to myself, that where I am you may be also" (John 14:3, ESV). For the saints to go to heaven, which would include Jesus' apostles to whom He was speaking, along with the Old Testament prophets, kings, judges, and so forth, Jesus would have to come back. He states in John 14:3 that He will come again to take His apostles to heaven with Him. Was this literal, His coming, or was it figurative? Just go back and look at all the Old Testament figurative apocalyptic language. God came in judgment throughout the OTC era, yet no man had ever seen God. I would love to have been there when the floods clapped their hands and the hills showed their joy. *"Let the floods clap their hands: let the hills be joyful together before the LORD; for He cometh to judge the earth: with righteousness shall he judge the world, and the people with equity"* (Psalm 98:8–9, KJV). I misspoke. No, I am glad that I was not there during Judgment Day/Resurrection Day/The Day of the Lord. It was hades on

earth for the living. It was glorious to the ones who were raised from the dead. Do you reckon every knee bowed and every tongue confessed that Jesus was Lord? I think so.

Let's go back and look at the "to be absent from the body is to be present with the Lord" verse. I picked the King James Version because it is the closest to what you hear misquoted on radio, television, and from the pulpits. *"We are confident, I say, and willing rather to be absent from the body, and to be present with the Lord"* (2 Corinthians 5:8, KJV). What we must do when we hear a single verse quoted is to go back and look at the context, which means to go back and read many verses leading up to and sometimes several verses following the verse in question. The following verse is the one which impacts the true meaning of this often misquoted and misunderstood passage.

"For we that are in this tabernacle do groan, being burdened: not for that we would be unclothed, but clothed upon, that mortality might be swallowed up of life" (2 Corinthians 5:4, KJV). "This tabernacle" means the fleshly body. Eight of the English versions used in the BLB online site use the term "tent," one uses "body," and five use "tabernacle." Eternal life had not yet come. Mortality was still a part of life when Paul made this statement. Mortality was still part of the curse. Mortality is promised death at some point in time, and the believers' only hope was a future resurrection, which is not bodily but spiritual. Souls would awake on that appointed day that the Lord had declared as Resurrection Day. It was the future hope for King David, Job, Daniel, and others. Today it is a present reality. Until that Day occurred, all the past saints had was a future hope, but I guess those who slept weren't really thinking or hoping for anything. Hope was put on hold until reality took place. Let's look at another verse that will help to weld the true meaning of death during the time of the apostles.

> Indeed, I count everything as loss because of the surpassing worth of knowing Christ Jesus my Lord. For his sake I have suffered the loss of all things and count them as rubbish, in order that I may gain Christ and be found in him, not having a righteousness of my own that comes from the law, but that which comes through faith in Christ, the righteousness from God that depends on faith—that I may know him and the power of his resurrection, and may share his sufferings, becoming like him in his death, that by any means possible I may attain the resurrection from the dead. Not that I have already

obtained this or am already perfect, but I press on to make it my own, because Christ Jesus has made me his own. Brothers, I do not consider that I have made it my own. But one thing I do: forgetting what lies behind and straining forward to what lies ahead.

(Philippians 3:8–13, ESV)

Paul states in verse 10 that he has hope for a future resurrection. To be resurrected means that you have to die and experience "soul sleep." The Old Testament saints were not resurrected from life. Paul fully had the expectations that he would experience the same death that his Messiah had experienced, as well as all the Old Testament saints. The penalty for sin was death. Death was literal "soul sleep." No, Jesus did not go to heaven for three days when he was crucified, as I have heard many state. He paid the full price for our sins. Paul also states in verse 10 that he would "share his sufferings, becoming like him in his death."

After Jesus' resurrection, when He had the encounter with Mary, He told her not to touch Him because He had not yet ascended to His Father. *"Jesus said to her, "Do not cling to me, for I have not yet ascended to the Father; but go to my brothers and say to them, I am ascending to my Father and your Father, to my God and your God"* (John 20:17, ESV). So, this verse addresses the false assumption of the thief on the cross being with Jesus in heaven that day. Was the thief superior to Messiah? Was the thief the first to experience heaven? I think not. The thief would have to wait about forty years in a state of "soul sleep" before being resurrected into the presence of Messiah.

It is obvious that something had to occur for the old way (soul sleep) to pass and the new way (eternal life), to begin. Jesus had given them many signs to make them aware of the coming event. The day that it culminated all of the apostles, except John, would be in the grave. On that day, the dead in Christ arose. Those who were living and in Christ, but had heeded His signs and were spared, were changed in the twinkling of an eye. They put on immortality. They would never experience death. Immortality was never known by man until that day. Jesus even had to die to pay the penalty for sin and was raised on the third day. The dead in Christ put on incorruption. Their bodies had rotted and experienced corruption.

"So when this corruptible shall have put on incorruption, and this mortal shall have put on immortality, then shall be brought to pass the saying that is written, Death is swallowed up in victory" (1 Corinthians 15:54, KJV). The "corruptible" were the rotten and decayed bodies of

115

the dead saints. Actually, most of the bodies would have decayed away to nothingness since the beginning. They didn't use metal coffins back then. The mortal were the living saints. The Day of the Lord brought all of this to a head, and today we live under a New Light that is the Flood Light of Christ. There is no more death. Why would anyone under the OC dread dying if it meant a trip to heaven? Well, it is being preached in some churches. The penalty for sin has always been death, and it still is for the unrepentant sinner.

Upon death today, if you are in Christ, your spirit (soul) will ascend into the Kingdom of God, heaven, immediately. Your flesh will either be buried or burned. Either way, the flesh will return to the earth, ashes to ashes, dust to dust. We will put on immortal bodies that shall never know the weakness of flesh ever again. There will be no more sorrow or pain. Sorry, but you do not get to keep your old fleshly tent. Flesh is corruptible in two senses. The biblical view being expressed about "this corruptible shall have put on incorruption" is the rotting flesh. The mortal, before the consummation of the OTC era, at death, became the corruptible. Now, under the NC the mortal has put on immortality. The soul shall never experience "sleep" ever again in the sense that the Old Testament saints experienced death. The repentant sinners' soul will rise upon death and be given a glorified body incapable of entropy, aging, or corruption (rotting). I desire my new glorified non-fleshly super body. Be careful what you ask for. God may oblige you with a stinky fleshly body in heaven that will experience entropy and death. It is the very nature of flesh.

This is the thing that sets the NTC superior to the OTC. Under the OTC, even the saints experienced "soul sleep." All experienced the penalty for sin, which is death. Men's souls were not allowed into heaven during the OTC era. They ceased to experience life. Abraham's bosom is nothing more than a metaphor for the earth. What did Abraham purchase as a deathbed for Sarah and himself? A piece of earth called Abraham's Bosom. Were not Isaac and Jacob taken back to Abraham's place of rest? What about Joseph's bones being taken out of Egypt? It was more about symbolism. Under the NC the believer shall never experience the wages of sin. His presence is allowed into heaven, the Kingdom of God, immediately upon death. If souls got to go to heaven during the OC era and there was no "soul sleep," then what is superior about the NC? I am sorry, but nowhere will you find in the scripture that you are half present at any time. If the penalty for sin was death, and yet the soul went to be in heaven until "that Day," well, that isn't a penalty no matter what form you are in. Death is death. It is not to exist. This is the New Heaven and Earth now for the believer. Nothing changes for the unrepentant sinner. Now, that in itself is a deep subject. Our understanding must evolve a step at a time. It is much more difficult to overcome faulty programming. The garbage has to be taken out also. That is the great obstacle to overcoming false teaching. It is more difficult to change a mind that has been tainted due to the nature of man believing that he is always right. Well, if it contradicts the word of God, it is wrong. Out with the garbage and in with the knowledge.

I have kind of strayed away from the major theme of this section, but it is all interrelated and relevant. There are many issues within one theme. It is difficult not to get off on a rabbit chase. I just pray that my rabbit chases are enlightening to the seeker of what God's word actually states and that it will open your eyes to the heresies that are being taught today. Now, back to the theme: the consummation.

"Therefore, preparing your minds for action, and being sober-minded, set your hope fully on the grace that will be brought to you at the revelation of Jesus Christ" (1 Peter 1:13, ESV). When did Jesus reveal Himself to man? The Epistle of Peter was obviously written before AD 70, or surely he would have mentioned the destruction of the temple and the city of Jerusalem. It was written at least twenty years after Jesus' death, burial, resurrection, and ascension. Jesus revealed Himself to His apostles about three years before His crucifixion. Pretty much everyone in the local area surrounding Jerusalem would have heard about Him, His ministry, opposition, and His miracles. Yet, Peter is writing about the "revelation of Jesus Christ." This revelation was a future event to Peter. Peter saw all the miracles, but he fled Jesus' side when the Roman soldiers came. He even denied Christ three times before the rooster crowed. If he had really believed Jesus was Messiah, would he have fled? Would the other apostles have fled? I believe that you and I would have fled. Human nature would have taken over.

After Jesus was crucified, I imagine that all of His apostles had come to the conclusion that He was not who He claimed to be. The "destroy this temple, and in three days I will raise it up" had not yet become a reality. On the third day, it became a reality. From this point until death, all the apostles would "walk on water" for their Savior. Still, though, the writing of Peter's epistle is at the very least twenty years into the future from the crucifixion. The apostles and others that had seen the Risen Savior knew that He was Messiah. Others heard about this Jesus and were convinced, but those who pierced Him had no idea yet, that Jesus was whom He claimed to be. The law was still in effect. The wages for sin was still death for the saint and sinner alike. Grace, the pardon of the death penalty for the repentant sinner, was not yet a reality, as seen in this verse. It was still a future hope when Peter penned this epistle.

> And he shall confirm the covenant with many for one week: and in the midst of the week he shall cause the sacrifice and the oblation to cease, and for the overspreading of abominations he shall make it desolate, even until the consummation, and that determined shall be poured upon the desolate. (Daniel 9:27, KJV)

There was a time in the first century when temple sacrifices were forbidden. It occurred after the city of Rome burned and Nero blamed it on the Christians. Galba, the predecessor of Nero after his suicide, set up an image of Nero in the temple and demanded that it be worshipped. Because of a lack of history, or a lack of effort, we will never know all the facts about this era of time. There are events and people who we shall never be able to put a name to. The exact timing of Daniel's prophecy here is uncertain, but rest assured, it occurred during the first century between AD 30 and AD 70. The OTC was to be made desolate. This was the consummation, the end of the OTC. The temple and the city were made desolate. This was an all-consuming event.

> In speaking of a new covenant, he makes the first one obsolete. And what is becoming obsolete and growing old is ready to vanish away. (Hebrews 8:13, ESV)
>
> In that he saith, a new covenant, he hath made the first old. Now that which decayeth and waxeth old is ready to vanish away. (KJV)

From this scripture, it is obvious that the OTC was still in effect but was on the very edge of extinction. It had not become obsolete, but it would shortly vanish away and the entry of the NC era would begin for all time. Hebrews was written twenty-plus years after Jesus ascended to heaven. I think I have mentioned this in another section, but I will mention it again here because of relevance. Contrary to what you believe or have been taught, if the scripture is your authority and not the teachings of man, then Jesus never lived in the New Covenant era. He lived in the latter days of the OC era. It was time, God's timing, for the old to pass and the new to come in. Death would forevermore lose its sting for the repentant sinner. One reason the OC decayed was because it had the weight of the blood of the prophets and saints from ages ago upon it. It could not stand the weight of Messiah's blood. Something had to give.

"Otherwise, He would have needed to suffer often since the foundation of the world; but now once at the consummation of the ages He has been manifested to put away sin by the sacrifice of Himself" (Hebrew 9:26, NASB). Again, the writer of Hebrews is reiterating that the end was near. Another issue that he brings to the forefront is the issue of sin. The consummation of the ages had not yet taken place. Jesus died forty years prior to the consummation. Both events are in the "latter days," but the consummation is a separate event from the sacrifice of Christ. They are forty years apart, a generation. Death still reigned until the consummation of AD 70. The price had been paid in AD 30, but there was a timeframe allotted for man to get right with his Creator. A faithful remnant did. The ones professing Christ that lived through the consummation were the 144,000 mentioned in Revelation. Was it a literal number? I dare say no. The majority of Jews did not get right with their Maker and were destroyed at the consummation. The New Covenant would be manifested for all time at the consummation of the ages, which was the end of the Old Covenant era. It was time for a new beginning.

The purpose of this whole undertaking is to alert people that the Bible does not warn us of the end of the world. It is not about that at all. It is about creation, the fall of man, man's rebellion, and eventual judgment by God. God judged the nation of Israel, the house of God, in AD 70. *"For it is time for judgment to begin at the household of God; and if it begins with us, what will be the outcome for those who do not obey the gospel of God"* (1 Peter 4:17, ESV)? The unrepentant sinner shall face the judgment of God upon his last breath in this life. Shall you rise or shall you descend?

I hope this has opened the eyes to your heart and your mind. The consummation is an event that is not taught in church on Sunday mornings today. It should be a major topic of all churches and schools and even in colleges.

I hope after this chapter that you have a true understanding about what the *end* was about. It was not about the end of the world, but about the end of the age, the Old Covenant era. Out with the old and in with the new. This ushered in the reality of "to be absent from the body is to be present with the Lord" that had never been a possibility until the destruction of the temple, the city of Jerusalem, and the nation of Israel. Judgment did begin at the house of the Lord. It also ended there for the repentant believer. Judgment is still there for the unrepentant, and the wages is still death. God has given His people a new name, and it is not "Jew." It is Christian. The Jews were not a race of people. God covenanted with Abraham, who was from Ur, which is present-day Iraq. Today there is not a single pure race of people on this planet. No matter your nation, ethnicity, or skin color, what matters most is if you are one of His: a Christian.

Coming:
What Is It and When Is It?

Thy Kingdom Come

And it came to pass, that, as he was praying in a certain place, when he ceased, one of his disciples said unto him, Lord, teach us to pray, as John also taught his disciples. And he said unto them, When ye pray, say, Our Father which art in heaven, Hallowed be thy name. Thy kingdom come. Thy will be done, as in heaven, so in earth. (Luke 11:1–2, KJV)

There has been much confusion about "Thy kingdom come" over the last two millennia. These are the first two verses of the Lord's Prayer. The confusion lies around what is the kingdom of God, where is the kingdom of God, and when is the kingdom of God?

I will attempt here to answer this to the best of my ability based on what the scriptures say, not on what man says. Jesus never would have asked His disciples to pray for something that would be two millennia away from their deaths on this earth. This would entail the death of fifty generations and billions of people. When we pray, we expect an answer to our prayers in our lifetimes, don't we? Otherwise our prayers are in futility. If our prayers are hopeless, then why should we pray?

But you, when you pray, enter into your inner chamber, and having shut your door, pray to your Father who is in secret, and your Father who sees in secret will reward you openly. (Matthew 6:6, HNV)

Therefore I tell you, whatever you ask in prayer, believe that you have received it, and it will be yours. (Mark 11:24, ESV)

These two verses say nothing about waiting two millennia for an answer to prayer. Jesus is telling his disciples to pray and to expect an answer in their lifetime from their Father who is in heaven. Otherwise, their prayers would be in vain, or fruitless, as would ours.

We will first take a look at "what is the kingdom of God?" I imagine if I asked this in a class setting, I would probably get as many answers as there are people in the class. We will begin with John in the book of Revelation.

"Then I saw a new heaven and a new earth, for the first heaven and the first earth had passed away, and the sea was no more" (Revelation 21:1, ESV). The old earth and heaven were different from what we have today due to the sacrifice that Jesus made on the cross. God no longer required or honored animal sacrifices after the cross. All of the Old Testament saints of God experienced "soul sleep." Animal sacrifice never took away the experience of "soul sleep," which was the wages of sin. They awaited the coming resurrection in the grave in a state of nothingness. The resurrection was their great far-future hope when they took their last breath in this life. During the age of the Old Covenant, to be absent from the body was to be present in the dirt. The old earth consumed life upon death, "Ashes to ashes, dust to dust." The old heaven allowed no man, as Jesus states in the following: *"And no man hath ascended up to heaven, but he that came down from heaven, even the Son of man which is in heaven"* (John 3:13, ESV). The new heaven, once inaugurated, would allow the presence of man. I go to prepare a place for you . . . In my house are many mansions . . . . Eye hath not seen, nor ear heard . . ." Catch my drift? No. Well, when John wrote his Gospel about twenty years after Jesus' death and ascension, he uses Jesus' statement that "no man hath ascended up to heaven." Consensus is that John wrote his gospel no earlier than AD 50. It is obvious that it was written prior to AD 70, or surely John would have mentioned the destruction of the temple and city of Jerusalem, as well as the death of around 1 million Jews in the streets of Israel, according to Josephus in his *Wars of the Jews*. At the time John wrote his gospel, no man was allowed into heaven, still, at least twenty years after Jesus' death. No, the thief on the cross did not go to heaven on that day. Jesus did not go to heaven the day He was crucified. He went into the earth. The thief actually experienced the corruption of the flesh, ashes to ashes, dust to dust. I tell you today you are going to die. Well, you are going to die, just not likely today. The Greek and Hebrew languages use no punctuation marks. They were inserted by the Bible interpreters. They got it wrong. Scripture does not contradict itself.

The new heaven and earth would usher in life eternal, everlasting life. This was the future hope of the Old Testament saints. They all experienced "soul sleep." Daniel states in Daniel 12:2 (ESV): *"And many of those who sleep in the dust of the earth shall awake, some to everlasting life, and some to shame and everlasting contempt."* Daniel is speaking about a future event that would not take place during his lifetime. A great event would have to take place before this great hope was realized. If they were to awaken then they had to be experiencing "soul sleep," or death. John writes in John 6:47 (ESV): *"Truly, truly, I say to you, whoever believes has eternal life."* Jesus was speaking to his contemporaries, the ones who would live through the consummation of the OC. Some would be martyred and experience "soul sleep" and the resurrection. If you do an Old Testament King James search in the Blue Letter Bible, you will notice that the terms "eternal life" and "life eternal" only show up in the New Testament. If you do a search for "everlasting life" and "life everlasting," you will get only one result that shows up in the Old Testament, and that is the verse in Daniel listed above. Everlasting life was not a reality in the days of the Old Testament saints. It was for a future time and only after certain events took place. Death on the cross was part of it, but it was not ushered in until the consummation of the old way, the OC, which was consummated in AD 70. The wages for sin was death even for Abraham, Moses, and David, the man after God's own heart under the Old Covenant. All who breathed life under the OC would experience death, the wages of sin.

I believe that the above paragraph gives a great clue as to where the kingdom of God is. Many people believe that Jesus is coming again to reign on this earth and that He will be conducting temple sacrifices. If He died once for all, then why would animal sacrifices need to be re-implemented? This is beyond comprehension, not to me but to God. "It is finished," said Jesus when on the cross. No more bloody animal sacrifices would be necessary forevermore.

Here are just a few verses that will attest to the location of the kingdom of God.

> Blessed are the poor in spirit: for theirs is the kingdom of heaven. (Matthew 5:3, KJV)

> And he answered them, "To you it has been given to know the secrets of the kingdom of heaven, but to them it has not been given." (Matthew 13:11, ESV)

> But Jesus said, Suffer little children, and forbid them not,
> to come unto me: for of such is the kingdom of heaven.
> (Mathew 19:14, KJV)

> But Jesus called them to him, saying, "Let the children
> come to me, and do not hinder them, for to such belongs
> the kingdom of God. (Luke 18:16, ESV)

Now, if there is any doubt as to the kingdom of God and the kingdom of heaven being one and the same, well, the answer is in the last two verses that represent the same account of Jesus' sayings by two different authors. Matthew states "kingdom of heaven," and Luke states "kingdom of God." They were both speaking of the very same event when Jesus spoke these words. Not that it is an issue, but it makes the point for the few who would take issue with it. There is a great heresy in the world today that was likely fostered back in the late 1800s. I have not devoted much time to studying it yet. It is the "Two Kingdoms" heresy. Well, Matthew 19:14 and Luke 18:16 knock that heresy in the head. There are those who believe the church will go to heaven and that the Jews will live on this earth after the "end" comes. This is a fabrication that came out of an ignorant view of scripture from C.I. Scofield. It is taught as fact today in many seminaries that use the Scofield Bible.

There is only one Kingdom of God and only one people of God. Thus says Paul; "There is neither Jew nor Greek . . ." It would take much space to list all verses that account for the location of the kingdom of God (heaven). There are sixty-eight verses in the New Testament that have "kingdom of God," and "kingdom of heaven" shows up 31 times. What I found astonishing was the fact that "kingdom of God" and "kingdom of heaven" is not mentioned a single time in the Old Testament. Yes, it speaks of heaven, but not in the context as it is mentioned in the New Testament. The kingdom was on the horizon. It was imminent. I suppose that is why it, all of a sudden, became such a subject of conversation and concern. There was no near hope of the kingdom of God (heaven) for the saints hundreds of years before Jesus advent. Things were changing, though. Messiah had come, and the end was near. That which is perfect was about to come, the New Covenant, which ushered in the new heaven and earth. The new heaven and earth is also synonymous with the New Covenant.

And he said, "See that you are not led astray. For many will come in my name, saying, "I am he." and, "The time is at hand." Do not go after them. (Luke 21:8, ESV)

Repent, for the kingdom of heaven is at hand.
(Matthew 3:2, ESV)

The end of all things is at hand; therefore be self-controlled and sober-minded for the sake of your prayers.
(1 Peter 4:7, ESV)

The revelation of Jesus Christ, which God gave him to show to his servants the things that must soon take place. He made it known by sending his angel to his servant John, (Revelation 1:1, ESV)

And he said to me, "These words are trustworthy and true. And the Lord, the God of the spirits of the prophets, has sent his angel to show his servants what must soon take place." (Revelation 22:6, ESV)

Many who read the Bible believe that the words are specifically for them and their generation because of a flaw in teaching and in man. Man is so self-centered that we think the world revolves around us and that it is all about us. Thank God Jesus did not feel that way.

The verses above all have terms or phrases that we recognize as relating to time. "At hand" means near, or close. "Soon," of course means soon, unless you are an end-times doomsday sayer. We know that God is not going to answer prayers from a person that is evil and wicked, one who does not obey his word. Peter admonishes his hearers to be self-controlled and sober-minded so that they will pray the will of the Father and can expect an answer in their lifetime for their prayers. Another theme you hear today is all the panic about false teachers and such that is prophesied by the apostles. It is as if the warnings are for our generation, yet it was for their generation. *"Beloved, do not believe every spirit, but test the spirits to see whether they are from God, for many false prophets have gone out into the world"* (1 John 4:1, ESV). It is obvious that this verse is not for us today, but for those who John was addressing. Maybe it is for us. Any that profess that what has happened almost 2,000 years ago is still in our future is not a false prophet, for there are no prophets today. They have

127

been misled by false teachings and are so obstinate that they have no heart for truth. To repent and confess before the people that they are wrong and have been misled by what is popular in the culture and even the seminaries would be to admit that they have taught a false theology and history. I admit that I was misled as a child, but once I realized that the scriptures and current end-times doomsday theology did not align, I began to shift. I started off in first gear. Now I am in overdrive!

> But understand this, that in the last days there will come times of difficulty. For people will be lovers of self, lovers of money, proud, arrogant, abusive, disobedient to their parents, ungrateful, unholy, heartless, unappeasable, slanderous, without self-control, brutal, not loving good, treacherous, reckless, swollen with conceit, lovers of pleasure rather than lovers of God, having the appearance of godliness, but denying its power. Avoid such people. (2 Timothy 3:1–5, ESV)

The above verse is probably the most used verse by the end-times doomsday sayers today. It is as if no other generation in all of time has ever been wicked. Well, that generation killed the Son of God. I dare say that this generation would do likewise if He were here walking the earth today, and many of these doomsday sayers would be the leaders of the pack. I believe that if Jesus would state that there is only one people of God today and only one plan for salvation for all mankind, then those of the end-times doomsday sayers would want to preach against Jesus and call Him a liar. They would tell their congregation to avoid one such as him. Well, the word of God says to avoid the one preaching anything that goes against His word and His ways. There is only one people of God today, not two. There is neither Jew, not Greek, nor... .

> And when the LORD smelled the pleasing aroma, the LORD said in his heart, "I will never again curse the ground because of man, for the intention of man's heart is evil from his youth. Neither will I ever again strike down every living creature as I have done.
> (Genesis 8:21, ESV)

Man has been evil from the beginning. I hear many today who want to blame the devil for everything that goes wrong. But this is wicked in itself. If you recall Cain and Abel, you will notice that there is no mention of Satan or the devil involved in this fracas. If all evil and wickedness resonates from Satan, then where is he during this fracas? He is not present. Man is evil enough on his own accord and always has been since the fall of man. I shall always take responsibility for all of my faults and calamities. Every bad thing that has ever happened to me has been because of a decision that I made. Sometimes the decisions of others do affect us, but still, it is the mind of man and not of Satan. Today you would think that in the past children have never disrespected their parents, lovers of money never existed before, arrogance is Johnny-Come-Lately, pride never existed before now, I am sorry, but all of these things have been around from the beginning. Why did God destroy the world with a flood? It was because man had become so evil.

Never think that this generation is the most evil generation that ever existed. This generation may be as evil as any generation that ever existed, but we are not "this generation" that Jesus mentions: *"And he sighed deeply in his spirit, and saith, why doth this generation seek after a sign? Verily I say unto you, there shall no sign be given unto this generation"* (Mark 8:12, KJV). This is the generation that would go through the tribulation that Jesus spoke of, as well as John. As long as life is on this planet there will be tribulation on this earth. Yet, Jesus has charged the church, the leaves on the Tree of Life, to be a force that brings healing to the nations: *"...and the leaves of the tree were for the healing of the nations"* (Revelation 22:2c, KJV). Currently the church is a leading force in the world that has created hate, enmity, and division. There are no superior people groups with God today. When the people figure this out, then this world shall be one step closer to what Jesus intended.

Jesus contemporaries would live to witness His Kingdom come upon this earth.

> And when he was demanded of the Pharisees, when the kingdom of God should come, he answered them and said, The kingdom of God cometh not with observation: Neither shall they say, Lo here. Or, lo there. For, behold, the kingdom of God is within you.
>
> (Luke 17:20–21, KJV)

He told the Pharisees that His kingdom was not by observation. If it is not observable from an earthly perspective, then how is it observable? The kingdom is not of this world; otherwise it would be observable by the human eye in the here and now. Sadly, many, or perhaps most, have been deceived into thinking that Jesus is going to set up His kingdom on earth and reign over it for a thousand years, but that is not what the word of God says. Since this is the case, I think this does away with the earthly millennial reign. His kingdom is the place where there shall be no more death, sorrow, crying, or pain, as is related in the following: *"He will wipe away every tear from their eyes, and death shall be no more, neither shall there be mourning, nor crying, nor pain anymore, for the former things have passed away"* (Revelation 21:4, ESV). When you pass from this life into eternity, you will have passed away from the former things. I also believe that this verse had tremendous meaning for the first-century survivors who heeded Jesus' warnings and survived the carnage that they had been warned of. If we had a true worldview and perspective, we could even experience much of Revelation 21:4 in this world. If heaven is your eternal destiny, then why fear death? America has built another beast called the Health Care System because of our fear of certainly, death. A funeral for a saint should be a festival and not a pity party. I am not of this world. I look forward to leaving this world and entering eternity. The saints put on immortality the moment they repent and the Holy Spirit indwells them.

"Jesus answered, "My kingdom is not of this world. If my kingdom were of this world, my servants would have been fighting, that I might not be delivered over to the Jews. But my kingdom is not from the world" (John 18:36, ESV). Jesus shall never set up His kingdom here on Planet Earth because His kingdom is not of this world. His kingdom is in a paradise that has never experienced the fall of man. We shall never get a glimpse of His glory this side of heaven. There are many in the pulpits across America today awaiting the thousand-year reign of Christ to begin on earth. I am sorry, but that is not what you are going to get. You shall never see Christ until you take that last breath of life, and then with eyes wide open, you will see Him in the kingdom of eternal life. *"Yet a little while, and the world seeth me no more; but ye see me: because I live, ye shall live also"* (John 14:19, ESV). This verse is my standard. He is speaking to His apostles. We will go into more detail on this subject in another chapter, Coming on Clouds.

There shall never be eternal life on earth. The believer has put on immortality in the here and now, but immortality is for His kingdom in heaven. Death has lost its sting, but these fleshly bodies shall pass away. The flesh shall never inherit the kingdom of heaven. Many say that these bodies will be resurrected in the end. Well, that is a standard

THY KINGDOM COME

of man and not the word of God. Here is the word: *"Now this I say, brethren, that flesh and blood cannot inherit the kingdom of God; neither doth corruption inherit incorruption"* (1 Corinthians 1 15:50, KJV). The Resurrection was for the dead saints who were under the Old Covenant. It was a spiritual resurrection and not a bodily resurrection, as this attests to. If the flesh cannot enter heaven, then a bodily resurrection would be pointless. The Old Testament saints' spirits rose to heaven, and they inherited incorruptible bodies at the Resurrection, the Wedding Supper of the Lamb. Under the New Covenant, the repentant soul never experiences death. The soul goes directly to heaven upon death and does not experience "soul sleep," or death.

In the Old Testament Covenant era prior to AD 70, no man had ever gone to heaven, as attested to by John's gospel. Jesus stated in the above passage that His kingdom could not be seen. If it was of this world it could be seen. Another issue is that His kingdom had not yet come. Jesus told His disciples, *"After this manner therefore pray ye: Our Father which art in heaven, Hallowed be thy name. Thy kingdom come. Thy will be done in earth, as it is in heaven"* (Matthew 6:9–10, KJV). His kingdom was yet in their future and would begin with the resurrection of the saints.

Resurrection Day had not yet occurred as Timothy attested to in (2 Timothy 2:17, ESV): *"and their talk will spread like gangrene. Among them are Hymenaeus and Philetus, who have swerved from the truth, saying that the resurrection has already happened. They are upsetting the faith of some."* I have seen posts online where people use this verse today to defend that the resurrection has not yet happened in our day. Well, it has had almost two millennia to occur since this verse was written. This verse is not a defense today as it was at the time it was written. Paul fully expected the resurrection during the generation that Jesus walked, talked, and performed miracles among. He would experience it within a decade of his death.

For the Lord himself will descend from heaven with a cry of command, with the voice of an archangel, and with the sound of the trumpet of God. And the dead in Christ will rise first. Then we who are alive, who are left, will be caught up together with them in the clouds to meet the Lord in the air, and so we will always be with the Lord. (1 Thessalonians 4:16–17, ESV)

I tell you this, brothers: flesh and blood cannot inherit the kingdom of God, nor does the perishable inherit the imperishable. Behold. I tell you a mystery. We shall not all sleep, but we shall all be changed, in a moment, in the twinkling of an eye, at the last trumpet. For the trumpet will sound, and the dead will be raised imperishable, and we shall be changed. For this perishable body must put on the imperishable, and this mortal body must put on immortality. When the perishable puts on the imperishable, and the mortal puts on immortality, then shall come to pass the saying that is written: "Death is swallowed up in victory." "O death, where is your victory? O death, where is your sting?" The sting of death is sin, and the power of sin is the law. But thanks be to God, who gives us the victory through our Lord Jesus Christ. Therefore, my beloved brothers, be steadfast, immovable, always abounding in the work of the Lord, knowing that in the Lord your labor is not in vain.

(1 Corinthians 15:50–57, ESV)

Death lost its sting at the consummation of the Old Covenant. Paul is speaking of the same event to the Thessalonians and the Corinthians. To get a better understanding of what actually took place when the event that Paul was speaking of took place, you have to parse through both encounters. Paul states in First Thessalonians 4:17 that those who are alive will be "caught up together with them in the clouds to meet the Lord in the air . . ." In Corinthians, Paul is speaking of the same event, but he goes into more detail. The dead will be raised, which is the resurrection. They will put on incorruptible bodies, not of corruptible flesh. Flesh will not inherit eternity. This is a spiritual resurrection. Those who are alive are the mortal. They would put on immortality. This is only for the repentant believer. After the consummation of the OC, death was banished for the believer. It says nothing about being "caught up" in Corinthians. The believer will be caught up when he takes his last breath here on Planet Earth. He will leave his fleshly body in the grave, or "ashes to ashes, dust to dust." The soul shall rise to heaven, and there he will receive an imperishable body. To understand the resurrection, you must put these two verses together. There are many instances in the scriptures where this must be done. You cannot truly understand the New Testament without understanding the Old.

First Thessalonians 4:17 is where rapture theory comes from. Rapture was not believed by the early church fathers. Augustine never mentions it, nor does John Calvin or Martin Luther. As mentioned before, John Nelson Darby is accredited with this heresy back in 1830. If you will do your research, you will find that he came up with this after hearing of a woman who claimed to have had a vision, or spiritual encounter. It is obvious that man gives men too much credit in the area of spiritual discernment sometimes. "And the LORD said to me: *"The prophets are prophesying lies in my name. I did not send them, nor did I command them or speak to them. They are prophesying to you a lying vision, worthless divination, and the deceit of their own minds"* (Jeremiah 14:14, ESV).

The mind of man is wicked. He can sit around and imagine the world away. Vain imaginations can be very destructive to the one imagining or to the ones who he/she sells his goods to. Those who are not discerning can compromise their faith with false teachings, or they can literally be led astray and into eternal damnation. Paul wrote the following to the people of Corinth:

> "Love never ends. As for prophecies, they will pass away;
> as for tongues, they will cease; as for knowledge, it will
> pass away. For we know in part and we prophesy in part,
> but when the perfect comes, the partial will pass away"
> (1 Corinthians in 13:8–10, ESV).

Paul is stating here that once the "perfect" has come, then prophecy and speaking in tongues shall be done away with. Jesus asked His disciples to pray "Thy kingdom come." Well, Resurrection Day/Judgment Day would be the beginning of the Kingdom of God. There would no longer be speaking in tongues, or prophecy. This event took place in AD 70. His kingdom has come, but it is not of this world, nor is it observable. Tongues have been abolished, along with prophecy. If prophecy has passed away, then there are no more prophets. That which is perfect is the New Testament Covenant. What makes it superior to the Old Covenant? Well, there will never again be "the dead in Christ." Those who live for Christ shall live forevermore now. Under the OC saint and pagan experienced the wages of sin, death. This was the Marriage Supper of the Lamb. It was for the dead in the grave, the ones who experienced the resurrection event. The OC was consummated and the saints were joined to the NC. Contrary to what some believe today, death has always meant not to exist. It is not to be present anywhere with half of your assets waiting to receive the other half of your assets. Today the repentant believer arises upon death, and the unrepentant sinner descends at death.

Can you think of any religions that have sprung up since AD 70 that have prophets? There are prophets in Islam, Mormonism, Jehovah's witnesses, as well as many other variations or denominations of the Christian church. I have even heard it stated that God has gifted certain denominations with certain gifts, meaning, of course, speaking in tongues. I am sorry, but God is not into division among his church. He will divide the true believer from the lost upon death, but he is never into denomination. The church was meant to be of one mind. The problem is that men have twisted the scriptures, and most do not comprehend what has taken place. This is the number one reason for all the division in America today. If the church was united, the world would advance and not recede. Corruption abounds today, but it is more prevalent among politicians, the ones who take bribe money and call it "soft monies." God will call it what it is. "Depart from me. I never knew you."

All the answers to mankind's problems are in the scriptures. The problem is that most men have held to the teaching of man and not the teaching of scripture. We are at war now with the Muslims because they have believed a false prophet. Another reason is that America thinks that the Jews are God's chosen people, but I am sorry. Today there is neither Jew nor Greek before God Almighty. He does not favor a group of people today. That was nullified when the OC was consummated in AD 70. Actually, it was annulled when the veil was torn the day Jesus was crucified, but God gave the nation of the Jews forty years to repent. Then He came on clouds to destroy the nation once and for all time. What God has put asunder, let no man put back together. That is the number one reason that peace is not prevalent in the world today. Do unto others as you would have them to do unto you. Hmmm—I wish that someone would kick me out of my house and country, and stick me in a refugee camp. I reckon that is what Jesus had in mind with His statement about doing unto others as you would have them to do unto you. I think not! I highly recommend reading *The Apocalypse Code* by Hank Hanegraaff. It astonished me as to what many governments around the world sponsored when they allowed the Jewish military to go in and take the nation of Israel after World War II. Still, it is a two-way street. Prophecy ceased with the destruction of the temple. Any prophets who came along after AD 70 are nothing more than liars and highly likely thieves. Christians profess Jesus as Messiah. Jews are still awaiting their messiah, which is not Jesus. Their Bible, the Talmud, states that Jesus is the bastard son of a harlot and Roman soldier. It also states that He is now in a boiling pot of excrement for all eternity. That sounds like antichrist rhetoric to me.

I believe that if I ran for political office on the grounds that I would take every home of every non-native American citizen and give it and all other property owned by the non-native to the native, I would get very few votes. Yet, that is what America sponsored in the 1948 rebirth of a Jewish nation. There very well may never be peace on this earth until this issue is addressed. I believe that God will favor a person who believes that Jesus was a great prophet over a person who believes that Jesus is the bastard son of a harlot and Roman soldier. That is what the Jewish Bible teaches. The Talmud is their Bible, not the KJV.

A true understanding of the word of God is much needed in this world today. Also, a true understanding of historical events associated with biblical prophecy is needed. The first-century church most definitely understood who "this generation" was. They comprehended the signs of the times. They did not know the day or hour that He would come, but they certainly knew that it was in their generation. Paul's letter to the church at Corinth was imminent and relevant to them, and it still is to us today. *"Love never ends. As for prophecies, they will pass away; as for tongues, they will cease; as for knowledge, it will pass away"* (1 Corinthians 13:8, ESV). Knowledge of what happened in AD 70 has certainly passed away. Until man has a better understanding of this history and fulfilled prophecy, there will never be peace in this world. We shall never know all the intricacies of the prophecies leading up to the consummation of the OC in AD 70, such as who all the characters were, but we should very well be aware of the event and of fulfilled prophecy. Not one jot or tittle was left unfulfilled.

If you have read Revelation as many times as I have, you have come to the conclusion that it is a very difficult writing to understand. It is obvious that those who reigned with Jesus during the "thousand years" were those who had taken up the cross of Christ, His contemporaries, "this generation." You will garner this out of Revelation 20. This would mean that the OTC saints were still in the grave awaiting the second resurrection. Now, if neither had happened yet, then all who ever died from the beginning of time are still experiencing death. If only the first has occurred, then all the OT saints, at the least, are still experiencing death, which would include Abraham, Isaac, Jacob, Job, King David, Daniel, Jeremiah, and so on. A resurrection is an event, not something that goes on continuously, as "to be absent from the body is to be present with the Lord." The main issue is that it has occurred. It was part and parcel of the consummation of the Old Covenant. To those who seek the Lord, He will make Himself known to them, but it will be made known through

His word. Anyone who contradicts His word and bows and twists the obvious meaning of His word is not of Him.

I hope that by the time you get to the end of this book, that your interest will be tweaked and that you will do your own research with a discerning heart. It matters not what man says if it contradicts the word of God. If the word of God seems to contradict itself, then man has mistranslated or misinterpreted what the original intent was. God does not contradict Himself, yet we have men on the radio, television, and pulpits contradicting each other, as well as His word, any given day. Many contradict themselves from sermon to sermon. Most are in it for profit, for surely there are no prophets today, so says the word of God.

Coming On Clouds

here are several verses in the New Testament KJV of the Bible that use the descriptive image of "clouds" or "cloud." "Clouds" is mentioned eight times in the New Testament KJV, but not all are speaking of His coming. We will look at the relevant verses.

"And then shall appear the sign of the Son of man in heaven: and then shall all the tribes of the earth mourn, and they shall see the Son of man coming in the clouds of heaven with power and great glory" (Matthew 24:30, KJV). What was the sign that Jesus was speaking of here? I encourage you to make a note and go to your Bible and read this whole chapter and particularly take notice of the verses that directly precede this one. It becomes obvious that a battle is going to break out within the Jewish province of the Roman Empire. When these things began to happen, it would be a sign to the people. This would be the event that all the prophets had prophesied that had not yet happened. This would be the fulfillment of the prophecy of Daniel, as well as the not-yet-given prophetic revelation of John. "Coming in the clouds" is Old Testament apocalyptic judgment language. It has nothing to do with a literal appearance, as we will reveal. This language is also used in the Old Testament, yet no one ever literally saw God. God used the force of other nations, as well as the forces of the creation, to judge in the generations leading up to the advent of Jesus. He would do likewise here at the end, the consummation, of the Old Covenant era. The destruction of the temple in AD 70 was the consummation of the Old Covenant. It was also akin to the divorce decree that God had issued the northern tribes of Israel that created the Lost Tribes.

And then shall they see the Son of man coming in the clouds with great power and glory. (Mark 13:26, KJV)

And then shall they see the Son of man coming in a cloud with power and great glory. (Luke 21:27, KJV)

137

To put into context the meaning of this verse, we must know what is taking place here. Jesus is speaking to Peter, James, John, and Andrew here. Jesus had just mentioned that the temple would be destroyed and that not a stone would be left unturned. They wanted to know when this would happen. He went into some detail describing to *them* what *they* could expect to see that would be signs of the times. According to extra-biblical sources it is believed that John is the only one who would live to see the destruction of the temple. Was he actually there? I dare say no. I imagine that he was a considerable distance from Jerusalem when this event took place. It is highly possible that after the event took place that he would have gone and seen it. It would have been a tremendous thing to have seen the very heart of the Jewish nation destroyed. If Jesus had been the very heart of the Jewish nation, it would still be there today as it was. Sorry, but God does not recognize the still-apostate nation of Israel that believes that Jesus is the bastard son of a harlot, as His chosen ones. He had a chosen One, and He was Jesus. We can choose to accept or choose to reject Him. Your fruit will bear you out. *"Whoever has my commands and keeps them is the one who loves me. The one who loves me will be loved by my Father, and I too will love them and show myself to them"* (John 14:21, NIV). Do you love Him? If so, obey Him. Jesus stated that He did not come to do away with the law but to fulfill the law. Death is still the wages for sin. Jesus paid the price for the repentant. Before the consummation the price for all, sinner and saint alike, was death. Their future hope was the resurrection. Our future hope is death of this corruptible body. At that time, the saint shall rise and never experience death. The unrepentant shall descend.

Jesus tells His apostles what must be done before the end is accomplished. He even states that He has told them all things; *"But take ye heed: behold, I have foretold you all things"* (Mark 13:23, KJV). They asked for signs. He told them what to expect. He did not tell them what we can expect. It would be irrelevant to them. That is why the angel told Daniel to seal up his prophecy, for the time was not near, but far off, about 550 to 650 years from the day he heard it. At what time was Daniel's prophecy unsealed? I imagine that since it was sealed, it was not propagated to all the fourteen to sixteen generations that had lived prior to the times that the apostles were in. I would imagine that a good time to have unsealed it was when Israel was defeated by the Roman general Pompey in 63 BC. Of course over the course of the years from Daniel's prophecy until AD 70, there were events that current history shall never reveal because we are not knowledgeable of that epoch of time. Yet, since

Daniel was told to seal it, we know that it was irrelevant to Daniel and his contemporaries. Our generation is right about at the fiftieth generation mark from Jesus' death, resurrection, and ascension. Our timeframe is over three times the distance in years of Daniels' prophecy for the ones who would experience the destruction of the temple, the city of Jerusalem, and the nation of Israel. Surely Jesus would have told John to seal up the book of Revelation if it was meant for a far-future generation—fifty generations, and almost 2,000 years into the future.

"And Jesus said, I am: and ye shall see the Son of man sitting on the right hand of power, and coming in the clouds of heaven" (Mark 14:62, KJV). Jesus was speaking to the high priest, chief priests, elders, and the scribes, here. This was right after he had been seized in the garden. The high priest had asked Jesus if He was the Christ, the Son of the Blessed. This was Jesus' answer to them. This group of men would have been very familiar with the Old Testament apocalyptic language that Jesus used here. We will look at some verses in the Old Testament shortly to confirm the terminology. If what Jesus had just told them was taken in a literal sense, they probably would have laughed at Him and joked. That is not at all what they did. It so incensed them that the high priest ripped his own clothes. Some of the others began to spit on Him and mock Him. "Coming on clouds" was language that they would have been familiar with. They knew that what Jesus had just spoken to them was akin to a threat of death and destruction. If they had thought that He was just speaking of a glorious return where all of mankind would see Him sitting on a cloud hovering over the earth, they would not have been so angry. Jesus had just done the equivalent of spitting in their faces. I imagine that the high priest and the others had an image of what Jesus had just spoken that would have been more aligned with what Amos had spoken in his day—the 700s BC.

I will avert to another modern story about this same scripture. Today it is scripture. When Jesus spoke the saying, it was not yet legend. It has become quite the legend, but in a very wrong context. I was reading an article earlier this year, I believe it was. In the article the woman writing the article was speaking about her daughter, a child under six years of age, singing a song of praise to Jesus. She spoke about how sweet it was and lovely. The article was basically a longing to see Jesus coming on clouds. This is also tied to the "coming day of the Lord." Well, let's just look and see what that day is really all about, just in a very short revelation here. Amos had a much better idea of what the coming day of the Lord was all about.

> Woe to you who desire the day of the LORD. Why would
> you have the day of the LORD? It is darkness, and not
> light, as if a man fled from a lion, and a bear met him, or
> went into the house and leaned his hand against the wall,
> and a serpent bit him. Is not the day of the LORD dark-
> ness, and not light, and gloom with no brightness in it?
> (Amos 5:18–20, ESV)

God came in judgment many times in the OTC era. He used a flood once. He used other nations, His own people, famine, pestilence, and so forth. It was never a day of jubilation. It was always a day of death and destruction. Jesus "coming on clouds" was nothing more than an apocalyptic prophesy of destruction, where not one stone would be left unturned. It would not be a day of joy, as the little girl had sang. There are hymns and contemporary Christian songs that have glorified this day as if it would be the most glorious and joyful event that will ever happen to all of humanity that has bowed the knee to Jesus. Well, I will allow the word of God to be my standard and not the writers of songs, little girls singing, and others that have distorted what the true meaning of "day of the Lord" and "coming on clouds" truly means. This is one and the same day. Actually, it transpired over the waning days of the generation that crucified Jesus and was the consummation of the OC. Was it a literal day? Nope. It was a several-year process that began with the crucifixion of Jesus. They had forty years to get it right before the coming day of the Lord. Did the temple literally fall in a day? I wasn't there, thank God. This was only for the "elect" generation. Thank God that we are not the "elect! "Again, I highly encourage all with a yearning to know more about the destruction of Jerusalem and the temple, and the fulfilled prophecy of Daniel, the Old Testament prophets, John the Revelator, and Jesus, to read *The Wars of the Jews* by Josephus.

One afternoon as I was reading *The Wars of the Jews*, I came upon a portion that attested to the fact that the Son did come. His coming was as Amos had stated. It was a day of gloom and doom, a day of darkness, and not light. Josephus was standing with the soldiers of the Roman Empire as they were catapulting stones that weighed about a talent, a hundred pounds, over the wall of the temple or the city. Josephus states that the Jews on the wall were shouting "The Son cometh! The Son cometh!" Josephus even states that prophecy is being fulfilled upon these events. Is there any scripture that prophesies this event? *"From the sky huge hail-stones, each weighing about a hundred pounds, fell on people. And they cursed God on account of the plague of hail, because the plague was so terrible"* (Revelation 16:21, NIV). This was the "coming on clouds" event that Jesus had prophesied. The Jews on the wall recognized it for what it was: fulfillment of prophecy and Jesus coming on clouds.

One thing that kind of surprised me was what I saw on the notes at the bottom of the page. These notes, of course, are not notes from Josephus. They are notes from those who have read his writings and were critiquing them. The notes state that the saying "The Son cometh! The Son cometh!" is an error in Josephus's writing. They insist that he meant to state "stones." It is also noted that they checked another manuscript that Josephus wrote in another language. He probably did a Hebrew, Greek, or Latin version. The commentators checked the other language and it stated the exact same thing, "The Son cometh! The Son cometh!" Even after this, the commentators still came to the conclusion that it was an error in the text. Well, I am sorry, but I will go along with the ones who were standing there and experienced those "hailstones" falling out of the sky. Actually, they were shooting out of the catapult. Josephus knew what the Jews on the wall were shouting. He was there. The commentators were not there. The commentators were centuries removed from the event. Scripture states that the Father had left the judging of the ones who crucified the Son to the Son. They recognized this as Jesus "coming on clouds." "Coming on clouds" is Old Testament apocalyptic judgment language that is not meant to be taken literally, yet they were literally experiencing the judgment of the Son. I will allow the ones who were standing on the temple wall at the time of judgment and the greatest historian of that epoch of time to be my standard above the modern commentators that are almost 2,000 years removed from this event. It is mighty ironic that it also aligns with the prophecy of Daniel, John, and Jesus. Extrabiblical sources attest to the accuracy and validity of fulfilled prophecy here. Not one jot or tittle is left out. Take notice; all my sources are from those who prophesied the event and the ones who experienced the prophesied event. My source is not from a seminary or pulpit two millennia away from the fulfillment of the consummation of the Old Covenant. Nor is my source from an individual that wants to start his own denomination and cause another schism in the church.

Amos's statement above could certainly apply to us today. "Woe to you who desire the day of the Lord." God could choose to pour out His wrath on this world again to get the people's attention. People are seeking this day now, yet this day is in our past. Jesus is light and not darkness, yet this verse states that the day of the Lord is darkness and not light.

Amos is basically stating that the people of God were about to jump out of the frying pan and into the fire. God is saying jump high, and I will catch you. Jump up and not down. There are people in the church today praying for the day of the Lord. They are praying to see Jesus coming in the clouds. Quit! You are praying for your own destruction, as well as those you claim to love.

Peter is on a rant here against the corruptible, the sexually immoral, the liars, cheaters, and thieves of Israel. This included the priests, the average person, the sluggard, and the rich and famous. I include this verse strictly to show how clouds are used as a metaphor. Actually every subject matter in this verse is used as a metaphor. All represent the evil people of first-century Israel, the ones who crucified Messiah. The wells are a representation of the people as are the clouds. The "mist of darkness" could actually represent ignorance and death here. As "clouds" here is a metaphor for people, so is the "coming on clouds" verse about Jesus a metaphor for judgment. *"These are wells without water, clouds that are carried with a tempest; to whom the mist of darkness is reserved for ever"* (2 Peter 2:17, KJV).

This is a very interesting verse that many I know would be the subject of Jude's rebuke here. Jude was rebuking those who despised authority, were sexually immoral, and spoke evil of the dignities of that day and age. The reference to the clouds without water is a reference to people without substance. Yet, he said that even Michael the archangel, when contending with the devil over the body of Moses, did not bring forth a railing accusation against the devil but said "the Lord rebuke thee." I know many that should give this serious consideration. *"These are spots in your love feasts, while they feast with you without fear, serving only themselves. They are clouds without water, carried about by the winds; late autumn trees without fruit, twice dead, pulled up by the roots;"* (Jude 1:12, NKJV).

"Behold, he cometh with clouds; and every eye shall see him, and they also which pierced him: and all kindreds of the earth shall wail because of him. Even so, Amen" (Revelation 1:7, KJV). This was one of those verses that always perplexed me before I made the word of God my standard and not the teachings of man. I hope it is as obvious to you as it was to me. Do you see it yet? Well, if those who pierced Jesus were to see Him coming on clouds, they would either have to be over 2,000 years old today and still living, or Jesus coming on clouds was to happen shortly. Otherwise, "this generation" was about to pass. It had been about forty years since Jesus' crucifixion and about a decade since John wrote it for the people of "this generation." Many of "this generation" had died,

but some were still left. I am sure, absolutely, that God made sure that certain ones were alive to see the coming judgment on those who crucified His Son. This would have been the instance when every knee bowed and every tongue confessed that Jesus was Lord and Messiah—the One whom He professed to be. The destruction of the temple would have been the leading indicator that Jesus was whom He claimed to be, Messiah. Mission accomplished; the OTC was consummated, and that which is perfect had come. We are now under the NTC, which is perfect. The repentant sinner no longer has to experience death. However, the wages for sin has not changed. The unrepentant shall still suffer the wages of sin. Work out your own salvation with fear and trembling.

"And he that sat on the cloud thrust in his sickle on the earth; and the earth was reaped" (Revelation 14:16, KJV). This verse has nothing to do with the actual sitting on a cloud. It also has nothing to do with the actual sickle. This verse represents the reaping of the harvest. The verses that follow this actually speak of the gathering of the fruits of the vine, the grapes, and not the wheat and tares, but it is just another representation of the same event. The clusters of grapes were thrown into the winepress of the wrath of God. This was part of the judgment on the generation that killed Messiah. No one was sitting on the cloud. This was just a metaphor representing the agents that God ordained to carry out the judgment on Israel.

I believe at this point we can break away to the Old Testament and see where the apocalyptic images of the "clouds" as judgment comes from. Let's allow scripture to interpret scripture. How was "clouds" used in the Old Testament? What was the meaning to the ones using the word and how was it interpreted by those hearing the word? Let's see.

> He made darkness his covering, his canopy around him, thick *clouds* dark with water. Out of the brightness before him hailstones and coals of fire broke through his *clouds*. The LORD also thundered in the heavens, and the Most High uttered his voice, hailstones and coals of fire. And he sent out his arrows and scattered them; he flashed forth lightnings and routed them. Then the channels of the sea were seen, and the foundations of the world were laid bare at your rebuke, O LORD, at the blast of the breath of your nostrils. (Psalm 18:11–19, ESV)

"Clouds" is here used as a metaphor to show God's judgment against the enemies of David. This was not a literal battle cloud doing the fighting. It is just language that is used to show defeat of David's' enemies. David had actually done the fighting, along with his soldiers.

"Ascribe ye strength unto God: his excellency is over Israel, and his strength is in the clouds" (Psalm 68:34, KJV). Is God's strength literally in the clouds? Can God not control the clouds? God controls every aspect of creation. He does not control it with the clouds. The stars and the planets are above the clouds. Are they beneath His control? I think not. "Clouds" is used here as a metaphor of God's strength. He is speaking in terms that man can comprehend. I do not think that man can truly understand the rumblings of thunder in the clouds, but it is an awesome show of power. That is one rumble that I do not want to have an encounter with. God controls the clouds. He is the One you do not want to get crossed up with.

"Who layeth the beams of his chambers in the waters: who maketh the clouds his chariot: who walketh upon the wings of the wind" (Psalm 104:3, KJV). This verse is not fashioned in the form of a question but in the form of a statement. We know that God is omnipresent. He needs no form of transportation. He need not walk to be present. Clouds are used here to speak to man in a way that he can understand what God is communicating.

"Whoso boasteth himself of a false gift is like clouds and wind without rain" (Proverbs 25:14, KJV). "Clouds" is not used here in the sense that goes along with this section, but it was just too enticing not to kick it in here. There are many that boast of false gifts today, as obviously there was during Solomon's days. They too, are as clouds and wind without rain. They are without substance. I will allow the word of God to be my authority and not the teachings of man, which are traditions, and often heresies that Jesus spoke of. Man loves to set him up some traditions!

> Charity never faileth: but whether there be prophecies, they shall fail; whether there be tongues, they shall cease; whether there be knowledge, it shall vanish away. For we know in part, and we prophesy in part. But when that which is perfect is come, then that which is in part shall be done away. (1 Corinthians 13:8–10, KJV)

Paul is referencing the consummation of the OC here and the coming of that which is perfect, the NC. The New Covenant annuls the wages of sin for the repentant believer. Paul stated that when the NC era begins then the OC is consummated, and prophesy will fail because there will be no more prophets. Obviously there would be those prophesying events that would not come to fruition. We have that going on even today. Hal Lindsey was wrong, as was Harold Camping, John Hagee, and gazillions of others. Also, speaking in tongues would cease at that time. This is not my opinion. This is the standard of God, His word, which is His opinion. Sorry, but that is my authority.

"Behold, he shall come up as clouds, and his chariots shall be as a whirlwind: his horses are swifter than eagles. Woe unto us. For we are spoiled" (Jeremiah 4:13, KJV). Jeremiah is speaking of a coming judgment of God against His chosen ones. Clouds have a way of sneaking up on you, if you know what I mean. You cannot hear them coming. The next thing you know, you look up and "woe is me!" "Clouds" is used again as a metaphor for judgment.

"A day of darkness and of gloominess, a day of clouds and of thick darkness, as the morning spread upon the mountains: a great people and a strong; there hath not been ever the like, neither shall be any more after it, even to the years of many generations" (Joel 2:2, KJV). Joel was a prophet to the southern kingdom of Judah. There is much discrepancy as to the timing of his life. The sources that I looked at had him living between the years of 835 BC to 537. Joel states in verse fifteen of chapter 1 that the day of the Lord is at hand. He states in this chapter in verse 1 that "the day of the Lord cometh, for it is nigh at hand." Well, we know from the timeframe of his life that the next judgment event to take place in the scriptures is the Babylonian exile. Later on in the chapter, Joel states that the nation will be restored, as we know that it was. It was even in a safe state as part of the Roman Empire before Jesus' birth. Joel is also where we get the prophecy of the Day of Pentecost that happened after Jesus' death. Joel covers a large range of territory. Oops! I meant time. There I go using a metaphor.

"A day of darkness and of gloominess, a day of clouds and of thick darkness" is again just Old Testament apocalyptic language. It was describing a day of judgment upon Judah. Joel even goes on to state that "there hath not been ever the like; neither shall be any more after it, even to the years of many generations." This same language is used about the destruction prophesied by John that took place in AD 70. John was not the first to use that language. I dare say that anyone who has ever had an "A" bomb dropped on them would contest either event. Catch my drift? It is just language to describe judgment.

"That day is a day of wrath, a day of trouble and distress, a day of wasteness and desolation, a day of darkness and gloominess, a day

of clouds and thick darkness" (Zephaniah 1:15, KJV). Zephaniah was a prophet to the Kingdom of Judah prior to the Babylonian Exile and the first destruction of the temple that occurred in the early sixth century BC. He uses "at hand" and "near" when describing the timing of the event. He even states "The great day of the Lord is near, it is near, and hasteth greatly." Zephaniah uses the same terminology that John uses in Revelation to convey the timing of the event. It is believed that Zephaniah documented his prophecy around 620 BC. This would have been around thirty-three years before the first destruction of the city and the temple by the Chaldeans of the Babylonian Empire. He deemed that this thirty-something-year period was not lengthy enough to state that it was other than "at hand" and "near." Of course he probably did not know the day or hour, but he knew it was at hand. There is great evidence that John wrote Revelation at least within no more than sixteen years of the second and final destruction of the temple in AD 70.

The Babylonian overtaking was also a day of wrath, a day of trouble and distress, as we see in this verse from Zephaniah. Here again we have the metaphor of clouds used as a day of judgment, wrath, day of trouble, and great day of the Lord. The word *trouble* here brings to mind the "day of Jacob's trouble." This was obviously one of those days, but there was still one many centuries in the future.

> Alas. For that day is great, so that none is like it; and it is the time of Jacob's trouble, but he shall be saved out of it.
>
> For it shall come to pass in that day, says the LORD of hosts, that I will break his yoke from your neck, and will burst your bonds; foreigners shall no more enslave them. But they shall serve the LORD their God, and David their king, whom I will raise up for them.
>
> (Jeremiah 30:7–9, NKJV)

I thought this would be a great place to insert this verse, even though it is not a "clouds" verse. Jeremiah prophesies here of the coming Messiah, Jesus. David was not literally raised up. This is a simile, language that is used every day in our conversations, yet many attempt to make every word in the Bible to be literal. John the Baptist is referred to as Elijah the prophet, but it was certainly not literal. Jesus was the Seed of Abraham, not David or the Jews. Jesus speaks of the same event that Jeremiah calls the "time of Jacob's trouble." The time of Jacob's trouble is when Jesus came on clouds. Jesus is using the same Old Testament apocalyptic language that was used by the Old Testament prophets. Coming on clouds is judgment.

"For the day is near, even the day of the LORD is near, a cloudy day; it shall be the time of the heathen" (Ezekiel 30:3 KJV). It is obvious here that Ezekiel is speaking of an event that is right on the horizon. Nebuchadnezzar attacked Egypt early in his reign as king of Babylon, either in the late 600s or early 500s. Now when you are going from BC to AD the early 500s would be like 599, 598, and so forth. The late 600s would be 602, 601, and 600. The first attempt was a failed attempt. He again attacked them in his thirty-seventh year as king with success. This second attempt is the likely event that Ezekiel is prophesying, but it could have been a combined event. Again, the main issue here is the term used to describe the event. Here "cloudy day" is used, and not "day of clouds." Was it a cloudy day? Was it even a day? Most of Egypt today receives less than two and a half inches of rain per year, and the area along the Mediterranean Sea gets about eight inches per year. So, there are very few dark cloudy days in Egypt. They probably do have many days of beautiful white cumulus clouds though. This battle also lasted more than a day.

"As a shepherd seeketh out his flock in the day that he is among his sheep that are scattered; so will I seek out my sheep, and will deliver them out of all places where they have been scattered in the cloudy and dark day" (Ezekiel 34:12, KJV). This is referencing those who were scattered during the Babylonian Exile. They had to be brought back to rebuild the temple and reconstruct the city. When the event took place in AD 70, the event that Jesus and John prophesied, as well as many of the Old Testament prophets, including Ezekiel, there was never to be deliverance back to the land. The Promised Land is now heaven, the Kingdom of God, which is also the Kingdom of Heaven. The "cloudy and dark day" is here referred to the whole time of the exile, which was a seventy-year period. This makes it obvious then that a day of the Lord can mean an event that occupies many years of time. The day of the Lord referenced in the New Testament was not a literal, one-day event, either.

"You have covered yourself with a cloud, so that no prayer can pass through" (Lamentations 3:44, HNV). "Cloud" in this verse is not representative of judgment, but it was penned by Jeremiah during the Babylonian Exile, which was God's judgment on Israel for playing the harlot. Cloud here is used as a barrier between God and the southern kingdom of Judah. I imagine that all the Old Testament apocalyptic cloud language was demonstrative of a barrier between God and the Jews. *"And I saw a new heaven and a new earth: for the first heaven and the first*

earth were passed away; and there was no more sea" (Revelation 21:1, KJV). The "sea" used in this verse is representative of a barrier. Before the Old Covenant was consummated in AD 70, no man was allowed into heaven, the Kingdom of God. Jesus removed this barrier, but only for those who profess Him as Messiah. Without Jesus, the barrier is still there. With Jesus, there is no barrier. The cloud is used in this verse to represent a barrier as the sea is used to represent a barrier to eternal life in heaven. Know Jesus; no barrier. No Jesus; a barrier.

This is pretty much the end point for the "cloud" verses. We will look at a few other verses here just to show the similarities of other verses that speak of the same event, using like language.

"The sun shall be turned into darkness, and the moon into blood, before that great and notable day of the Lord come" (Acts 2:20, KJV). As I have stated elsewhere, scientist today claim that the sun has enough energy to last over 4 billion years. Man could not even bomb the sun out of the universe because the weapon chosen would be destroyed by the heat of the sun long before it reached the sun. We had another "false prophet" (there are no prophets today) prophesy about a blood moon event that was to happen last September. Well, it came and went. I am sure his church is still full, though. If you will watch the moon when it is coming up in the east over the horizon, you will notice that it is almost always a red-pinkish color as it begins to rise. As it gets higher in the sky, it gets whiter and brighter. Of course the moon does not always rise. Early in its cycle, you will see it in the sky before the sun even sets. Late in the cycle, once it has reached full moon status, is when it rises in the east. There is information that testifies of three lunar eclipses in AD 70, as well as two solar eclipses. You can research this on the Internet and find it on Wikipedia. They have a list of lunar and solar eclipses.

Let's look at another aspect of how figures of speech are used in the Bible. Have you ever had a dream that got you in trouble? Sometimes it is best to keep our dreams to ourselves. Family and friends can get very angry sometimes when we reveal our dreams. Do you have a clue where I am going with this?

> Then he dreamed another dream and told it to his brothers and said, "Behold, I have dreamed another dream. Behold, the sun, the moon, and eleven stars were bowing down to me." But when he told it to his father and to his brothers, his father rebuked him and said to him, "What is this dream that you have dreamed? Shall

I and your mother and your brothers indeed come to bow
ourselves to the ground before you?" And his brothers
were jealous of him, but his father kept the saying in
mind. (Genesis 37:9–11, ESV)

What is the sun in this dream? The ones Joseph was sharing it with
knew for sure. Who was the moon? Who were the eleven stars? The sun
is Jacob, the father, the moon was the mother, and the eleven stars were
his brothers. They understood very well what Joseph was sharing with
them. They would one day bow down to him, and they did not like that
at all. It almost cost him his life. Let's look at a couple of other verses.

"*But in those days, after that tribulation, the sun will be darkened, and
the moon will not give its light, and the stars will be falling from heaven,
and the powers in the heavens will be shaken*" (Mark 13:24, ESV). What
were the heavenly bodies representatives of in Joseph's dream? They were
representatives of the nation of Israel. They were the third and fourth generation of the covenant people of God. The sun was Jacob, the moon was
the mother, and the stars were Joseph's brothers. In this verse, the nation of
Israel will lose its light. It was no longer a light on a hill. She would lose
all of her glory, and the overwhelming majority of her sons and daughters
would be destroyed. The apple of His eye was falling from the sky. The
OC was being consummated. That is what this language is symbolic of.
The stars, the moon, and the sun shall never fall from the sky. If you ever
look up and see Jesus sitting on a cloud, you had better skedaddle. He ain't
coming to bring joy, peace, and light! He is coming in judgment.

Behold, he is coming with the *clouds*, and every eye will
see him, even those who pierced him, and all tribes of
the earth will wail on account of him. Even so. Amen. "I
am the Alpha and the Omega," says the Lord God, "who
is and who was and who is to come, the Almighty."
(Revelation 1:7–8, ESV)

Here we are over two thousand years after Jesus' death and ascension,
and I would like for someone to introduce me to someone who pierced
Jesus. I know that Jesus died once for all, but all did not pierce Him.
This was strictly the generation that shouted, "Crucify Him! We have
no king but Caesar!" As Jacob and family were incensed by Joseph's
dream, so were the Pharisees when Jesus spoke this same "clouds" language before them. I imagine that they were thinking as Joseph's family

thought, "How dare He! Who does He think He is?" Well, He is the One who created the clouds.

There have been many who have fallen away from the church because of the false perceptions of what people believe Jesus meant about "His coming." It was not literal. Let's look at what was meant to be taken literally. Jesus used no symbolism in this instance. He meant for His apostles and all of mankind to take this literally: *"I will not leave you comfortless: I will come to you. Yet a little while, and the world seeth me no more; but ye see me: because I live, ye shall live also. At that day ye shall know that I am in my Father, and ye in me, and I in you"* (John 14:18–20, KJV). It is obvious here that when Jesus states "I will come to you" that He is speaking of the coming Holy Spirit on the day of Pentecost. A few more verses and this becomes fact. *"But the Comforter, which is the Holy Ghost, whom the Father will send in my name, he shall teach you all things, and bring all things to your remembrance, whatsoever I have said unto you"* (John 14:26, KJV). He was not speaking of a literal coming. He goes on to state "Yet a little while, and the world seeth me no more; but ye see me: because I live, ye shall live also." The world would see Him no more because He would no longer be on this earth. Jesus is also telling the apostles here that they can expect to see Him only after death and the resurrection. He is assuring them that they would live after death, and that is when they would see Him again, when they were resurrected. This is the meaning of John 14:19. I encourage you to read John 14 in its entirety. It becomes obvious that the only encounter that man will have in this life will be a spiritual encounter, which is the indwelling of the Holy Spirit. It is also apparent in this scripture that "at that day" is the "coming on clouds" judgment of apostate Israel. It was not a literal one day but an event. Of course, all of His apostles, except John, were dead by the time the temple fell. The "world seeth me no more" is a verse that is never addressed by those who have a false view on the end-times. There is no symbolism used here to get confused about. The actual Greek word used when Jesus made the statement is the word κόσμος, which should always be literally translated as "inhabitants of the earth" or even possibly a certain geological area. It is according to the context. Jesus meant here the people of the Roman Empire, the nation of Israel, as well as the entire world.

"For yet a little while, and he that shall come will come, and will not tarry" (Hebrews 10:37, KJV). The writer of Hebrews expected Jesus' "coming on clouds" to occur in a little while. Why? Because that is what Jesus told them. He told them that "this generation" would be the one

to experience the end, the end of the Old Covenant, the consummation of all things with the nation of Israel. I am sorry, but 2,000 years and 50 generations will never be considered a little while to anyone on this earth. The scriptures say what they mean and mean what they say, or you can just chunk it. Of course, if we do not comprehend the symbolism being used it could be very detrimental to mans' understanding.

> Be patient therefore, brethren, unto the coming of the Lord. Behold, the husbandman waiteth for the precious fruit of the earth, and hath long patience for it, until he receive the early and latter rain. Be ye also patient; stablish your hearts: for the coming of the Lord draweth nigh. (James 5:7–8, KJV)

James, the brother of Jesus, is the one who documented this scripture. He expected the events that Jesus prophesied during his generation. It would be ludicrous to ask anyone to be patient about an event that was fifty generations away. "No man knoweth the hour or the day" is not a defense. As we demonstrated in a previous section, they certainly knew that it was their generation. No, God would not have all generations of man to be experiencing sleepless nights awaiting what was not a joyous event, but a day of darkness. James states in verse 8 that the coming of the Lord is drawing nigh, or near. He knew what he was talking about. The timing of this writing is not certain, but it was obviously before the destruction of the temple and the city of Jerusalem. I will date it to prior to Rome burning in AD 64. If persecution was going on from the Romans at the time of this writing it would have surely been made known by the contents of the letter. The persecution that is documented within the writings of James is among the Jews, those Judaizers persecuting true Israel, the Christians. James is speaking of the same coming that the writer of Hebrews spoke of, the only coming that Jesus ever mentioned. It was His coming on clouds in judgment. This would be proof that He was whom He claimed to be and that He was sitting at the right hand of the Father who is in heaven.

> But when they persecute you in this city, flee ye into another: for verily I say unto you, ye shall not have gone over the cities of Israel, until the Son of man be come.
> (Matthew 10:23, KJV)

> But whenever they persecute you in one city, flee to the
> next; for truly I say to you, you will not finish going through
> the cities of Israel until the Son of Man comes. (NASB)

Jesus gives His apostles a time indicator in this verse of His coming. He tells them that they will not have even gone through the cities of Israel before His coming. No matter the version of the Bible you use, all make it obvious that this was a coming that was not fifty generations, two millennia, away. "Verily I say unto you" is the King James interpretation, but "truly I say to you" is a better rendering to our current language. Now, if Jesus stated, "verily," "truly," or "assuredly," surely He was telling the truth. If not, He should have stated "unverily I say unto you," "for falsely I say unto you," or "for unassuredly I say unto you." He assures them that they will not have even covered the cities of Israel before His coming. They would have forty years before the destruction of the temple and the city to cover the cities of Israel, yet they would hardly cover this territory. Was Jesus lying to them? If He did not come by the time they had covered the cities of Israel, then He was a liar. "No man knoweth the hour or the day" does not fly here. If He did not know, He should not have spoken as fact His timing prophecy. I will side up with Jesus here. Who shall you side up with? The teachings of man or the standard of God?

This next verse is not a "clouds" verse, but it is very relevant for this section. Words have meaning and intent. The revelation, or revealing, in this verse, shows that there are discrepancies in the scriptures. It takes a discerning soul to parse it out.

> So that ye come behind in no gift; waiting for the coming
> of our Lord Jesus Christ: (1 Corinthians 1:7, KJV)

> so that you are not lacking in any spiritual gift, as you
> wait for the revealing of our Lord Jesus Christ; (RSV)

> so that you come short in no gift, eagerly waiting for the
> revelation of our Lord Jesus Christ, (NKJV)

I noticed that there is an obvious difference between a "coming" and a "revealing," or "revelation." The Greek word that the translation comes from is ἀποκάλυψις. The meaning of this word is revelation or revealing. Let's look at another verse that has a variant of the same word:

> The Revelation of Jesus Christ, which God gave unto
> him, to shew unto his servants things which must shortly
> come to pass; and he sent and signified it by his angel
> unto his servant John: (Revelation 1:1, KJV)

All fourteen of the English versions translate *apokalypsis* (English transliteration) in Revelation 1:1 as revelation, which is correct. It could have also been stated as "a revealing." This is not a "coming." There is inconsistency with the way the KJV translators interpreted the original word denoting "revelation" or "revealing." There is also inconsistency within the other versions, but the KJV is most often the worst when it comes to important timing issues. The abomination of desolation that Daniel prophesied, as well as Jesus, would have certainly been a revealing that the end was near for this generation that killed Messiah. This was when Galba, the seventh caesar, set up an image of Nero in the temple after Nero had committed suicide. We will address this later in "The Beast & Other Characters of the Last Days" section. Actually, God had snuffed Nero out. This event would certainly qualify as a revealing that Jesus was whom He claimed to be. A better to the nth degree revealing would have been when the temple was destroyed and not a stone was left unturned in AD 70.

We have all of the revelation of the Creator and Messiah that we shall ever receive or ever need. Those who see the light shall experience His light forevermore. I pray that after all the symbolism and figures of speech that we have looked at in this section that your brain has grown to the size of a whale. Josephus attests to the fact that the *"Son cometh! The Son cometh!"* He was there. He experienced it, along with those Jews that were standing on the wall, and the soldiers that were loading the catapult with the hundred pound stones. *"Coming on clouds"* is the only mention in the scriptures of this world seeing Jesus again after His departure, and it is obvious Old Testament apocalyptic language not to be taken literally. His statement of *"Yet a little while, and the world seeth me no more"* was to be taken literally. There is no symbolic language used with this statement. We use much figurative language in our talk every day. Go to South America and use figurative language, and you just may get slapped or punched. Cultural idioms oftentimes do not translate well into other languages. I know this from experience. We must learn to read the scriptures in light of the scriptures. We must become familiar with the images used in the Hebrew culture. It is a difficult thing to do and we will never nail it down 100 percent of the time, but rest assured, you will never see Jesus literally sitting or standing on clouds. Yes, He could, but that is not what was meant in the scriptures. Interpret scripture in light of scripture, and you will get a better understanding of God's communication to the Hebrews of ancient times and apply what is relevant to your life and you will rise up as on eagles' wings.

THE END DAYS ARE NOT
THE LAST DAYS

New Testament Scriptures Designating the End of an Era

*O*oday the church is so engrossed with the end-times scenarios that are being touted on television, radio, and the Internet. We are going to look at some "end" verses now in the New Testament that are relative to the issue. All "end" verses are not relative for this subject matter. For instance, in Matthew 24:31 it speaks of "from one end of heaven to the other." "End" in this sense is not the "end" that was imminent for the first-century believer. The word *end* is used fifty-six times in the KJV New Testament. We are only going to look at the verses where "end" is the event. Every time that *end* is used in this section, it is referring to the same event. We will do this chronologically, as the books of the authors are placed in the Bible. Many of the fifty-six "ends" are repeats from the different authors of the same statements Jesus made. We will not rehash all of those instances.

"And ye shall be hated of all men for my name's sake: but he that endureth to the end shall be saved" (Matthew 10:22, KJV). Jesus is speaking to His apostles here. He is telling them what they can expect in the coming years. From the time of His death until the time of His coming on clouds was a generation, about forty years. There are two ways to look at this verse, since it is now history to us, but it was future for Jesus' apostles. We know that most of Jesus' apostles were martyred before the destruction of Jerusalem and the temple in AD 70 and that John is likely the only one who lived through the consummation of the OC and got to experience the perfection of the NC. Remember the time that Jesus stated to Peter concerning John that John would remain alive until Jesus came back?

> Jesus replied, "If I want him to remain alive until I return, what is that to you? As for you, follow me." So the rumor

> spread among the community of believers that this dis-
> ciple wouldn't die. But that isn't what Jesus said at all.
> He only said, "If I want him to remain alive until I return,
> what is that to you?" (John 21:22–23 NLT)

There are theologians today, scholars, and preachers that gloss over this as if Jesus was clueless as to what He was actually saying. Yes, Jesus was stating to Peter that John would live to see His second coming. After AD 70, there is historical evidence that John was still living. This would not have even been mentioned in the scriptures if it were not a forth telling of what would be. Obviously, there was some confusion among those who heard it because there was a controversy as to whether John would live forever or long enough to see the events of AD 70. For the deep thinker, I recommend you go to this scripture in John and study it, particularly verse 23. Contrary to what people think about the afterlife, all shall experience bodily death in this life. At that point under the NC, you will be taken into heaven in the presence of Messiah and the Father. Under the OC, you experienced soul sleep. Peter and all the other apostles were to experience soul sleep in this life and then the resurrection of the dead on "that day," whatever day it was that the Lord chose.

Peter and the others endured all types of persecution, but they were faithful to the end. What end were they faithful to? The end of their lives. What end was John faithful to? He was faithful to the end of the OC era, the consummation. I am sure that after that he was faithful to the same end as the other apostles, death of the fleshly body. The only difference is that John did not have to experience soul sleep. Under the Old Covenant all experienced "soul sleep," both the sinner and the saint. Under the New Covenant the repentant sinner shall never experience "soul sleep" but shall rise to His kingdom on that day (the day the believer takes his last breath in this life.) Ascension upon death is the culmination, or highest degree, of the differences between the two covenants.

"But the one who endures to the end will be saved. And this gospel of the kingdom will be proclaimed throughout the whole world as a testimony to all nations, and then the end will come" (Matthew 24:13–14, ESV). Many today believe that the gospel has not gone out to the world as of yet. I take issue with that. The teaching of man is not my standard on this issue but the word of God and knowledge of language. The Greek word used for world here is *oikoumenē*. We know that this Greek term is never used to define the whole world. It is most often used in the scriptures to define the Roman Empire. Now this is something that a rational

person will conclude once knowledge of the Greek language is understood. Yet, this is not my only source for making this conclusion. Let's look at the source that is the most important: the word of God.

> We give thanks to God the Father of our Lord Jesus Christ, praying always for you, having heard of your faith in Christ Jesus, and of the love which ye have toward all the saints, because of the *hope which is laid up for you in the heavens*, whereof ye heard before in the word of the truth of the gospel, which is come unto you; even as it is also in all the world bearing fruit and increasing, as it doth in you also, since the day ye heard and knew the grace of God in truth. (Colossians 1:3–6, ASV)

When this word was spoken by Paul, which would have been prior to Nero's death in AD 68, the early believers still only had a hope laid up for them in heaven. This hope had not yet become a reality. The old had to pass away before the new would take effect. This was part of the gospel message; death was to be conquered for the believer, but not until the consummation, which was still on the horizon. Paul also states that the gospel is also in all the world. I was surprised to see that the actual Greek term used here in the TR is *kosmos*, which is the proper term to use when speaking of the whole world. Yet, this is not the final nail in the coffin about the gospel reaching the territory that Jesus meant for it to reach before His coming.

"If ye continue in the faith grounded and settled, and be not moved away from the hope of the gospel, which ye have heard, and which was preached to every creature which is under heaven; whereof I Paul am made a minister" (Colossians 1:23, KJV). I have been randomly picking versions of the Bible as I list scripture references, but here I purposely chose the KJV version for the KJV-Only advocates. Paul states here to his peers that the gospel had been "preached to every creature which is under heaven." Now, for the literalist, why do you not take this literally? It appears that people want to pick and choose what they believe is literal and what is not. I hear people today talking about how bad things have gotten in the world. They will even make statements about people who are falling away from the church and sound doctrine, as if we are living in the age that Jesus warned His apostles about. It is all over social media and YouTube videos galore. No, Paul was speaking to his peers. Yes, some fell away when the pressure rose. When family members were

being killed by family members because of their faith in Jesus, many departed from the faith. Josephus reports the Zealots' persecution of the Christians, as well as the Judaizers (followers of the Law of Moses). He also gives the best historical account of the Roman persecution that began in AD 64 under the Caesar Nero after Rome burned while Nero was fiddling. If you will research this you will see that the fiddle did not even exist when Nero committed suicide. It would be hundreds of years later, almost a millennia, until even something that resembled a fiddle was invented. There are even sources that reveal the fiddle did not come on the scene until the twelfth century.

I believe this would be a good place to state another tragedy. There are many today fiddling with the facts of history and the minds of man for tremendous financial gain. God Almighty has broken the strings to my fiddle. There shall be no more fiddling with my mind and life. Again, though, "every creature which is under heaven" used in this verse is just symbolic language representing the area within the Roman Empire that Jesus had intended and not literally every creature which is under heaven. I do not believe the monkeys had yet learned Hebrew!

"And you will hear of wars and threats of wars, but don't panic. Yes, these things must take place, but the end won't follow immediately" (Mark 13:7, NLT). If you were to do a study on the history of the Roman Empire, which Israel became part of in 63 BC, you will discover that there were wars and rumors of wars, as the KJV states, throughout the Roman Empire and beyond. The Roman Empire was still attempting to take other territories to expand their borders and to enrich the empire. At times the ruling caesar would even send out soldiers with no intent of making war, but as a scare tactic to intimidate other kingdoms, nations, territories, and so forth. Caligula was about as ghastly a figure as was Nero. In AD 39 he marched with his troops to Germania in a mock campaign to intimidate the Germanic people. In AD 40 Caligula marches to the English Channel with intentions of invading Britannia. They did not cross the channel. His troops collected sea shells, and no war was pursued. Caligula returned to Rome and celebrated a fabricated victory. Caligula was assassinated in AD 41, and Claudius ascended to the throne. In AD 43, the Roman Empire began to invade Britannia. In AD 47, the Roman general Corbulo defeats the Frisians, which was a Germanic ethnic group that held land in the coastal area of the Netherlands and Germany. Also, part of Denmark made up this area. Claudius died in AD 54, and Nero succeeded him. Claudius was deified at this time. In AD 58, General Corbulo conquered Armenia. In AD 61, Boudicca, the queen of the Iceni tribe, led a revolt against Roman

occupation. In AD 62, the first signs of volcanic activity were recorded in Mount Vesuvius. The great fire of Rome occurred in AD 64. There are many more revolts and attempts to take territory going on in and around the Roman Empire at that time. Persecution of the Christians and the nation of Israel began in earnest by the Roman Empire after the fire that burned Rome was blamed on them. There were many more skirmishes going on within the Roman Empire and bordering territories at that time. In AD 70, the city of Jerusalem was taken, and the temple was destroyed. Not a stone was left unturned.

I advise the earnest seeker to do the research for themselves. The writings of Josephus will confirm some of this. You can also search on the Internet for the first-century Roman Empire. There were wars, rumors of wars, threatenings of wars, and so forth going on in the Roman Empire at this point in time. It was a time of "hell on earth," the likes as had not been experienced in that region since the Jews took the Promised Land. What is going on today in that area pales in comparison to what was going on then. There was actually much activity going on with the expansion of the Roman Empire before Jesus was born. All the instances that I mentioned in this section are post AD 30 after Jesus' death. Israel was taken into the Empire in 63 BC, and the taxation process began that the Jews hated so much.

"When you hear of wars and uprisings, do not be frightened. These things must happen first, but the end will not come right away" (Luke 21:9, NIV). This verse in Luke is the same account as the previous scripture in Mark, but a different author penned it. As I listed numerous accounts of events going on within and bordering the Roman Empire previously, it is the same here. The message is this: when you hear of these things, take heed. It is the beginning of the end. It would take many years to eventually lead to the consummation of the OC. It was a process that had been in the making for years. God set up the Roman Empire to conquer the rebellious "Great Whore," the "Great Harlot," Israel. The leaders that were in place at that time were God ordained. That is why the people were admonished to pray for their leaders, as well as to be compliant with their commands. This was for that specific people and that specific time. The point here is that such activity was to be viewed as the beginning of the birth pangs. The end was not yet. It was still many years off from happening. As things heated up, the closer it got to AD 70, surely the ones warned by Jesus would flee to the mountains before that great day.

"After that the end will come, when he will turn the Kingdom over to God the Father, having destroyed every ruler and authority and power"

(1 Corinthians 15:24, NLT). Who is actually in charge here? It is Jesus. He is in command. He is out to destroy His enemies and to put them under His feet. His enemies were many. The leaders of the Jewish people, who happened to be the priests of the temple, were among His enemies. Anyone who was at war with the first-century church was an enemy, which would have included Roman Emperor Nero, the Beast (666), as well as the zealots, false teachers, false prophets, and so on. The Beast that was known by 666 was the Roman Empire. Nero was just a representative of the empire. Satan was alive and well during this time. Jesus actually used Vespasian to destroy the temple and the city of Jerusalem. I dare say that Jesus did not consider Vespasian to be an enemy of His. He was actually His ally.

Paul is telling the Corinthians in this verse that even though all experienced "soul sleep" prior to Jesus coming, the end for such was about to be. The martyrs for Jesus would be the first to rise. They would be with Him at His throne in heaven, judging the nation of Israel with Him. Is this literal? Ask when you get there. After this would come the second resurrection, which was for those who were under the Old Covenant and died prior to Messiah's birth. This likely happened just prior to the destruction of the temple and city of Jerusalem. All of this would culminate with the end of the OC.

Death has lost its sting for the believer. Each believer will be taken up in his own order, upon his last breath on this earth. The dates and timing of these resurrection events would be impossible for anyone today to declare with precise accuracy. Both resurrections happened between AD 64 and AD 70. The Christians, after this event, shall never experience "soul sleep." Also, you will not be in heaven with half of your assets, contrary to what many say today. Of course, you have sects and individuals today that believe in a future resurrection, which does away with the superiority of the NC. This is a subject, believe it or not, where there is much disagreement. Suffice it to say, I will allow the word of God to be my number one authority, and second goes to extra-biblical historical sources, such as Josephus. He was a contemporary to the first-century believers. He walked the earth in the very same generation as did Peter, Paul, and Mary. I will put my confidence in a man that walked the earth in the same generation as the apostles before I put my faith in a heresy that came along in 1830, or the 1900s. Again, do an online search on John Nelson Darby. You will be enlightened. Just make sure that you read at least five to six sources. There have been many in the world like him within this generation, such as Pat Robertson, John Hagee, Tim LaHaye,

Hal Lindsey, Jonathan Cahn, and Harold Camping. Actually, Camping died in 2013, and LaHaye in June of 2016. The Mormon religion and Jehovah's Witnesses were born out of this "end-times doomsday" foolishness. It was prevalent in the 1800s because of ignorant men who were seeking celebrity. Woe be unto them that continue to propagate such lies.

"To the end he may stablish your hearts unblameable in holiness before God, even our Father, at the coming of our Lord Jesus Christ with all his saints" (1 Thessalonians 3:13, KJV). The first-century believers needed to have their hearts strengthened. Most of these people did not actually witness Jesus' miracles. Most of them had never seen Him. What they were hearing from the apostles at that time and what they saw going on in the Roman Empire gave them reason to believe that something earth-shattering was about to happen. It would be the greatest event to ever happen in history forever. This was not a literal coming of the Lord and His holy ones, or saints. This is just Old Testament hyperbolic apocalyptic language. Mountains have never sung, nor have trees clapped their hands. *"For ye shall go out with joy, and be led forth with peace: the mountains and the hills shall break forth before you into singing, and all the trees of the field shall clap their hands"* (Isaiah 55:12, KJV). Take literally only what was meant to be taken literally. Otherwise you may be found leading the fig trees in song and dance.

"For we have become partakers of Christ if we hold the beginning of our confidence steadfast to the end" (Hebrews 3:14, NKJV). The writer of Hebrews is speaking to the last generation of the nation of Israel as God's chosen people. Not all that claim to be of Israel are of Israel. Those who failed to profess Jesus as Messiah were not true Israel. *"Not as though the word of God hath taken none effect. For they are not all Israel, which are of Israel:"* (Romans 9:6, KJV). Paul is stating that only those who hold on unto the end will be considered partakers of Christ. There would be many who would fall away due to the stress and torment that would ramp up as the end approached. There would also be many who would literally partake of what Jesus went through. Many would have to die for their faith. Many would heed the signs and flee to the mountains. It was appointed to most of Jesus' apostles to partake of death for their faith in Him. John was the only apostle that was allowed to put on immortality. The rest experienced death and corruption of the flesh before AD 70. I believe that most scholars and theologians would concede that the majority of Jesus' apostles, if not all, were put to death several years before AD 70 and that their flesh would have literally been turned back to dust.

"And we desire each one of you to show the same earnestness to have the full assurance of hope until the end" (Hebrews 6:11, ESV). This first generation of Christians was as bold a generation that has ever lived on this earth. Their hope was in the reality of Jesus being the very Son of God. If He was not, then their faith was in vain. If He was not, the faith of the first-century Christians would have ended there. Evidence of the reality of Jesus being the very Son of God was the destruction of the temple. What greater evidence for the proof of Jesus' claim to be the Messiah than fulfilled prophecy? Not one jot or tittle was left unfulfilled. He is the Prophet, the Priest, and the King.

The end was not the end of the world but the end of the covenant. That is a crucial element in the understanding of the Bible. It is amazing to me that there is also scripture that states that the world will go on forever, but no one preaches that or discusses it. Yet, the scriptures state the "end is near," and the people get all excited. Well, the end isn't near. It is approaching two millennia in our past. We need to quit living in the past, so we can change the course of history. His story needs to be understood in the light of reality and not as a fairy tale. Doom and gloom is nothing more than a horrific fairy tale, worse yet, a nightmare for little ones. The victory is the Lord's, and His soldiers are the believers. All the ammo we need is a true understanding of His story and a love for our fellow man. The leaves on the Tree of Life are for the healing of the nations.

"But the end of all things is at hand: be ye therefore sober, and watch unto prayer" (1 Peter 4:7, KJV). This is another of those verses that the people must come to understand what "end of all things is at hand" means. Well, what did it mean to Peter? After all, he is the one addressing the people with this letter. To whom was he writing? He was writing to the people of Pontus, Galatia, Cappadocia, Asia, and Bithynia. All of these areas were within the Roman Empire. Peter knew that the end was near. The end he had in mind was the one which Jesus had warned him and the other apostles about. It was also the event that the Old Testament prophets had foretold. Contrary to what some scholars and theologians think, the epistles of Peter were all written prior to the destruction of the temple and the city of Jerusalem in AD 70. Many scholars and theologians believe that Peter did not write this epistle. It could be possible that he had someone else to pen it while he spoke it, but he is the originator of it. If the temple and Jerusalem had already been destroyed when this epistle had been written, surely Peter would have mentioned it.

It is mighty intriguing that many scholars and theologians attribute the books of the New Testament to authors other than the apostle claiming authorship. The fact that none mention the destruction of the temple and the city of Jerusalem is evidence enough that all were written prior to AD 70. This has caused many who are not firm in the faith to fall away or have doubts. Woe be unto those who profess such lies. They are attempting to cover up their ignorance of reality. The "end" that Peter was speaking of was at hand; it was near. He did not know what day, year, or time, but he certainly knew it would occur within the generation that Jesus spoke. It occurred about forty years, a biblical generation, from Jesus' death. No, Jesus did not die in AD 33. No, He was not born in AD 1. He was born 3–6 BC and was crucified between AD 30 and AD 33 (I say AD 30.) There is an error in the calendar. Man can't even get that right, but this planet still rotates on its axis once every twenty-four hours at a speed of about 1,000 mph and around the sun once every 365 days at a speed of about 66 thousand miles per hour.

"At hand" means near. Many claim that Peter and the other writers of the New Testament were ignorant of the time that Jesus had warned them about. They even claim that Jesus was ignorant of the time, because of this verse: *"But of that day and hour knoweth no man, no, not the angels of heaven, but my Father only"* (Matthew 24:36, KJV) Again, I am sorry, but they did know the generation that would experience it. Here is food for thought: Did Jesus not claim to be One with the Father? Does the left hand not know what the right hand is doing when the same mind controls both?

"Now faith is the substance of things hoped for, the evidence of things not seen" (Hebrews 11:1, KJV). We may not have seen the destruction of the temple and the city, but it occurred. That is a *fact*. Facts are as important as faith. Otherwise fulfilled prophecy would be meaningless. Why did Jesus and the apostles state many times that "such and such was done so as to fulfill this prophecy?" Our faith should be greater than the apostles' due to the knowledge of fulfilled prophecy. Not one jot or tittle . . . .

"For it is time for judgment to begin at the household of God; and if it begins with us, what will be the outcome for those who do not obey the gospel of God" (1 Peter 4:17, ESV)? The judgment that Peter had in mind here was the judgment at hand. I imagine that Peter knew how literal his statement was. The children of Israel were the household of God, but also the temple was the house of God. God was about to judge the very people responsible for the death of His Son. One of the symbols that Jesus had given as the greatest sign of His messiahship was the destruction of the temple. The Romans loved grandeur. One of the grandest things in the Roman Empire was the city of Jerusalem and the temple building. The

Romans did not want to destroy such grandeur. Such grandeur added to the splendor of the Roman Empire. Josephus attempted to get the Jews to surrender, so the city and the temple would not be destroyed. The Jews were obstinate and self-centered. They even thought that God was on their side and would never allow them to be defeated, much less allow the destruction of the temple. Boy, were they wrong! The Jews always loved to hear the false prophets because they always prophesied of God's blessings upon Israel. They ridiculed and killed the true prophets of God who spoke the truth. They had become self-righteous and self-centered. You will notice in this verse that a responsibility had been placed on man for his eternal state. Obedience is required.

"To all who are victorious, who obey me to the very end, to them I will give authority over all the nations" (Revelation 2:26, NLT). Jesus was revealing to John what was about to happen shortly as stated in the introduction of Revelation: *"The Revelation of Jesus Christ, which God gave unto him, to shew unto his servants things which must shortly come to pass; and he sent and signified it by his angel unto his servant John:"* (Revelation 1:1, KJV). Shortly does not mean fifty generations away. Shortly has always meant shortly, except in the time of the end when it could actually mean a few more years or even decades. There are many references from Matthew to Revelation that give the sense of shortness of time for the event that the prophets and Jesus had foretold. To get a sense of how that generation possibly viewed time we need to go back to the time of Abraham. God made His covenant with Abraham around 2,050 years before Jesus came on the scene. This is over fifty biblical generations, quite a length of time. America became an independent nation in 1776, two hundred and forty years ago—a mere six generations ago. Shortly to us today would mean very soon. If I were to tell you I will be there shortly, you would assume that I am coming the same day, if not the same hour. Shortly to us would almost certainly always mean at least within the month and not six months away. Shortly has never meant fifty generations away. That is about how far we are from when all the books of the New Testament were written, prior to AD 70.

Jesus is telling John here that the "elect of Christ," the first-century Christians, who heeded His warnings and fled from the destruction of Jerusalem and the temple, would be given influence over the kings of the nations. If we truly had a better understanding of history, we would see that this was the case. Under certain kings, the Gospel of Jesus spread tremendously across this world. This world will ebb and flow as the Gospel of Jesus Christ is believed and understood. The Gospel of Jesus

Christ is not doom and gloom. It is victory over this world and evil. Those who perpetrate evil and call it good shall never inherit eternity. Doom and gloom is defeat. Jesus will not be defeated. You may be defeated, but the Gospel will not. If you are representing a false gospel, you will be defeated. You may also be held accountable for all time. You need to educate yourself and allow the word of God to be your standard and not the teachings of man. Otherwise you may be considered among the last in the kingdom of God.

The "end" that is referred to in these verses is clearly speaking about an event that was shortly to take place. Men today do not have a proper understanding and knowledge of history. We also do not have a proper understanding of the language of the people and time of the first-century church. If the mayor asked you how the game went Friday night and you told him that "We killed them," he would comprehend what you are stating. If this were in writing and it was found by someone two thousand years in the future, they very well may believe that this was about a terrorist attack. This is not a literal statement, but 2,000 years in the future, it may become historic fact. Now, "shortly," "near," and "at hand" are literal statements that were meant to be taken literally almost two millennia ago. Sadly, many today take them literally for our generation. Wake up, people. The end ain't near!

Day of the Lord

*M*ost people today have a false belief about the Day of the Lord; actually, many false beliefs are circulating. The main error is that it is in our future. If this is the case, then Abraham, Isaac, Jacob, Job, Noah, Jonah, King David, Jeremiah, Ezekiel, and others are still in the grave, experiencing "soul sleep."

Another error is that this will be a wonderful day, a day of blessing and awesome wonder. That is a false belief, too. What did the Old Testament prophets prophecy? The Day of the Lord and the Day of Wrath are the same day. The prophets prophesied the destruction of Jerusalem. Jesus' prophecy of the destruction of the temple was just another prophecy about the same event, but it was only about forty years after His death. If there is any doubt about the definition of the Day of the Lord, I believe that Amos gives the most accurate definition.

> Woe to you who desire the day of the LORD. Why would you have the day of the LORD? It is darkness, and not light, as if a man fled from a lion, and a bear met him, or went into the house and leaned his hand against the wall, and a serpent bit him. Is not the day of the LORD darkness, and not light, and gloom with no brightness in it? (Amos 5:18, ESV)

This describes the events that took place during the waning days of the northern kingdom of Israel. The Day of the Lord was not just a once-in-a-lifetime event. It occurred many times within the scriptures. The Day of the Lord that occurred in AD 70 was really much more than a one-day event. It was also the timeframe of the resurrection of the Old Testament saints, which would have been a glorious day for the dead but a horrific day for the living. Josephus's account of the destruction of the Jewish nation in his *The Wars of the Jews* gives a grand description of the last days of the Old Testament covenant era, even though he may not have been a Christian, according to many scholars and theologians. If he recognized Jesus as Messiah, then he was a Christian. He did not beleaguer the point, though. He was the historian of that era of time. Without his writings, we would have very little history of this era and particularly of this event. He was a Jew and was well aware of prophecy. This was the waning years of the OC era.

All the scriptures had been written by the time the temple was destroyed, despite what some may say. I am sorry, but if the temple had been destroyed in AD 70 and John had written the book of Revelation in the 90s AD, he certainly would have brought up the prophetic event of the temple being destroyed in AD 70 to show the fulfillment of Jesus' prophecy about the temple being destroyed and not a stone was left unturned. Irenaeus is the only source that gives the late dating of the book of Revelation. He is also the only one who states that Jesus' ministry lasted until Jesus was in his fifties. Well, Josephus was a contemporary of the apostles. Irenaeus was not born until between AD 115 and 125, which was forty-five to fifty-five years after the destruction of the temple and the city. Irenaeus was the likes of the heretics that Jesus and the apostles warned their generation about. His teachings contradict the teachings of John. Therefore, he is not an "early church father" as some profess. People pick and choose bits here and there to fit their preconceived notions. It takes a real man to admit that he was taught a lie and has discovered the truth. The truth will set you free. Even though Amos was prophesying of the end of the northern kingdom of Israel, he gives a definition of what the Day of the Lord was, a day of destruction, but highly likely not a one-day event.

Daniel prophesied of the end of the southern kingdom of Judah, which was the event that Jesus and John prophesied. We will look at some verses in chapter 12 now.

> And at that time shall Michael stand up, the great prince which standeth for the children of thy people: and there shall be a time of trouble, such as never was since there was a nation even to that same time: and at that time thy people shall be delivered, every one who shall be found written in the book. And many of them that sleep in the dust of the earth shall awake, some to everlasting life, and some to shame and everlasting contempt.
>
> (Daniel 12:1–2, KJV)

This verse mentions nothing of a rapture. Jesus warned His contemporaries about the signs of the times. When the people began to see the signs, then it was time to flee to the mountains. This is why possessions and property would be of no value to them. As a matter of fact, if you had lots of property and possessions, woe be unto you. This is where the verse about gaining the whole world only to lose your soul is most relevant. If you had lots of possessions, then things of the world had become your God. About a year before I repented and came back to God, I had just bought a condo on the Mississippi Gulf Coast. I traveled down to the condo at least two weekends a month. I was in the process of researching information about a center console boat that would be sufficient for bay fishing as well as offshore fishing. I would have bought it very quickly if I had not gotten that knock on my door that Thursday night in 1998. If I would have bought the boat, I would have felt obligated to use it, and God would have been put on the back burner. I thank God that I had not yet made that boat purchase. If my memory serves me correctly, I think that I made one more trip to the condo after I repented, and then I rented it out until it finally sold. Possessions can destroy one's relationship with God or certainly make it second, third, fourth, and so on priority. He should be the number one priority in one's life. If He is, it will show.

It is obvious from this verse in Amos that, as I have stated before, the Day of the Lord was so much more than the average Christian realizes. It was a day of horror, terror, and judgment—the very wrath of God. Coming on clouds is typical Old Testament judgment language. Judgment in the Bible is the punishment. When God pours out His judgment on you, it is the sentence. That is why "Judge not, that ye be not judged" is written. When we are offended or angry at another, we are not to strike out at them but to turn the cheek. To many, that is a slap in the face. Well, Jesus was saying "Just take your slap and go on," not "Take your slap and slap back." This verse is the most quoted verse by non-professing Christians, but it is quoted out of context and without the true meaning that was intended.

"But go your way until the end. And you shall rest and shall stand in your allotted place at the end of the days" (Daniel 12:13, ESV). The first verse tells of a time of tribulation, but those in Christ would be delivered. That would also include the Old Testament saints, prophets, judges, and so forth. They would be delivered from death and the grave. The living would be spared—the ones who heeded Jesus warning signs and fled. Verse 13 was spoken to Daniel. Daniel would not be around when the end came. Daniel would experience "soul sleep," but would be resurrected on that day in the far future from his prophecy date, some 550 years prior to the event.

> Everyone then who hears these words of mine and does them will be like a wise man who built his house on the rock. And the rain fell, and the floods came, and the winds blew and beat on that house, but it did not fall, because it had been founded on the rock. And everyone who hears these words of mine and does not do them will be like a foolish man who built his house on the sand. And the rain fell, and the floods came, and the winds blew and beat against that house, and it fell, and great was the fall of it. (Matthew 7:24–27 24, ESV)

Jesus was speaking to the crowds when He spoke these words. He was not talking about literal rain, nor floods, and winds. What He was speaking of was the torment that lay ahead of the nation of Israel after His crucifixion and departure from this world. The rain, floods, and winds would be persecution from their Jewish brethren and the forces of the Roman Empire. Those firmly rooted in the faith would not fall back but would rise to the task that lay ahead. It was appointed to His apostles to preach the Gospel message throughout the Roman Empire and then to die, except for John. Jesus also gave warnings to the crowds to flee to the mountains when they saw the signs that He spoke of. These were spared. If there was to be a rapture, why would they need to flee? Their safety was in believing and trusting in what Jesus told them to do: to acknowledge the signs and flee. Those who heeded the signs and warnings did flee and were spared.

> And if anyone will not receive you or listen to your words, shake off the dust from your feet when you leave that house or town. Truly, I say to you, it will be more bearable on the day of judgment for the land of Sodom and Gomorrah than for that town. (Matthew 10:14, ESV)

People who believe the judgment is in our future need to know that there are probably only a remnant of those cities left since the destruction of AD 70 and all of the wars that have occurred since then. It is obvious that this J-Day was on the horizon. Judgment was going to take place during "this generation." This coming judgment has nothing to do with receiving rewards for a job well done. This judgment was destruction. That is what judgment was in the OC era. The judgment was the punishment.

Many today think that Jesus' mandate to preach the Gospel to the world is still left unfulfilled, yet the following verse states otherwise:

"When they persecute you in one town, flee to the next, for truly, I say to you, you will not have gone through all the towns of Israel before the Son of Man comes" (Matthew 10:23, ESV).

Jesus' apostles had about forty years to achieve His mandate, and they did, but barely. This is another verse that the end-times doomsday sayers have only one answer for. They must state that Jesus was ignorant of the day and hour, but also of the generation and millennia. Was Jesus ignorant? I think not. If you go along with the end-times doomsday sayers then you must claim that Jesus was ignorant of the times He was living in, yet the consummation of the OC is what this "elect generation" was all about. He elected that generation to do away with the wages of sin, but many had to experience death during that generation, even Jesus' best friends. No, you are not an elect of God. If you were, you would have lived and died during the first century AD.

We will look at six verses here in the KJV that mention the day of the Lord. I am always tempted to put it in capitals, but it is not done that way in the scriptures. The "Day of the Lord" is only mentioned five times in the New Testament KJV, but there are several other terms used for this same day, such as "day of judgment," "that day," "the day of our Lord Jesus Christ," "come in a day," and a few others.

"Behold, I will send you Elijah the prophet before the coming of the great and dreadful day of the LORD" (Malachi 4:5, KJV). I listed the Malachi verse because it is obvious that this was a prophecy about John the Baptist, who appeared onto the scene in Israel before Jesus began his public ministry. The following conversation with Jesus and His apostles confirms this:

> And the disciples asked him, "Then why do the scribes say that first Elijah must come?" He answered, "Elijah does come, and he will restore all things. But I tell you that Elijah has already come, and they did not recognize him, but did to him whatever they pleased. So also the Son of Man will certainly suffer at their hands." Then the disciples understood that he was speaking to them of John the Baptist. (Matthew 17:10–13, ESV)

Did John show up 2,000-plus years ago to warn his contemporaries of an outpouring of God's wrath that was still in the future? Jesus even stated that "he will restore all things," speaking of John the Baptist. What did he restore? His appearance would be the sign of the times that

172

---

everlasting life was about to be restored, but only for those who hear the knock at the door and respond accordingly. Knock-knock!

I guess we have Hal Lindsey, John Hagee, Tim LaHaye, and Pat Robertson who are our Elijah's. Not! There are many others out there. There are nights that I am bored and want to just sit back and catch some fiction or fairytale. I will just get on YouTube and watch a short video or two about the world ending in the next few weeks or months, prophesied by false prophets. They arc truly fairytales. Sadly, it is really not at all entertaining. Such as these shall be considered least in the kingdom of God for all eternity, or more than likely they will not even be there. They have called Jesus a liar through their false beliefs and teachings. The only way that they can pull off their shenanigans is to claim that Jesus was ignorant. If Jesus did not mean "this generation," the very generation to whom He was speaking, then He was surely not aware of the timing of the event He was prophesying. If that is the case then, according to Moses, Jesus would have been a false prophet. Regardless of whether these end-times doomsday sayers literally state that Jesus is a false prophet; they are quite literally stating that Jesus was ignorant. No. No. Noooo! Jesus is the Creator of the universe, very Son of God, and God Himself. If you believe that Jesus was ignorant of the generation that would experience the outpouring of God's wrath and the consummation of the OC, then you do not believe that Jesus is part of the All-Knowing Godhead. You may want to consider cleansing your mind and reprogramming yourself to truth. Only those who have the Truth shall enter the Pearly Gates. I hope that by the time you reach the end of this book, the reprogramming is well under way. It is a slow process to overcome the false teachings and heresy that have infiltrated the minds of the church. End-times doomsday sayers preach defeat. They must be on the same side as Satan. He lost. Jesus won. I am on His side.

"The sun shall be turned into darkness, and the moon into blood, before that great and notable day of the Lord come" (Acts 2:20, KJV). If you are not familiar with the Old Testament, I recommend that you familiarize yourself with it. There is much language in the Old Testament about the sun, moon, stars, and clouds. It sounds much like the language in this verse. The language is the same Old Testament apocalyptic language that was used back in that day. The language may change, but the subject matter is the same. It was never about the sun, moon, and clouds. It was about judgment. I believe that the coming on clouds study should have tweaked your knowledge of symbolic language and how it was used when writing the scriptures. It was used in a "swang" that the people

of that day and age would have comprehended it. It is obvious that the Jews on the temple wall comprehended that Jesus was Messiah and that He was actually sitting at the right hand of the Father who is in heaven. Jesus was not actually there at the wall, but those whom he chose to judge the nation of Israel. Not a stone was left unturned—not one jot or tittle.

"To deliver such an one unto Satan for the destruction of the flesh, that the spirit may be saved in the day of the Lord Jesus" (1 Corinthians 5:5, KJV). Satan was not out killing his people. He was killing the saints of the Lord. If you opposed emperor worship and the apostate harlot Jewish synagogue of Satan, you would be offered up for destruction during the waning days of the OC era. Actually, a better rendering of the last part of this verse would be "that the spirit (soul) may be revived in the day of the Lord Jesus," for that is what happened at that time. The souls of those who had their names written in the Book of Life had been at rest (soul sleep) and were resurrected and rose to heaven. It is obvious from this verse that the soul did not arise at the time of death. It experienced a time of "unawareness" until the day of the Lord, which was the Day of Wrath and Resurrection Day. Today it is different. To be absent from the body is to be present with the Lord in heaven under the NC.

"And the seventh angel sounded; and there were great voices in heaven, saying, The kingdoms of this world are become the kingdoms of our Lord, and of his Christ; and he shall reign forever and ever" (Revelation 11:15, KJV). The scripture actually states that after all of this is completed that God will be in control. All of Jesus' saints are with Him, all that have ever lived and died. This verse says nothing of the earth being destroyed. God is in control today and reigning on high. There are many in the world today waiting on Jesus. Well, He is in heaven waiting on man. It is His desire that we repent and fall away from the sinful, evil, wicked ways of man and administer the love of God to our fellow man. There is neither Jew nor Greek today. The KJV of the Bible never uses the word *Gentile* in this context, yet a Greek is a Gentile. The leaves on the Tree of Life are the believers. The believers are for the healing of the nations. Man is made in the image of God, and we have the responsibility to bring the healing and peace to the nations. Racism and nationalism are enemies to the process of peace. If you are a racist and nationalist, then you are an enemy to the cause of Christ.

> Stand therefore, having your loins girt about with truth,
> and having on the breastplate of righteousness; And your
> feet shod with the preparation of the gospel of peace;

Above all, taking the shield of faith, wherewith ye
shall be able to quench all the fiery darts of the wicked.
(Ephesians 6:14–16, KJV)

The message that Jesus came to give, the Gospel, is a message of
peace, and not division. It is what the healing of the nations is about. That
is for this earth and not for heaven. There will be no division in heaven.
God divided the people into nations after the Tower of Babel dispersion.
Heaven will be about unity and not division, which will exclude nations.
If there are no nations in heaven, then the healing is for the here and now.
Now, is it heretical to think that God desires for Christians to bring the
healing of the nations to this world? It appears that the leaves are for the
poisoning of the nations. Woe be unto those who preach doom and gloom,
as well as national supremacy and favoritism.

Wake up, America! Wake up, world! Jesus is longsuffering, but He
will not allow disregard, as well as downright heresy, against His word
to continue into eternity. He could decide to do to us what He did to the
elect in AD 70. He could pour out His wrath on this generation, but there
will not be a rapture before the event. If you don't believe it, if you get
to heaven, ask the first-century believers who will be there. They were
not spared tribulation. They were aware of the signs, sold their property
and goods, and fled for safety.

*"As also ye have acknowledged us in part, that we are your rejoicing,
even as ye also are ours in the day of the Lord Jesus"* (2 Corinthians 1:14,
KJV). The Corinthians rejoiced in the fact that Paul and Timothy had
shared the Gospel with them. They had the assurance of the resurrection
of their souls on that day of the Lord. Paul and Timothy also knew that
on that day, it would bode well for them to have evangelized as many as
possible into the kingdom. The more the merrier. The more that heeded
the warnings and fled to safety, the more there would be to evangelize
and plant the roots of the early first-century church. Also, the rewards
would be greater for Paul and Timothy in heaven. It is more of a numbers
game than we realize.

*"For yourselves know perfectly that the day of the Lord so cometh
as a thief in the night"* (1 Thessalonians 5:2, KJV). Paul is basically
repeating what Jesus stated in Matthew 24:43–44 (NLT): *"Understand
this: If a homeowner knew exactly when a burglar was coming, he would
keep watch and not permit his house to be broken into. You also must be
ready all the time, for the Son of Man will come when least expected."* It
is obvious that Paul had been schooled in what Jesus taught His apostles,

as he was not a disciple of Jesus during His life. Jesus made this statement as they were leaving the temple grounds, right after he made the statement about "Not one stone will be left on top of another" in verse 2 of the same chapter. It should be obvious that He was talking of the same event, the temple destruction, and the thief that comes. No man may have known the exact hour, but many saw the signs and fled to safety. Since Jesus was the One who was ruling from heaven, it is obvious that the Father had clued Him in on the day and hour of the "coming of the Son of man"; otherwise, He would not have known when to come.

"But the day of the Lord will come as a thief in the night; in the which the heavens shall pass away with a great noise, and the elements shall melt with fervent heat, the earth also and the works that are therein shall be burned up" (2 Peter 3:10, KJV). Peter is restating the same material we just discussed above. This was not a literal burning of the earth. It was the destruction of the apostate harlot nation, Mystery Babylon (Jerusalem), the place where the prophets and Jesus were killed. Again, this is Old Testament apocalyptic language. This was the consummation of the Old Covenant. The world is going nowhere. You and I shall pass, but the world shall go on. How long? Who knows? I dare say that the evolutionists are probably closer to the truth on this than the church is. The Creator can maintain His creation and the uniformitarian principle of "everything is as it always was" is not a fact. He maintains. He did not just set the universe in motion and sit back to see what happens. He is active in maintaining His creation. Man is His biggest problem. I am not referring to the way man treats the planet but the way man treats man.

In the next section we will look at "Day of Wrath" scriptures and demonstrate that it is the same event.

Day of Wrath

The "day of wrath" is a term that can also be associated with other days in the OTC section of the Bible. The "day of the Lord" and "judgment day" are used synonymously, as well as other terms. There were many days of wrath and days of the Lord in the Old Testament era.

Another term that is flung around in Christian circles is the term *saved*. Salvation is of imminent importance to all mankind of all times, whether they realize it or not. However, salvation to the generation that was living when Jesus walked the earth was much different from what the term means today. Salvation in that era was to be absent from the city of Jerusalem when God poured out His wrath on the Jews and nation of Israel. Even Jesus' apostles were not spared from the torment of the destruction of that era. His apostles were not killed by God, though. They were killed by the great harlot, Mystery Babylon, Israel, the Jewish nation, in alliance with the beast of the Roman Empire. God had been patient with Israel ever since He led them out of Egypt. He poured out His wrath on this world many times, beginning with the banishment of Adam and Eve from the Garden of Eden and the flood in Noah's day. The flood was judgment on the world. There are other times when He judged the nation of Israel. The day of wrath is used in the Old Testament to describe the destruction of Jerusalem by the Chaldeans, which resulted in the Babylonian exile. This was God's wrath against the southern kingdom of Judah. God had already divorced the northern kingdom of Israel with the Assyrian captivity, which resulted in the lost tribes of Israel. God poured out His wrath on the Egyptians at times. The prophesied day of wrath that was not fulfilled in the OTC era was against the people who God had made a covenant with that began with Abraham. We will now look at some verses where "day of wrath" is used. The exact phrase "day of wrath" is used only four times in the KJV Bible. Three of those occurrences are in the Old Testament. There are other terms used for God's judgment, such as "day of His fierce anger," "day of His wrath," and "day of the wrath of the Lord," as well as others. "Day of wrath" is not just a specific one-time event. There were many days in the scriptures that were days of wrath, some against Israel's enemies and some against the very nation of Israel.

"That the wicked is reserved to the day of destruction? They shall be brought forth to the day of wrath" (Job 21:30, KJV). The day of wrath here does not refer to the AD 70 destruction and consummation. This is referring to the final destruction of the individual. Job was speaking to his tormentors. This is a verse that could be used to paint a picture that it does not paint. Many verses of scripture are taken out of context. This verse here could easily be used to paint a picture of a final end-times event. But, that is not what it is referencing. Let's look at the verses that follow this verse:

> Who shall declare his way to his face? And who shall repay him what he hath done? Yet shall he be brought to the grave, and shall remain in the tomb. The clods of the valley shall be sweet unto him, and every man shall draw after him, as there are innumerable before him. How then comfort ye me in vain, seeing in your answers there remaineth falsehood? (Job 21:31–34, KJV)

The wages for sinful man is death. This is the wrath of God. Each man prior to the New Covenant had experienced a day of destruction, a day of wrath. If it were not for the perfection of Jesus Christ and His sinless blood, every man that has ever been born and ever would be born would have to experience death for all time. The New Covenant allows one not to experience the wages of sin, but only for those who bow the knee to Jesus. Those who do not profess Christ shall experience a day of destruction, a day of death. They shall never know eternal life—only the wages of sin.

"Riches profit not in the day of wrath: but righteousness delivereth from death" (Proverbs 11:4, KJV). Proverbs is the book of wisdom. It reveals much about how to live a wise life. Today we have these social-ists who believe it is biblical to take money from the worker and give it to the sluggard. This is not biblical, and God will consider it as what it is: thievery. God's word does not contradict itself. The generation that crucified Jesus was an "elect" people who were under special circum-stances. If they held onto the riches of this world, they would be killed by the Roman forces, the Judaizers, or the Zealots. They needed to sell what

they had and distribute it among the believers, so they could just subsist. When Nero led the persecution that began in AD 64, I imagine that many of Jesus' followers recognized what was going on as what He and John had prophesied, as well as Daniel's prophesy, packed up, and fled. The lighter your load, the quicker you can move to safety. A heavy load could have guaranteed your delay and your death or imprisonment. Just getting by was sufficient for them. Christians can go back and live the wisdom of Solomon now. Otherwise, you are not a "good man." *"A good man leaveth an inheritance to his children's children: and the wealth of the sinner is laid up for the just"* (Proverbs 13:22, KJV). Woe be unto them who attach a death tax to a person's estate so that his generous inheritance to his children and grandchildren is stolen by the government. Those who do not oppose this will have it attributed to them as if they had entered a man's house and stolen his goods. There will be no thieves in heaven. Government makes no decisions. Man makes decisions and will be held accountable. Take heed.

"That day is a day of wrath, a day of trouble and distress, a day of wasteness and desolation, a day of darkness and gloominess, a day of clouds and thick darkness" (Zephaniah 1:15, KJV). This verse is actually associated with the defeat of the Jewish nation by the Chaldeans and the Babylonian exile, which began between the latter 600s and 586 BC. I mention it here to get an idea planted in your head about Jesus coming in the New Testament. Remember, He said they would see the Son coming on clouds: *"And Jesus said, I am: and ye shall see the Son of man sitting on the right hand of power, and coming in the clouds of heaven"* (Mark 14:62, KJV). The language used in Zephaniah is Old Testament apocalyptic language, describing judgment. A day of clouds is a metaphor for judgment, which was often carried out by other nation's armies. Also, if you live in the southern part of the United States, you know that there are more sunny or fair days than cloudy days. I imagine that God poured out His judgment many times on sunny days, but still it was as a day of gloominess—a day of clouds. We addressed "clouds" in a previous section. It just felt like a great place to plant a seed. The harvest is coming.

"But because of your stubbornness and your unrepentant heart, you are storing up wrath against yourself for the day of God's wrath, when his righteous judgment will be revealed" (Romans 2:5, NIV). The day of Gods' wrath was on the horizon. This was not someday two millennia away. Paul is warning his contemporaries in Rome about what was about to happen. He did not know the day or the hour, but he certainly knew the generation that would experience it. Judgment day was the day of

wrath, the day of the Lord. What good would it do for our local high school coach to browbeat his current team about a future game that is twenty years away? None whatsoever. If he was found guilty of doing so, he would probably be deemed a lunatic and would lose his job. There are those who would say that Paul's contemporaries were browbeaten for our benefit today. I believe that God would diagnose such people as schizophrenics and unfit for everlasting life, or maybe they are the ones who will be considered the least in the kingdom of God because they are causing many to stumble. They are also causing many to fall away. The devil could do no better job.

"The Lord is at Your right hand; He shall execute kings in the day of His wrath" (Psalm 110:5, NKJV). We know from history that Nero committed suicide in AD 68, after a three and a half-year tribulation period over the Jewish nation. He was caesar, not a king, but the Jews viewed them as kings. Remember what the Jews shouted before Jesus' crucifixion? "We have no king but Caesar." So, from Nero to the destruction of the temple in AD 70, there were five kings. After Nero, there was Galba, Otho, Vitellius, and Vespasian. Galba reigned seven months and was murdered. Otho succeeded him and reigned three months before committing suicide. Vitellius reigned about eight months before being murdered. Vespasian succeeded him and reined from December 21, AD 69 to June 24, AD 79. He supposedly died of natural causes created from a horrendous episode of diarrhea. Vespasian was caesar when the city of Jerusalem was taken and the temple was destroyed. There were four caesars in the year 69 AD. You can go to the Internet and research this on Wikipedia. Rome lost two caesars due to suicide and two to murder between June AD 68 and the end of 69. Since America's first president, George Washington until now, a period of time that covers 227 years (Washington became President in 1789), there have only been four presidents killed in office, yet Rome had four new caesars due to death between June AD 68 and the end of AD 69. People talk as if the world has never experienced more tumultuous times than we are living in today. I think the facts of ancient history reveal that current thoughts are vain imaginations.

> They will throw their silver into the streets, and their gold will be treated as a thing unclean. Their silver and gold will not be able to deliver them in the day of the LORD's wrath. It will not satisfy their hunger or fill their stomachs, for it has caused them to stumble into sin. (Ezekiel 7:19, NIV)

If you will, study *The Wars of the Jews* by Josephus. You will see this verse really come to life. Josephus states that some of the Jews had eaten their gold and were hoping to escape the city without the gold being detected. Many were killed and their stomachs were cut open to retrieve the gold. I suppose that if it had reached the bowels, it would certainly have been considered an unclean thing. I certainly would not want to handle coins covered in dung. If the Jews had attempted to flee the city with their gold and silver in bags or containers, they likely would have been detained by the Zealots and robbed, as they were causing as much tribulation on their own nation as the Romans and Judaizers.

I was recently sharing with a friend some of the history in Josephus's writings and showed how it confirmed biblical prophecy. He stated to me "Well, Josephus is not scripture, so I can't put much weight on his writings." Well then, the American Revolution, the Civil War, World Wars I and II, must not be true history, either, because they are not in scripture. I got mugged in New Orleans on Fat Tuesday in 1987 and was shot by the mugger. That wasn't in the scriptures, but it is a fact. That is very poor reasoning or, really, no reasoning at all.

"Neither their silver nor their gold shall be able to deliver them in the day of Jehovah's wrath; but the whole land shall be devoured by the fire of his jealousy: for he will make an end, yea, a terrible end, of all them that dwell in the land" (Zephaniah 1:18, ASV). When reading this verse and the previous verse, it appears that they are speaking of the same event. Ezekiel and Zephaniah began speaking about the Chaldean destruction of Jerusalem and the temple, but it appears that they extend their prophecy to another event farther in the future that would be the end of all things. Actually, it would be the end that Moses had told of, as well as all the prophets from Samuel on. It would be God's divorce decree from the nation of Israel after they murdered their Messiah, the very Son of God. This was the AD 70 destruction of the temple and Jerusalem. There are commentaries out there that state that this is a future event that will be fulfilled when Russia invades the Jewish nation. I am sorry. It is not. It is in our past. God would have the United States to be at peace with Russia. Woe be unto you who keep causing not only little ones to stumble, but even those who should be partakers of solid meat, yet are still babes in the word. We are to be peacemakers and healers of the nations.

"For the great day of their wrath has come, and who is able to stand" (Revelation 6:17, NASB)? Eight Bible versions state "their wrath" and six versions state "His." From a literal standpoint, we know that God is Father, Son, and Holy Spirit. We also know that God appointed to the

Son to judge the ones who crucified Him. It is very obvious that John is speaking to his contemporaries about an historical event that would affect them.

I have made this observation before, but it is relevant here also. Daniel was told to seal up his prophecy. He would not be around to unseal the prophecy anyway. John was told not to seal up his prophecy. Well, that would be because the time was at hand—at the door. It was time to get the word out to the people. The day of wrath was not a literal day. It was a period of time. It began with the persecution of the antichrist Jews and ended when Vespasian's forces leveled the city and the temple.

It appears that John wrote the book of Revelation prior to the beginning of the Neronian persecution. He could have had his vision years before he penned it. My first experience with the beast and 666 happened at least forty years ago, but I am just now penning it. John may have waited until he perceived that Nero was the prophesied Beast before he penned it. Regardless, the temple was still standing when John penned Revelation, which means that it was written prior to AD 70. Irenaeus is credited with dating the writing of Revelation post-AD 70. He also states that Jesus lived into His fifties. I am sorry, but if he can't get that right, I am prone not to accept much weightier issues from him. He is the only source that dates Jesus's life this late. I have other issues with this source, too, but that is for another study. He was a heretic, yet many are beholden to his false teachings. I am sorry, but if John had written any of his compositions of the Bible after AD 70, surely he would have mentioned the destruction of the temple. He wrote five books of the Bible, yet wrote at least one of them (Revelation) after the destruction of the temple and consummation of the Old Covenant, yet He never mentions the fulfilled prophecy of Jesus' statement of "not one stone here will be left upon another"? I am sorry. That does not correspond to the facts. All five of John's books were written prior to AD 70, and I dare say before AD 64. Is scripture your standard? If so, here is the answer: *"There are also seven kings. Five have fallen, one is, and the other has not yet come. And when he comes, he must continue a short time"* (Revelation 17:10, NKJV). The five that have fallen are all dead caesars. The "one is" would be the one who was ruling at the time John delivered Revelation to the seven churches, the sixth caesar. This would be Nero. Galba would be next, but he would rule for a short time, only eight months. This one verse destroys Irenaeus's false assumption of John writing Revelation after the fall of the temple. Have you been fleeced by the teachings of man? Man up and admit it. Many have.

The day of wrath is in our past, at least the one that was prophesied in the Bible. God could certainly pour out His wrath on the world at any time and any place. The whole world is ripe for judgment because of idolatry, corruption, immorality, and so on. Man is more likely to pour out his judgment on mankind. Man is willing to sacrifice the sons of others for his victory, which leads to the death of many on both sides. God was willing to sacrifice the life of His Son for man's victory — the One died for the many. *"In the midst of the street of it, and on either side of the river, was there the tree of life, which bare twelve manner of fruits, and yielded her fruit every month: and the leaves of the tree were for the healing of the nations"* (Revelation 22:2, KJV). It is obvious that the church has not taken up the mandate to be a force that brings about the healing of the nations. It sounds like the church has been defeated, but by whom? These end-times doomsday sayers. The healing of the nations will take place. Will it begin now, or will the church continue to be divisive and racist? Remember this; Abraham was from Ur of the Chaldeans, which would be in modern-day Iraq. So, Abraham was an Iraqi. God is not a favorer of nations, nor races of people. In His eyes, there is only the human race.

I hope that this has enlightened the reader to the awareness of whom the scriptures state would experience the wrath of God. This is so very important. So much so that we will look at many other aspects of the same event, but spoken of in other terms, such as "end," "latter days," "last days," and so forth.

The End of the World or End of an Age?

*T*he English word *world* is found 241 times in the King James Version (KJV) of the New Testament using the Blue Letter Bible online search tool. The Greek words that the interpreters of the KJV attached the word *world* to are listed below, along with the Greek transliteration of the word and the definition as found online at billmounce.com.

Aion—36 times
Aion—a period of time of significant character; life; an era; an age: hence, a state of things marking an age or era; the present order of nature

Kosmos—188 times
Kosmos—the world, the material universe, the lower world, the earth

Oikoumenē—14 times
Oikoumenē —the habitable world, world

There are variants of these words that actually have a different meanings than what is defined in dictionaries and concordances. A man-assigned definition is not the correct way to define a term in every instance. Context is everything. The definition assigned to a term does not always meet the need. For instance, the KJV uses *world* where oikoumenē is used, and it is obviously not referring to the whole world, but a defined location. This has been addressed in a previous section, but it is a critical issue.

Without knowledge of the Greek language, I noticed immediately that the word *aion* would certainly not qualify for what we would define as world. Even a novice would know to associate this word with *time* and not *world*. I can't even begin to think of the number of times that I have stated "That was eons ago." The most obvious thing that I noticed as I studied the context of the word "world" is that every time the Greek word *aion* is used, it is referring to a particular time, era, or epoch of time, or even what we would call an age. I think that if I were to state the term "modern age," most would discern that I am not talking about the first century, or even the eighteen or nineteenth century. I would be talking about the here and now, the computer age, the age of technology. It is obvious to even the casual observer who has had experience in a foreign culture where a foreign language is spoken that something is awry here. The word *aion* means something totally different than the other terms for world. Every time that the word *aion* is used the interpreters of the King James Version (KJV) of the Bible inserted the word "world." This was either done out of error or intentionally. If it was done intentionally, then it appears that there was an ulterior motive. The ulterior motive could be an eschatological (end-times) motive to paint a picture of a preconceived view based on current convictions, whether true or false. I will list some KJV and ESV scriptures that were interpreted from the Greek *aion* and a few with other words, such as *kosmos*, which is the most used Greek term to describe the world, as well as a few others.

> And whosoever speaketh a word against the Son of man, it shall be forgiven him: but whosoever speaketh against the Holy Ghost, it shall not be forgiven him, neither in this world, neither in the world to come.
>
> (Matthew 12:32, KJV)

> And whoever speaks a word against the Son of Man will be forgiven, but whoever speaks against the Holy Spirit will not be forgiven, either in this age or in the age to come.(ESV)

Aion is used in this verse. Jesus is stating that anyone who blasphemes the Holy Spirit in either the Old Covenant Age (current during his lifetime) or the coming New Covenant Age (to begin in about forty years), there would be no forgiveness. This is not about a new world coming. This world is all that there is for man this side of heaven. The coming age was the New Covenant era. The passing age was the Old Covenant era. No, it did not pass the day Jesus was crucified. It would be forty years after His death and resurrection. Hmmm—forty years to wander and wonder around and repent or perish.

The enemy that sowed them is the devil; the harvest is
the end of the world; and the reapers are the angels.
(Matthew 13:39, KJV)

and the enemy who sowed them is the devil. The harvest
is the end of the age, and the reapers are angels. (ESV)

Jesus is speaking here of the destruction of Jerusalem in AD 70, which
was on the horizon for Israel. They would be given about forty years to
repent after they had crucified Him. This was not about the end of the world.
The followers of Jesus were separated from the defiant. They heeded Jesus
warnings and fled to the mountains. I am sure some probably even fled to
valleys. The main thing was that they were to separate themselves from
those who denied the deity of Jesus. This was the separating of the wheat
and tares. It was about the end of the Old Covenant, the end of an era. A
new heaven and earth were on the horizon, the New Covenant.

As therefore the tares are gathered and burned in the fire;
so shall it be in the end of this world.
(Matthew 13:40, KJV)

Just as the weeds are gathered and burned with fire, so
will it be at the end of the age. (ESV)

The above verse has nothing to do with hellfire and the end of the
world. Jesus is stating that as man gathers weeds and burns them to destroy
them, so too will be the destruction of those who deny His deity until the
end of the age, the Old Covenant Age. At harvest time the tares are separated and destroyed, and the wheat is what is left behind to be productive
and useful. Hmmm—left behind. That should be your desire. If you are
taken, you are destroyed. This would be the very generation, "this generation" that would reap what they had sown. They had sown death and
destruction upon the Messiah, so they thought. You reap what you sow.

So shall it be at the end of the world: the angels shall
come forth, and sever the wicked from among the just,
(Matthew 13:49, KJV).

So it will be at the end of the age. The angels will come
out and separate the evil from the righteous. (ESV)

Josephus states in his writings that out of the magnitude of dead bodies in the streets of Jerusalem that there was not a single known Christian among the dead. Now, did the angels literally separate the righteous from the evil, or had the righteous heeded the signs and warnings of Jesus and the Old Testament prophets, and fled to the mountains on their own? Regardless, they were obviously not present in Jerusalem when the Roman forces attacked the city. Hmmm—end of the age and not the world.

> And as he sat upon the mount of Olives, the disciples came unto him privately, saying, Tell us, when shall these things be? And what shall be the sign of thy coming, and of the end of the world?
> (Matthew 24:3, KJV)

> As he sat on the Mount of Olives, the disciples came to him privately, saying, "Tell us, when will these things be, and what will be the sign of your coming and of the end of the age?" (ESV)

If the destruction of Jerusalem was 2,000-plus years in the future, I do not think "this generation" would really have cared much about the signs of His coming. I am sorry, but they could have cared less if it did not pertain to their generation. Even if it was 2,000 years away, I could care less. What can I do to change it? Now, if it was forty years away, I would be highly concerned. That could affect my life.

> Who shall not receive manifold more in this present time, and in the world to come life everlasting.
> (Luke 18:30, KJV)

> who will not receive many times more in this time, and in the age to come eternal life. (ESV)

The current age, the Old Covenant Age, did not allow for eternal life. The wages for sin was death (and still is), and it still reigned. It would reign forty more years after Jesus' death and resurrection until the Old Covenant was consummated and the dead in Christ arose, along with the Queen of the South and the Ninevites to judge the nation of Israel. Of course that was Old Testament apocalyptic language that was not to be taken literally, for God used the Roman Empire to judge the nation of Israel. But, the rising

187

of the Queen of the South and the men of Nineveh would be sufficient evidence that Judgment Day, Resurrection Day, and the Day of the Lord are in the same timeframe. It is also sufficient to say that this was the second resurrection because these were not involved in the forty-year reign of Jesus and those who were martyred for His namesake. Sorry, but Moses, Abraham, David, Daniel, Zechariah, and so forth did not give their lives for Christ's namesake. This was for the martyrs of Jesus generation, those who died for His namesake. We will probably never understand all the details about the resurrections mentioned in Revelation until we get there. Yes, it speaks of two, but none involve those under the New Testament Covenant.

> Now all these things happened unto them for ensamples: and they are written for our admonition, upon whom the ends of the world are come. (1 Corinthians 10:11, KJV)

> Now these things happened to them as an example, but they were written down for our instruction, on whom the end of the ages has come. (ESV)

If we read only the King James Version of the Bible, we would have a very schizophrenic view on reality. Two thousand years has never been considered a short span of time. Even the angel that prophesied to Daniel events that were to take place over 500 years in his future told him to seal up the prophecy. This was the same event that Jesus prophesied, as well as John. John was told not to seal up the prophecy because the time was near. Paul states in this verse that the "end of the age" had come upon his generation, which was "this generation." This is proof positive that the Old Covenant did not end at Jesus' death and resurrection. It was still yet future. I have never seen an "end" last 2,000 years, and I am sorry, but "that one day *is* with the Lord as a thousand years" does not cut the muster here. Only an obstinate one would take that view. This is one of the most out-of-context verses of scripture quoted. God speaks to man in terms that man can comprehend; otherwise why speak at all? The "day as a thousand years" scriptures basically mean that God can do more in a day than man can do in a thousand years, but literally, God can do more in a second than man can do in a trillion-plus years. Sorry, but that is the God that I serve. Those without discernment attempt to do the same thing that evolutionists do. If you do not discern reality, just add time and chance and you become a brilliant scholar. Sorry, that is insufficient and will not suffice in the presence of the One True Righteous Judge.

We will now take a look at some verses where the Greek word *kosmos* is used. It is obvious here that "world" is the true meaning as it was meant to be, but not so when they translated the previous verses with the word *aion* to "world."

> Ye are of God, little children, and have overcome them: because greater is he that is in you, than he that is in the world. (1 John 4:4, KJV)

> Little children, you are from God and have overcome them, for he who is in you is greater than he who is in the world. (ESV)

The above verse is reflecting John's encouraging words to the new Christians who were wise enough to discern the garbage that false prophets were spouting out among them. We need more wise men today pointing out the false teachers/preachers of today. It is as if there is total ignorance of the events that took place in AD 70 to "this generation," not our generation. I have never heard it preached as a major event in the church. I have, however, heard several preachers state that all that is left to happen today is the rapture, or Jesus coming back. Well, the signs of the times were for the generation that Jesus lived in and the signs were for their survival if they heeded them and fled. You never hear a preacher today warning his audience that they should flee when they see the signs, yet everyone today is yapping about the "signs of the times" being fulfilled before our very eyes. Jesus warned His generation to flee when they saw the signs. If you flee, you are spared. If you are ignorant and do not heed the signs, you die. Why is no one fleeing today, yet they claim that we are living in the "end times?"

> They are of the world: therefore speak they of the world, and the world heareth them. (1 John 4:5, KJV)

> They are from the world; therefore they speak from the world, and the world listens to them. (ESV)

There are two words used here that represent world. The third meaning is obviously different. The world does not have ears. People do. If you do a New Testament word search, using the Greek word κόσμος in the Textus Receptus version of the Blue Letter Bible online, you will get thirty-two occurrences. The following verse is another example.

> He was in the world, and the world was made by him,
> and the world knew him not. (John 1:10, KJV)

> He was in the world, and the world was made through
> him, yet the world did not know him. (ESV)

In John 1:10, a more literal translation would be as follows: He was in the world, and the world was made by Him, yet the people did not know Him. An even more accurate translation would be "He was among the people, and the people were made by Him, yet the people did not know Him."

In America we say things like this. "This world sure is evil," or "This world is crazy." Well, we are not speaking of the literal world. We are speaking about the people of the world, or the cultural norms that have come to be accepted. Only living things can be evil or crazy. The world, the earth, is neutral. The earth does not premeditate hurricanes, tornadoes, earthquakes, and so on. Those are just the result of a fallen world.

> Now all these things happened unto them for ensamples:
> and they are written for our admonition, upon whom the
> ends of the world are come. (1 Corinthians 10:11, KJV)

> Now these things happened to them as an example, but
> they were written down for our instruction, on whom the
> end of the ages has come. (ESV)

Paul is speaking to his contemporaries here of past judgments of God on the children of Israel for such sins as fornication, idolatry, murmuring, and such. He is telling them that the end is about to be—then. He was not speaking to us today. The end of the Old Testament Covenant age was on the horizon. It would not be a passing such as from 1699 to 1700, 1799 to 1800, or 1999 to Y2K. Now, for those who remember Y2K (passing from December 31 to January 1, 2000), well, thank God it was just as any other year, but those who were into the doomsday end of time anti-intellectual scenario it was supposed to be a catastrophic event. Well, it came and went, and most have forgotten about the non-event. Many profited from it, however, as we see, men are still promoting book after book today of a false end of the world scenario.

I believe that most reading at this point have surely come to the conclusion that the world is still here and has not ended. If you are a big proponent of the KJV of the Bible, well, what happened? If Paul prophesied that the end of the world had come upon that generation, then he is a false prophet. Of the fourteen English versions represented in the Blue Letter Bible, twelve of them get it right. Only two versions use the word "world" where the Greek word αἰώνων (*aion*) is used: the King James and the Webster Bible.

Paul was well aware of what age they lived in. He was very familiar with the prophets and Old Testament saints. He was well aware of Daniel's prophecy about the increase in knowledge that would take place as the end of the age began to close in on that generation. As the events of the age began to unfold, it was obvious to those who were steeped in the word of God that the events prophesied by the Old Testament prophets were being fulfilled before their eyes. That was the increase in knowledge. It was an increase in the awareness of the times and events that they were experiencing that Daniel had prophesied, not the age of technology.

> For then must he often have suffered since the foundation of the world: but now once in the end of the world hath he appeared to put away sin by the sacrifice of himself. (Hebrews 9:26, KJV)

> for then he would h0ave had to suffer repeatedly since the foundation of the world. But as it is, he has appeared once for all at the end of the ages to put away sin by the sacrifice of himself. (ESV)

The KJV represents the time of Jesus' crucifixion as being the time for the end of the world, but obviously it was not. It was the end of the Old Covenant era, but only after the events that Jesus, John, and the Old Testament prophets had prophesied came to fruition. This would be the end of that age and the beginning of the new age. This was the beginning of the new heaven and earth. The earth would never again be the home of deceased saints. Heaven, for the first time ever, would allow those humans who are in Christ to enter into Paradise. This is the new heaven and earth. What we are experiencing in the here and now is life. After life under the OTC, you had no access to heaven. The saint and the pagan experienced the same effects of death. Today, under the New Covenant, the repentant sinner shall experience "to be absent from the body is to be present with the Lord."

> And the world passeth away, and the lust thereof: but he that doeth the will of God abideth for ever.
> (1 John 2:17, KJV)

And the world is passing away with all its desires, but the person who does the will of God remains forever. (NET)

(TR) καὶ ὁ <u>κόσμος</u> παράγεται, καὶ ἡ ἐπιθυμία αὐτοῦ ὁ δὲ ποιῶν τὸ θέλημα τοῦ Θεοῦ μένει εἰς τὸν αἰῶνα

The Greek word κόσμος is used here. If you do a Blue Letter Bible word search in the Textus Receptus, you will discover that 99 percent of the time, if not 100 percent of the time, this word is used it is a reference to people and not the world. The people of the world will pass away, but those who are not of this world, the repentant, shall never experience the death of the soul, or "soul sleep." However, when John stated this, if you were to die before the revealing of Christ in the latter days of the Old Covenant, prior to AD 70, you did experience "soul sleep." We are under the New Covenant since the consummation of the Old Covenant in AD 70. Oh, death, where is your sting? It is still there for the unrepentant. This verse in no way makes reference to the end of the world. All men shall pass from life to death of the flesh. Your status with the Savior will determine eternal life or perdition.

The believer still has much work to do. The main thing for the believer to do today is to educate himself to true history and learn what it had to do with His story. When the facts are made known, there will still be scoffers, and sadly, many of those scoffers will come from the pews and pulpits of the churches. Education to true history is far more important and relevant to modern-day success than an anti-Christ education system that perpetuates racism and hate. Woe be unto the leaders of any nation that allow such anti-Christ education to be propagated to the future. That is why America and the world seem to be shuffling toward Gomorrah. It may create hell on earth, but you reap what you sow.

I hope that you have seen the error that the King James translators made by taking what should have been translated as *age* and making it into *world*. There are many people today in the world that believe, due to the KJV of the Bible, that the world is going to end shortly. The end of the Old Covenant era is what the prophets, Jesus, and John prophesied about. The end of the world is never prophesied in the Bible. There is much scripture that attests that this world will go on forever. Man may blow each other off the face of the earth, but a few will always survive and start over. Pray that it does not come to that. Knowledge of true history and of His story would increase peace and love across this planet. Those who deny truth will have it accounted unto them at death. If you are a hinderer, at the very least, you will be considered least in the kingdom of God.

The Last Days/A Little While

*T*he *last days*, or *times*, has become a major issue in our day, when in fact it should not be of imminence to us, but of relevance. What is astonishing, though, is that I see no one selling their possessions and sharing their assets with others. The apostles admonished their peers to do such as this since they lived in the last days. Guess what? They did it. Wealth would not profit them in the last days. Wealth would be a hindrance to them and could be the very cause of their demise. The ones who were the followers of Jesus would have been singled out and killed in the streets in the waning days of the OC era if they had loaded all their possessions into a cart and fled. The Zealots of Israel, as well as the Roman soldiers, would have taken them prisoner or killed them, and taken all their possessions. The writings of Josephus paint the best picture of what that generation experienced. This is what the Zealots were doing, and they were Jews. The Christians had to fear them as much as they did the Roman forces after late AD 64. We will now look at some verses that are associated with the last days of the OTC era.

> And it shall come to pass afterward, that I will pour out
> my Spirit on all flesh; your sons and your daughters shall
> prophesy, your old men shall dream dreams, and your
> young men shall see visions. (Joel 2:28, ESV)

> And in the last days it shall be, God declares, that I will
> pour out my Spirit on all flesh, and your sons and your
> daughters shall prophesy, and your young men shall see
> visions, and your old men shall dream dreams.
> (Acts 2:17, ESV)

What Joel had prophesied was the day of Pentecost. This was the day that God poured out His spirit on the followers of Jesus. What is of utmost importance here is that we recognize the timing of the event. Peter was not ignorant of the times he lived in. Peter stated that God declared in the "last days" He would pour out His Spirit on all flesh. Well, we know that is exactly what took place, so it is obvious that when God spoke this prophecy to Joel that God was speaking about the first generation of the followers of Christ. This would mean Jew and Gentile. It was not meant for all flesh. It was meant only for those who bowed the knee to Jesus as Messiah. This was for that time and that time only. It was "signs and wonders," which indicated consummation of the OTC era. Paul states in First Corinthians 13:8 (ESV) that "Love never ends. As for prophecies, they will pass away; as for tongues, they will cease; as for knowledge, it will pass away." This statement that Paul makes here is relevant for all time. When the passing of the OC era was consummated in AD 70, there would be no more prophecy from God, no more speaking in tongues inspired by God, and knowledge of those first-century events would pass. I think all can agree with that today. We shall never know in minute detail all the facts of the characters that were prophesied about by Daniel and John. I guarantee you that "this generation" was well aware of what was about to happen to them and by whom the destruction would come. As the "end" approached I am sure the followers of Christ realized that the Roman Empire was the beast prophesied by Daniel and John.

> But understand this, that in the last days there will come times of difficulty. For people will be lovers of self, lovers of money, proud, arrogant, abusive, disobedient to their parents, ungrateful, unholy, heartless, unappeasable, slanderous, without self-control, brutal, not loving good, treacherous, reckless, swollen with conceit, lovers of pleasure rather than lovers of God, having the appearance of godliness, but denying its power. Avoid such people. (2 Timothy 3:1–5, ESV)

Who was Paul speaking to here? Was he not speaking to his contemporary companion, Timothy? If they were not living in the "last days," then what Paul was saying would be irrelevant to Timothy. He would have been just blowing steam for nothing. The wise and discerning Timothy knew exactly the times Paul was speaking of. He saw it all around him. Many today use this verse to convince others that we are the only generation that has ever acted like this. Well, we are not the generation that crucified Jesus. I believe our generation probably would crucify Him. Those who are preaching a prosperity gospel today would certainly

THE LAST DAYS/A LITTLE WHILE

want to crucify Him if He were to walk into one of their Sunday morning services with His whip and went to cleaning house. Now, I want to clarify something here about the prosperity gospel. The prosperity gospel is where the preacher pitches to his audience that if they will sow into his ministry, God will bless them materially, possibly tenfold, one hundred fold, or a thousand fold. It has to do with you giving money to his or her ministry. Do not allow one of these guilt manipulators to take advantage of you. I am sure that you probably have some family members who could use your financial help. Family is not relegated to just mother, dad, and siblings. A man that will not take care of his family is considered to be worse than an infidel in the eyes of God. Does this eliminate women? Eternity is far too long to risk your eternal rewards forevermore. Your family comes before the church.

For some reason, the church seems to think that this is the only generation in which people love money and are prideful, arrogant, abusive, disobedient to parents, ungrateful, and unholy. Well, read Josephus. There was a Jewish woman that had killed her baby and cooked it. It sickened the Roman soldiers when she offered some to them. As sickening as many have thought the invading Roman soldiers were to the first century Jews, well, this topped anything they did to the Jews. There was a time in Jewish history when they sacrificed their children to false gods. They got this custom from the pagan society around them. It is going on today in America. Sorry, life begins in the womb at conception. Yet, if you spoil the nest of a sea turtle or bald eagle, you are likely to be prosecuted and spend time in prison. Maybe it *is* our generation. Hardly. Yet, we are just as wicked. Those in authority, though, shall pay the maximum penalty because they have the power to do something about it but won't. If you sanction it, you are guilty of it.

During this time, mothers and fathers were turning their kids in to the authorities, as well as children turning on their Christian parents. Relatives who were anti-Christ were turning on their family members. Pride was a major issue, especially among the Zealots. Again, that generation killed the very Son of God, their Creator. Sure, I imagine that there have been generations all over this world at any point in time that would have done likewise, as I do believe this current generation would. They yell "Spare the murderers and rapists. Kill the babies." Actions speak louder than words. All generations are evil. That is why God sent His Son to pay the price for sinful humanity. Believe and receive. Reject and be-decked.

"But in these last days he has spoken to us by his Son, whom he appointed the heir of all things, through whom also he created the world"

195

(Hebrews 1:2, ESV). There is no consensus on who wrote the book of Hebrews. Some say that it was Barnabas, some say Clemens of Rome, and others say it was Luke. The majority back in Matthew Henry's (1662–1714) days credited it to Paul. Regardless, whoever wrote it completed it before AD 64 and believed that they were living in the last days of the OC era. From my studies I have come to the conclusion that they had no delusion that the world would end with their generation. They knew that a new heaven and earth, the kingdom of God, was on the horizon for them and all eternity.

"Your gold and silver have corroded, and their corrosion will be evidence against you and will eat your flesh like fire. You have laid up treasure in the last days" (James 5:3, ESV). Wealth is not a sin. For wealth to become your god is a sin. In the last days, however, it was a hindrance that could condemn you to death. The time was imminent. The danger was real. That is why that generation of Christians sold off their material assets to assist their fellow brethren in time of need. In times like that, it is sinful not to assist your Christian brethren in need. This is a voluntary measure and not one mandated by the government. Robbery from one group of people to enrich another group of people is sin, and it will be judged as such. God has mandated that the family take care of the needs of the family. His word states that a man that will not take care of his family is worse than an infidel. This still applies today. His word never changes. When your ways are perfect, there are no needs for upgrades and enhancements. Perfection needs no improvement. Solomon states in Proverbs 13:22 (KJV), *"A good man leaveth an inheritance to his children's children: and the wealth of the sinner is laid up for the just."* There are many scholars and theologians that say that the Bible contradicts itself. If you believe that, you may need to rethink your interpretation of the contradicting scriptures. There are times when what is considered the wise and prudent thing to do is just not possible because of special circumstances. I can assure you that post AD 64 through AD 70 was a very special time that had circumstances that would not apply to the average day-to-day routine. It is a sin not to take care of one's family members who are not able-bodied and self-sufficient. Any government policy that creates enmity between people groups is of the evil imaginations of man. Let me just say, "Woe be unto you." This would include the takers and the receivers. It will be accounted as thievery.

"Knowing this first of all, that scoffers will come in the last days with scoffing, following their own sinful desires" (2 Peter 3:3, ESV.) A scoffer is someone who shows derision or scorn. They mock others, as

well as show contempt. This is nothing new. There are many sermons preached that mention this verse. You would think that this was a new phenomenon for our time only. No. This has happened throughout all of time. You can look at several online dictionary sites, and you will see that mockery, or mocker, is associated with scoffer. Job accused his friends of being mockers. David laments in Psalm 35:16 about hypocritical mockers. Isaiah and Jeremiah speak of mockers. This is nothing new. I find it kind of ironic today when I hear people quote this verse or post it on social media. No one is mocking or scoffing at the ones posting it.

The timeframe for this was the first century, before AD 70. Jesus had promised that "this generation" was the one who would experience the consummation, the end of the OC that God had with the Jews. It was the far-future event that all the Old Testament prophets had prophesied. There were Jews back then, and even now, that did not believe God would abandon them. Well, what did all the Old Testament prophets speak of? Moses even speaks about the event. The covenant was conditional. It was all a foreshadowing of the state of things going into eternity here on earth.

Those who departed Egypt in the Exodus and did not trust God and obey Him were not allowed to enter the Promised Land. The land of Israel was not the focus. The focus was God Almighty and loyalty and obedience to Him and His ways. What happened in AD 70 was the final countdown with the Jews. Those who accepted Messiah, Jesus, would be allowed to enter the true Promised Land—heaven. Those who rejected Jesus as Messiah were allowed a period of forty years to repent and get right with their Maker. Some did, but most did not. Those who did not shall never enter His rest in heaven. Paul states the following in Romans 9:6 (KJV): *"Not as though the word of God hath taken none effect. For they are not all Israel, which are of Israel."* This very verse is communicating not only to Paul's peers, but also to all of mankind for all time that it isn't about being a Jew. It is about being a Christian. Those who rejected Him were not of Israel. Ever since Jesus' crucifixion, death, burial, resurrection, and ascension, there has been neither Jew nor Greek, slave nor free, male nor female. All are one in Christ, which means that there are no groups with favor. Now, it would be a right aim to pursue to be a man after God's own heart, as was David, but He shall not favor one group, or sector, over another. All are equal in His sight.

These are all the verses in the New Testament that use "last days." Now let us look at some other terms which connote the same era of time, just different terminology.

> For yet a little while, and he that shall come will come, and will not tarry. (Hebrews 10:37 KJV)

> For, yet a little while, and the coming one will come and will not delay; (ESV)

The writer of Hebrews knows not the hour, day, or time, that the Lord will come, but he does know that it is on the horizon and not two thousand years in the future. Otherwise, surely He would tell them to seal it up. The time is not near. But, that is not what He tells them. The author tells his peers that in just a little while Jesus will come. He even reiterates that the time is short when he states that He will not tarry or delay. Now, if this event did not occur in a little while then the writer, be it Luke, Barnabas, or Paul, would fail the test of a prophet, and this book should not be allowed into the cannon of scripture. Now, I know that this event has come and gone, but for those who insist that it has not, they should take their scissors and cut the book of Hebrews out of their Bible because it conflicts with their beliefs. Therefore, to them it is a book of false prophetic events. Live what you believe and believe what you live. He came on clouds.

"Be patient, therefore, brothers, until the coming of the Lord. See how the farmer waits for the precious fruit of the earth, being patient about it, until it receives the early and the late rains" (James 5:7, ESV). The writer of this epistle is James, the brother of Jesus. He is admonishing his peers to be patient until the coming of his brother, Jesus. Has anyone ever asked you to be patient? I imagine that you have at least heard this from your mother, or possibly even your dad, if by no one else. I can recall some instances when I was asked to be patient. Never was I asked to be patient about an event that was not going to happen in my lifetime. It would be ludicrous to ask someone to be patient for something that is about two thousand years into the future. What you would be telling them is that this is a hopeless situation as far as you are concerned. You may as well tell them not to be patient. It will not matter to them anyway. They will have long been dead and gone. This would also be cruel and unusual punishment. It would be even worse than attempting to still convince your children that Santa Claus is real even after they are in their thirties. I dare say that they would make a correct assumption and just assume that you have lost your mind. If a high school teacher today was found attempting to convince students that World War I and World War

ll never happened, I believe that individual would lose their job because they are too ignorant to be teaching history.

One issue that I have always had with the end-times view of the majority in America is that God would not want all generations for about two thousand years to sit up and not sleep awaiting the return of Jesus. That would be akin to the mother of a child and wife of a soldier telling her five-year-old child that "Daddy is coming home tonight. Stay up and wait for him so you can greet him at the door," after he has been gone for two years, yet knowing that he got killed after three months and is never coming home again. Yet, she is still telling her fifteen-year-old son years later that Daddy is still coming home. If anyone in the government were to find this out, I believe that they would take the child from the mother and convict her for cruel and unusual punishment, and rightly so. Now, I know that Jesus came in AD 70 on clouds and judged apostate of Israel. I am in no way stating that Jesus was killed and that's that. If that was my case, I would be an atheist. I believe that most people who know me will tell you that I am about as passionate a person about Jesus as they have ever met. The scoffers today are the ones who say Jesus has not come back yet.

"You also, be patient. Establish your hearts, for the coming of the Lord is at hand" (James 5:8, ESV). James answers the question in his next words as to how long they can expect to wait. Be patient for how long? If something is at my hand, it is about to be grabbed, slapped, touched, tickled, shoved, or punched. Two millennia is not at hand. Also, "a thousand years, is as a day with the Lord" does not fly here. God would not communicate to people in terms that they cannot comprehend. If He does, then communication is pointless. It would be like saying He doesn't mean what He says, and doesn't say what He means. I am sorry, but that isn't the God that I serve.

James was well aware of the generation that wandered in the wilderness and was not allowed to enter the Promised Land. He knew the very date that Jesus had been crucified and knew that it was likely going to be within forty years. There are some that credit James with writing of this epistle prior to AD 50, but that would mean that the event was twenty-plus years away. It could have been. Again, he knew the generation, just not the hour, day, or time.

"Who by God's power are being guarded through faith for a salvation ready to be revealed in the last time" (1 Peter 1:5, ESV). "Ready to be revealed" means that the time is near. I have never gotten ready (gotten dressed) for an event that was fifty years out. The "last time" was very

near. Now, no man knew the hour, day, or time, but they knew the generation. James was stoned to death in AD 62, according to some sources. Others give later dates, and some give much earlier dates. We do know that Jesus stated that "this generation shall not pass until all these things be fulfilled."

"How that they told you there should be mockers in the last time, who should walk after their own ungodly lusts" (Jude 1:18, KJV). Jude is speaking to his peers here about what is going on in their lives at that time. They were witnessing upheaval in their culture. People had denied the very Son of God and crucified Him. Their culture was degenerate and getting worse by and by. Jude was not speaking about a generation that was about 2,000 years into his future. He was warning them that the signs that they saw in their culture were the signs prophesied by the Old Testament prophets. "Get ready. The end is near."

"Who verily was foreordained before the foundation of the world, but was manifest in these last times for you" (1 Peter 1:20, KJV). Peter is speaking of Jesus, Messiah, in this verse. It is obvious that Peter was aware that he and his contemporaries were living in the "last times." Peter was not ignorant of the timing of prophecy. Jesus had made His apostles aware of the times they were living in. It was the time of the end of the covenant with the Jews. It was time for a new heaven and a new earth. They were the elect generation that God had foreordained to consummate the old and bring in the new.

> And this is the Father's will which hath sent me, that of all which he hath given me I should lose nothing, but should raise it up again at the last day. And this is the will of him that sent me, that every one which seeth the Son, and believeth on him, may have everlasting life: and I will raise him up at the last day. (John 6:39–40, KJV)

The Father had given Jesus the "elect." That generation was the elect that God chose to use to consummate the Old Covenant. There is no other elect generation or people of God. This was His elect. Many of the elect generation would perish to perdition. Those who bowed the knee to Messiah would be raised up on that day. Now, if we are awaiting the last day, then the elect of God are still in the dirt, experiencing "soul sleep" over two thousand years since their death. If this were the case, then the Old Covenant is still in effect today, but that is not the case. The "last days" was within the generation that walked the earth with Jesus. He departed forty years prior to the last day or days. Still, many that were responsible for His crucifixion were still alive forty years later. If these believers were going to be in heaven upon their Old Covenant death, then there would be no need for a new and better covenant. The Old Covenant had not yet been consummated and Jesus' death would not be the consummation either. He gave them forty years to get it right. Some would. Most would not.

I know there are those who believe the New Covenant era began with Jesus' death on the cross, but according to scripture, that is not the case. God is a merciful God, full of grace, mercy, and forgiveness. He allowed "this generation," a literal biblical generation, to repent and come to Jesus. The consummation of the OC had to become a reality first. The reality of Jesus as King of kings also had to be confirmed. This would be the event that would lead to every knee bowing, and every tongue confessing that Jesus is Lord. This was a past event—fulfilled prophecy. All prophecy has been fulfilled. Not one jot or tittle has been left unfulfilled. What is unfulfilled is our knowledge of historical facts and biblical language. Fulfilled prophecy is all the hope that we shall ever need. Without a true knowledge of history one shall never realize the greatness of Messiah in our generation. It is time for the leaves on the Tree of Life to begin the healing process and quit the racism and bigotry. Oh, by the way, it is a two-way street.

DEATH AND RESURRECTION

Death under the Old Covenant and the New Covenant

I once heard a pastor preach a message that really gave me an eerie feeling. Actually, I have heard many sermons over the years that have given me an eerie feeling due to not being biblical and consistent with all of scripture. This particular sermon contained portions that concerned Old Covenant death versus death under the New Covenant. He stated in his sermon that when Jesus took his last breath on the cross, He went to heaven, and on the third day He was sent back to earth to be resurrected with his fleshly body. He also stated that since man is made in the image of God, even those under the Old Covenant were in heaven awaiting their bodies. This would include Adam and Eve, Abel, Job, Noah, Jonah, King David, Samuel, Ezekiel, Nehemiah, Zechariah, and all God's people who lived under the Old Covenant. My understanding, and the biblical teaching on death, is that it is the penalty for sin. All have sinned. None are righteous. Jesus came to bring a better covenant than the one which the Jews were currently under, as well as to bring the Gentiles into the kingdom of God. He came to pay the penalty for sin. *"For the wages of sin is death, but the free gift of God is eternal life in Christ Jesus our Lord"* (Romans 6:23, ESV). All men who ever lived, from Adam to the consummation of the Old Covenant, experienced what I call soul sleep. I state it this way because there are many references in the Bible where "sleep" and "asleep" are used as symbolic words for death.

> And the LORD said unto Moses, Behold, thou shalt sleep with thy fathers; and this people will rise up, and go a whoring after the gods of the strangers of the land, whither they go to be among them, and will forsake me, and break my covenant which I have made with them. (Deuteronomy 31:16, KJV)

What the Lord stated to Moses is that he would experience the same thing that all of his ancestors had experienced, death, not to be alive. There is no mention here of Moses' soul ascending to heaven. Moses was certainly not beneath any of the Old Testament saints of God. Abraham, Isaac, and Jacob experienced the same death, as did Job and the prophets of Baal. *"Yea, though he live a thousand years twice told, yet hath he seen no good: do not all go to one place"* (Ecclesiastes 6:6, KJV)? All went to the "one place" under the OC. That place was the grave.

> But I would not have you to be ignorant, brethren, con-
> cerning them which are asleep, that ye sorrow not, even
> as others which have no hope. For if we believe that
> Jesus died and rose again, even so them also which sleep
> in Jesus will God bring with him.
> (1 Thessalonians 4:13–14, KJV)

If one sleeps in Jesus, would this not be soul sleep? Let's look at the most definitive verse in the Bible on this issue. It is stated by Paul in First Corinthians 15:50 (KJV): *"Now this I say, brethren, that flesh and blood cannot inherit the kingdom of God; neither doth corruption inherit incorruption."* Flesh and blood are corruptible, which means that there is a day appointed for the body, the flesh, to die. It will rot away. Flesh is not for everlasting life. When the repentant soul gets to heaven, a new glorified body will be given to him or her that shall never experience the effects of entropy. If flesh and blood "cannot inherit the kingdom of God," then what were all those souls in the pastor's sermon waiting for? If they were waiting on flesh and blood, well, it ain't going to happen! Also, do you think that they would have been there, some for over five thousand years, with half of their assets? I am sorry, but you will not find that anywhere in the word of God. You must put all the scriptures together. Symbolism often represents what something is like and not what it truly is.

Death was likened to sleep because there was the legend of the future resurrection, which was on the horizon for the generation that Jesus lived in. Not only did the flesh die, but the soul also ceased awareness. I imagine that it was much like a deep sleep with no dreams and no awareness of anything, except there is no life. Pretty soon the flesh rots. It is a state of nothingness. If Jesus paid the price for our sin, then He experienced the penalty for sin, except He was not in the grave long enough for the flesh to experience corruption, rotting. To get to go to heaven for a few days, years, or millennia was not the price for sin. Otherwise, there would be no reason for a Savior, and why would anyone need to repent? If the New Covenant is a better covenant and the Old Testament saints' souls are in heaven since death and the New Covenant saint, at death, rises spiritually to heaven and both are awaiting their fleshly bodies, then what is so much better about the New Covenant? It is false teaching.

I believe that there are some preconceived faulty notions involved here. It has much to do with the false rapture theory of John Nelson Darby that began in 1830. I will not go into details here. There is much information out there on the subject. Just do an Internet search on John Nelson Darby, and your search begins. I just caution you to use biblical discernment as you research this. There is much information available on this subject. Just keep in mind, the resurrection is in the past. Any site that states otherwise has bought into Darby's theory, just as modern science has bought into the theory of evolution.

The message of this pastor's sermon contained the concept that when the Christian passes from life to eternity, he will be in the kingdom of God with half of his being until the future resurrection. At the future resurrection, bodies will be restored and believers will be made whole. Until then we will be half present in heaven. I ponder what I will be able to do without all of my faculties. I have given this subject much study and thought. The first thing to do is to see if the Bible confirms this "half-present" theory. Nowhere in the word of God will you find a statement that professes that souls go to heaven at death for the Old Covenant believer and that both Old Covenant saints and New Covenant saints will be awaiting Resurrection Day for their bodies to rise from the earth so that there will be a reunion with soul and body. The only way you can come up with that is to read or induce something into the word that is not there. We will go back to the Old Testament and start there with *death* and base our decision on what God's word says and not on preconceived notions that come from the false teachings of man.

The first time that death is mentioned in the Bible is in the second chapter of Genesis. *"And the LORD God commanded the man, saying, "You may surely eat of every tree of the garden, but of the tree of the knowledge of good and evil you shall not eat, for in the day that you eat of it you shall surely die"* (Genesis 2:16–17, ESV). Adam and Eve experienced spiritual death that day that would in the future lead to physical death. This scripture was the warning against going against God's word, which is defined as sin. The next place death is mentioned is in the next chapter.

> And the woman said to the serpent, "We may eat of the fruit of the trees in the garden, but God said, "You shall not eat of the fruit of the tree that is in the midst of the garden, neither shall you touch it, lest you die." But the serpent said to the woman, "You will not surely die."
>
> (Genesis 3:2–4, ESV)

> Then the LORD God said, "Behold, the man has become like one of us in knowing good and evil. Now, lest he reach out his hand and take also of the tree of life and eat, and live forever—" therefore the LORD God sent him out from the garden of Eden to work the ground from which he was taken. He drove out the man, and at the east of the Garden of Eden he placed the cherubim and a flaming sword that turned every way to guard the way to the tree of life. (Genesis 3:22–24, ESV)

These are the first passages in the Bible that mention death. No, God did not kill Adam and Eve. The consequences of their actions is seen in the preceding verses (Genesis 3:22–24). They were allowed to continue on in life, but they were not allowed to live forever. After the flood, the life expectancy of man was diminished greatly due to atmospheric, climatic, and other changes in the laws of nature. God knew that if man lived forever under the burden of sin, he would become more and more evil. We see this in worldwide politics today, especially in America. Corruption seems to rule when there is no end in sight. That is just one more reason that heaven will be heaven. There will be no lifetime politicians. There will only be God the Father, Son, and Holy Spirit as rulers of heaven. He who is first shall be last, if he even makes it there.

Death was not immediate, but it was to be the norm for future generations. Adam lived for 930 years, which makes it obvious that "everything is as it always was (uniformitarianism)" is not truth. The atmosphere on earth was highly likely much different before the flood of Noah's age. The gravitational force was probably much less than what it is today, so that life could persist for over 900 years. The flood would change that, as the world was turned on its axis. Check out the book, *The Face that Demonstrates the Farce of Evolution*, by Hank Hanegraaff, president of the Christian Research Institute.

A term that is used to describe death many times in the Bible is sleep. That is where I get my term *soul sleep* from. It was literal death as defined by the Old Testament, which would also fit the secular definition of death as found online at Dictionary by Farlex, which is as follows:

1) The act of dying; termination of life.
2) The state of being dead.
3) The cause of dying: Drugs were the death of him.
8) The termination or extinction of something.

I actually prefer definition number 8. The termination of life is something that most people of below average intelligence would understand. I like my definition even better: to cease to exist. I think that most people catch my drift here. Even a man with an IQ of over 200 can come up with no better definition than to cease to exist. However, there are those who have come up with their own definition, based on faulty interpretations of the scriptures. I am sorry, but death from the beginning until the consummation of the Old Covenant was not "to be absent from the body is to be present in spirit only with the Lord until the far-future resurrection." We will look at some scriptures in the Old Testament now and then at some New Testament scriptures that will make my point. Death was death for all under the Old Covenant because all had sinned. Their only hope was in a future Messiah and the destruction of the Old Covenant. Until that date, all experienced "soul sleep."

"When your days are fulfilled and you lie down with your fathers, I will raise up your offspring after you, who shall come from your body, and I will establish his kingdom" (2 Samuel 7:12, ESV). Samuel was speaking to David here. When David's days were over and all was accomplished through his life that God had planned for him, he was laid to rest with his fathers, his predecessors. It says nothing about his spirit going to heaven. He experienced "soul sleep." What inspires me about this verse is that God has a purpose for our lives. Our lives need not be empty and void. When we put 101 percent of our focus on the Messiah, then the purpose He has for each individual life should begin to become a reality. I can promise you this. After you have been on that path for many years, you will look back one day and thank God. You will thank Him for getting you out of the rut you were in and putting you on the straight and narrow path that leads to peace, joy, and purpose. There was a day when I was seeking to gain the whole world and all it had to offer. Life was void of peace, joy, and purpose. Now that I have found Him, ohhhhhh, what joy, peace, and life everlasting!

"Why did I not die at birth, come out from the womb and expire" (Job 3:11, ESV)? Job was speaking here that he would rather have died at birth than to be experiencing what he was going through at this time in his life. Heavy burdens can do this to people. Most people have had times like this in their lives when they may have wished that they had never been born. It is normal for the human this side of heaven. My personal experience with this phenomenon has been that given time and a persistence to stay the "straight and narrow path," it will lead to more peace and joy than you ever imagined. The key is to not lose focus on the One who gave His life for yours. Longsuffering creates patience and endurance.

To expire means to come to an end, terminate; to breathe ones' last breath; die, as defined by Dictionary by Farlex (online). I believe that most people understand what it means to expire. It means to cease to exist. Another way to look at it is to think of what happens when you attempt to use an expired debit card at a swiper. The plastic card is still there, but it no longer has a function, or purpose. It is a lifeless piece of material. I can remember a time in my life that I felt like that, but I was still in the flesh. Oh, well. You catch my drift.

> Now a word was brought to me stealthily; my ear received the whisper of it. Amid thoughts from visions of the night, when deep sleep falls on men, dread came upon me, and trembling, which made all my bones shake. A spirit glided past my face; the hair of my flesh stood up. It stood still, but I could not discern its appearance. A form was before my eyes; there was silence, then I heard a voice: Can mortal man be in the right before God? Can a man be pure before his Maker? Even in his servants he puts no trust, and his angels he charges with error; how much more those who dwell in houses of clay, whose foundation is in the dust, who are crushed like the moth. Between morning and evening they are beaten to pieces; they perish forever without anyone regarding it. Is not their tent-cord plucked up within them, do they not die, and that without wisdom? (Job 4:12–21, ESV)

This scripture sums up even before the times of the Messiah, Jesus, of what happens to those who have no wisdom. They perish forever. There is no hope for them. What we are doing here in this chapter is showing the difference in Old Covenant death versus New Covenant death. OC death was hopeless. To be absent from the body was to be present in the dust.

> My days are swifter than a weaver's shuttle and come to their end without hope. "Remember that my life is a breath; my eye will never again see well. The eye of him who sees me will behold me no more; while your eyes are on me, I shall be gone. As the cloud fades and vanishes, so he who goes down to Sheol does not come up; he returns no more to his house, nor does his place know him anymore. (Job 7:6–10, ESV)

The description given here of death is what the Old Testament saint had to look forward to at the time of their death. There was no hope of life everlasting at that time. *"I loathe my life; I would not live forever. Leave me alone, for my days are a breath; why do you not pardon my transgression and take away my iniquity? For now I shall lie in the earth; you will seek me, but I shall not be"* (Job 7:16, 21, ESV).

Iniquity was the cause of death but if one is pardoned, life everlasting (not yet available). There was no pardon for sin until the time of Messiah. Jesus is the key. Without the key, there was no entry. That still applies today. The penalty for sin, and all of mankind were sinners, was death. Job was a servant of God, yet he suffered what was the lot of man under the burden of sin. The law had not yet come onto the scene, but that is really irrelevant here. Law does not bring life because all have broken the law. The blood of Christ is for the remission of sins. Accept and rise. Reject and bedecked.

"Remember that you have made me like clay; and will you return me to the dust" (Job 10:9, ESV)? To be returned to the dust was the only hope that the OC believer had. His hope was for Resurrection Day. The price he paid was soul sleep and corruption of the flesh, the rotting of the flesh. It is believed that Job lived during the time of Moses' father. This would mean that he very likely slept for over 1,500 years before the resurrection in AD 70.

> Are not my days few? Then cease, and leave me alone, that I may find a little cheer before I go—and I shall not return—to the land of darkness and deep shadow, the land of gloom like thick darkness, like deep shadow without any order, where light is as thick darkness. (Job 10:20–22, ESV)

Job had no hope of eternal life. If he had any hope at all, it would have to be in a far-future resurrection. He knew that he would not return to the land of darkness and deep shadow, the land of gloom and doom. This would be the Planet Earth. During the Old Testament Covenant era, there was no hope. Something would have to happen to change all of that, but it was so far away from Job that he may not have even been aware of it. Actually, he makes statements that lead one to believe that he was aware of Messiah. I have been on this planet for a little over a half century. Job spent over fifteen centuries in the dust. I would have lamented, too.

> For there is hope for a tree, if it be cut down, that it will sprout again, and that its shoots will not cease. Though its root grow old in the earth, and its stump die in the soil, yet at the scent of water it will bud and put out branches like a young plant. But a man dies and is laid low; man breathes his last, and where is he? As waters fail from a lake and a river wastes away and dries up, so a man lies down and rises not again; until the heavens are no more he will not awake or be roused out of his sleep. Oh that you would hide me in Sheol that you would conceal me until your wrath be past, that you would appoint me a set time, and remember me. If a man dies, shall he live again? All the days of my service I would wait, until my renewal should come. You would call, and I would answer you; you would long for the work of your hands. For then you would number my steps; you would not keep watch over my sin; my transgression would be sealed up in a bag, and you would cover over my iniquity. (Job 14:7–17, ESV)

Even a tree had the hope of sprouting out again and continuing on in life after a catastrophic event, such as a tornado or hurricane that breaks it at the surface of the earth or halfway up. When man died in the days of Job, his hope was far future. The heavens in the days of the OC era were often used as a simile to portray the current state of matters, such as under law versus grace. "Till heaven and earth pass away" in the scriptures refers to the Old Covenant. "Till the heavens are no more" is about the consummation of the Old Testament Covenant. Law meant death for all, good and evil. Grace means life for the believer. Under the Old Covenant, the only hope was far future for Job and near future for the apostles until the consummation of the Old Covenant in AD 70. Jesus Christ was the

212

one who would seal up the sinners' transgressions, and His blood would cover the repentant man's iniquity (sins).

> O earth, cover not my blood, and let my cry find no resting place. Even now, behold, my witness is in heaven, and he who testifies for me is on high. My friends scorn me; my eye pours out tears to God, that he would argue the case of a man with God, as a son of man does with his neighbor. For when a few years have come I shall go the way from which I shall not return. (Job 16:18–22, ESV)

There are many in the world today that believe God is going to set up His kingdom here on this earth one day for Jesus to rule for at least a thousand years. However, Jesus states the following: *"Jesus answered, "My kingdom is not of this world. If my kingdom were of this world, my servants would have been fighting, that I might not be delivered over to the Jews. But my kingdom is not from the world"* (John 18:36, ESV). Job knew that his years were numbered, as are ours. He had no hope of being instantly transferred to heaven. He would literally rot away to nothingness. Now, I am not an archeologist, but I imagine that a body covered over with dirt and not in a coffin as we do today would probably rot away to nothingness. Even the bones would rot away given enough time. Otherwise, without the special intervention of a catastrophic flood and the circumstances it would render for fossil production, there would be no fossil record that would date back over probably not even a few hundred years without coffins. One thing that this 2,000-year-old era that we are now in, the New Covenant era, has in common with the last era, the Old Covenant era, is that our days on this earth are still numbered. Each individual person is allotted an amount of time to achieve God's purpose for that life. If all were 100 percent successful, earth would be a paradise. None are 100 percent successful because man wars with the flesh and others. Most are not even involved in kingdom work of any sort. Sitting on a pew every Wednesday night, Sunday morning, and Sunday night is not kingdom work. Educating the world to the Redeemer is priority one. Sadly, we live in a time today that people must be educated to the realities of fulfilled prophecies. The "end" is in our past, not in our future.

> Oh that my words were now written. Oh that they were inscribed in a book. That with an iron pen and lead. They

were graven in the rock for ever. But as for me I know that my Redeemer liveth, and at last he will stand up upon the earth: And after my skin, even this body, is destroyed, then without my flesh shall I see God; Whom I, even I, shall see, on my side, and mine eyes shall behold, and not as a stranger. My heart is consumed within me. (Job 19:23–27, ASV)

Oh that my words were now written. Oh that they were printed in a book. That they were graven with an iron pen and lead in the rock for ever. For I know that my redeemer liveth, and that he shall stand at the latter day upon the earth: And though after my skin worms destroy this body, yet in my flesh shall I see God: Whom I shall see for myself, and mine eyes shall behold, and not another; though my reins be consumed within me. (KJV)

There is an obvious conflict in these verses. The conflict is in verse 26 where Job states that "without my flesh" in the ASV, and "in my flesh" in the KJV. When you do an interlinear search, you notice that the ASV is not used. The Blue Letter Bible uses only the KJV, HCSB, and the NASB for interlinear (language) searches. Two of the fourteen English translations represent the encounter as being outside the flesh, the ASV and the DBY. Four other translations state in the body, or flesh, but put in a notation the following: NLT—without my body I will see God; NIV—apart from; ESV—without; HCSB—apart from.

So, we have fourteen English versions represented, and four allude to a discrepancy with the original Greek translation, two versions use the "out of body" version, and eight versions show "in the body (or flesh)" as the translation with no mention of a discrepancy. When you go to the Matthew Henry (untainted pretrib rapture commentary), you will see that he interprets it as a spiritual encounter, and not of the flesh or body. He states, "So that we must necessarily understand him of the redemption of his soul from the power of the grave, and his reception to glory, which is spoken of, Psalm 49:15." Matthew Henry believed in "soul sleep," as well as a future resurrection of Jobs soul. He had no inkling that there would ever be a resurrection of the flesh. This shall be my standard:

> Now this I say, brethren, that flesh and blood cannot
> inherit the kingdom of God; neither doth corruption
> inherit incorruption. (1 Corinthians 15:50, KJV)

> But God will redeem my soul from the power of the
> grave: for he shall receive me. Selah.
>
> (Psalm 49:15, KJV)

There is no evolution from one specie to many. Man did not come from monkey. Only those who profess they did are monkey men. Only a follower of Christ evolves. He evolves from an ignorant, depraved individual to a soul in heaven one day, where he will be a spiritual entity with His Father who is in heaven forevermore with his glorified, incorruptible body. Evolution in man is more of a spiritual and thought process than a visible morphosis. Of course, a man who is growing into a true spiritual relationship with the Creator should show obvious outward appearance of spiritual growth. Self-control is one of the fruits of the spirit. Our language should be an obvious change to those who know us best. Our appearance should also improve. Our countenance should be brighter. Our demeanor should reflect a positive change. Our appetites, amounts of food included, should also reflect our relationship with the Father who is in heaven. The only One and the only thing we should idolize is Him. Our purpose is to glorify Him and not self, and oh, what a life it is.

"For in death there is no remembrance of you; in Sheol who will give you praise" (Psalm 6:5, ESV)? David knew what "soul sleep" was all about. It was to be inanimate. If David's soul was in heaven, surely he would have been praising God. Old Testament "soul sleep" rendered a person incapable to do anything. Dead flesh and a dead spirit know no praise. They only know nothingness. Due to a lack of information, there is no definitive date for Jobs' lifetime. The best timeframe that can be given is between 2350 BC and 1350 BC, approximately. So, he would have experienced "soul sleep" for about 1,420 to 2,000 years. That sounds pretty hopeless. Just think about the timeframe from Jesus' death to today. That would be about 1,985 years (circa 2016). That is a long time to be waiting around, unless you are unaware. King David would have to suffer "soul sleep" for about 1,040 years. Is unawareness capable of suffering? To lie in a state of "nothingness" for decades, hundreds, or even thousands of years, is likened to anguish and suffering, yet there is no awareness, so state Job and David.

> Behold, the eye of the LORD is on those who fear him, on those who hope in his steadfast love, that he may deliver their soul from death and keep them alive in famine. Our soul waits for the LORD; he is our help and our shield. For our heart is glad in him, because we trust in his holy name. (Psalm 33:18–21, ESV)

Notice that it states, "deliver their soul from death." It also states, "Our soul waits for the Lord." It was the soul that would be delivered from death and the soul that waits on the Lord. It is not our flesh, but our soul (spirit). When I state "our," I do not mean us in the here and now, but those in the Old Covenant era, prior to the consummation of AD 70. It is not about the flesh. Jesus was resurrected in the flesh because He was still of this earth. Remember, He stated to Mary after His resurrection the following from John 20:17 (ESV): *"Jesus said to her, 'Do not cling to me, for I have not yet ascended to the Father; but go to my brothers and say to them, "I am ascending to my Father and your Father, to my God and your God."* If Jesus had appeared to them in spirit, would they have heard Him? Could they have seen Him in spirit form? I think not. Demons (spirit beings) of old had to possess the flesh to be able to have communication or interaction with the human realm. We have read much more into this verse in Psalms than was intended. There are far more verses that speak of the spirits and souls of men after death than speak of the flesh. Also, some of the ones who do, as I have demonstrated, are conspicuous at best.

One thing that is paramount about Jesus resurrection was the fact that His flesh had not experienced corruption, or rotting. Otherwise, He would have been walking around looking pretty ghastly. If Jesus had experienced the effects of death, probably a few days longer, His flesh would have experienced the effects of rotting. King David was not only king, but he was also a prophet. He prophesied the following: *"For You will not leave my soul in Sheol, nor will You allow Your Holy One to see corruption"* (Psalm 16:10, NKJV). Peter alludes to this prophecy in the following: *"...having foreseen, he did speak concerning the rising again of the Christ, that his soul was not left to hades, nor did his flesh see corruption"* (Acts 2:31, YLT). If Jesus flesh had experienced "ashes to ashes, dust to dust" then there would be nothing left for His soul to occupy upon the resurrection of the soul. He inherited His fleshly body that had not been dead long enough to experience the effects of rotting because He was present here on earth. Say what you may, but today, upon the death of this fleshly tent, the believer will inherit an incorruptible, nonfleshly, everlasting body. Flesh is corruptible, capable of rotting. The glorified, incorruptible body that believers shall have in heaven will be incapable of rotting. It is not flesh and blood.

> You love evil more than good, and lying more than speaking what is right. Selah
>
> You love all words that devour, O deceitful tongue. But God will break you down forever; he will snatch and tear you from your tent; he will uproot you from the land of the living. Selah
>
> The righteous shall see and fear, and shall laugh at him, saying, "See the man who would not make God his refuge, but trusted in the abundance of his riches and sought refuge in his own destruction."
>
> (Psalm 52:3–7, ESV)

The tent is the human body. The flesh will surely rot upon death after some time has passed, but the soul (spirit) is another matter. God can obviously extend to the soul eternal life or eternal damnation. The land of the living in this scripture is earth. God either rewards or condemns the soul where it is at. Before AD 70, it was somewhere in the realm that we live in. Where? I suppose in the earth, but to be sure I will have to ask Jesus on that day I am called home. Those in the here and now who trust in the Lord as their Refuge shall in the blink of an eye be in His presence upon that last breath. The Old Covenant people had to wait, some for millennia and some for just a few days. John transitioned from the Old Covenant era into the New Covenant era. He is the only apostle who did not have to experience "soul sleep."

"You who have made me see many troubles and calamities will revive me again; from the depths of the earth you will bring me up again" (Psalm 71:20, ESV). The Psalmist is not listed on this chapter in the Psalms, but it sounds like it was highly likely David. Regardless of who wrote it, it is obvious that upon death, he expected to descend into the earth and experience "soul sleep." To revive means to bring back to livelihood. Life must cease for this to happen. When this happens, there is no awareness. There is no pain and suffering. There is only nothingness. If this individual were to pass from this life into heaven, I do not believe that he would be contemplating a future resurrection. If you know that you will be in God's

presence for all eternity and you feel incomplete, then I am sorry, but that isn't heaven. Heaven is perfection. It is either perfection from the beginning, now, and for all eternity, or it is not heaven. In heaven, you will be lacking nothing. You will not be there lamenting the loss of your fleshly body until some future resurrection occurs. Heaven is completeness and fullness in the glory of the Father who is in heaven.

> For my soul is full of troubles, and my life draws near to Sheol. I am counted among those who go down to the pit; I am a man who has no strength, like one set loose among the dead, like the slain that lie in the grave, like those whom you remember no more, for they are cut off from your hand. (Psalm 88:3–5, ESV)

The sons of Korah are attributed to writing this psalm. Sheol is defined as the abode of the dead, or of departed spirits (souls). The reality to the living at that time was that he would experience a state of nothingness for an undetermined length of time. The sons of Korah date back to the days of Moses. Their father, along with others, had questioned Moses as to whether he was their deliverer out of the land of Egypt. Moses prayed to God that He would devour these men alive with the earth and that they would be consumed by the earth. Obviously, the sons of Korah were more attuned to God than their father was. Those that God remembers no more are those who are not written in the Lamb's Book of Life. Sheol, the graveyard, was the near hope for the departed in the days of the Old Testament saints. They had no hope as repentant sinners have today. Today there is that instant transfer from earthly death to heavenly life everlasting. Oh, what hope for man today versus the hope of the Old Testament saints. That is why the New Covenant is superior to the Old Covenant. Paul referred to the coming New Covenant as that which is perfect.

> The dead do not praise the LORD, nor do any who go down into silence. (Psalm 115:17, ESV)

> It is not the dead who praise the LORD, those who go down to the place of silence; (NIV)

> The dead do not praise the LORD, nor do any of those who descend into the silence of death. (NET)

I listed three translations above to show that there is a difference. Of the fourteen English versions in the Blue Letter Bible, twelve take the path that the ESV takes. Only the NLT and NIV take what I believe is the correct meaning. Who else goes down into silence, but the dead? Now, we assume that the place of silence is the place of the dead, and that is a correct assumption. This is no major issue, but it does make one wonder. The dead here could possibly mean those who are absent from the Book of Life. There will be no Lazarus's and rich men having conversations in Sheol. It is a place of silence, a place for dead bodies. That parable by Jesus was just that: a parable. Otherwise, the Bible contradicts itself. The point of the parable was that the people had not heard Moses or the prophets. Eventually there would be one raised from the dead, one who performed miracles, one who walked on water, turned water into wine, made the lame to walk, and the blind to see, yet they would not even believe He was Messiah after He rose from the dead. We must interpret scriptures in the light of the whole scripture. If the Bible contradicts itself in any way, then I would be inclined not to believe any of the scriptures. It is either all right or all wrong. Again, if it appears to contradict itself, from my experience, I need to look at my interpretation and see if I can reconcile it with other scriptures and history. I have yet to find an instance where I cannot reconcile the scriptures with scriptures.

"Even though he should live a thousand years twice over, yet enjoy no good—do not all go to the one place" (Ecclesiastes 6:6, ESV)? Where is the one place that the good, the bad, the ugly, the beautiful, the child, the old man, the brilliant, and the ignorant go? That place is sheol, the grave. Solomon is not asking a question here. He is making a statement. Over the lifetime of the earth there have been untold numbers who died and were not buried. They were actually eaten by the vultures, buzzards, crows, and so on. Were their souls (spirits) eaten? Of course not. Those souls still went to the place of silence. This is one verse that shows the superiority of the NC over the OC. The repentant sinner shall rise at death, and the unrepentant shall experience eternity in sheol.

We have looked at mostly Old Testament verses here that involved death. I noted elsewhere that Jesus and His apostles lived during the latter days of the Old Covenant. Some would say that this statement is heretical, but the way the Bible is laid out is in error. We have looked at this elsewhere, but I want to knock it home. Jesus and His apostles did not live under the New Covenant. Under the Old Covenant, the sinner and the saint experienced death, the wages of sin. Death is often referred to in the scriptures as "sleep" and "asleep." This is done in both testaments of the Bible, as it is designed by man. Well, if that which is perfect had come, the New Covenant, then death would not be the wages for sin anymore using the premise that Jesus and the apostles lived under the New Covenant. Let's just go ahead and show the proof that it was still on the horizon for the first-century church. *"And he kneeled down, and cried with a loud voice, Lord, lay not this sin to their charge. And when he had said this, he fell asleep"* (Acts 7:60, KJV). This was right after the stoning. Stephen had to experience "soul sleep" for a number of years before the New Covenant was inaugurated and the Old Covenant was consummated. The repentant believer today shall never have to experience "soul sleep," which is death for sinner and saint. Stephen did not rise on that day. He likely spent over twenty years in the dirt and in a state of "soul sleep."

"After that, he was seen of above five hundred brethren at once; of whom the greater part remain unto this present, but some are fallen asleep" (1 Corinthians 15:6, KJV). Most scholars believe that First Corinthians was written between AD 50 and 55. This was twenty to twenty-five years after Jesus left the earth. Those who witnessed the miracle of Jesus' resurrection from the dead are the ones who Paul is referencing here. Paul states that some of them have "fallen asleep." He is using the same terminology that is used in the Old Testament scriptures when a saint of God died. This was not just a fleshly sleep. The flesh would rot. The soul would be preserved, but in a state of sleep—so say the scriptures. The very essence of man is spirit. If the very essence of man had ascended at this time to heaven it would not state that man was in a state of sleep.

> Six days later Jesus took with Him Peter and James and John his brother, and led them up on a high mountain by themselves. And He was transfigured before them; and His face shone like the sun, and His garments became as white as light. And behold, Moses and Elijah appeared to them, talking with Him. (Matthew 17:1–3, NASB)

I have heard preachers use this event as a defense for the Old Covenant saints being in heaven at that time and they were transfigured to earth. This account is spoken of not only in Matthew, but also in Mark and Luke. When this is being taught erroneously, the Mark and Luke verses are generally the ones being used. This is an error on the part of the one propagating this lie. This was not a real encounter. After the encounter, as they were heading down the mountain, Jesus stated the following: *"As they were coming down from the mountain, Jesus commanded them, saying, "Tell the vision to no one until the Son of Man has risen from the dead"* (Matthew 17:9, NASB). Mark and Luke do not mention this being a vision, but they do state that Jesus warned them not to tell anyone until He had risen from the dead. A vision in the scriptures is generally about a forthcoming event. The apostles probably did not truly understand the meaning of what they had witnessed until later. Moses got to stand on Mount Pisgah and peer over into the Promised Land, but he was not allowed to enter, but died and was buried. Elijah's being taken up in a chariot was not a journey to heaven, but highly likely to the safety of the mountains. The Transfiguration was a vision to the apostles that the resurrection was on the horizon, but still was about a generation away. The Promised Land was about to be made available to those who had been faithful to God, as well as those who bowed the knee to Jesus. It was still a way out, though. Still, it was within their generation, the "elect generation." The Promised Land to them was just a shadow of what was to come, His Kingdom, which is in heaven. You can have Israel. I choose Messiah, who leads to heaven. It was not about the land. It was just a shadow of that which is greater. There is no "Holy Land" today apart from His Kingdom, which is in heaven. Those who take a stance for land on this earth as the Holy Land just may get to receive it for all eternity, ashes to ashes, dust to dust. It was not about the land. It was about the Promised One who was rejected. The Holy Land today is heaven. The tainted land today is earthly Israel. What God has put asunder let no man bring back together. The price just could be sheol forevermore.

> Your fathers did eat manna in the wilderness, and are dead. This is the bread which cometh down from heaven, that a man may eat thereof, and not die. I am the living bread which came down from heaven: if any man eat of this bread, he shall live for ever: and the bread that I will give is my flesh, which I will give for the life of the world. (John 6:49–51, KJV)

To be dead is not to be alive, no matter the flesh or the spirit. All that had ever lived experienced "soul sleep" until the consummation of the OC. Jesus was speaking to the crowds here. There were those in His presence who would die before AD 70 and some that would live through the destruction of the temple and Jerusalem, which was the consummation of the Old Covenant. Until that event took place, that which was obsolete and waxeth old was still in existence. If all of those events did not take place, then the new and better covenant is not yet a reality. Make

221

sure your beliefs stack up with the facts. Otherwise you may find *your-self* under the law for all time, which brings death to all.

> As the living Father hath sent me, and I live by the
> Father: so he that eateth me, even he shall live by me.
> This is that bread which came down from heaven: not as
> your fathers did eat manna, and are dead: he that eateth
> of this bread shall live for ever. (John 6:57–58, KJV)

Eternal life was not possible or available until the advent of Jesus. No man had ever experienced heaven until the consummation of the OC in the latter days of the generation that walked the earth with Messiah. The "eating" in this verse was literal for the ones in the wilderness, but it was not literal for those under the NC. There is scripture that literally speaks of eating the words of God, yet it is not literal. It is nothing more than hyperbolic language describing what the true believer should be doing with God's word. We should be eating it up. Once you begin to eat it up, you will begin to notice that there are many who are not speaking truth when they speak of the scriptures. Any man that believes humans had access to heaven before the consummation of AD 70 has not rightly digested the word of God. Likely, he has digested the teachings of an inferior teacher.

This chapter was an attempt to show that there is a difference in Old Covenant death versus New Covenant death. Under the OC, the sinner and the saint went to the place of silence, sheol, the grave. Under the NC, the unrepentant sinner does not rise on D-day (day of death), but shall experience all eternity with the Old Covenant nonbeliever. The dead in Christ will be, upon their last breath, transferred to heaven, in the blink of an eye, in an instant. The repentant sinner shall not have to experience what David, Moses, Ezekiel, Nehemiah, and Abraham, experienced — nor what Paul, Peter, Stephen, and all the first-century believers that passed from life prior to AD 70 experienced. Messiah had come, but the consummation had not yet taken place until AD 70. All who died prior to AD 70, the sinner and the saint, experienced the wages of sin: "soul sleep." Those who lived wandered in the wilderness for forty years and were given a chance to repent. A remnant of the Jews was allowed to enter that which is perfect, the New Covenant era, along with John the Revelator. You can chalk this up to the 144,000. These were left behind to propagate the Gospel and the history of that event where there was no more death, nor sorrow, for the repentant. The old heaven and earth passed away in AD 70 and not at Jesus' birth, death, resurrection, or ascension.

Resurrection: Past or Future?

$\mathcal{T}$his is a subject that must be addressed within the covers of this book. I thought that I could just leave it out and do a future work that addresses the resurrection. As usual, I always feel compelled to capitalize such events as this, but out of the forty-one times it is used in the KJV scriptures, it is not capitalized a single time. It is also not found in the Old Testament. There is not a single mention of the word *resurrection* in all of the 987 pages of the Old Testament of the Gideon Bible. Yet, it is mentioned forty-one times in forty verses of the 300 pages of the New Testament of the Gideon Bible. As I have made mention of in another section, Jesus and His apostles did not actually live in the New Testament Covenant era. It had not yet been consummated, and the wages for sin for the believer and non-believer alike was still death until the consummation.

Whether you are familiar with this or not, there is approximately a 400-year period where the southern kingdom of Judah did not hear from God. The last prophetic messages were delivered during the Persian Period of dominance in the Middle East. Malachi and Nehemiah spoke of the same abuses going on in Jerusalem in their writings, so it appears that they lived at the same time. The main point, though, is that the word *resurrection* is not mentioned at all in the Old Testament scriptures that cover time from the creation to just before the Roman persecution began in late AD 64. This is a period of time of about 3,600 (400 years of silence taken into account) years. The New Testament scriptures cover a period of time that is only about sixty years. So, there are zero mentions of resurrection in the Old Testament that covers about 3,600 years and forty-one mentions of resurrection in a period less than sixty-four years. Surely, it seems like something was going on. The resurrection was on the horizon. It was just a few years off, if you can call forty years after the crucifixion of Jesus a short time. Now, I am not saying that there was no hope for the

Old Testament saint. They did have a hope for a far-future awakening, but they did not use the term *resurrection*. Of course, English was not their language, but the same event in Hebrew and Greek would still use the same word when translated into the English word *resurrection*.

What had happened all of a sudden that there would be much talk of this event? Well, the afterlife was relevant to Noah, Abraham, Job, Moses, Daniel, David, Malachi, and the other saints of that time, but it was not imminent. It was far future to them. It was now imminent to the ones living in the latter days of the Old Covenant. At Jesus' death, resurrection, and ascension, they were a biblical generation away from the resurrection, which was the Marriage Supper of the Lamb. This was the event that reconciled those under the Old Covenant into the New Covenant. The Marriage Supper of the Lamb was not for those under the New Covenant. We do not have to be married into the New. We are born under the New. Man still has a decision to make even under the New. If Jesus is your Messiah, then you shall rise on that day when you take your last breath. If not, you shall descend to perdition.

It is critical that we understand this, though. Even though a resurrection is not mentioned a single time in the Old Testament scriptures, it does not mean that they had no hope of eternal life. Also, another very important issue that man needs to understand today is that there are many who believe the resurrection will be bodily, but no, it was not. What is your standard? Here is mine: *"Now this I say, brethren, that flesh and blood cannot inherit the kingdom of God; neither doth corruption inherit incorruption"* (1 Corinthians 15:50, KJV). The bodies that we live in today are referred to many times in the scriptures as tents. Tents are occupied. These fleshly bodies are occupied. The very essence of man is spirit. The saints that lived hundreds of years before Jesus, and even back to the beginning, did have a hope for a far-future resurrection. They just did not talk about it much because it was far in the future to them. They had also not attached the moniker *resurrection* to the event at that time.

Paul says that flesh and blood, our earthly tents, cannot inherit the kingdom of God, which is heaven. These fleshly bodies are not capable of lasting forever. When we get to heaven, we will put on the incorruptible. Under the New Covenant, we will be caught up to the kingdom upon the death of these fleshly bodies. It will not be a singular event at the "end." The end has already been. The living will be caught up upon death. We shall never experience the wages of sin, "soul sleep." This was for those under the Old Covenant. This is where the heretical teaching of being in heaven with half of your assets comes from. A false understanding of the resurrection that occurred in the "last days" or "latter days" of the Old Covenant is where this false teaching comes from. Nowhere in the scriptures does it say that humans, bodily or spiritually, were allowed into heaven prior to AD 70. There were visions about heaven, but a vision is not reality. There is only one key to heaven, and that key is Jesus. Without the key there is no entry. It is not biblical and also requires that the ones teaching it do not believe that Jesus did what He came to do. "It is finished" was for real, but there was still forty years to go before the effects took place. They were given forty years again to wander in the wilderness, so to speak. Few would repent. Those who did, and lived through the AD 70 event, would never experience soul sleep. They would be taken up, each at his own end, to the kingdom. The believers that died before the consummation in AD 70, which included the apostles, would go through the resurrection and the Marriage Supper of the Lamb. Our hope today is "to be absent from the body is to be present with the Lord." This was not a possibility until the consummation, the end.

> So will it be with the resurrection of the dead. The body that is sown is perishable, it is raised imperishable; it is sown in dishonor, it is raised in glory; it is sown in weakness, it is raised in power; it is sown a natural body, it is raised a spiritual body.

> If there is a natural body, there is also a spiritual body. So it is written: "The first man Adam became a living being"; the last Adam, a life-giving spirit. The spiritual did not come first, but the natural, and after that the spiritual. The first man was of the dust of the earth; the second man is of heaven. As was the earthly man, so are those who are of the earth; and as is the heavenly man, so also are those who are of heaven. And just as we have borne the image of the earthly man, so shall we bear the image of the heavenly man.
>
> (1 Corinthians 15:42–49, NIV)

Entry into heaven for mankind was still yet future when Paul wrote this letter to the Corinthians. We can gather from these verses that until Christ came, there was no entry for man into heaven. God created man in His image, but this had nothing to do with being in heaven before Christ came and the consummation of the Old Covenant. It was an impossibility

225

before the Old Covenant was consummated in AD 70. Before that time all that died experienced "soul sleep" and the rotting of the flesh. The flesh shall remain in the earth upon passing from life to death for all time. Only the soul rises. When it reaches heaven it will be given a glorified imperishable body, not of flesh.

> Now at that time Michael, the great prince who stands guard over the sons of your people, will arise. And there will be a time of distress such as never occurred since there was a nation until that time; and at that time your people, everyone who is found written in the book, will be rescued. Many of those who sleep in the dust of the ground will awake, these to everlasting life, but the others to disgrace and everlasting contempt. Those who have insight will shine brightly like the brightness of the expanse of heaven, and those who lead the many to righteousness, like the stars forever and ever. But as for you, Daniel, conceal these words and seal up the book until the end of time; many will go back and forth, and knowledge will increase. (Daniel 12:1–4, NASB)

Did you notice that the NASB version stated "end of time"? Out of the fourteen English versions used in the BLB, this is the only translation that takes this route. All the others state "time of the end." It was not the end of time. It was the time of the end, the end of the Old Covenant era. I could have used any of the thirteen English versions that got it right, but I am out to disclose the fact that there are many errors in the scriptures. None are perfect, not even the best. Even the KJV gets this right. Overall, the NASB version is superior to the KJV. It is one of my favorites, but it gets it wrong here. If you are a deep, discerning thinker, it is obvious that "end of time" and "time of the end" are in no way congruent. I will experience the time of my end, but time shall not end.

Daniel is obviously speaking here of the same event that John and Jesus foretold. The difference, though, is the timeframe. For Daniel it was far future, so far forward that he was told to seal the scripture up. It was so close to those to whom John related his prophetic event that he was told not to seal it up. Daniel's prophecy would have been penned about 600 years before the destruction of the temple and city of Jerusalem in AD 70. John would have penned Revelation no sooner than six years before AD 70. It could have been within sixteen years at most, due to the fact that "five are fallen, and one is." Nero was the "one" since he was the sixth caesar over Rome, and he took the throne in AD 54. Twas not imminent to Daniel, only relevant. It was very imminent to the ones who received the Revelation from John prior to AD 70. Judgment was about to come upon the house of God, but also the resurrection of the Old Covenant saints was shortly to take place. This was Daniel's far-future hope: *"But go thou thy way until the end be: for thou shalt rest, and stand in thy lot at the end of the days"* (Daniel 12:13, KJV). Do you think that Daniel was going to get into his La-Z-Boy recliner and rest for about 600 years, awaiting this event? No, his rest would be as the rest of Abraham, Isaac, and Jacob. He would experience "soul sleep" until the far-future resurrection that occurred in AD 70, forty years after Jesus' ascension.

"Verily, verily, I say unto you, the hour is coming, and now is, when the dead shall hear the voice of the Son of God: and they that hear shall live" (John 5:25, KJV). Jesus spoke this verse and even gives a time-frame reference in His statement. He even allowed His apostles to see a vision of Moses and Elijah on the mountain later. It was a vision of the forthcoming resurrection. It was a revealing of an event that would happen within their generation and also an event that would affect all of the apostles but John. The vision was the assurance of their future resurrection. Jesus stated that "the hour is coming, and now is." It was still over forty years away, but the resurrection was still within their generation, and not for a future elect. This was part and parcel with the elect of God. That elect generation got to experience Messiah, God's wrath, and the often spoke of resurrection of the dead. It is in our past and not imminent to our generation. There is no future resurrection. It was part of the consummation of the Old Covenant with the descendants of Abraham. Abraham rose on that day. If you do not believe this, then you believe that Abraham is still in a state of "soul sleep," along with all that have ever died from the beginning. Under the New Covenant you either rise or fall the day the flesh dies.

"And God hath both raised up the Lord, and will also raise up us by his own power" (1 Corinthians 6:14, KJV). It is obvious from Paul's statement here that he fully expected to go through the resurrection. It was not at that time "to be absent from the body is to be present with the Lord." This was still future for that generation. No, Paul had no inclination that he and all the faithful would be in heaven with half of their essence or being. This was not reality and is the figment of a very erroneous and faulty teaching.

I can remember hearing sermons on the Marriage Supper of the Lamb that date back to my childhood days in the 1970s. Current teachings have always put this event into the future and have always associated it with the saints of old and those under the New Covenant. It has always been associated with the end of the world, but we have addressed that earlier. I also want to mention this here, and I encourage you to follow up and see it for yourself. We also have touched on this issue here, too, but it is critical to comprehend the facts. After the great white throne (not capitalized in the KJV) judgment, which takes place in heaven, there is still life going on here in the new heaven and new earth. There is also sin still going on at this time. After the new heaven and earth come, there is still sin? Yep. It is the time we are living in today. Man has a choice. He can accept Jesus as Messiah and live for eternity, or he can reject Him and experience perdition.

> And I saw a great white throne, and him that sat on it, from whose face the earth and the heaven fled away; and there was found no place for them. And I saw the dead, small and great, stand before God; and the books were opened: and another book was opened, which is the book of life: and the dead were judged out of those things which were written in the books, according to their works. And the sea gave up the dead which were in it; and death and hell delivered up the dead which were in them: and they were judged every man according to their works. And death and hell were cast into the lake of fire. This is the second death. And whosoever was not found written in the book of life was cast into the lake of fire. (Revelation 20:11–15, KJV)

The resurrection and the white throne judgment was a far-past event that involved only the Old Covenant dwellers. I invite you to read Revelation 19 through 22, which confirm this. There is no mention whatsoever of the raptured saints being present at the great white throne judgment because there is no rapture spoken of in the scriptures. We will all be taken up separately today upon the believer's last breath on earth. The white throne judgment was only for the dead saints that were under the Old Covenant. There is no mention whatsoever of the living being present here at the judgment. Those under the New Covenant will experience judgment upon death. You either rise or fall. That is your judgment. Your final destination will be determined by your relationship with Jesus. Your fruit will bare you out. The absence of the living at the great white throne refutes rapture theory. There is a verse that addresses judgment. Judgment was the outpouring of wrath on the Mother of Harlots, the Jewish nation. Those who believed and heeded Jesus' signs and warnings, along with His apostles' warnings, were spared judgment. *"Very truly I tell you, whoever hears my word and believes him who sent me has eternal life and will not be judged but has crossed over from death to life"* (John 5:24, NIV). The white throne judgment was for Old Covenant dwellers. The Key to everlasting life had not yet come when they lived. At the Consummation of the Ages the dead were judged, as well as the living, the rebellious, whoring nation of Jews. This verse states that the repentant shall forgo the judgment. You either rise or fall today.

I was not planning on doing a section on the resurrection, but it is just too important for the times that we live in. There is much information out there on it. As I have stated elsewhere within these covers, do a search online on John Nelson Darby. I have researched this issue enough that I have come to the conclusion that it is just another false teaching born out of misinterpreting, or reading something into the scriptures that just isn't there. We know from scripture listed earlier in this section that flesh and blood shall not inherit the kingdom. Only the soul goes to heaven. Will the believer inherit a solid material body? Again, it is not a definite. Just because Jesus appeared in the flesh certainly does not mean that this is reality in heaven. Jesus was not in heaven. He was on earth. He had to appear in a form that humans would be able to sense. We will not know what kind of bodies we will have until we get there, in our own timing, each upon his own death. Most modern commentators believe in a fleshly future resurrection, but Paul eats that heresy alive when he stated that flesh and blood could not inherit the kingdom of God. We are going to look at the verses now that have been used to develop "Rapture Theory."

> But I would not have you to be ignorant, brethren, concerning them which are asleep, that ye sorrow not, even as others which have no hope. For if we believe that Jesus died and rose again, even so them also which sleep in Jesus will God bring with him. For this we say unto you by the word of the Lord, that we which are alive and remain unto the coming of the Lord shall not prevent them which are asleep. For the Lord himself shall descend from heaven with a shout, with the voice of the archangel, and with the trump of God: and the dead

> in Christ shall rise first: Then we which are alive and
> remain shall be caught up together with them in the
> clouds, to meet the Lord in the air: and so shall we ever
> be with the Lord. (1 Thessalonians 4:13–18, KJV)

I heard a preacher recently deny "soul sleep." *"And no man hath ascended up to heaven, but he that came down from heaven, even the Son of man which is in heaven"* (John 3:13, KJV). As mentioned elsewhere, according to biblical scholars, John penned his gospel twenty-plus years after Jesus' ascension. If this statement had been made null and void, surely John would have stated that this is no longer the case. He did not because this was still the status quo and would continue to be until the Lord resurrected those who died for Him in the first century, and then those who lived before His advent, which would include all the Old Covenant faithful. Well, if no man had ascended up to heaven over twenty years after Jesus' death, resurrection, and ascension, where are the souls of the repentant preserved? Do they sleep? *"And he kneeled down, and cried with a loud voice, Lord, lay not this sin to their charge. And when he had said this, he fell asleep"* (Acts 7:60, KJV). This was Stephen after he was stoned right before he experienced "soul sleep." Well, obviously the soul must be preserved somewhere. These two verses from the word of God are my standard on this issue. I know that "sleep" and "asleep" are references to death, but no man had ever gone to heaven twenty years after Jesus' death. We have addressed Abraham's bosom elsewhere. It is just symbolic language representing the grave. The scripture in Acts attests to "soul sleep" contrary to what anyone else says on this issue. This is my standard, not the teachings of man. Those who were dying in the days that the apostles lived prior to AD 70 were still under the Old Covenant as we have shown elsewhere. They were still experiencing "soul sleep." The language that Paul uses in Thessalonians is not literal. It is symbolic. You shall never hear a trumpet from heaven. Paul states that the dead would rise first. This was the resurrection. It occurred in AD 70, either prior to or shortly after the destruction of the temple and the city of Jerusalem.

Paul states next that those who are alive and remain shall be caught up. Let's look at another place in scripture where Paul addresses this same issue but with more detail. This more detail is what always gets left out in a teaching session. Paul is addressing the same issue, but a different audience.

> Now this I say, brethren, that flesh and blood cannot
> inherit the kingdom of God; neither doth corruption

inherit incorruption. Behold, I shew you a mystery; we shall not all sleep, but we shall all be changed, in a moment, in the twinkling of an eye, at the last trump: for the trumpet shall sound, and the dead shall be raised incorruptible, and we shall be changed. For this corruptible must put on incorruption, and this mortal must put on immortality. So when this corruptible shall have put on incorruption, and this mortal shall have put on immortality, then shall be brought to pass the saying that is written, Death is swallowed up in victory. O death, where is thy sting? O grave, where is thy victory? The sting of death is sin; and the strength of sin is the law. But thanks be to God, which giveth us the victory through our Lord Jesus Christ.

(1 Corinthians 15:50, KJV)

Heaven is the incorruption that Paul is speaking of here, and corruption is the fleshly body. Only in heaven will there ever be incorruptible bodies. Without the cleansing blood of the Lamb, none shall enter the incorruptible kingdom of God, heaven. He addresses the key to entryway into the kingdom in the last verse, which is our Lord Jesus Christ. Paul is stating in symbolic language that when the last trump is heard, the New Covenant would begin. The Old Testament saints were under the Old Covenant. This is what the Marriage Supper of the Lamb was about. They had to be married into the New Covenant. If you lived through the consummation, you did not have to experience the resurrection because your soul would never sleep if you were a repentant believer. The dead were raised incorruptible. This means that they were raised forevermore.

Death no longer reigns for the believer. Those living are not taken up here, yet Paul is speaking of the same event he spoke of in First Thessalonians. He goes into more detail here. Those Christians that lived through the consummation, the mortal, or living at that time, then put on immortality, which did not exist before the Old Covenant was consummated. Under the Old Covenant it was appointed to man to die, soul and flesh. Under the New Covenant the flesh still dies. This is the first death. All of mankind will experience this death. The second death is the death of the soul. Under the New Covenant those who are in Christ shall never have to experience this death. Death has lost its sting forevermore for the believer. The law still applies today. The wages of sin is still death, but for those who have bowed the knee to Messiah, Jesus, they shall never experience the sting of death. The unrepentant shall, and for them, there is no future hope at this time nor will there ever be. Eternity is decided when you take your last breath in the here and now. You either rise or fall. It is for all eternity.

Paul states nothing in this scripture about being "caught up." I imagine that the people who lived at that time had a better understanding of the resurrection of the dead than we do today. Paul gives a partial explanation to the Thessalonians and a bit here to the Corinthians. We infer that those who have put on immortality, salvation through Jesus Christ, shall upon death of these fleshly bodies be caught up into His kingdom. Under the New Covenant this will be a singular event for each believer, not as the resurrection that was for all the dead. Based on what we do know, we can infer from these two passages that the resurrection was in the past and only for those under the Old Covenant. The New Covenant has come, and the believer today does not go down to perdition to await a future resurrection. Under that which is perfect the believers are spared death and are caught up upon that last breath in the here and now. When Paul made this statement the Old Covenant still reigned. Paul knew that he would have to suffer "soul sleep" and go through the resurrection, but he is planting hope for the Corinthians when he stated the following: *"But when that which is perfect is come, then that which is in part shall be done away"* (1 Corinthians 13:10, KJV). Paul was speaking about the consummation, the end of the Old Covenant and the entry of that which is perfect, the New Covenant. It was still on the horizon, but it would arrive in a few more years.

Paul fully expected to experience what Jesus had experienced. This makes it obvious that the price Jesus paid for the sinner was not yet in force until the consummation of the Old Covenant with the Jews. Paul would experience the same thing that Job, David, Elijah, Enoch, and others had experienced, the death of the flesh and "soul sleep." His time in the earth would not be for long, though, just a few years. *"My goal is to know Him and the power of His resurrection and the fellowship of His sufferings, being conformed to His death, assuming that I will somehow reach the resurrection from among the dead"* (Philippians 3:10–11, HCSB). Paul's future hope was for the resurrection of the soul. He trusted that Jesus would do what He had promised. *"For this reason I also suffer these things; nevertheless I am not ashamed, for I know whom I have believed and am persuaded that He is able to keep what I have committed to Him until that Day"* (2 Timothy 1:12, NKJV.)What had Paul entrusted, or committed, to Jesus? He had committed his soul unto Him. What "day" was Paul looking forward to? This would be the once for all time Resurrection Day, the Marriage Supper of the Lamb. This was the prophesied event that all the Old Covenant believers had a future hope for. This event was for the Old Covenant believers only and not for those under the New Covenant. Otherwise, what is superior about the New Covenant? These are the facts and the major difference in the New and Superior Covenant over the one that "waxeth old" that Paul was still living under.

In Revelation, it is revealed that there are two resurrections. Two different groups are taken up at different times. We will address the thousand year reign of Jesus in another section, but the first resurrection takes places during this timeframe, prior to AD 70, as the martyrs of Jesus were taken up first, those who walked the earth with Him.

> And I saw thrones, and they sat upon them, and judgment was given unto them: and I saw the souls of them that were beheaded for the witness of Jesus, and for the word of God, and which had not worshipped the beast, neither his image, neither had received his mark upon their foreheads, or in their hands; and they lived and reigned with Christ a thousand years. But the rest of the dead lived not again until the thousand years were finished. This is the first resurrection. Blessed and holy is he that hath part in the first resurrection: on such the second death hath no power, but they shall be priests of God and of Christ, and shall reign with him a thousand years. And when the thousand years are expired, Satan shall be loosed out of his prison,
>
> (Revelation 20:4–7, KJV)

It is obvious that those present here are the ones who were among the first-century believers after Jesus left the earth. This would include His apostles. These were the ones who "had no king but Jesus." I have seen commentaries that stated this was not a literal resurrection and that this actually refers to the living saints of Jesus that had experienced a spiritual resurrection, equivalent to what we consider salvation. They state that the "dead" here are the unrepentant. Well, if that is the case, then why can't we just use that reasoning every time we see "dead"? No, this is incorrect. This verse talks about the beheaded and the dead. I have never seen a headless person walking this earth. The beheaded were those who walked the earth with Jesus and were decapitated for their faith, hung on crosses, killed in the arenas, and so on. The "rest of the dead" were those who died prior to Jesus birth. Both groups are deceased at the time this scripture was penned, prior to AD 64. This is one of those areas where there will likely never be consensus. If we just take what the scripture states, then it appears that there is a resurrection of those who experienced death from the time Jesus ascended to heaven and a future date prior to the AD 70 consummation. There is no way that we could attach a date to this. If I had to give a date, I would say that it was after the city of Rome burned and the Roman persecution began in earnest against the first-century church. Now, I am taking a literal approach on this scripture, but should I be? I will ask when I get there. All I know for sure about this particular scripture is that it is in my far past, for sure.

The next resurrection is when the white throne judgment takes place, the one who has no living, or raptured saints, present. This would be all who had died prior to Jesus' advent. These had experienced the first death, which is a physical death that also included "soul sleep." The second death entailed the destruction of the soul. Verse 12 states that those under this judgment were judged according to their works. That was the Old Covenant. The repentant believer today is judged by the works of Jesus, what He did on the cross. You are either in Christ or not. Jesus stated that He did not come to do away with the law but to fulfill it. He paid the wages for sin. Those under Him will obey Him.

> If ye love me, keep my commandments.
>
> (John 14:15, KJV)

> Jesus answered and said unto him, if a man love me, he will keep my words: and my Father will love him, and we will come unto him, and make our abode with him.
>
> (John 14:23, KJV)

Do you keep the commandments of Jesus? Do you keep His words? Do you know His commandments and words? It is critical that you do, lest you offend Him and violate what He has commanded in either an affirmative or negative way.

God's word is still relevant to man today. The world is in the shape it is in today because man is ignorant of His word. Your reward will be based on His word. It pays to know His word. *"Therefore shall ye lay up these my words in your heart and in your soul, and bind them for a sign upon your hand, that they may be as frontlets between your eyes"* (Deuteronomy 11:18, KJV). God was speaking through Moses here to the children of the Exodus. We know that because they were unfaithful to God's word they wandered in the wilderness for forty years. The first generation that encountered Jesus, Messiah, on this earth was allowed to wander, or wonder, for forty years because they did not heed the words of Jesus. The majority from both generations did not enter into the Promised Land.

"Thy words were found, and I did eat them; and thy word was unto me the joy and rejoicing of mine heart: for I am called by thy name, O LORD God of hosts" (Jeremiah 15:16, KJV). Have you ever eaten the words of God? You should eat them as often as possible. It should be your passion, as well as your hobby. It should be what dominates your spare time. The more man becomes familiar with His ways through His word, the more disciplined lives we will live. Self-control is a fruit of the Spirit. Without the Spirit, there is no self-control. Without knowledge, self-control is pointless. I admonish you to get deep in the word of God and allow the scriptures to be your standard and not the teachings of man. If the scripture says it, you can trust it. Do not allow anyone to refute what is written. Yes, there are difficult passages, but a better understanding of the symbolic language used in that epoch of time will give greater insight into what is being conveyed. The bottom line is this. The "end" has come and is about 1,950 years in our past. The resurrection was for those who dwelt under the Old Covenant. It is not imminent for us. The relevance is in the fact that it is fulfilled prophecy. This world isn't going to end no time soon. Your life will end within the next hundred years, for sure. The world will go on long after we are gone.

Before we close this chapter, I feel compelled to add just a bit more that will put to rest the heretical teaching of a future rapture of the saints.

> For as in Adam all die, so also in Christ all will be made alive. But each in his own order: Christ the first fruits, after that those who are Christ's at His coming, then comes the end, when He hands over the kingdom to the God and Father, when He has abolished all rule and all authority and power. For He must reign until He has put all His enemies under His feet. The last enemy that will be abolished is death. (1 Corinthians 15:22–26, NASB)

It is believed by scholars that First Corinthians was written in the first half of the fifties AD. Paul states here that "in Christ all will be made alive. But each in his own order." Obviously this was still a future event when he penned this scripture. He also makes it clear that all will not rise at once—"each in his own order." This confirms that those who died for the cause of Christ were raised up prior to the end of the OC and before the saints who died prior to the advent of Jesus. Being "caught up in his own order" is also how the New Covenant operates. Upon death of the flesh, each believer will be caught up in his own order. All of those who were the enemies of Jesus were defeated prior to and at the destruction of the temple and city of Jerusalem by the Roman Empire, the beast. Death has been abolished for the repentant today. John never experienced death or "soul sleep."

Rapture theory is a heresy that began about 1830 with John Nelson Darby. He was obviously not familiar with all of scripture concerning life on this earth and the way to heaven. Paul admonishes the Corinthians about this issue. Obviously there was ignorance of the resurrection of the dead, as well as the state of matters beyond the resurrection, as there is today. We know that the Samaritans did not believe in the resurrection. Paul goes a step further in this verse to shred the false rapture theory. Only those who have experienced the death of the flesh shall enter heaven. This would eliminate all the living being taken up to heaven in a future rapture.

> Do not be deceived: "Bad company corrupts good morals." Become sober-minded as you ought, and stop sinning; for some have no knowledge of God. I speak this to your shame. But someone will say, "How are the dead raised? And with what kind of body do they come?" You fool. That which you sow does not come to life unless it dies; and that which you sow, you do not sow the body which is to be, but a bare grain, perhaps of wheat or of something else. But God gives it a body just as He wished, and to each of the seeds a body of its own.
> (1 Corinthians 15:33–38, NASB)

Paul is going a step farther here with what happens at death for the believer. Verse 36 is the definitive verse. This is a literal statement. The fleshly body of the believer must go through the death of the flesh before the believer can go to heaven. This was the state of the flesh before the New Covenant took effect and is the status for all flesh forevermore.

When you reach heaven, you will get a glorified, incorruptible body that will last for all eternity. There are those who will state that this is a literal dying to self and not literal death. That is false. For rapture theory to be correct, then God would have to destroy all the believers on the earth before they could enter heaven—no death of the flesh and no heaven. This eliminates rapture theory. Rapture theory has put the church on hold. While man is waiting on Jesus, God is waiting on man. It is time that the leaves on the Tree of Life rise up and bring about the healing of the nations. That is a mandate from God for the believers, but if you have a false end-times view, you are sitting back and waiting on God. He is waiting on the faithful to bring about the healing of the nations. If you are not for the healing of the nations, you are not attached to the Tree of Life.

The Thousand-Year Reign

I am sure that you are familiar with the old saying, "Garbage in, garbage out." Most individuals in this world believe that most other individuals in this world are programmed the wrong way. Now, do you program a human being? Yes, you do. The word of God says the following: *"Train up a child in the way he should go: and when he is old, he will not depart from it"* (Proverbs 22:6, KJV). Even a seventy-year-old man is considered a babe in Christ if he has just made a profession of faith and was never brought up under the admonition of the Lord. It is my hope that most church leadership would not allow a man to teach a class just because he is seventy years of age. Age is not a determiner of wisdom. A relationship with the Lord is, but what about the teaching of an individual? I believe that all humans can comprehend that bad teaching, or input, can destroy lives. It can make people compromise their lives. There are many religions out there that claim to be truth, but there is only One who died for the sins of mankind. That One is Jesus Christ.

Buddha abandoned his newborn son immediately after birth and went off into the outdoors, supposedly seeking enlightenment. Well, it is obvious to me that what he was seeking was to have his load lightened from the burden of being a responsible adult, father, and husband. He was twenty-nine years old when he did this. It is believed that he had no contact with his child until the child was about seven years old, and this was just a brief encounter. I dare say if Buddha would have been brought up in America today, his son would likely not even know who his "sperm donor" was. Buddha would probably have many different children by many different women. He would also likely be on the taxpayer dole, feigning disability. God disdains any man who shirks his responsibility as a father and as a husband.

It is a fact that children who are brought up without fathers in the house are at a disadvantage in life. When they get into their teen years, they tend to develop disrespect for authority, particularly the males. Our prisons are full of such men. The majority of prison inmates are made up of minority populations in the United States. I think by now that you are catching my drift. Buddha was no better than most in our prison population today. He ran from his God-given role as a husband and father because he did not want the responsibility. Yet, today there are those who worship Buddha and seek enlightenment. Well, Buddha did not have it. Seek elsewhere.

> My son, be attentive to my words; incline your ear to my sayings. Let them not escape from your sight; keep them within your heart. For they are life to those who find them, and healing to all their flesh. Keep your heart with all vigilance, for from it flow the springs of life. Put away from you crooked speech, and put devious talk far from you. Let your eyes look directly forward, and your gaze be straight before you. Ponder the path of your feet; then all your ways will be sure. Do not swerve to the right or to the left; turn your foot away from evil.
>
> (Proverbs 4:20–27, ESV)

Solomon is speaking words of wisdom here for all of mankind for all time. Where does wisdom come from? God, of course. He is wisdom. We can also take this as an admonition from God to be attentive to His words. We are to incline our ear to His sayings. Well, where are His sayings? What are His sayings? The Bible is where you will find what His sayings are. Let no man lead you astray as to what the word of God says. If man contradicts the word of God, then that man is either ignorant or evil, and could be both. Regardless, a lie told, whether intentional or not, can have devastating consequences. As the theory of evolution has expanded in our world today, the value of life has decreased. Our culture fosters murder. If the punishment for murder is three square meals a day, regular exercise, and possibly even an education, well, such as this promotes murder. If the death penalty were enforced the world over, you would see a tremendous decrease in the murder rate. In America and most of the world, if a man murders the son of another, he is imprisoned and then the family of the victim is forced to pay for the welfare of the murderer the rest of their lives through taxation. This is an abomination to the Father in heaven. All of the innocent hard workers of the society are forced to pay for the welfare of the murderer. Heaven shall be heaven because those who stand for such will not be there. Crime should not profit a man, yet in America it gets you free food, clothes, free amenities, heat and air, and so forth. I am sorry, but prison is a place that should be hell on earth. If it were, the recidivism rate would not be so high. It is mighty peculiar that there is no mention of Jesus visiting the prisons. He admonished His apostles and the first-century believers to visit the prisons because the innocent were going to be imprisoned as religious tyranny broke out within the streets of Israel. These were not criminals but the innocent, as were Paul and Silas as they sang the midnight hymn.

I thought this would be a great place to mention this observation. Today our prisons are such a pleasurable place to be compared to what they were back in the biblical day and even in earlier times in the United States. The lash used to be very prevalent in the penal systems of the world. A pleasurable cool or warm environment was not considered for the criminal generations ago, nor is it in many nations today. There is nothing advanced about this. If anything, it is backward. In America today, there are many people there who have been imprisoned three to six times. If it were not such a place of pleasure compared to what it was meant to be, you would see the recidivism rate go way down. It is obvious that criminals do not view it as a place of punishment. Three square meals a day, an exercise regime, and heating and air-conditioning are not punishment. The church takes great pride in prison reform.

Here are statistics from the National Institute of Justice from a study done in 2005:

Bureau of Justice Statistics studies have found high rates of recidivism among released prisoners. One study tracked 404,638 prisoners in 30 states after their release from prison in 2005. [1] The researchers found that:

Within three years of release, about two-thirds (67.8 percent) of released prisoners were rearrested.

Within five years of release, about three-quarters (76.6 percent) of released prisoners were rearrested.

Of those prisoners who were rearrested, more than half (56.7 percent) were arrested by the end of the first year.

Property offenders were the most likely to be rearrested, with 82.1 percent of released property offenders arrested for a new crime compared with 76.9 percent of drug offenders, 73.6 percent of public order offenders and 71.3 percent of violent offenders.

Well, what led to prison reform is a false understanding of the scriptures and the times that the apostles lived in. Jesus admonished His apostles to visit the prisons because the innocent would be there, as were Paul and Silas. If Jesus was so into criminals, why is there no documentation of His ever visiting a prison? God demands punishment for the criminal. A false understanding of the scriptures is what has made the prisons of the United States such a pleasurable place today. The innocent hard worker is robbed by the government, so the thuggish sluggard can sleep in comfort and live without responsibility. Woe be unto those who propagate such. A false understanding of scripture is what has led to this. If prisons were a place of discomfort and torment, criminal activity would be greatly reduced. Instead, the church has led the cause here. False understandings of the scripture will be no excuse before God. The church has encouraged crime and violence because of ignorance of the word. When the innocent is robbed to feed the criminal, the one doing the robbing will be considered a thief.

Just a few days ago I heard a woman on a news program make the statement that the death penalty in America has not proven to reduce the murder rate. I thought to myself how ignorant her statement was. If a man has at least thirty years to abuse the evil appeals process, then that is part of the problem. If the death penalty was mandated for the murderer, and it was mandated to be carried out within two weeks of the verdict, the murder rate would take a nosedive. It should also be shown to the public as it is being carried out. A few years ago, I heard a news commentator state that attorneys for a certain murderer had received in excess of a million dollars from the taxpayer dole while defending a murderer. The key was the appeals process. It had gone on for about thirty years at the expense of the honest hard-working American. This is a system that is set up to enrich corrupt individuals who have no respect for the innocent, yet devote their lives to fleecing the innocent while defending the dogs of this world. Is that statement off base? *"Outside the city are the dogs—the sorcerers, the sexually immoral, the murderers, the idol worshipers, and all who love to live a lie"* (Revelation 22:16, NLT). Well, the city referred to here is just symbolic language for heaven, the kingdom of God. It was never meant for the innocent to pay for the defense of a murderer or for any criminal defense. Say what you will, but this is evil personified. "Depart from me," thus saith the Lord. I have a solution, but I do not imagine any government official will ever seek my advice.

We are going to take a look at a very important part of Revelation that can really cause one to stumble if he is not well versed in the Bible. If you do not understand the language of the Old Testament, you will flounder greatly when reading the prophecies of the New Testament. There is much Old Testament prophetic apocalyptic language that is used in the New Testament. I am learning as I go, but there could be a book written on that subject alone. There are those who claim to be literalists when it comes to scripture. Generally, these tend to be the end-times doomsday sayers. They truly only pick and choose what they want to be taken literally, though. Would you take the following verse literally? *"For you shall go out in joy and be led forth in peace; the mountains and the hills before you shall break forth into singing, and all the trees of the field shall clap their hands"* (Isaiah 55:12, ESV). I have spent a great deal of time in the mountains. I loves me some mountains! It matters not how high they are. When you are in them experiencing the glory of God, the fact that you are at the highest point in the Ozarks, at around 2,700 feet in no way takes away from the grandeur of the Ozarks. The highest point in the Appalachians is 6,684 feet at Mount Mitchell in North Carolina, the highest point east of the Mississippi River. The San Bernardino Mountains in southern California peak out at about 11,500 feet. The highest peak in Death Valley, Telescope Peak, is 11,049 feet. Mount Hood in Oregon is 11, 239 feet, Mount Rainier in Washington is at 14,411 feet, Black Mountain in Kentucky is at 4,154 feet, Mount Rodgers in Virginia peaks at about 5,729 feet, Spruce Mountain in West Virginia at 4,863 feet, and Clingmans Dome in Tennessee peaks out at 6,643 feet. I have experienced all of these mountains, plus the Andes in Peru, which peak out at over 20,000 feet. I can tell you that the Ozarks of Arkansas and Missouri are just as scenic as the highest mountains in the United States and in the world. The mountains do speak, no matter how short they are. They speak of the glory of the Creator and His majesty. I guess they speak in tongues, too! They speak a language that everyone can comprehend in his own language. I sure am glad, though, that the trees have always chosen not to clap their hands when I am in their midst. Otherwise, I would probably be a mist of "Ash to ash, dust to dust." Those redwoods have long arms and huge hands. I hope that you have figured out that the last six or seven sentences are not literal. I am using hyperbole, and metaphors that are not meant to be taken literally, not once in a thousand years.

Well, let's get back to the main issue, the thousand-year millennial reign. This part of Revelation is really the only part that had me stumped as I began to acquire extra-biblical knowledge of history. As I have stated elsewhere, when scripture seems to contradict itself, man needs to go back and rethink what he perceives the meaning to be. When the scripture seems to contradict itself, the reader needs to parse much deeper into the word to get a true understanding of what is being communicated. Revelation begins with a "time" statement of when its hearers can expect *all of it to take place*, not in part. *"This is a revelation from Jesus Christ, which God gave him to show his servants the events that must soon take place. He sent an angel to present this revelation to his servant John"* (Revelation 1:1, NLT). John did not state that parts of this revelation must take place. All of these events are a package deal. This package is for "this generation," not ours, or one in the future. Other versions of the Bible use the words "shortly," "quickly," and "very soon." If it was to be two thousand years into their future, I believe Jesus would have told John to seal it up; the time is not near. However, that is not at all what He says.

God would not have His children to be schizophrenic for fifty generations. Daniel's prophecy, about 600 years prior to John's Revelation, was about the same event. Daniel was told to "seal the book, even to the time of the end." John was told not to seal up his book: *And he saith unto me, Seal not the sayings of the prophecy of this book: for the time is at hand"* (Revelation 22:10, KJV). Again, there is a time indicator here: "time is at hand." This is not John speaking here. This is Jesus speaking to John. *"He which testifieth these things saith,* (Jesus speaking)-*Surely I come quickly. Amen.* (John speaking)-*Even so, come, Lord Jesus"* (Revelation 22:20, KJV). Again He gives a time indicator: "quickly." These are the last words recorded in the scriptures of Jesus speaking to man. Surely His last statement to man that was to be recorded for all eternity is not a lie, and I am sorry, but in no way did Jesus mean that "I am not coming shortly, but in about 2,000 years. When I come, though, I will come quickly." I am sorry, little boys. Get out of the sandbox. Yes, people, there are those who preach this. They state that Jesus did not mean that He was coming soon, or shortly, but that when He does come it will be quickly. That sounds like a conversation with a three-year-old, do you not agree? I would love to know who the first to preach/teach this was. It sure has been parroted out of many pulpits today. It just goes to show that the teachings of man are a greater standard to many in the pulpits than is the standard of God's word.

John begins Revelation with a time indicator in the very first verse with the word "shortly", and he ends the book of Revelation with a time indicator in the next to last verse of Revelation. Jesus is speaking in the last use, and John is introducing in the beginning of Revelation the idea of "nearness" that was derived from all of Jesus' revelation about what was about to take place—soon, or as Jesus states in Revelation 22:20, "quickly." Read through Revelation and see how many time indicators there are. I promise you will find it interesting. It means what it says and says what it means. Otherwise, it is a lie and cannot be trusted. Trust the word. Do not trust one who says the word says something that it does not say. Flee from such as this.

All the time indicators reveal that a great event is about to happen. Near has always meant near. Shortly has always meant shortly, and quickly has always meant quickly. Now, the only times these words lose their meaning is when they are being spoken by a liar. By now, surely you have discerned that I base my life and beliefs on the Bible. I have found that it is the greatest source of wisdom there is. It affirms science in far more ways than the average atheist is willing to admit. It is historically, scientifically, geologically, and archeologically spot on. You know that you are a child of Gods' when all those "thou shalt nots" are recognized as a great blessing to life and not a hindrance.

I will now list the verses that contain the "millennial reign," as well as Satan being bound for a thousand years. We will then look at some other scriptures where "thousand" is used and allow scripture to interpret scripture. We do not get to pick and choose when something used in the same context gets changed to mean something else. That leads to a mis-understanding that can have a negative impact on an individual, as well as a whole culture, and even the world.

> And I saw an angel coming down out of heaven, having the key to the Abyss and holding in his hand a great chain. He seized the dragon, that ancient serpent, who is the devil, or Satan, and bound him for a thousand years. He threw him into the Abyss, and locked and sealed it over him, to keep him from deceiving the nations any-more until the thousand years were ended. After that, he must be set free for a short time.

> I saw thrones on which were seated those who had been given authority to judge. And I saw the souls of those who had been beheaded because of their testimony about Jesus and because of the word of God. They had not worshiped the beast or its image and had not received its mark on their foreheads or their hands. They came to life and reigned with Christ a thousand years. The rest of the dead did not come to life until the thousand years were ended. This is the first resurrection. Blessed and

holy are those who share in the first resurrection. The second death has no power over them, but they will be priests of God and of Christ and will reign with him for a thousand years. (Revelation 20:1–4, NIV)

Now, let's take a look at the time indicator that causes all the confusion, the "millennial reign" and Satan being bound a thousand years, as one and the same. Is there any other place in the Bible that speaks of this "millennial reign"? No, there is not. Revelation is the only place it is mentioned. Actually, there is never a mention of a "millennial reign," only the thousand years. There is only one other place in the KJV of the Bible where a "thousand years" is used in the New Testament. The way it is used, however, is not as a time indicator. It is used as a means to show totality, or completeness. Second Peter 3:8 (KJV) says, *"But, beloved, be not ignorant of this one thing, that one day is with the Lord as a thousand years, and a thousand years as one day."* Is "thousand years" in this verse being used as a time indicator? Nope. It is used as a hyperbole here, an exaggeration to create a strong impression but not meant to be taken literally. My interpretation of this verse has always been that God can do more in a day than man can in a thousand years. I dare say a literal interpretation would be that all of mankind, the 7 billion that now inhabit this world, and the gazillions that existed before, all put together, could not do in all their lifetimes combined the things that God can do in a thousandth of a second. This verse also gives the sense that God is out of the realm of time. Time does not affect Him one iota. God is not limited by time, but man is. Our lives in the here and now are limited by time. We shall all take our last breath here on Planet Earth one day and then the judgment. You will either rise or fall. You will not be in heaven waiting, for possibly thousands of years, for a judgment with half of your assets. If you make it to heaven, you have passed God's judgment. Each believer will be caught up in his own time upon death.

We will now look at some Old Testament verses where the "thousand years" is used in the same context as it is used in Revelation. Thousand is found 467 times in 353 verses of the Old Testament of the KJV. It is found fifty-four times in the New Testament KJV. We shall allow scripture to interpret scripture. The word of God is a far better interpreter of His word than man. The word of God is not biased, nor is it tainted with false end-time beliefs. The majority of times that it is used, it is used as a numerical value representing a number of people, such as soldiers. We

FOR SUCH A TIME AS THIS: LET MY PEOPLE Go

will use only the ones that are used to show not exactness, but a totality or completeness.

"And five of you shall chase an hundred, and an hundred of you shall put ten thousand to flight: and your enemies shall fall before you by the sword" (Leviticus 26:8, KJV). The speaker here is God. God has the children of Israel's back. Did God mean that if six chased one hundred and one, they would fail, or that if four chased a hundred that they would not be successful? Does this mean that ninety-nine will not put ten thousand to flight, or that 101 will not have success over 10,001? When God has your back, numbers mean nothing. God is communicating to the nation of Israel that He is with them. If they trust Him, all will go well. God could put to flight a hundred thousand or a million with one if he had a mind to. Just let the rumbling of an earthquake break forth or the fierceness of a tornado or hurricane. This would put gazillions to flight. Numbers are not mighty. God is Almighty.

"The LORD your God hath multiplied you, and, behold, ye are this day as the stars of heaven for multitude. (The LORD God of your fathers make you a thousand times so many more as ye are, and bless you, as he hath promised you)" (Deuteronomy 1:10–11, KJV). Moses is speaking to the children of Israel here. This was before they entered the Promised Land. Today most scientists agree that there are innumerable stars in the heavens. Some say that there are an estimated 70,000,000,000,000,000,000,000. That is a huge number. If the current population of earth was to grow each year by today's estimated rate of about 7 billion people, then in 6,000 years, you would have 42,000,000,000,000. There are ten less zeroes in the population using this figure than there are stars. We will use a conservative figure for the number of children that Moses led out of Egypt. We will assume that the men were adults and that the majority were married with children. Most had many more children back then than people have today. We will use a total figure of 900,000. If you multiply nine hundred thousand times a thousand you get 900,000,000. The number of Jews in the world today is estimated to be between thirteen million to sixteen million. So, the Jewish population will have to grow about sixty times what it is right now to attain to this saying of Moses. Hmmm, we are about 3,462 years away from Moses' statement, and we have only fifteen million Jews? I guess at this rate, we won't have to worry about a rapture in the next several thousand years. Well, if God is going to multiply the ones who He led out of Egypt, the Jews, by a thousand times the number that Moses was speaking to, we have a long way to go—if you are a literalist.

"Know therefore that the LORD thy God, he is God, the faithful God, which keepeth covenant and mercy with them that love him and keep his commandments to a thousand generations" (Deuteronomy 7:9, KJV). Does God annul His agreement with man after a thousand generations? If so, in about forty thousand years after you have been in heaven, you could get booted out. After all, His covenant is only good up to a thousand generations, which would be forty thousand years. Actually, if this were a literal statement then we still have over 36,000 years until God annuls the Old Covenant with the nation of Israel. If that is the case, then our generation has nothing to fear. The end is nowhere in sight, which means that all will still experience the wages of sin—death and "soul sleep." This would mean that Christ's sacrifice on the cross would have no effect until the Old Covenant is consummated and that which is better is brought in.

"And he found a new jawbone of an ass, and put forth his hand, and took it, and slew a thousand men therewith" (Judges 15:15, KJV). I heard a guy state to another after a fishing trip that he and his partner had caught a ton. Well, do you think that I took it literally? I asked a friend of mine how the ballgame went Friday night. He said "We killed them." Should I take him literally? If so, I should have called 911. This statement about Samson was not meant to be taken literally. It is a statement that indicates that he slew a great number and highly likely nowhere close to a thousand. I heard a young fellow ask one of his friends about how a basketball game had gone the night before. He states "We beat them by a thousand points." That must have been some game. How do you score a thousand points in thirty-two minutes? That's thirty one and a quarter points per minute.

> And the man said unto Joab, Though I should receive
> a thousand shekels of silver in mine hand, yet would
> I not put forth mine hand against the king's son: for in
> our hearing the king charged thee and Abishai and Ittai,
> saying, Beware that none touch the young man Absalom.
> (2 Samuel 18:12, KJV)

There is no way that you could hold a thousand shekels of silver in your hand. Think about a thousand pennies in your hand. A roll of pennies is only fifty cents. You cannot hold twenty rolls in your hand at one time, or even both hands. The weight would not be the issue. It would only weigh about five and a half pounds. It is obvious here that this is just a figure of speech that is not meant to be taken literally. It is just another

247

way to use "thousand" to show how committed this man was to King David's wish for none of his troops to lay a hand on his rebellious son, Absalom. They did not have to lay a hand on him. God would use the hands of an oak tree to snatch him off of his horse and hang him. Well, that is literally what happened. He went under an oak tree on his horse, obviously galloping, and was caught up by a limb and hanged.

"Be ye mindful always of his covenant; the word which he commanded to a thousand generations" (1 Chronicles 16:15, KJV). Ezra wrote here of an event which included King David delivering a psalm. If David is referring back to the statement made by Moses, then we are still about 36,000 years away from the end of the Old Covenant. Surely God would not end the world before His covenant is complete, would He? Well, the consummation was in AD 70. I guess He did end it before the thousandth generation. Otherwise, that which is inferior, the Old Covenant, is still in place and eternal life has not yet come.

"For every beast of the forest is mine, and the cattle upon a thousand hills" (Psalm 50:10, KJV). Does God just own the cattle of a thousand hills? Who owns the cattle that are on the 1001 hill, 1002, 1003, and so forth? This is not a figure that is used to place a numerical value on anything. It is used as a reference to completeness, totality. God owns the cattle of all the hills, be it a thousand, two thousand, ten thousand, or 10 gazillion. Again, thousand is used here to show a sense of completeness, or totality.

"For a day in your courts is better than a thousand elsewhere. I would rather be a doorkeeper in the house of my God than dwell in the tents of wickedness" (Psalm 84:10, ESV). What about that 1001 day? Will that day surpass the greatness of being in the courts of God? Is one day in the courts of God not better than ten thousand days elsewhere, or what about a million elsewhere? I believe that one day in the court of God is certainly better than 240 years in the courts of America. There is no justice here. The innocent are punished, and the evil are rewarded. Those who cannot determine correctly *the standard of justice* shall not harken the doors of heaven. That is why heaven will be heaven—no corruption is there.

"For a thousand years in thy sight are but as yesterday when it is past, and as a watch in the night" (Psalm 90:4, KJV). A thousand years in the sight of God is as a day. Basically, a thousand has no value to God. He is timeless. He is not bound by a twenty-four-hour cycle, a seven-day cycle, a thirty-day cycle, a 365-day cycle, an eighty-year cycle, nor any cycle that concerns time. He will be around forever. Those who choose Jesus as Messiah will experience about eighty years of life as we know

it and will enter eternity when you take your last breath in this life. At that point, life truly begins. That is when the chains that bind will truly be gone for all eternity. After a million years, there will be a gazillion more and then eternity.

"He hath remembered his covenant for ever, the word which he commanded to a thousand generations" (Psalm 105:8, KJV). If we believe in literalism, then I believe that we may have come up with the definition of "forever," or "eternity" here. It appears that the definition is forty thousand years. I guess that will be a great adventure like none we have ever taken before. The key, though, is that this would limit each individual to a forty-thousand-year term in heaven. I guess after spending three-quarters of a century in this life, that over 500 three-quarter centuries in heaven will feel like eternity. Is that all that we can expect? Well, only if you are a literalist. There is scripture in the New Testament that states that if you believe that something is sinful, yet you do it, it shall be accounted unto you as sin. Paul states this about such as God has not called sin, such as eating of certain types of meat, drinking certain things, and so on. In other words, don't call sin what God has not called sin. You could be judged for it. What if God decided that those who claim to be literalists should be held to the very nth degree of literalism? You may get kicked out of heaven after forty thousand years. Or what about those who believe the resurrection is in the future? What if He allows their souls to descend upon death and remain there for about forty thousand years? It would really be no big deal. When you awake you will still have eternity to look forward to. It will just be forty thousand years shorter. No big deal!

"Yea, though he live a thousand years twice told, yet hath he seen no good: do not all go to one place" (Ecclesiastes 6:6, KJV)? This is among the writings of Solomon. This is not a literal statement. Surely Solomon has seen some good in his lifetime. I would like to think that living a life of luxury such as Solomon lived that he would have had a different perspective on life. Actually, he was a realist. His life was far superior to most that have ever lived before, during, and after his life. Surely his children brought some joy into his life as they were learning to walk and talk. Yet, life is life.

During the OC era, all did go to the "one place." This was the grave, where all experienced the wages of sin, death—nonexistence. The difference under the NC is that the believer bypasses the wages of sin, the sting of death. There is no documentation of anyone ever living beyond 969 years of age. This was the age Methuselah reached. Just because there is no documentation of it, though, is not sufficient to declare that no man ever lived longer. There are many cultures that have existed that we have no written record of. I would love to know when the American Indians arrived on this continent and how they got here. Sadly, there is no documentation. If you are a Christian, you must know that they migrated here after the flood. When did the continents split? Was it during the flood, or post-flood? If post, then how long afterward? Was man upon all the land when the schism took place? If so, then it sure simplifies things. Otherwise, there were men far braver than Christopher Columbus out there.

Solomon is not being literal here. No matter how bad you perceive your life to have been, all is not doom and gloom and misery. Surely a life with just seventy-five years shall experience some joy. Solomon states here that after twenty-six lifetimes, no one should expect any good in this life. Well, I am sorry, but life isn't that bad. To have wisdom and knowledge is one thing. To make decisions based on that knowledge and wisdom is another. It is obvious that even the wise do not always make wise decisions. Solomon had 700 wives and 300 concubines (a secondary wife, usually of lower social rank; a cohabitator). It is hard enough to please oneself, much less attempt to please a thousand. The more the merrier just isn't true in this situation, particularly when it goes against the very word of God. That is the good thing about God's word. If it were a fairy tale, it would leave out facts that would diminish the character of its leading characters. The Bible includes all the flaws to show that all men are sinful, even the wise. A man after God's own heart is even capable of sin, Solomon's dad, King David.

If you read all the commentaries on Revelation 20:1–6, you will get many different opinions. Commentaries are nothing more than opinions. Do you value the opinions of men over the word of God? Some things we shall never know, as Paul states, *"whether there be knowledge, it shall vanish away"* (1 Corinthians 13:8, KJV). Paul makes this statement based on the reality of the consummation of the OC and the arrival of the New Covenant, *"that which is perfect . . ."* (1 Corinthians 13:10). We are about 1,985 years in the future from Jesus' death in AD 30 and 1,945 years from the destruction of Jerusalem and the temple in AD 70. Most professing Christians are aware of the AD 30 event, even though they may not be aware that it was in AD 30 and not AD 33 (no consensus among theologians and scholars). Most are not aware of what happened in AD 70 because it is not preached in the pulpits. If it is mentioned, it is glossed over as some minor event in history, even though it was the prophetic event that Jesus foretold containing the destruction of the temple and *"shall not be left one stone upon another, that shall not be thrown down"* (Luke 21:6, KJV).

> And I saw an angel come down from heaven, having the key of the bottomless pit and a great chain in his hand. And he laid hold on the dragon, that old serpent, which is the Devil, and Satan, and bound him a thousand years, And cast him into the bottomless pit, and shut him up, and set a seal upon him, that he should deceive the nations no more, until the thousand years should be fulfilled: and after that he must be loosed a little season.
> (Revelation 20:1–3, KJV)

There is no consensus on these verses. Some claim that the angel is Jesus. This may not even be a literal event. Does hades have a doorway that is opened by a key? Is Satan literally bound by a chain for a thousand years, or is his influence on humanity just limited for this timeframe? We shall never know in this life. Would it take God a thousand years to get His plan to line up, even though Jesus had stated *"This generation shall not pass until all these things be fulfilled"*? God had spent probably centuries lining things up for this event. He had placed kings (caesars) and nations into positions of power for such a time as this. All things were in place to fulfill the consummation of the OC and the reigning in of the NC, that which is perfect.

Nero was the Beast, or the representative of the Beast, which was the Roman Empire.

"For the mystery of lawlessness is already at work; only He who now restrains will do so until He is taken out of the way" (2 Thessalonians 2:7, NKJV). Israel was at peace with the Roman Empire until the time of Nero. Claudius was caesar before Nero. History reports that Claudius was poisoned by his wife and that Nero succeeded him as caesar. Some believe that Claudius was the one who restrained. I take no issue with that. Nero had no power until the restrainer had been taken out of the way. This occurred in AD 54. The Roman persecution of the church and Israel did not begin until AD 64. The Gospel of Jesus Christ had been allowed to go over all the Roman Empire until AD 64. Claudius believed in freedom of

religion. Up until AD 64, the major persecution that the church received was from among their non-Christian Jewish peers. After Rome burned, Nero began a horrendous persecution of the Christians. They were forbidden from entering Rome. Many would die over the next few years in the arena, some by beast and others by the sword. Many would be used as torches at night to light the streets of Rome. The "restrained" had been loosed. Hmmm—that sounds like hell on earth, the Great Tribulation. It appears that Satan must have been released for a little while.

> And I saw thrones, and they sat on them, and judgment was committed to them. Then I saw the souls of those who had been beheaded for their witness to Jesus and for the word of God, who had not worshiped the beast or his image, and had not received his mark on their foreheads or on their hands. And they lived and reigned with Christ for a thousand years. (Revelation 20:4, NKJV)

There are some who believe that this was literally the living Christians who reigned on earth as Christ's agents doing His will, but the scripture states that the beheaded came to life and reigned with Jesus. It appears that there was a resurrection prior to AD 70. When did it occur? Was it a one-time event or an on-going event, rising at death? Heaven knows. We shall never know until we get there, but I do have my opinion. The living were reigning on this earth, doing the will of Jesus the King, and the dead in Christ were resurrected. This would only be those who died as martyrs for the name of Jesus. The Old Testament saints would not have been resurrected at this time. It was to come shortly, in a few years, at the consummation date of the OC in AD 70.

> But the rest of the dead did not live again until the thousand years were finished. This is the first resurrection. Blessed and holy is he who has part in the first resurrection. Over such the second death has no power, but they shall be priests of God and of Christ, and shall reign with Him a thousand years. (Revelation 20:5–6, NKJV)

Those in Christ that were killed for His namesake were accounted as righteous. They got to view the judgment of Israel from the vantage point of heaven. The balance of the dead of all times past would not be judged until the consummation was fulfilled. At that point, death would lose its sting. The sacrificial blood of the Lamb would forevermore wash the sins away from the repentant sinner and allow immediate entry into heaven upon our last breath here in this life. The old saints, prophets, patriots, and so forth had to undergo judgment after the consummation or just prior to the consummation. This was the time of determination for all souls who experienced death prior to Jesus' advent. To die after this event and into eternity would mean to literally experience the wages of sin for all time. If you do not experience death, then you are in heaven. The wages of sin is death. The wages of surrender to Christ is life eternal in heaven, yet these fleshly bodies must die. After the apostles experienced martyrs' deaths, as well as their proselytes, they had the opportunity of a lifetime to be priests of God and Jesus in heaven until the appointed time of the end of the OC. They were the very elect of God. As stated earlier, we shall not know if this was a one-time event or an ongoing resurrection upon death in the pre-AD 70 era. They would reign with Him not a thousand years literally, but until the time had been fulfilled. They are probably doing whatever man is expected to do in heaven for all eternity now.

"Now when the thousand years have expired, Satan will be released from his prison" (Revelation 20:7, NKJV). Was this when Nero declared persecution against the Christians in AD 64? Obviously we will never know the exact date or time. We can be assured of one thing, however, because Jesus said it. "This generation shall not pass . . ." I cannot give you the day or the hour, but I can state with much certainty that it occurred after Jesus' birth and prior to AD 70.

Now, for the literalist out there, if there are any left, I will advance another view that I have never heard mentioned before by anyone. If you do your research you will find that the name *Satan* is mentioned nineteen times in the Old Testament KJV of the Bible. Satan is mentioned by that name thirty-six times in the New Testament of the KJV of the Bible. *Lucifer* is mentioned only once in the KJV of the Bible and it is in Isaiah in the Old Testament. *Serpent* is mentioned thirty times in the Old Testament version of the KJV and eight times in the New Testament. *Beelzebub* is mentioned only seven times in the KJV, and all are in the New Testament. *Dragon* is used as a representative of Satan only three times in the KJV of the Old Testament, and one of these is questionable. Of the thirteen times dragon is used in the KJV of the New Testament, only eight or nine are a direct reference to Satan. *Devil* is not used in the KJV of the Old Testament but occurs sixty-one times in the KJV of the New Testament. *Accuser* is used only once in the New Testament of the

KJV. All of these instances are not in direct reference of Satan. Dragon is used interchangeably as Satan, as well as a beast of the earth. After whittling it down, it appears that there is mention of Satan, using these various names, fifty-two times in the KJV of the Old Testament, which has 987 pages in the Gideon hotel/motel version. He is mentioned 121 times in the KJV of the New Testament, which contains only 300 pages in the Gideon Bible. Of the 173 times that Satan is mentioned in the Bible, 69.942 percent are in the New Testament. The New Testament contains only 23.23 percent of the pages in the Bible. So, it appears that Satan was let loose when Messiah was on the scene. Of course, many of the New Testament mentions are repeats because they are documenting the same accounts in the gospels. Still, the Old Testament of the Bible covers a period of just under 4,000 years, and the New Testament covers a period of time from the birth of Jesus to about AD 64, when the last scriptures were written. All that Jesus prophesied, which was the same that all the Old Testament prophets prophesied that had not yet been fulfilled, was fulfilled between Jesus' birth and the destruction of the temple in AD 70. Why do I have this belief? Because Jesus stated that *"This generation shall not pass until all these things be fulfilled."* I am sorry, but Jesus is my standard. He was not confused about who this generation was, nor am I. He may not have known the day or hour, but He knew the generation. The temple was still standing when Jesus made His prophetic statement about the temple being destroyed. The temple was still standing when John wrote the book of Revelation. I will allow common sense and the words of Jesus to guide me on this issue. Was the temple to be destroyed twice, yet Jesus made no mention of it? No, He pointed to the then-standing temple and was speaking of it and only it, not a future temple. Otherwise, He would have stated "This temple will be destroyed during this generation, in about forty years, but this is not the sign. It will be rebuilt two millennia in the future, and that is the one I am speaking of. Not this one. Do not be confused." Now, why is there so much confusion? Because the teachings of man have become the standard for all men, even the ones in the pulpit. Let's take a much closer look at this.

I am sure that there are a few more times that Satan is mentioned in the Bible under different names or terms, but this is sufficient to make the point. Satan is mentioned fifty-two times in the Old Testament timeframe of the Bible, which covers just under 4,000 years. He is mentioned 121 times in the New Testament, which covers less than seventy-five years. The term *demon* is not used in the KJV of the Bible. It uses the term *devils* for demons. In the Old Testament, every time that devils is used, which is only four times, it is in reference to false gods or idols in the KJV. The term is used fifty-one times in the New Testament, and over 90 percent of them are references to demons or their master. This could be a study in itself, another book and much time. Why does it seem that the activity of Satan and his minions had increased all of a sudden? Had he been bound for a thousand years until Jesus arrived? Well, Messiah was born in the beginning of this epoch of time, 3–5 BC to AD 70. If Messiah was going to crush the head of the serpent, then that old serpent had best get at it!

The last encounter Satan had with man documented in the scriptures prior to Jesus' birth is in First Chronicles 21:1, KJV: *"And Satan stood up against Israel, and provoked David to number Israel."* David reigned as king from 1010–970 BC. All sources vary on an exact date. This encounter was obviously before 970 BC. The next time Satan is documented in the scriptures is in Zechariah. Zechariah states that the word of the Lord came to him in the second year of the reign of King Darius, which ruled over Persia. This would have been in the year circa 520 BC.

"And he shewed me Joshua the high priest standing before the angel of the LORD, and Satan standing at his right hand to resist him" (Zechariah 3:1, KJV). This encounter is not an earthly event. It appears that it is in heaven before the throne of God. We know from the writings of John that no man had ever gone to heaven at the time he penned this declaration from Jesus. This would relegate this encounter to a vision and not an actual encounter. This being the case, we can eliminate this encounter with Satan.

Isaiah mentions an encounter with Satan within the last millennium BC within the KJV. Again, it is not a real encounter, but a revelation, or vision, from God. The serpent as being referenced as Satan is used by Isaiah in the following: *"In that day the LORD with his sore and great and strong sword shall punish leviathan the piercing serpent, even leviathan that crooked serpent; and he shall slay the dragon that is in the sea"* (Isaiah 27:1, KJV). This is not an earthly event here, but is a prophecy about the forthcoming consummation event that was to take place in AD 70. For other "serpent" encounters with reference to Satan you have to go all the way back to Genesis because the balance has no reference to Satan. The encounters with a "dragon" that are listed in the Old Testament are spurious at best. I believe that if you really parse through the six mentions of dragon, you will come to the conclusion that none are a direct reference to Satan. Of the thirteen times *dragon* is used in the KJV of the New Testament, ten of them are in direct reference to Satan.

Now, to the point; the last documented encounter that a human being had with Satan was when he enticed David into taking a census. This would have been between 1010 and 970 BC. There are no other earthly encounters documented in the scriptures, until Jesus shows up a thousand years later. Actually, the next time Satan is mentioned is when Jesus went into the wilderness to be tempted of the devil. This was right after He was baptized by John the Baptist and prior to the beginning of His earthly ministry. He had no apostles yet. He was probably in his late twenties, but there is no consensus as to His age when he was crucified. He was between the ages of thirty-three and thirty-eight. This would have put the last documented advent of Satan on the earth at about 1,000 years prior to this encounter, give or take. Hmmm—could this be the time that Satan was bound for a thousand years? Of course, just because there is no documentation about the whereabouts of Satan for over a thousand years does not necessarily mean that he was not active. But why all of the inactivity, and then all of a sudden it appears that the doors were blown off? Demonic possession went through the roof. I cannot think of a single demonic possession that is mentioned in the Old Testament. This was the appointed time for Messiah. It would be the time if you were His enemy to bring all of your minions to the battlefield and let the battle begin. If you must have a literal thousand-year binding of Satan, it appears that this could have been it.

I am a human being and am far from perfect. I am also an evolutionist. I evolve each time I read the scriptures. I evolve as a person, not as a specie. We need more evolution in the church, but we need to get it out of the classrooms. If God is not perfect, then He is not God. There is plenty of evidence out there that refutes evolution, as I am revealing information that refutes these "end-times" doomsday sayers. Scientists need to reveal the lies and fiddling going on within the scientific community today. You will be judged accordingly. You will rise or fall when you take your last breath in this life.

I have used many verses to attempt to show that "thousand" is not to be taken literally, but as symbolism for completeness or fullness of time. Some may state that I am dead wrong here. Well, let's allow *the standard*, scripture, to inform us of truth and not the opinions of man. *"But when the fullness of the time was come, God sent forth his Son, made of a woman, made under the law, To redeem them that were under the law, that we might receive the adoption of sons"* (Galatians 4:4–5, KJV). It is obvious that the fullness of time had come. It was this generation that would experience the consummation of the Old Covenant and the penalty for having killed the prophets of the past, as well as Jesus, Messiah. This "fullness" is what was represented by the "thousand years" and the "seven seventies" in Daniel. It was not literal. It was always about the fullness of time appointed by God.

Back to my point. As I research and study, my views change and evolve. One thing that is absolutely irrefutable, though, is that the "end times," the "day of the Lord," "day of wrath," prophesied by the Old Testament prophets, John the Revelator, and Jesus, has come and gone. It isn't in our future. I would have to become a devolutionist to backslide to this fatal ignorant view. Ignorance is a lack of information or knowledge about certain subjects. It is my desire to be as Christ has made me to be, an enlightener. The thousand-year reign was not literal. Thousand in their lingo meant fullness of time or completeness. We have idioms and such in our current language that could stump future generations if they had no knowledge of such. Language differences and symbolism can wreak havoc when a foreigner is attempting to comprehend the writings of another culture. As I showed elsewhere, I have never lived in a pepper and my missionary friend does not live in a cherry tree, but if you were not familiar with the terms being names of towns, you would think just that using an online interpreter.

I hope that you come away from this session more enlightened to the language and symbolism used in the ancient Greek and Hebrew cultures. We are just as colorful today in all cultures of the world with symbolism and idioms. Unless you have spent time in a foreign culture, you will not truly comprehend this one hundred percent. What is critical for man to understand today is that the end is nowhere in sight. God has given the believers, the leaves on the Tree of Life, the mandate to heal the nations and bring peace upon this world. We aren't even a quarter of the way there yet. It is time to blast the past and change the future!

A New Heaven and a New Earth

After the millennial reign of Christ and the thousand years binding of Satan are over with, what's next?

> And when the thousand years are ended, Satan will be released from his prison and will come out to deceive the nations that are at the four corners of the earth, Gog and Magog, to gather them for battle; their number is like the sand of the sea. And they marched up over the broad plain of the earth and surrounded the camp of the saints and the beloved city, but fire came down from heaven and consumed them, and the devil who had deceived them was thrown into the lake of fire and sulfur where the beast and the false prophet were, and they will be tormented day and night forever and ever.
>
> (Revelation 20:7–10, ESV)

The likelihood that we will ever know who are all the characters and nations involved in the book of Revelation is a longshot at best. These events were "shortly" to take place. They are far in our past, about one thousand, nine hundred, and forty-six years. The information may be available, but it would be an immense, time-consuming project. A thousand years may be as a day to the Lord, but God communicates to man in terms that are relevant and comprehendible. Revelation is a revealing, not a hiding. It is not an attempt to hide from man but to reveal to man. It was not meant to reveal to us, but to the first-century church. God would not have told man that it was "at hand," "this generation," "shortly," and so on if He had meant a people fifty generations into the future. Moses was considered one of the "Ancient Fathers" to the generation that Jesus lived in. Moses wrote the Pentateuch (Genesis, Exodus,

Leviticus, Numbers, and Deuteronomy) between circa 1391–1271 BC, but there is no consensus on these dates. This would have been about thirty-five generations before the generation that would face the wrath of God in AD 70. The Pilgrims landed on Plymouth Rock in 1620, a mere ten generations ago and we already have "scholars" and liberals rewriting the historicity of this event and even of this nation. My main point about this is that we do not even have a firm grip on our own history from ten generations ago. How can we ever expect to totally understand events and characters involved in those events close to two thousand years ago? We see history being revised around us in the United States right now. Characters who were once villains to this nation are becoming heroes to the university faculty and secular media. Also, time is bearing out that men we thought were righteous men just a few years ago are being revealed to be seedy characters. Time will tell. I wonder what people in ten generations will think about this generation when they read *The Late Great Planet Earth*, *Left Behind*, *Four Blood Moons: Something is About to Change*, *The Harbinger*, and so on. I believe they will have much to say about this generation, and this isn't the generation that Jesus lived in. Do you reckon "that generation" four hundred years from now will mistake our generation for their generation? It is food for thought.

The scripture referenced at the beginning of this section shows that Satan has been put down. It mentions Gog and Magog. Magog was a territory or nation that is now within present-day Turkey. There is history that reveals that Alexander the Great had dealings with Gog and Magog. The Alexandrian Empire was the third beast mentioned in Daniel, which existed in the latter years of the 300s BC. Alexander died in 323 BC, a month before his thirty-fifth birthday. Man is evil enough on his own, but he always wants to blame Satan when things go wrong. If you will, open your Bible and read the account of Cain and Abel. You will see that there is no mention of Satan or the Devil. Cain did not need the influence of Satan to become a murderer. Do you need the influence of Satan to become a liar, a thief, a fornicator, an adulterer, or other? Sorry, but I believe the word of God over the teachings of man.

> And the LORD smelled a sweet savour; and the LORD said in his heart, I will not again curse the ground any more for man's sake; for the imagination of man's heart is evil from his youth; neither will I again smite any more every thing living, as I have done. (Genesis 8:21, KJV)

> For the children of Israel and the children of Judah have only done evil before me from their youth: for the children of Israel have only provoked me to anger with the work of their hands, saith the LORD.
>
> (Jeremiah 32:30, KJV)

There is no mention of Satan in either of these two verses. It speaks of the evil of man without the influence of Satan. Man likes to play the blame-game with Satan. The sins of man were not accounted to Satan. The sins of man will be accounted to the perpetrator. I am responsible for my sin. I am also responsible for my ignorance. It is up to me to educate myself to the teachings of God as a man. It is up to parents to teach their children about the ways and will of God. If they fail to do so, they will be held accountable. The degenerate will produce the degenerate.

Okay, back to the Revelation 20:7–10 scripture introduced at the beginning of this section. Satan was put down. What is the next grand event mentioned in God's word? The great white throne judgment (Not capitalized in any verson).

> Then I saw a great white throne and him who was seated on it. From his presence earth and sky fled away, and no place was found for them. And I saw the dead, great and small, standing before the throne, and books were opened. Then another book was opened, which is the book of life. And the dead were judged by what was written in the books, according to what they had done. And the sea gave up the dead who were in it, Death and Hades gave up the dead who were in them, and they were judged, each one of them, according to what they had done. Then Death and Hades were thrown into the lake of fire. This is the second death, the lake of fire. And if anyone's name was not found written in the book of life, he was thrown into the lake of fire.
>
> (Revelation 20:11–15, ESV)

One fact that should jump out at the astute here should be the "living" or the lack of the "living." There are no living involved in the great white throne judgment. Why? Well, this involves the resurrection of those under the Old Covenant. The great white throne judgment was for the dead only. It is not for the living. Those who had died before the NTC had begun were under the law. They had to be judged by the law. The wages for sin was death, and it still is. The key was Messiah. What all did this entail? Well, I was not there. We will never know what all took place at the white throne judgment. If your name was written in the Book of Life, you were spared eternal damnation. It says nothing of the living here. What happens to the living? Hmmm—that would include you and me today. It would have also included John, the Revelator, as well as all the others that accepted Jesus as Messiah during the lifetime ministry of Jesus and also lived beyond the consummation of the OTC in AD 70. We are experiencing it in the here and now. Yet, what was the next event recorded in Revelation?

> Then I saw a new heaven and a new earth, for the first heaven and the first earth had passed away, and the sea was no more. And I saw the holy city, new Jerusalem, coming down out of heaven from God, prepared as a bride adorned for her husband. And I heard a loud voice from the throne saying, "Behold, the dwelling place of God is with man. He will dwell with them, and they will be his people, and God himself will be with them as their God. He will wipe away every tear from their eyes, and death shall be no more, neither shall there be mourning, nor crying, nor pain anymore, for the former things have passed away."
>
> And he who was seated on the throne said, "Behold, I am making all things new." Also he said, "Write this down, for these words are trustworthy and true." And he said to me, "It is done. I am the Alpha and the Omega, the beginning and the end. To the thirsty I will give from the spring of the water of life without payment. The one who conquers will have this heritage, and I will be his God and he will be my son. But as for the cowardly, the faithless, the detestable, as for murderers, the sexually immoral, sorcerers, idolaters, and all liars, their portion will be in the lake that burns with fire and sulfur, which is the second death." (Revelation 21:1–8, ESV)

The next event was the new heaven and new earth. Is this to be paradise on earth, a utopian society? Well, God makes his dwelling place with man. He no longer abides in a temple. Our bodies have become the temple for the Spirit of God. *"Do you not know that you are a temple of God and that the Spirit of God dwells in you"* (1 Corinthians 3:1, NASB)? The church building is not the temple of God. God's presence was in the temple of Jerusalem until the death of Christ. He abandoned the temple when the veil was torn. Still, the OTC was not yet consummated upon Jesus' death. The children of Israel were given forty years to repent and trust that Jesus was the prophesied Messiah. If we truly understood the word of God and all that had transpired, we may never shed another tear. I imagine when you hammer that fingernail or drop that weighty item on your toe that you just may shed a few tears. This is not literal. It is figurative. God is in our midst in the here and now. We do not mourn at funerals as if we will never see our Christian loved ones again. We grieve for the loss, but we do not mourn as if we shall never encounter them for all eternity. Death has lost its sting for the believer. The believer shall rise upon death of this corruptible body to eternal life and the nonbeliever shall descend to sheol, hades. The former things have passed away. The old heaven that would not allow the presence of humanity and the old earth that consumed the body of all dead, pagan, as well as believer, has passed away. Jesus was the first being that occupied human flesh to enter heaven, yet flesh and blood did not enter heaven, contrary to what many say today; *"Now this I say, brethren, that flesh and blood cannot inherit the kingdom of God; neither doth corruption inherit incorruption"* (1 Corinthians 15:50, KJV). The fleshly body is referred to here as the corruptible, as well as in other places in the scriptures. The term actually means a body that is capable of rotting. Heaven is incorruptible and only glorified, non-fleshly bodies will be among the inhabitants of heaven. Jesus was the first and the last. Jesus was the first that ever adorned human flesh to enter the kingdom of God and the last saint that would have to experience the penalty for sin: "soul sleep." Actually, he was the representative of the last. Still, any that died before the first resurrection had to experience death. This involved only the first-century believers who died for Jesus' name and sake. From that time and forevermore, He will be there to give water to those who thirst after Him without pay. Hmmm—makes one think.

Was He speaking about literal water when He met the woman at the well? He spoke of "living water," the very thing He is speaking of here. No, it was not literal H_2O. The heritage that would be from this point on would be those who are in a right relationship with God, those who have bowed the knee to Jesus. He will be their God, and their lives will reflect it. When they take their last breath here in this life, they will take their next in heaven, in the presence of God and Jesus forevermore. That is why the living are not mentioned in the great white throne judgment. It was not for the living. It was for the dead only. The living are judged upon death. You either rise or fall. That is your judgment.

"For, behold, I create new heavens and a new earth: and the former shall not be remembered, nor come into mind" (Isaiah 65:17, KJV). Isaiah had prophesied of the new heaven and new earth about 800 years prior to the consummation of the Old Covenant. It is amazing to me that regardless of whether these end-times doomsday sayers realize it or not, they are still awaiting the new heaven and earth today. They are basically living their lives as if Jesus did not actually come and do what He claimed to do. He was to usher in the New. The Old had to pass, but it was still a generation after His death and ascension before the new earth and heaven came, which was the New Covenant that did away with death for the repentant believer and gave the Gentile nations access to His kingdom. If you are a victim of the end-times heresy going on today, then you must not believe that Jesus did away with the Old yet. Sorry, but that is part and parcel with this heresy. Whether they realize it or not, they are proclaiming that the old heaven and earth are still in effect, which is the Old Covenant.

"In that he saith, a new covenant, he hath made the first old. Now that which decayeth and waxeth old is ready to vanish away" (Hebrews 8:13, KJV). We have looked at this verse in another section, but it is very relevant here. Actually it is imminent. The book of Hebrews was written prior to AD 64, as the Roman persecution had not yet begun, yet the Old Covenant was still in place. It "decayeth and waxeth old," but it still reigned. The prophesied "end" was still in the future at this time, but it was on the horizon. What Isaiah had prophesied was coming to fruition. Isaiah also prophesied the birth of Messiah. I dare say that the birth of Messiah had everything to do with "out with the old and in with the new." Those who were loyal and faithful to God knew what it was about. They had to go through sheol on this earth, but what peace they had afterward.

"Heaven and earth shall pass away, but my words shall not pass away. But of that day and hour knoweth no man, no, not the angels of heaven, but my Father only. But as the days of Noe were, so shall also the coming of the Son of man be" (Matthew 24:35, KJV). Many people misinterpret this verse. In no way is this verse stating that heaven and earth will pass away. If earth passed away, mankind would have no dwelling place. If heaven passes away, the angels, Jesus, and God would have no dwelling place. The Kingdom of heaven is His dwelling place. We have shown in

other places where these terms are also used as the OC system that the nation of Israel was under, that went back to the days of Abraham. The passing was on the horizon but was not yet history. You can rest assured that it is history now. Otherwise, the repentant believers today shall have to spend an unknowable length of time in the grave in a state of "soul sleep." I thought that we lived under a new and better covenant. Well, for those who do not believe that this prophesied event is in our past, they are saying that it is not finished. It was finished on the cross, but God gave sinful Israel, the Great Harlot, Mystery Babylon, forty years to get right with their Maker.

We are experiencing the new heaven and earth now. Yet, we still have cowards, the faithless, the detestable, murderers, the sexually immoral, sorcerers, idolaters, and liars. These will not pass judgment. Upon death they will descend to sheol, or hades. That is their judgment. The repentant shall rise upon death, and the unrepentant shall descend. This is the state of things now. Will it go on forever? Well, there is much scripture that states that it shall. The verses that state this state it in a literal fashion.

> His name shall endure for ever: his name shall be continued as long as the sun: and men shall be blessed in him: all nations shall call him blessed. Blessed be the LORD God, the God of Israel, who only doeth wondrous things. And blessed be his glorious name for ever: and let the whole earth be filled with his glory; Amen, and Amen. (Psalm 72:17–19, KJV)

If His name is to continue as long as the sun, well, I would be satisfied with 4.5 billion years more of life either here, or in heaven, preferably heaven, with my glorified, non-fleshly body. As stated elsewhere, evolutionists claim that the sun has enough energy to last at least this length of time. I believe that David had the impression that the sun would last forever. I believe that God maintains all, and "everything is as it always was," uniformitarianism, is hogwash. I know that He is in control and that eternal life is everlasting. I also do not believe that heaven will be made up of nations. We will be one people of God and not separated by nation. Heaven will be about unity and not division. The world is divided by nations, which is division. We have man to thank for this because of the fall of man. If all the wicked were under one nation, woe be unto that people.

"And he built his sanctuary like high palaces, like the earth which he hath established for ever" (Psalm 78:69, KJV). We can also look at

this from another angle, the contradiction issue. Does the Bible contradict itself? If so, we need to readjust our perception of the contradictions. What we have is a bad translation or a faulty understanding. We know that Jesus stated that His kingdom is not of this world nor was it by observation. You cannot see it from an earthly vantage point because it is not earthly but heavenly. Has the earth been established forever? Is this literal? It will take many more millennia to gander a guess. The moon and sun shall continue to give light, and the stars shall never fall into the earth. If one star were to hit earth, there would be nothing left, probably not even a speck of dust. The smallest star would be larger than the earth. The moon shall never turn to blood. Men have taken figurative Old Testament apocalyptic language and have preached it as fact today. I am sorry, but as Hank Hanegraaff of the Christian Research Institute would say, such teaching should make your "baloney meter" go off the charts. I tell you this today, my baloney meter has been recalibrated and the teachings of man are no longer my standard. God's word is my standard.

"Who laid the foundations of the earth, that it should not be removed for ever" (Psalm 104:5, KJV). We know that God laid the foundations of the earth. This verse is not asking a question but making a statement. Knowing that God made a statement that He would never destroy life on this earth again with a flood, and knowing that He poured out His judgment on apostate Israel in AD 70, well, I just don't see Him literally destroying this world and its inhabitants again. The inhabitants of this earth may destroy each other. That could happen. Man does not need the influence of Satan to do evil things. Atheism has killed far more people over the last 120 years than all the religions combined. Also, a false understanding about the "end times" can even make a Christian do things that God will condemn as sin. Ignorance is not an excuse with God. *"Therefore shall ye lay up these my words in your heart and in your soul, and bind them for a sign upon your hand, that they may be as frontlets between your eyes"* (Deuteronomy 11:18, KJV). Ignorance of the word of God has never been an excuse that was acceptable by Him. Write the words upon your heart.

> And I saw no temple in the city, for its temple is the Lord God the Almighty and the Lamb. And the city has no need of sun or moon to shine on it, for the glory of God gives it light, and its lamp is the Lamb. By its light will the nations walk, and the kings of the earth will bring their glory into it, and its gates will never be shut by

day—and there will be no night there. They will bring
into it the glory and the honor of the nations. But nothing
unclean will ever enter it, nor anyone who does what is
detestable or false, but only those who are written in the
Lamb's book of life. (Revelation 21:22–27, ESV)

The verses from between Revelation 21:8 and 21:21 goes into great detail describing the holy city. Is this describing a literal city? Is this the heavenly city, or is this an earthly city? Is it really even a city? I do know this. It is by His light that I see all things. After all of this metaphorical, hyperbolic, symbolic language is ended at verse 21, we see that the city has no temple in it. Where does God dwell now on Planet Earth? He abides in the believer. He is the Light of the world. We have no need for light anymore. The gates of the heavenly city are open now. Do we have access to the holy city now? Can we go back and forth? The holy city is open to all believers who make a genuine confession of faith in Jesus as Messiah. It is a one-way street into the holy city. People are entering the city but not leaving it. It is the eternal destination for the ones who have glorified God and honored Him. Take notice here that in verse 27 that the unclean and the ones who do what is detestable, or false, are still living. I could take several more months and go through the scriptures and compile a list of all things that are detestable to God. I could also work up a list of things that are false to God. We know that there are no more prophets at this point because that which is perfect has come. Those who pretend to be prophets today and those who profess that God has two people and two plans will be deemed false and not true, maintaining a lie that is detestable to God.

This is the time that we live in today. What I have stated in this compilation is not prophetic. It is what is in the word of God. There are no more prophets today. There are also no more "tongue speakers" today, as there were back then. Yes, there are many different languages out there, but until you go into another nation and comprehend their languages without knowledge of their language, do not declare that you are more spiritual than any other. This is a detestable abomination to God. God is not a god of division. He is not a God of denomination. He is the God of one people, the ones who choose Him and make Him the center of their lives, and not self. Do not allow yourself to be played upon and manipulated by crowd dynamics.

Any religion that came on the scene after AD 70 that claims to have prophets is an abomination to God. It is detestable and a false religion, denomination, or cult. That is not my opinion. Those are the facts based on knowledge of His word. God's word says to test it. There are religions, sects, and cults out there that discourage their followers from reading or researching material outside of their beliefs. God's word says to test it, and know that it is truth. As I have stated before, all of those "thou shalt nots" I have tested, to my own demise. They are there for our best interest. They are truly not a burden, but a delight. They keep one from much misery.

"But we have renounced disgraceful, underhanded ways. We refuse to practice cunning or to tamper with God's word, but by the open statement of the truth we would commend ourselves to everyone's conscience in the sight of God" (2 Corinthians 4:2, ESV). Many have tampered with God's word and bowed and twisted it to mean whatever they want it to mean. As I have documented elsewhere in this endeavor, Hal Lindsey declared that the following verse is Israel becoming a nation again in 1948: *"Now learn a parable of the fig tree; When his branch is yet tender, and putteth forth leaves, ye know that summer is nigh"* (Matthew 24:32, KJV). Well, Lindsey predicted that the rapture would take place and the tribulation based on the 1948 date of Israel becoming a nation again. Based on his view of a false "Rapture Theory," 1981 would have been the year of the rapture, and 1988 would have been the end of the world. Heck, I missed both. Actually, the scriptures talk about a three and a half year tribulation, not seven years. Do your biblical research and you will find that there is no mention of a seven-year tribulation. It does speak about a three and a half year ordeal, but we can tie that in with Nero's persecution that began in AD 64 and ended in 68 AD, when he committed suicide. It would be quite the undertaking, but attempt to do a study on biblical commentaries dated prior to Hal Lindsey's book, *The Late Great Planet Earth*, which was published in 1970. I believe you will discover that most, if not all commentaries dated prior to 1970 give a totally different perspective to Jesus' teaching about the fig tree. After Lindsey paraded his interpretation before the world, well, the number of commentaries written after this heresy that spout out the same thing is amazing. All those commentators have allowed the teachings of Hal Lindsey to become their standard and not the word of God. Lindsey could have been subjected to this false teaching while in seminary. It may not have originated with him, but he sure touted it and popularized it to the point that it is more biblical than scripture today.

The end of the world is not near. The end of your life may be near. Set the word of God as your standard, and you will be enlightened to His truths, and you will be lightened of the burdens of false teachings and prophecies. Do not get bogged down in false end-times teachings. If you are going to walk on water for your Father who art in heaven, you must rise up out of the mire and muck of end-times teachings. The "end" has passed. We are in a new era of time. The prophesied "end" was the consummation of the OTC, not the end of the world. The only end the believer will experience will be the end of his time on earth, which as of late, has become somewhat of a prison sentence for the believer. Do not fret, though. There will be none of the following in heaven: *"Outside the city are the dogs—the sorcerers, the sexually immoral, the murderers, the idol worshipers, and all who love to live a lie"* (Revelation 22:15, NLT). Those who will not bow the knee to Messiah in this life will not be in heaven because paradise will not allow such dogs. That is not my opinion; it is God's word.

I hope that this section has at least opened the eyes of a few hearts that are truly seeking knowledge and wisdom from the scriptures. No, I do not understand every event that took place at the end of the OC era. I certainly do not know who every character was, but I do know that "this generation" has come to pass. It is almost two millennia in our past. The majority that read this will likely take issue with it because it does not line up with the teaching of their favorite pulpit preacher, radio preacher, or televangelist. Fret not. It lines up with what the word of God says, and extra-biblical sources affirm the truth of history prophesied in Revelation, Daniel, Matthew, and so on. What is your standard? It could determine your final destination, as well as your rewards in heaven.

The major point that I hope to have made with this chapter is that even after the new heaven and earth have come, there is still no paradise here on earth. There are still liars, cheats, and thieves. There are still the sexually immoral, murderers, and so forth living in the new earth. The following verse precedes the "new heaven and earth" verse in a chronological fashion: *"And God shall wipe away all tears from their eyes; and there shall be no more death, neither sorrow, nor crying, neither shall there be any more pain: for the former things are passed away"* (Revelation 21:4, KJV). The above description is prior to the Revelation 22:15 verse. Even after *"no more death, neither sorrow, nor crying, neither shall there be any more pain"* there are still *"dogs—the sorcerers, the sexually immoral, the murderers, the idol worshipers, and all who love to live a lie."* What do you think about this? Is this your idea of a new heaven and earth? Well, it states that *"Outside the city are the dogs."* The city it is referencing is not of this earth. His kingdom is heaven. "Outside the city" is earth. All of this symbolic language is used in a fashion that the first-century hearers would not have taken it literally.

We will probably never comprehend even all the Psalms because there is much imagery used in them. I have learned to see through much of the imagery that the people and culture of that day used. It certainly enhances the scriptures. We are living in the new heaven and earth now. We have access to heaven now. No man had access to heaven until the first resurrection prior to AD 70 and not at Jesus' crucifixion. The saints of God no longer have to "bite the dust" before entering heaven. The new heaven and earth are in the here and now, and this earth will always have dogs, the unrepentant sinners, upon it. It is God's desire, though, that the leaves on the Tree of Life would bring healing to the world. The leaves on the Tree of Life are the repentant believers. Those who think that God has two peoples and two plans are not attached to the Tree of Life. They are deceived by their imaginations. If their plans considered the plans of God, there would be no schism in the church today. They have their own plans, and God is excluded. God despises double standards. Double standards will separate you from God for all eternity. God's standard needs to become man's standard. That standard leads to life everlasting that begins in this life on this earth.

The new heavens and new earth are not literal. This is symbolic language that is used to convey the passing of the Old Covenant and the bringing in of the New Covenant, the superior covenant. We will rehash some verses here that we used within this section that are all speaking of the same thing. Isaiah prophesies about this coming event around 750 years prior to the birth of Messiah and about 820 years before the realization of the New Covenant in AD 70. Jesus spoke of the passing of the Old Covenant around forty to forty-three years prior to the AD 70 event. The writer of Hebrews mentions the passing of the Old Covenant as if it is in their very near future. Some scholars date the writing of Hebrews around 64–65 AD, which was five to six years from the consummation of the Old Covenant. I believe it was obviously written before the Roman persecution began in earnest after the city of Rome burned in AD 64. Surely the warnings were sent out before the persecution began.

> For behold, I create new heavens and a new earth; And the former things will not be remembered or come to mind. (Isaiah 65:17, NASB)

> Heaven and earth shall pass away, but my words shall not pass away. (Matthew 24:35, KJV)

> When God speaks of a "new" covenant, it means he has
> made the first one obsolete. It is now out of date and will
> soon disappear. (Hebrews 8:13, NLT)

Isaiah and Jesus are speaking of the same thing, just about 780 years apart. The old heaven and earth would have to pass away. The law that they were under was the Old Covenant that had become obsolete. Isaiah had prophesied of Jesus coming, and about 780 years later, Jesus was speaking of the same event that Isaiah spoke of. The coming of Messiah was the beginning of the end of the Old Covenant. As was common with God, He gave the nation of Israel, the southern kingdom of Judah, forty years to wander (wonder) in the wilderness after they had killed Jesus. The Gospel was going out across the southern kingdom of Judah and the Roman Empire for about thirty-four years prior to the beginning of the Roman persecution, which began in earnest in late AD 64. The writer of Hebrews was very aware that the Old Covenant was about to pass. As I have made mention of elsewhere in this book, Jesus and the apostles did not live under the New Covenant. This verse in Hebrews should make it obvious. This is confirmation that the designers of the Bible made a huge error in having two testaments. Scripture was inspired, but the canonization and design of the Bible was obviously not inspired. Maybe it is this current generation that I live in that is not inspired. I am inspired by the word of God, and through that inspiration I have parsed out this issue with the two testaments. That which is old has passed, and that which is new is here. We live in the new heaven and earth today. It is not in our future. It was never about a literal new heavens and earth. It was about the Law versus the superior New Covenant, grace over the law. We have much work to do to bring the healing of the nations. It is time that we walk on water for our Father who art in heaven.

Not One Jot or Tittle

For verily I say unto you, Till heaven and earth pass, one jot or one tittle shall in no wise pass from the law, until all be fulfilled. (Matthew 5:18, KJV)

For truly, I say to you, until heaven and earth pass away, not an iota, not a dot, will pass from the Law until all is accomplished. (ESV)

*J*esus spoke these words very early in His ministry. He had gone up into a mountain, and His disciples came to Him. This was part of the famous Sermon on the Mount. Who was Jesus speaking to? Many today insist that Jesus was speaking to us in the here and now. Well, what He spoke that day is certainly relevant to us today, but it was of great imminence to that generation. This is also called the "Blessed Sermon." I suggest that you go to the scriptures and read this sermon. It is located in Matthew, chapters 5 thru 7. My point here is that we must always discern the situation at hand and the audience that is being spoken to. In the KJV of the scriptures "kingdom of heaven" and "at hand" is mentioned three times by Jesus. Jesus did not mean that those hearing Him were standing next to heaven. What He meant was that the timing of what the prophets had foretold was near, at hand, to occur shortly. He was not saying, "Reach out and touch me, and you have touched heaven."

The events that were about to transpire upon "this generation" were being signified by the very presence of Messiah, the one who would lay down His life and do away with the Old Covenant system of death for all. The wages for sin under the OC was death for all, the sinner and the saint. There are those out there who believe that the wages for sin under the OC was "to be absent from the body is to be present in heaven" with half of your being. They believe that the soul went to heaven, but the body stayed in the earth. There are also those who believe Abraham's bosom is the place that all the believers' souls go to upon death and that the souls are conscience entities. Abraham's bosom is just another metaphor used in the Bible to describe the place of death. Remember, Abraham bought a place to bury his wife, Sarah. Genesis 23 records this. It was not only a cave, but also a field. If you drive through the countryside of the United States, you will see that most cemeteries are in fields. Isaac and Jacob were also returned upon death to this place of burial. Joseph's bones were also returned from Egypt upon their Exodus with the intent of burying him in the same place. Those who reach heaven will discover that Abraham's bosom is nothing more than symbolic language for the grave. There are many verses in the Bible that give a truer sense of what death was to the OC believer than what is preached in the pulpits today. Death was total unawareness, experiencing nothingness. The verses are there. You have to read it with eyes wide open. There are many instances in the scripture where metaphors, hyperboles, and similes are used when describing death. You have to have a true biblical understanding of death in order to catch the true meaning of what is being conveyed by the author of that particular scripture. We use much symbolic language today. "It is raining cats and dogs" is hyperbolic language describing a rain event. If you were to state that in a foreign nation using an interpreter, you may get a mighty strange look. It is crucial when speaking to a foreign audience not to use idioms and symbolic language. If you state in another nation that your favorite tennis player killed his opponent last week, do not be surprised if someone walks up to you and inquires if this killer has been jailed.

> And it shall come to pass, that every soul, which will not hear that prophet, shall be destroyed from among the people. Yea, and all the prophets from Samuel and *those that* follow after, as many as have spoken, have likewise foretold of these days. (Acts 3:23–24, KJV)

Peter is speaking to the crowds here after healing the lame man, the one who he and John told they had no silver or gold, but they gave him what they did have: the power to stand and walk. Being able to walk in His light is far greater than silver and gold. If you are familiar with the Old Testament you must know that the Jews, the very chosen of God, were an obstinate group of people. They were self-centered and arrogant. They thought that they were the locus of the kingdom of God. Sorry, but that role is for Jesus. Peter is not really singling out a single prophet here. All that had prophesied, or spoken for God, were mocked, resented, persecuted, and many were put to death. Many of the Old Testament prophets had foretold of these "final days" that had come upon "this generation" of the Jews. They had recently killed John the Baptist during Jesus' ministry in Israel. The next prophet on the "kill list" would be Jesus, the very Son of God. Peter, Paul, Stephen, and likely all of Jesus' apostles died martyrs' deaths. It is believed that John was the only apostle who lived through the consummation. He never had to experience "soul sleep." Hmmm—that's what you call love!

Peter is stating here that all prophecy that is not yet fulfilled is about to be fulfilled during their generation. Jesus had stated that "not one jot or tittle" would pass from the law until all be fulfilled. When Peter made his statement, and Jesus made His statement, they were speaking to the same audience—their contemporaries of "this generation." The serpent would be crushed, and eternal life would be reinstated for the repentant believer only. Eternal life is not for earth since the fall of man. The kingdom of God is also the kingdom of heaven, not of this earth.

I believe that it would be appropriate to rehash this here. The "kingdom of heaven" is not mentioned a single time in the KJV of the Old Testament. Of course heaven is heaven. It appears that the kingdom of heaven gained significance in the books of the New Testament because of what was about to happen. It had everything to do with the passing of the old heaven and the old earth. Eternal life is never mentioned in the KJV of the Old Testament. It is mentioned thirty times in the New Testament. Eternity is mentioned once in the KJV of the Old Testament. It is mentioned in Isaiah, but the reference here is to a place and not a state of eternal life. It states "lofty One who inhabiteth eternity." Eternity is associated with a destination, which is heaven. No heaven means no eternity. It is only there that eternity will be experienced and not here on earth. Everlasting life is mentioned once in the KJV of the Old Testament. It is mentioned in the following: *"And many of them that sleep in the dust of the earth shall awake, some to everlasting life, and some to shame and everlasting contempt"* (Daniel 12:2, KJV). The only mention of everlasting life in the Old Testament is a reference to what happened at the end of the OC era. The reason that eternal life has taken on a sense of urgency all of a sudden is because it was now a possibility. Until Messiah came on the scene, there was no possibility; therefore, no one even considered it an option until Jesus' advent. There was a key that had to be inserted into the key hole. If I dropped the key here, would there be anyone to pick it up?

Well, the key has been dropped. Did you pick it up? I just took a fifteen-minute break. Did anyone pick up the key? The key is this, the old heaven and earth was the Old Covenant. The old heaven and earth would not allow humanity, in any form, into the kingdom of God. The old earth consumed the very spirit of man upon death under the Old Covenant. The flesh was consumed, but the saints' soul was preserved; it was dead but preserved. That was the Old Covenant. They were under the law, and the law led to death. The wages of sin was death for the sinner and the saint. By God's grace, the repentant sinner now has access to heaven once he takes his last breath in the here and now. The unrepentant sinner still suffers the wages of sin. This is what grace is. Grace is not for all. It is only for those who bow the knee to Jesus. Those who do shall experience life everlasting in heaven. Those who do not accept Jesus as Messiah in this life will never have another opportunity to get it right. Once that last breath passes from the nostrils, that is it. The new heaven and earth is the New Covenant. It is synonymous with life everlasting for the repentant believer. It is also kind of a metaphor for life everlasting. They are one and the same. Without the new heaven and earth, there is no eternal life. Of course, this takes place in His kingdom, which has come. It came in AD 70. No human, flesh or soul, ever entered heaven until the key had come. Jesus was the key. There can be no entry without the *key*.

Let's now go back to the Sermon on the Mount and look at what Jesus was saying and who He was saying it to. It was not only relevant to those who heard it, but it would also be imminent to many that heard Him. Surely some died natural deaths before the Roman persecution, and some under the persecution of the Jewish religious system, which had become apostate since the crucifixion of Jesus. What is known as the Beatitudes also comes out of this scripture. We will look at it one verse at a time and hopefully show how imminent it was to Jesus apostles.

> And he opened his mouth and taught them, saying:
> "Blessed are the poor in spirit, for theirs is the kingdom
> of heaven. Blessed are those who mourn, for they shall
> be comforted. Blessed are the meek, for they shall inherit
> the earth. Blessed are those who hunger and thirst for
> righteousness, for they shall be satisfied. Blessed are
> the merciful, for they shall receive mercy. Blessed are
> the pure in heart, for they shall see God. Blessed are

the peacemakers, for they shall be called sons of God. Blessed are those who are persecuted for righteousness' sake, for theirs is the kingdom of heaven. Blessed are you when others revile you and persecute you and utter all kinds of evil against you falsely on my account. Rejoice and be glad, for your reward is great in heaven, for so they persecuted the prophets who were before you.
(Matthew 5:2–12, ESV)

These verses are often misrepresented from the pulpit. Yes, there are situations where it is to our best interest to be humble, or poor in spirit, to mourn, to be meek, to hunger and thirst for righteousness, and so forth. But these words from Jesus were directly meant for His apostles. If I were to put a tape recorder in your living room and tape a deep conversation between you and your spouse or you and your children, would those conversations be of imminence to the rest of the world? I highly doubt it. Odds are that it would not even be taken seriously by all parties involved in the encounter. Could the world learn anything of importance from the taped conversation if it were made available to the public? Possibly. Let's take a look at the real situation at hand with Jesus and His apostles. I hope we can glean from this, knowing what they faced over the next forty years that they were going to be literally giving their lives for the faith. They would also lose loved ones to death and carnage and also be rejected by family members. The "end" was near. It was imminent. They needed to be especially prepared for the worst tribulation that anyone had ever faced. It is one thing to face rejection from this world, but to experience it from loved ones is not the norm. Have you ever been rejected by family for your beliefs? Have you ever faced death because of your religious beliefs here in America? I think not. His apostles would not only face death, they would suffer death by crucifixion, stoning, be-heading, and other means.

"Blessed are the poor in spirit, for theirs is the kingdom of heaven" (Matthew 5:3 ESV). I think that we have all faced people who are full of themselves. Everything they do is about them and only them. They never think about others. These people are self-focused and not others focused. Jesus was preparing His apostles for what they were going to face. We know that the kingdom of heaven is not of this world. It is not by observation, as he told the Pharisees. You can't see it in the here and now because it isn't ever going to be here, now or ever. Jesus was telling them to be of a lowly spirit and to put the interest of others before themselves. If they could acquire this spirit, they would do great and mighty

things for God. Well, most of the world knows who the twelve apostles were. They made history because they were willing to be of a poor spirit for the cause of Christ.

"Blessed are those who mourn, for they shall be comforted" (Matthew 5:4, ESV). Jesus' apostles and those first-century believers would be confronted not only with mocking, rejection, death of loved ones, and death of self, but also with relocation. Many would be forced to flee to the mountains to be spared religious persecution and the great tribulation. There would be much cause for mourning, such as the average American today has never faced. Sure, life is tough today, but most of us are not facing rejection from all of our family and friends, loss of property, and the necessity to flee for our lives. The apostles would never have the option of fleeing. They had to face up to the task at hand: getting the gospel out. Jesus was speaking to His apostles here and not the crowds. This was for their consolation. There would be much cause to mourn. Jesus was assuring His apostles that they would be comforted. I imagine that He had the Holy Spirit in mind. The "Comforter" is mentioned four times in the gospel of John, and he is of course speaking of the Holy Spirit. This would also be a great comfort for all of the first-century believers and all of Christianity forever. Tell me, how long is forever?

"Blessed are the meek, for they shall inherit the earth" (Matthew 5:5, ESV). To be meek is to exhibit patience, humility, gentleness, and to be submissive. If you look at the fruits of the Spirit, you will see that patience and gentleness are among them. From the words of Jesus, we know that earth is not where the kingdom of God is located. From the lives of the apostles, we also know that they did not inherit the earth. Those who belong to Christ have crucified the flesh with its passions and desires, according to Jesus in Galatians 5:22. The ones who accepted Jesus as Messiah and heeded His warnings and fled to the mountains were around to inherit what was left over after the destruction of Jerusalem and the temple. The nation of Israel was not restored, but the leftovers were there to be claimed, and much pillaging took place after the Jews were annihilated. Those who took to the sword were killed by the sword. Jesus warned His apostles the night He was taken into captivity by the Roman soldiers about taking up the sword: *"Then said Jesus unto him, Put up again thy sword into his place: for all they that take the sword shall perish with the sword"* (Matthew 26:52, KJV). Again, I highly recommend the reading of Josephus's *The Wars of the Jews*. The majority of Jews believed that God would never allow the destruction of Jerusalem, the temple, and the nation. Well, that is what the prophets prophesied. The

true prophets were deemed false prophets by the Jews. Judaism denies the deity of Jesus. They are still awaiting Messiah. Judaism today is a pagan religion to God Almighty. Any religion that denies the deity of Jesus is a pagan and antichrist religion. Judaism does just that. What God has put asunder, let no man bring back together.

Back to Josephus: in his *The Wars of the Jews*, he speaks much of a sect within the Jewish nation during the last days of the OTC era. The Zealots had taken up the sword. They were killing Christians as well as Roman soldiers. They were robbing their neighbors and pillaging the people of Jerusalem, even though they were Jews. These did not inherit the earth or the kingdom of God. They were not blessed of God. They were arrogant and full of pride. They were also murderers and thieves. They inherited sheol for all of eternity. The inheritance of the earth was a temporal inheritance. It was for the here and now, not for all eternity. Those who heeded Jesus' warnings and fled to the mountains were the ones who were spared and inherited the earth, not in a whole sense, but in a local sense. This was not and is not for us today. You can have the earth. I will take heaven.

"Blessed are those who hunger and thirst for righteousness, for they shall be satisfied" (Matthew 5:6, ESV). Do we truly hunger and thirst for righteousness today? Do we spend hours in prayer each week lamenting the status of our nation, as well as the whole world? Mississippi claims to be a mostly Christian populated state. Back in 2011, while I was out of the country for the gospel of Jesus Christ, there was a vote in Mississippi that fall on abortion, which determined when life began. I thought to myself that Mississippi, being as conservative as she claims to be, would overwhelmingly vote against abortion and vote that life begins at conception, as the scriptures state. *"Before I formed thee in the belly I knew thee; and before thou camest forth out of the womb I sanctified thee ...",* stated God to Jeremiah in Jeremiah 1:5, ESV. It was called Initiative 26. It was defeated by a 15.26 percent margin of 132,468 votes. I was very surprised to see the results. I would say that the majority in the "conservative" state of Mississippi are not hungering and thirsting for righteousness. The majority in the United States today do not hunger and thirst for righteousness.

What is righteousness? Well, we must look at it in the context that the generation that killed Messiah would have viewed it. The ones hungering and thirsting for righteousness would have been those seeking justice from the current evil system in the Roman Empire, but particularly in Israel. The other provinces and nations that Rome had conquered would rise up against the Jews and the Christians (true Israel). If you are familiar with the scriptures, you know that there are images of the dead Christians crying out to God for justice against their tormentors in Revelation 6:10. Their tormentors were the Jewish leaders, the Zealots, and the Roman armies and their allies. They cried the following: *"And they cried with a loud voice, saying, How long, O Lord, holy and true, dost thou not judge and avenge our blood on them that dwell on the earth"* (Revelation 6:10, KJV)?

When you are literally going through hell on earth, there seems to be no relief in sight. Jesus was assuring His apostles that the ones who hungered and thirsted for righteousness would be satisfied. Some would die and certainly be delivered from the earthly torment. Some would live through the consummation of the era and into the New Covenant era. Those would experience the relief of the torment of their fellow Jews and Roman Empire forces. They would experience a peace that many had not known in their lifetimes. Would children literally play with snakes and not fear getting bitten? Would the lamb and the wolf dwell together, as stated in Isaiah? I hope that you are becoming educated with the symbolism of the scriptures. Many times, the scriptures in the Old Testament and New Testament use the symbols of sheep as the children of God and wolves as the enemy. After the destruction of the temple and city of Jerusalem, the ones left behind would be the Christians. They would be able at this time to mingle with what was considered the wolves before the consummation. After the torment had ended, "true Israel" would experience peace for the first time in a generation. The children of God would also be able to handle those serpents. (Serpent is symbolic language for evil men, the wicked.)

"Blessed are the merciful, for they shall receive mercy" (Matthew 5:7, ESV). Jesus is telling His apostles here that if they will exhibit mercy, they will receive mercy. God would delve out mercy through other people. Many of the professing believers received more mercy from the Romans than they did from the Jews. This was a very special time and event. It was the event prophesied by Daniel, the other Old Testament prophets (prophecy that had yet to be fulfilled), prophecy from the book of Genesis, as well as future prophecy from Jesus and John that had not yet been made. Jesus particularly singled out orphans and widows as ones to show mercy to. There would certainly have been a burden on old women and little children who had no husband or father in their lives to provide necessities and protection. There were many more orphans and widows during that epoch of time. Many would lose their lives to the Judaizers before the persecution

of the Roman Empire began in late AD 64. An orphan was defined as a child who had a mother and a father in the house and had lost either one or both parents to death, or possible imprisonment of one parent or both. A widow was a woman that was married to a man and had lost him to death but possibly even lost a husband to imprisonment for the faith. Jesus was telling His apostles to be merciful and to preach mercy to the first-century church. They would need all the mercy they could find. Thank God, I am at a point in my life where I need no mercy. I have never been at that point. I was brought up to respect authority, to be self-sufficient, and not a burden to my family, friends, and the culture as a whole. When I get older, I may find myself in a position where I need mercy from others. I have been merciful to others, often to my own demise. It does not matter. It will be delved out to me as I delve it out.

There were many converts during the days of the apostles. Many heeded the warnings of Jesus and recognized the signs of the times. When they began to see the signs coming to fruition, the leaves popping out on the fig tree, they heeded His warning and fled to the mountains. Most of the apostles had likely been killed by then. God would put mercy into the hearts of the Gentiles who would take the Jewish believers in and provide safety and shelter for them. Mercy was shown by God through man.

"Blessed are the pure in heart, for they shall see God" (Matthew 5:8, ESV). Pure means to be of one spirit here. As a follower of Christ we are to be of a uniform composition, not mixed. This has nothing to do with mixed marriage. Moses married an Ethiopian after his first wife died. His sister spoke out against it, and God struck her with leprosy. A believer should not be of moral failing. He should be guiltless before God. I imagine that there are plenty out there who disagree with this, but that is what it says. If you will look up the word *pure* online using The Free Dictionary by Farlex, you will see that the definition of pure was gleaned from there. What would it take for man to be pure before God? I believe that if we will just obey the Ten Commandments, we will be well on our way. Those are achievable. Sadly, we live in a time now that man makes up sin, things that God has not declared as sin. It is not what goes into the body that defiles it, but what comes out, so says Jesus. This admonition that Jesus makes to His apostles was meant to give them strength and dogged determination. They would face all kinds of pressure and enticements to fall away from the faith. The biggest obstacle, however, that they would face would be the crucifixion of Jesus. They all fled his side that night. Peter followed at a distance and would deny he even knew Jesus three times before the sun rose.

If you know anything at all about roosters, they crow long before the sun even begins to rise. It broke Peter's heart when he heard that rooster crow. He knew that Jesus knew his heart. There would be an even greater event three days later when the tomb was found empty. I do not know how much hope this gave the apostles. It probably tweaked their spirits just a bit. There is no telling what all they imagined about the empty tomb. We know that the imaginations of man are wicked. Once Jesus appeared in their midst, though, they would have jumped out of a 747 jetliner five miles from the surface of the earth with no parachute. At that time they had no doubts as to what He was and who He was. He was truly the Son of man and the Son of God. At this point, they had all the fuel they needed to remain pure and holy for the One who died for them. He also rose for them. He also died and rose for us, but that first-century group of believers was an elect group.

I am sorry, but Calvinism doesn't fly with me. This was the "very elect" of God. God elected that generation to usher in the New Covenant. However, it did not truly begin until the temple and city were destroyed in AD 70. They were assured that if they remained pure, that they would see God. This still applies to us today. We are to be pure of heart. We are not to be mixed and mingled within our hearts. It is the same as being torn between two lovers. God will play second fiddle to no one. Do you want to hear, "Well done good and faithful servant" or "Depart from me; I never knew you"? Do not be fiddling with God. He may break out the banjo, and you may hear a bango and then a "go low."

"Blessed are the peacemakers, for they shall be called sons of God" (Matthew 5:9, ESV). There would be many factions over the next forty years within the Roman Empire. Some of these groups already existed, but many more would spring up. It was a time of great division. The Judaizers and the Christians would be two factions within the nation of Israel, but the Zealots were also a major faction that had emerged within the current generation. There would be groups organized around certain people, who were false teachers or false prophets. It would be a miraculous feat to maintain peace within the Roman Empire at a time like this. The ones who were peaceful would certainly be looked upon in a far more favorable light than the gang bangers.

The Zealots were far from peacemakers. They were nothing more than thugs robbing their own families, friends, and neighbors. Surely they were cursed of God. The Zealots were against the pagan Roman way of life, yet God had raised them up for such a time as this. The first-century Jews were admonished to comply with the laws and regulations of the authorities over them. This was not an admonition for all time. There is scripture that condemns God's people for the way they picked their own leaders. This elect generation was a regime that God had set up, and they were to comply with the laws for a short time; then they would be set free. This does not apply to us today, but that is for another time and place.

In Revelation, John speaks of the Tree of Life and its location in the garden. He states that its leaves are for the healing of the nations. This is an area that applies greatly to this generation today. Let me spell it out — *it is us*. The leaves on the Tree of Life are the Christians. Yet, the professing Christians of this generation are one of the biggest obstacles to peace. I dare say that the pure hearted is not a Zionist. What God has put asunder, let no man bring back together. His word states "Blessed are the peacemakers . . .," not "Blessed are the war-mongers . . ." If you want to be called a son of God, you shall desire and pray for the healing of the nations. There is neither Jew nor Greek (Gentile) today in the mind of God. He has cast out the old and brought in the new. The United States had better learn this and quit listening to the advice of false teachers, preachers and prophets. Cursed are the war-mongers. Sadly, many presidents, congressmen, and senators, are Biblically illiterate and listen to the likes of those that are into the heresy of Zionism.

"Blessed are those who are persecuted for righteousness' sake, for theirs is the kingdom of heaven" (Matthew 5:10, ESV). The apostles of Jesus spoke out against tyranny. They defined sin as sin. They did not attach politically correct terms to such as drunkards. Today people will talk about their alcoholic family members and friends. Well, according to the word of God, these people are addicted to sin. Alcohol actually has many positive attributes, but to abuse it will cause mayhem and destruction. It destroys families, relationships, minds, and bodies. I know of many individuals who have died long before the average age of humanity due to the negative effects of alcohol. The same can be said of drugs. Prescription drug abuse in America today has become a bigger issue than any will admit. In the minds of the people using these drugs, all is well with them. They are not drug addicts. That is a moniker for the illegal drug users.

There are many people today losing their minds at a much earlier age than what should be the norm. Hmmm. Is it normal to lose your mind at any age? It sure appears that way as of late. When I was much younger, I do not recall older people experiencing such as Alzheimer's or dementia at the rate you see today in America. I also notice that it is not nearly as prevalent in other nations that do not allow direct pharmaceutical advertising to the consumer. It has ramped up tremendously over the last couple of decades. It used to be illegal for pharmaceutical companies to advertise directly to the consumer. Once it became legal, through Washington, drug addiction skyrocketed, as did many memory-degrading diagnoses. Well, I am going to make a diagnosis here. There will be many that have allowed this atrocity to take place in America that will be diagnosed as "unrepentant sinner" and will be barred from heaven due to the contagious nature of sin. There will be those called doctor, pharmacist, pharmaceutical manufacturer or marketer, congressman, senator, president, and others who shall hear "Depart from me. I never knew you." Actually, those will hear nothing. This is just symbolic language that represents the demise of the unrepentant sinner. It is figurative language for the judgment that is passed upon the last breath of the New Covenant earth dwellers. Descension is the direction for the lost and not ascension.

I hope that you catch my drift. Those who speak out against unrighteousness are hated by the masses and the powers that be. Jesus spoke out against the corrupt religious authorities of His day, and He was eventually crucified for it. If they had just thought He was crazy, they would not have killed Him. They knew He was correct in His analysis of them and that He would convince the majority of the people if left unfettered. Therefore, they fettered Him to a cross, except they didn't use chains. They used nails. His apostles would also experience mocking, ridicule, persecution, and horrible deaths, except for John. They were persecuted for righteousness's sake. They spoke out against the status quo, and the authorities did everything in their power to turn the people against them.

It is a shameful thing, but the average person can be steered just like a car. Just look at political campaigns today. They promise the world to the sluggard for their vote, and they deliver very little, if anything. Of course, there are lobbyists in Washington who promise the legislatures much money if they vote a certain way for particular bills that come up. Obviously, these guys deliver. You can call it "soft monies" if you want. God will call it bribery. He will also call welfare theft, taking from the productive worker and giving to the sluggard. America rewards failure and penalizes success. Just think, if football, baseball, and basketball worked that way, I'd score and my opponent would get the reward, the points. That is ludicrous. Woe be unto you who promote such. God meant for families to take care of its own members. In America today, we have whole families on disability. I even know of mothers who have left their babies out in the scorching sun so the child would be disabled by the harmful effects of the heat in order to get a slow learning disability check. They are called "crazy checks" in the communities that do such wickedness. There are also mothers and grandmothers in the black community encouraging their daughters and granddaughters to get pregnant, even at the age of eleven, so they can increase the taxpay-er-robbed welfare income entering their homes. This dooms the daugh-ters' lives and begins a cycle of never-ending poverty of the victim and never-ending robbery of the honest hard-working class. Yes, this is going on in America. I dare say that God would deem such as this far worse than slavery. This devilish behavior dooms following generations to dis-ability and poverty. Such as this is a reproach to God and to the honest worker that is being robbed. If you speak out against injustice, you will be ridiculed and ostracized. It got Jesus killed, as well as His apostles and many more first-century believers.

There are those who see people in the grocery store who are obvi-ously of another ethnicity speaking in their native language, and they automatically assume that they are talking about them. We have such thin skin nowadays. I reckon our skin is thinner than it was a hundred years ago. I must be careful. Someone in another century, or another nation, may actually believe that man's skin used to be thicker in centuries past. This could really start a last day's doomsday era or error. "Our skin is growing thin. In another generation or two, man will be skinless. We are doomed." Surely, I jest.

"Blessed are you when others revile you and persecute you and utter all kinds of evil against you falsely on my account" (Matthew 5:11, ESV). Jesus was telling His apostles to expect ridicule. If you walk the walk, you can expect the talk—behind your back. The unrighteous will perse-cute you. They will hate you and mock you. They lived in such a culture back then that you could actually expect to be put to death. Now think about this for a moment. The Judaizers were doing the persecuting, the reviling, and the killing. These are those whose Bible today states that Jesus was the bastard son of a harlot and Roman soldier and is in hell for all eternity sitting in boiling excrement. If the Jews were the force today that they were back then, they would attempt to do the same today to those who profess Jesus as Messiah. God has seen to it that they shall never rise to that peak ever again. If they rise, it shall be on the shoulders of Jesus, and it will be with a totally different perspective on Messiah.

The first-century believers underwent persecution the likes of what we have never seen in America, nor ever shall. I do not believe the American government will ever sanction the beheading of a Christian; however, they may insist that you shut your mouth. If the first-century believers had not been so passionate about their faith, there would be no faith today. If we were as passionate about our faith today, the world would be a different place. People fuss about the movies, yet they attend them. They fuss about the liberal media, yet they watch it every day. They fuss about athletes not standing for the National Anthem, yet they go to the athletic events or watch them on television. We could steer the media if we were passionate about our beliefs. We feed the beasts, and then complain when the beasts feed us garbage.

Jesus was basically telling His followers that if you walk the walk, expect to be persecuted and reviled. If you aren't walking the walk and talking the talk, you can expect nothing. If you are making a difference, then you are going to offend the obstinate and the evil.

> Rejoice and be glad, for your reward is great in heaven, for so they persecuted the prophets who were before you. You are the salt of the earth, but if salt has lost its taste, how shall its saltiness be restored? It is no longer good for anything except to be thrown out and trampled under people's feet. You are the light of the world. A city set on a hill cannot be hidden. Nor do people light a lamp and put it under a basket, but on a stand, and it gives light to all in the house. (Matthew 5:12, ESV)

God intended for His people to be different from all the other people of the world. The Queen of Sheba had heard great and mighty things about the nation of Israel over nine hundred years before Jesus walked this earth. At that time, the Jewish culture had not drifted into what it would after much prosperity and success. Their culture was different from all the other cultures of the world. They had incentive to progress. All members of the culture had no barriers to hinder their success. Many people had become wealthy. The Jewish culture was a superior culture. It promoted the family with the father as the head. The father was to provide for his family, to teach his children responsibility, and to bring them up in the admonition of the Lord. Today, man has relegated this role to the government. That is not God's way. The man is to be the spiritual leader in the house, but that is a rarity today. God has His ways, and His way is the right way. Any other is the wrong way. Just look at our culture today. Dads shoved their responsibilities on the mothers. In the American culture, the mothers eventually shoved this responsibility on the day-care centers. Now we wonder why the children act as they do. God never meant for a baby to have to leave the arms of its mother to spend all day in the arms of a stranger. Yes, that is stranger than God ever imagined. You can call me crazy if you wish. God never intended for a child that young to be forced out into the world. It sure appears today that man has a more difficult time than ever dealing with reality. With age comes wisdom, but that is not a given. Wisdom comes from one place only. The ways of man is the wisdom of man, which is foolishness. The way of God is wisdom. His wisdom is found in His word. He says what He means and means what He says. Let no man tell you different.

The first generation of believers was truly salt and light. The world has been changed drastically for the better, in spite of what atheistic professors state. Without Christianity, there would be no colleges. These anti-Christ professors would not even have a pulpit to speak from if not for Christianity. The most technologically advanced nations in the world today are those who once had Christianity at the heart. Today, technology is being stolen from the "Christian" nations due to the corruption and greed behind the scenes that are pulling the strings in Washington. If you invent something today in the United States, it is yours for a brief time until the patent or copyright runs out. Then someone else "equates" your product at half the price. The originator has to tremendously inflate the price of his invention, drug, or other, until the patent runs out in order to make a generous profit. Once the "equates" kick in, the bottom falls out. This is why there are lobbyists in Washington. The copycats have to bribe in order to make this legal. If this corruption were ended, the consumers in this nation would save a fortune in their lifetimes. This is the main reason pharmaceuticals are so expensive. This is why the pharmaceutical industry is in Washington—so they can enrich themselves at the consumers' inflated expense. You can call it what you will. I believe that God will call it theft. Guess what? Thieves are on that "never shall enter" list. Think about this. Have you ever met a thief that was not also a liar? If you have to lie to cover yourself, you are likely committing sin.

What Jesus told His apostles that day on the mountain was of great imminence to them and extremely relevant. They would be facing issues that we in the United States will never have to face, at least for now. If we keep heading the direction we are going, that could change. Peter knew that he would die an untimely death. It is obvious from Paul's writings that he knew that his life would be lost for the cause, too. They were assured by Jesus that they would be justly rewarded with tremendous blessings. Most of those blessings would take place in the afterlife, though. Those blessings last for eternity. If being cursed by man in this life for righteousness's sake brings the blessedness of eternity in heaven, then bring it on!

Jesus prophesied much about the days ahead that His apostles would face. Peter stated to the crowds that they were living in the times prophesied by all the prophets. Jesus stated that not one jot or tittle would pass from the law until all is fulfilled. Heaven and earth is not literal. The Law is what all things hung from in the Jewish nation. It was the standard that God laid up for that people. They did not have the Bible that we have today. They had the Law only. It was heaven and earth to them. If they did not obey the law, the earth would consume them forever. Even the righteous perished. All the OC saints experienced the wages of sin, that is death. Death is nothingness, "soul sleep." The OC was about to expire on the Jewish nation. God was patient and long-suffering for many generations. They could mock and ridicule Him. They would disobey Him and blaspheme His name. He turned the other cheek. They murdered His Son, and He would not stand for this. The penalty for murder was death. God put the nail in the coffin for the generation that killed Messiah. He carried out the Law. After this, the Law would be for a different purpose, or handled differently. Today it is to convict the sinner of wrongdoing. If that sinner repents, he will not suffer the penalty for sin, death. Those who do not turn from sin will experience the penalty for sin forevermore. That is what is superior about the New Covenant.

All can come to Jesus now, all nations and peoples. All that do shall never experience death. If you never experience death, you will never experience the resurrection. That was only for the Old Covenant saints. It is in the past. As I have stated elsewhere, they are not sitting in heaven today waiting on the other half of their assets. They are complete. It isn't heaven if you are only half there.

When the repentant sinner takes his last breath in this life, he will take his next in heaven. Heck, who knows? Will we even breathe in heaven? That is not a given. The old heaven and earth passed away with the destruction of the temple and the city of Jerusalem. The new heaven and earth is the New Covenant era. There is much scripture in the Bible that says this world will go on forever, such as the following: *"Who laid the foundations of the earth, that it should not be moved for ever"* (Psalm 104:5). There are many references to His word going on forever. Well, in heaven the Word will be with us. We will have no need for the Bible in heaven because the Author will be with us. The word that is spoken of and referenced as going on forever is for this world. All who hear will not bow the knee to Jesus. All who do, however, shall experience eternity in His presence in heaven. Now, if we want to be literal here, if the ones who choose Jesus will be numbered as the sand of the seashores, well, we better get at it. If that is literal, then we have at least a gazillion years left.

In the beginning of this section we started out with the statement Jesus made about "one jot or one tittle shall in no wise pass from the law, until all be fulfilled." Let's take a look at the law.

Thou shalt have no other gods before me.
Thou shalt not make unto thee any graven image
Thou shalt not take the name of the LORD thy God in vain;
Remember the Sabbath day, to keep it holy.
Honour thy father and thy mother:
Thou shalt not kill.
Thou shalt not commit adultery.
Thou shalt not steal.
Thou shalt not bear false witness against thy neighbour.
Thou shalt not covet

The penalty for violating many of these laws was death. When Moses returned from the mountain with the Ten Commandments, the people had melted their gold and made an image of a calf. They were worshipping, dancing, and singing before it when Moses came down. God commanded, and Moses charged his men to do the bidding of God. Three thousand men died for this sin. Death was the penalty. The people had violated at least the first two commandments.

Jesus, the very image of God, had come and walked among the first-century Jews. They would not acknowledge Him as Messiah. They certainly took His name in vain. They certainly did not honor their Father who art in heaven. They killed the very Son of God. They had played the harlot with other god's. There is no mystery here. The Jewish nation had become "MYSTERY, BABYLON THE GREAT, THE MOTHER OF HARLOTS AND ABOMINATIONS OF THE EARTH." They certainly bore false witness against Jesus. Many false accusations were made against Him. The temple leaders coveted the attention that Jesus was getting. He was admired by the crowds for the great miracles He was doing, but also because of His teachings. His teachings were enlightening the people to truth and setting them free from the bondage of servitude to lying tyrants. The law was about to be fulfilled. The very nation that God had chosen to bring in Messiah had killed His Son. "This generation" was deserving of having the law poured out on them, and it was about to happen. All prophecy was about to be fulfilled, but so was the law. Death was coming to the harlot, Israel. This was the ultimate fulfillment of the Law. Not one jot or tittle was left unfilled. "Thy kingdom come" and the "new heaven and earth" have been addressed elsewhere. Earth shall never be heaven. If you can find one jot or tittle that has not been fulfilled, then you need to rehash your beliefs on that jot or tittle. If the Bible seems to contradict itself, then we need to either check the interpretation of the scripture or our misconception on what has actually been stated.

I hope and pray that this has given you a new perspective on the "end-times" and "last days." Learn to think for yourself. The Bible actually does say what it means and means what it says, in spite of what anyone else tells you. Cleanse your mind if you must and begin to read the scriptures from a new light. Get the garbage out and you will see *the light*. Well, I am going to go out here in the streets and play with some wolves. I hopes the sheep will come to my rescue!

The Beast and Other Characters of the Last Days

The beast of Revelation is a character that has gotten lots of attention at different times over the past forty-five years or so. It could be that even false teachers and preachers before my time have propagated lies based on ignorance in past generations that have started rumors about the coming beast before. I know that the founder of the Jehovah's Witnesses gave a false prophecy back in the 1800s. He prophesied that Jesus was coming back in 1874. When it did not happen, he taught that Jesus had secretly returned in 1874 and four years later was crowned King of heaven. He predicted that by the end of 1878, the resurrection of the dead would take place and that in 1914, the rapture would occur and Armageddon would begin. He died in 1916. Well, as usual with these false end-times doomsday preachers, nothing occurred or it was invisible. If he would have prophesied this garbage back in the days of King David or Solomon, he would have rightly been stoned to death or hung. He was a false teacher preaching lies to the people. His predecessor, Joseph Franklin Rutherford, predicted that Abraham, Isaac, and Jacob would come back by 1925 as rulers over the New World. Sorry, it ain't happening!

The prophecy of Revelation is about the consummation of the OC that occurred in AD 70, and the new heaven and earth was ushered in. By the way, Rutherford's predecessor, Nathan Knorr, predicted the world would end in 1974. His world did. He died that year. I was not born when the first two leaders were living. The third leader of the Watchtower Society was born in the year that my dad was born, 1942. I have no idea if there was talk at that time about the beast or not. The beast is scripturally tied to the "end-times," the "latter days." I imagine that anytime this false end-times garbage gets hyped that you are going to hear people predicting who the antichrist and the beast are. People even predicted that Ronald Wilson Reagan was the beast when he became president because all parts of his name contain 6 letters. Yet, today he is attributed as being tied for the number one position as best president ever. I am sorry, but if you can find anyone today that stated that Reagan was the beast, you need to let them know that they meet the biblical definition of a fool. People also attributed the role to Obama. I dare say that he certainly promoted many sins today that the word of God condemns. He is certainly anti-Jesus. You are either for Him or against Him. You do not get to pick and choose the parts of His word that tickles your fancy. Still, Barry Soetoro, who changed his name to Barak Hussein Obama, is not the beast.

In this chapter, we will look at some of the "end-times" characters and events that Jesus and John prophesied were to take place within their generation, which would have been shortly, near, and at hand. Some of the prophecies today have been twisted to mean something totally different than what was initially prophesied. Man has taken what was meant to be prophecy about events, or even religious beliefs or feelings of the time, and twisted it into persons. Who were the prophets? Jews. Who were they speaking to or warning? They were warning the Jews. They were not speaking to us today. Certainly we need to take heed and not repeat what the Jews did to Messiah, which was denial. All nations that have done this have failed. America is in "fail" stage today. Government has become the beast, and education has become a god. I hope that after this session you will have a better understanding of prophecy, events, and the figures involved in the latter days of the OTC era.

Nowhere in the scriptures is there mention of a seven-year tribulation. Below are scriptures that denote this end-times event from Daniel and John. Daniel prophesied of this event some five hundred years prior to its occurring. John prophesied of it within ten years of the beginning of the tribulation. A "time" is used in the scriptures to express a year in Daniel's prophecy. "Times" represents two years and a "half time," of course, represents half a year. John confirms this in Revelation with his 1,260 days and forty-two months. The Jewish calendar had only 360 days per year.

> He shall speak words against the Most High, and shall wear out the saints of the Most High, and shall think to change the times and the law; and they shall be given into his hand for a time, times, and half a time.
>
> (Daniel 7:25, ESV)

> The ruler will make a treaty with the people for a period of one set of seven, but after half this time, he will put

an end to the sacrifices and offerings. And as a climax to all his terrible deeds, he will set up a sacrilegious object that causes desecration, until the fate decreed for this defiler is finally poured out on him. (Daniel 9:27, NLT)

And she fled into the wilderness where a place had been prepared for her by God, so she could be taken care of for 1,260 days. (Revelation 12:6, NET)

Then the beast was allowed to speak great blasphemies against God. And he was given authority to do whatever he wanted for forty-two months.
(Revelation 13:5, NLT)

These are the major verses that denote the timetable for the tribulation. Actually, it did not end with the death of Nero. It continued on until the temple walls fell and the city of Jerusalem was destroyed. The key here is that those who professed Christ and heeded His warnings were spared this tribulation because they fled to the mountains. Those who were not Christian Jews were the ones who experienced one hundred percent of the tribulation and then some. Let's look at them characters!

Antichrist

If you get on social media today you will see all kind of garbage out there about the antichrist and the beast. This heresy is born out of ignorance mostly. There are also a few out there who are trying to profit from it. Never send money to one of these end-times doomsday sayers. That is a common theme among those who profess such. They always want donations to fund their "projects." Jesus would define them as heretics. We are going to look at some scripture in this section, and then we will look at historical figures who filled the roles that were prophesied by John the Revelator.

There are those today who propagate that the antichrist and the beast are one and the same. I have seen false teachings that state that the abomination of desolation is one and the same as the antichrist and the beast. Those who profess such have fallen for the false heretical teachings of Irenaeus (AD 115/125–202) and Hippolytus (AD 170–235), even though most sitting in the church pews have never heard of either. Odds are that if they have a seminary pastor and he teaches this heresy, then he got it from a seminary that propagates such. I have seen instances where pro-fessing Christians have quoted sayings of both as if they were quoting scripture. If it conflicts with the sayings of the apostles of Jesus, then it is a lie. Both conflict with what John taught about antichrist and the beast. Nowhere in the teachings of John is antichrist and the beast mentioned as being one and the same. Antichrist is not even mentioned as being an individual, but a spirit of the age. The beast is an individual. They would know him by his number. If an individual had zero knowledge of the characters in the Bible and read the epistles of John and Revelation, there is absolutely no way that they would infer that antichrist is an individual or that the beast and antichrist are one and the same.

We will start out with the antichrist. If I were to give a written test in most churches tomorrow with only one question, most people would make a zero on it. Where is the antichrist found in the Bible? The majority of people would list Revelation as the book. "Antichrist" is only men-tioned in four verses in the Bible. None of those verses are in Revelation. The author is John, but "antichrist" is only found in the epistles of John. I will list the verses, and we will parse through those verses. Hopefully you will come away with a more biblical understanding about "anti-christ" than you had before this encounter. We are also going to allow the scripture to be the standard here, the authority, and not the teachings of man. Read it, if possible, as if you have never seen it before and have no knowledge or preconceived notions about "antichrist." There are some translations of the Bible that capitalize the "A" in antichrist, but only four of them do it. The KJV is correct in their interpretation. The ancient Greek had no punctuation marks, as well as no distinction of capital and lowercase letters. They were all the same case. Preconceived notions and preferences come into play today with modern translations. John certainly never tied antichrist to an individual, but a spirit that was prev-alent among the first-century citizens of Judah.

Dear children, the last hour is here. You have heard that the Antichrist is coming, and already many such anti-christs have appeared. From this we know that the last hour has come. (1 John 2:18, NLT)

Children, it is the last hour; and just as you heard that antichrist is coming, even now many antichrists have appeared; from this we know that it is the last hour. (NASB)

Out of the fourteen English versions in the BLB, four of them capitalize antichrist. Even the KJV gets it right on this issue. John also gives a timeframe for the coming event, which would also be the same timing for the beast. If it was the last hour for the world, then what are we still doing here? It was the last days of the Old Covenant era. If this is a wrong assumption, then John was a liar and not a true prophet of God.

The astute will notice several things in this verse. Who is John writing to? You have to go back to verse one and read through to this point. You realize that John is not just addressing little children here. He is addressing the children of God, which also included old men and women. John is not speaking to us today. He is speaking to the ones in his generation, the very generation that Jesus walked among. There are "theologians" and "scholars" who claim the Epistles of John were written between AD 85 and 100. I am sorry, but I will state as fact that this is erroneous. Of course many of these "theologians" and "scholars" are agnostics or even atheists. Yes, there are atheistic theologians. Theology is the study of God. There are many heads of theology in the universities who are atheists. So, they have made a living off of something they do not even believe in. Actually, they criticize students' beliefs and turn many students into atheists and agnostics. Back to the issue, though; if John would have written his epistles after the destruction of the temple and the city of Jerusalem in AD 70, he most assuredly would have mentioned it. Many times Jesus noted fulfilled prophecy to His apostles as prophecy that was fulfilled as they were living. If John had written Revelation, his gospel, or the epistles after the destruction of the temple, he most definitely would have mentioned it at least once within five separate books of the Bible. Liberal scholars date all of John's writings after AD 70, and many later than 90 AD. Sorry, but that doesn't fit the facts. Surely if any one of Jesus' apostles had written a book of the Bible after the destruction of AD 70, it would have been included within the writing. It would have also been attested to as fulfilled prophecy by Jesus' prophetic story of "not a stone left unturned." All of the scripture was written before AD 70. Facts back this statement up. None of the books in the New Testament make mention of the destruction of the temple, the city, or the nation of the Jews in AD 70. Why? Because AD 70 had not yet occurred.

John also attests to the timing of antichrist. The KJV uses "last time." Eleven of the other English versions use "last hour," the HNV uses "end times," and the WEB also uses "last time." "It is" also has tremendous significance. If I state "It is raining" or "It is snowing," well, it either is or it isn't. If it is not, then I am a liar. I imagine the signs of the times were rampant when John penned his epistles. John was writing to his contemporaries about their current circumstances and not us today about a near-future event. Let the scripture be your standard and not the teachings of man. That is why the scriptures are provided for us today. It is history, which consists of His story, but much of its teachings are relevant for us today. Righteousness has no other standard bearer than the scriptures.

Now, what is antichrist? Is it an individual, a group, or a spirit? When I state spirit, I am not meaning a demonic or spiritual entity. If someone states to you that John Q has an air of supremacy about him, are they stating that an evil supreme spirit is about him protecting him? No, they are stating that he is arrogant. It is his substance, his beliefs. If he is in a position of authority, this could really cause some problems. If he is at the other end of the totem pole, it will only cause problems for him and those closest to him. It will not cause a meltdown in the culture. John states to his audience that there are many antichrists among them. Did his contemporaries believe that antichrist was a person? It appears that this could be the case, but it also appears that John is assuring them that antichrist is not an individual, but a spirit or movement. Let's parse a bit deeper here. Generally this next verse is left out when speaking of antichrist.

"They went out from us, but they were not of us; for if they had been of us, they would have continued with us: but they went out, that they might be made manifest that they all are not of us" (1 John 2:19, ASV). This is the verse that follows the first antichrist verse in the Bible. The subject matter that was being discussed in the previous sentence had not changed. The subject was still "antichrist." These were the antichrist. The antichrist was not an individual person. These people had associated with the first-century believers. Things were beginning to heat up. The Jewish leaders were persecuting the believers worse and worse as time went on. These antichrists disassociated with the first-century believers because they could not stand up to the persecution. To be a first-century believer could cost you your life. The Judaizers were the most likely ones to kill the Christians. They conspired with the Roman Empire to have Jesus crucified. They were the pushers. They were the ones who inspired the spirit of antichrist. The antichrist would rather deny Jesus as Messiah and live than to profess Him as King and die. The Roman persecution would not really heat up until the city of Rome burned and Nero blamed the Christians. His persecution would last three and a half years before he would commit suicide.

"And who is a liar? Anyone who says that Jesus is not the Christ. Anyone who denies the Father and the Son is an antichrist" (1 John 2:22,

NLT). One would not have expected the caesars to profess Jesus as Lord. One would not have expected the Babylonians, the Medes and Persians, the Greeks, or Romans to have professed Jesus as Lord. Most of them would have never heard about Him. One would not expect people who were in the very nation that produced Messiah to deny His Deity. This verse also states that antichrist is anyone who denies the Father and the Son. There were many antichrists in Israel 1,950 years ago, as there are in the United States today, as well as the world and Israel. We almost had an atheist as the democratic nominee for president in 2016. Bernie Sanders is an atheist. Yes, he is. Of course there are many politicians who claim to be believers, but their actions attest to their true beliefs. There will be no liars, thieves, or bribe takers (of soft monies) in heaven. John is not identifying any one person as antichrist. There were many back then and even more today. If you had witnessed the miracles of Jesus, I imagine that you were a convert. When He poured out His wrath on the nation of Israel and destroyed the temple in AD 70, surely every knee bowed and every tongue confessed that He was Lord. That was His "coming on clouds."

"And every spirit that confesseth not that Jesus Christ is come in the flesh is not of God: and this is that spirit of antichrist, whereof ye have heard that it should come; and even now already is it in the world" (1 John 4:3, KJV). Again, the timeframe is addressed in this verse. John tells his contemporaries that what they had heard was to come was already present. The temple authorities, the Pharisees, and the rulers of the Jewish nation all denied Jesus deity. Any one of these groups could have stepped up and spoken up for Jesus, and He would have been spared. They all denied His Messiahship. Were they all doggedly determined that He was not Messiah? Well, if they believed that He was the Messiah and did not man up, let's see what happened to them. *"Know ye not that the unrighteous shall not inherit the kingdom of God? Be not deceived: neither fornicators, nor idolaters, nor adulterers, nor effeminate, nor abusers of themselves with mankind"* (1 Corinthians 6:9, KJV). Effeminate here is not homosexual. That would be the next category listed. Effeminate are those males that will not man up. They are males that allow the women to rule the roost and will not live up to their God-given responsibilities as men. Man up!

All the prophets had foretold of a time when the people would be deniers and that God would pour out His wrath on them. Many had denied that God would ever do this to the Jews, yet it is what the prophets prophesied. Many today deny this. I will say it again. Today there is neither Jew nor Greek (Gentile). God is not a distinguisher of persons, unless you ask someone who is biblically illiterate. Let's address this here.

There are many who think that God has two peoples and two plans. That is a lie and not scriptural. It is also bigoted. I would say that it is racist, but there is only one race, the human race. There is also only one plan for salvation. *"Jesus saith unto him, I am the way, the truth, and the life: no man cometh unto the Father, but by me"* (John 14:6, KJV). Those who deny the deity of Jesus, His Lordship, and Messiahship shall never be admitted into the kingdom of God. God is in His kingdom. His kingdom is in heaven and is not of this earth. There is one plan and one people. The destruction of the temple and the city of Jerusalem marked the end of one people and began the new heaven and earth, which allows all people access to the kingdom—but only through Jesus. Jesus did not state "no man, but the Jew, cometh to the Father, but by me." There are no exceptions. Actually, the Queen of the South and the Ninevites were not covenant people. They are mentioned in the second resurrection, which consisted of those prior to the advent of Jesus the Messiah.

> The men of Nineveh shall rise in judgment with this generation, and shall condemn it: because they repented at the preaching of Jonas; and, behold, a greater than Jonas is here. The queen of the south shall rise up in the judgment with this generation, and shall condemn it: for she came from the uttermost parts of the earth to hear the wisdom of Solomon; and, behold, a greater than Solomon is here. (Matthew 12:41–42, KJV)

Salvation was available to others prior to the New Covenant. The Jews were not getting the job done. They had become nationalist and racist. The main difference with the covenants is that all experienced "soul sleep" under the OC. Under the NC, grace and not law, the repentant do not experience "soul sleep."

There are many preachers today that have stated this: "Those who bless my people I will bless, and those who curse my people I will curse." This is not scripturally correct. The scripture has to be twisted to get this heretical statement. What it states is the following: "And I will bless them that bless thee, and curse him that curseth thee: and in thee shall all families of the earth be blessed" (Genesis 12:3, KJV). God is speaking directly to Abraham here. He is telling Abraham that He will bless those who bless Abraham and curse those who curse Abraham. In no way is God stating that

He will bless the Jews. The Jews were of a covenant people. They were not a race. Abraham was of the present day area of Iraq. He was an Iraqi. His brothers and sisters, father, and mother were never considered Jews or of the covenant. It is obvious that even the Galatians may have had a false view of the Jews. Paul addresses it, though, once for all, but most miss it.

> Now to Abraham and his seed were the promises made. He saith not, and to seeds, as of many; but as of one, and to thy seed, which is Christ. And this I say, that the covenant, that was confirmed before of God in Christ, the law, which was four hundred and thirty years after, cannot disannul, that it should make the promise of none effect. For if the inheritance be of the law, it is no more of promise: but God gave it to Abraham by promise. Wherefore then serveth the law? It was added because of transgressions, until the seed should come to whom the promise was made; and it was ordained by angels in the hand of a mediator. Now a mediator is not a mediator of one, but God is one. Is the law then against the promises of God? God forbid: for if there had been a law given which could have given life, verily righteousness should have been by the law. But the scripture hath concluded all under sin that the promise by faith of Jesus Christ might be given to them that believe. But before faith came, we were kept under the law, shut up unto the faith which should afterwards be revealed. Wherefore the law was our schoolmaster to bring us unto Christ, that we might be justified by faith. But after that faith is come, we are no longer under a schoolmaster. For ye are all the children of God by faith in Christ Jesus. (Galatians 3:16–26, KJV)

The promises were made to Abraham and to Jesus, the coming Messiah. The promise was not made to the nation of Israel, the Jews. Jesus even states that He came to bless the Jew first. Why the Jew first? Because they were His lineage. They were also the ones who He interacted with on a daily basis. I have heard many television and radio preachers state false things about the Jewish people. There will never be peace on this earth until we interpret scripture as God meant for it to be interpreted. God is not a bigot or a racist. He is a favorer of those who choose the Seed that is Jesus the Christ. He shall never favor a people who hold to doctrine that states that Jesus is the bastard Son of a harlot. Sorry, these have "antichrist" written all over their foreheads.

It is very interesting how Paul stresses that the promise was to the "seed" and not "seeds." He is stating that the promise is not to the Jews, the nation of Israel. The promise it to Abraham and *the Seed*, which is Jesus the Christ, and none other. This verse has been in the New Testament biblical canon ever since its first canonization, in AD 170. Paul is stressing to the Galatians, who were Gentiles, that the promise was made to Abraham and his Seed. Paul stresses here that the Seed is not the Jew or the nation of Israel. I am sure that this is why none of Paul's writings ever made it into the Jewish Bible, the Talmud. If you bless God, you are a blessing to Jesus. If you bless Jesus, you are a blessing to God. If you are a denier of Jesus as the Son of God, you will not receive the blessings of God. Also, if you are a racist bigot, you will not receive the blessings of God. Eternal life is the ultimate blessing of God. If you are a racist with favoritism toward a group that believes that Jesus is the bastard son of a harlot, then you will hear, "Depart from me. I never knew you," as Jesus said.

"For many deceivers are entered into the world, who confess not that Jesus Christ is come in the flesh. This is a deceiver and an antichrist" (2 John 1:7, KJV). This is the last place where antichrist is used in the scriptures. John is the only one who uses the term. From this verse, we glean that deceivers are antichrist and that they were present in the world at that time. Nowhere does John prophecy of a coming antichrist. He states that antichrist is present "now," in their days. It is not for our future. Anyone who tells you that antichrist is for our near future is a deceiver. If they do not believe that every jot or tittle has been fulfilled, then they are not only deceiving the masses, they are deceiving themselves. Deception, either born out of ignorance or evil, has negative effects. There can be no rewards for negative effects. A lie is a lie regardless of intention or whether it is born out of a lie or out of ignorance. To be least in the kingdom of God is better than the alternative, but it is of low standing. Eternity is a long time. Yes, there are antichrists and deceivers today, but John was addressing his generation.

Mystery, Babylon the Mother of Harlots

> And upon her forehead was a name written, MYSTERY, BABYLON THE GREAT, THE MOTHER OF HARLOTS AND ABOMINATIONS OF THE EARTH. And I saw the woman drunken with the blood of the

> saints, and with the blood of the martyrs of Jesus: and
> when I saw her, I wondered with great admiration.
> (Revelation 17:5–6, KJV)

I must say that this verse was not a mystery to me until I heard a televangelist state something that was against common sense. There are many false teachers and preachers today who state this verse is speaking of another entity other than what John and God meant for those who are His to comprehend. Of course, this was written to the first-century believers and not us today. It is of relevance to us, but it was of imminence to them. Those who are familiar with the Old Testament recognize that there are many references to the nation of Israel, the Jewish people, as a harlot and a whore. Were the streets of Rome where the saints died? Did they die in the streets of Babylon or Greece? The saints were the Old Testament prophets and fathers of the nation of Israel. The martyrs of Jesus were those who died after His coming, which would have included His apostles and all who died for His name's sake prior to AD 70. None of the OT saints died in the streets of Rome or under Roman rule. We know that Paul and Peter died in Rome, but it was because of the persecution of the believers by the Judaistic leaders of the apostate harlot of the Jewish system. God's system was Jesus. The Jewish system was compromised and became the standard of man and not God. God sent them their prophesied Messiah, but they rejected Him. The events of AD 70 were God's rejection of apostate Jerusalem. This is a foreshadowing of what happens to the nonbeliever for all time.

America is in a state of decline now because the masses have rejected God. If Jesus is your Messiah, then your life will reflect it. Your fruit will bear you out. Nations will rise, and nations will fall based upon how they either accept God through Jesus the Christ or reject God by rejecting Jesus as Messiah. History has borne this out. Facts are facts regardless of your position. Every nation that has rejected God is a "has been" world power. Each nation was at its highest point when God was the God of that nation. Great Britain was the greatest empire this world has ever known until she rejected Messiah and has since pretty much become an atheistic nation. Yes, she was far greater than the Roman Empire. There was actually no comparison size-wise and population-wise. Spain has come and gone. France is another "has been." There are many nations that have been at their pinnacle of power and prosperity when God was at their heart. Heaven will be heaven because there will be no rejecters

299

there. Let's look at some Old Testament verses that attest to the harlot/ whore of the nation of Israel.

"How is the faithful city become an harlot. It was full of judgment; righteousness lodged in it; but now murderers" (Isaiah 1:21, KJV). The nation of Israel had split before Isaiah's time. He was a prophet to Judah, which included the temple that Solomon built, with the city of Jerusalem. His reference of "faithful city" is actually a reference to the nation of God's people. The nation had played a harlot with other nations, other gods, and so forth. The people had put their trust in other gods, which of course were no gods. Idolatry had taken hold of the people. They trusted in alliances with other nations rather than the might of Almighty God. This was an abomination to the One True God. Therefore God considered Israel a harlot or whore. He is never changing. Perfection need not evolve. He is the same yesterday, today, and forever.

> For of old time I have broken thy yoke, and burst thy bands; and thou saidst, I will not transgress; when upon every high hill and under every green tree thou wanderest, playing the harlot. (Jeremiah 2:20, KJV)

> The LORD said also unto me in the days of Josiah the king, hast thou seen that which backsliding Israel hath done? She is gone up upon every high mountain and under every green tree, and there hath played the harlot. (Jeremiah 3:6, KJV)

Jeremiah was a prophet to Judah about seventy-five years after Isaiah. He was prophet before the Babylonian exile and into the exile period, which began in the last years of the 600s BC. This would have been when the first group of prisoners was taken, which would have included Daniel. There were actually several different exiles that extended down to about 586 BC, which comprised the Babylonian exile. Symbolic language is very prevalent in the writings of the old prophets. Josiah was king of the southern kingdom of Judah from around 640 to 609 BC. Every high hill and every green tree is used here as symbolism for other nations or powers that be. The Jews trusted more in the power of nations than in the power of God Almighty. Therefore God attached the moniker, "harlot," to the nation of Israel.

"And I saw, when for all the causes whereby backsliding Israel committed adultery I had put her away, and given her a bill of divorce; yet

her treacherous sister Judah feared not, but went and played the harlot also" (Jeremiah 3:8, KJV). God had a covenant with all the nation of Israel; all twelve tribes would have been included. Because of the harlotry played by the northern kingdom of Israel, God had issued them a bill of divorce. There are those Zionists today who state that God would never divorce Israel. Well, He divorced the northern kingdom of Israel at the Assyrian captivity between 740 and 732 BC. Ever since then the ten tribes have been called the lost tribes. God's word says that He divorced the ten tribes for far less than the crucifixion of His Son committed by the southern kingdom of Judah. Yes, God signed a divorce decree with Judah in AD 70. *"And I saw, when for all the causes whereby backsliding Israel committed adultery I had put her away, and given her a bill of divorce; yet her treacherous sister Judah feared not, but went and played the harlot also"* (Jeremiah 3:8, KJV). This is God speaking in this verse. Jeremiah is documenting it. If the canon had not been sealed by man with the book of Revelation, then there very likely would have been a record of a divorce decree. It was delivered, but man has decreed that it be not known. Jesus declaration of *"There shall not be left here one stone upon another that shall not be thrown down"* was the divorce decree once it occurred. In the writings of Josephus is documented an instance when Galba took an image of Nero and had it set up in the Jewish temple. Galba reigned from June, 68 to January, 69. This event was very close to the end that the prophets and Jesus had foretold. We do not know the exact timing of Galba's setting the image of Nero in the temple, but obviously it was between June of 68 and January 69 AD. This would have been nineteen to twenty-six months prior to the destruction of the temple. A dear friend of mine commented that he would rather have received a divorce decree from God than to be annihilated by God. The city and temple were destroyed. What God has put asunder, let no man put back together.

"But thou didst trust in thine own beauty, and playedst the harlot because of thy renown, and pouredst out thy fornications on every one who passed by; his it was" (Ezekiel 16:15, KJV). Ezekiel was a prophet to Judah during the Babylonian exile. The language here is very symbolic. Obviously, the southern kingdom of Judah thought much of herself. She had been mightily blessed of God. She was renowned in that part of the world. Remember the Queen of Sheba? She had heard about the greatness of the nation of Israel and the wisdom of King Solomon. She went to visit Solomon and took him gifts of gold, spices, and precious stones. Solomon shared his wisdom with her based on questions that she had asked. She was very impressed with what she heard. She knew that this nation and this people group were far

different from other nations and peoples. The difference was in the God they served. All the other nations served false gods, which are no gods. Nature is no god. The sun and the moon are no gods. They were created by El Shaddai, the one True God. Allah was born out of a mythological local god in the Middle East. Allah was the moon god. Muhammed had knowledge of the One True God. He was familiar with the prophets. He mixed scripture with his vain imaginations and came up with Allah. This is a whole other subject that needs to be addressed. Actually, it has been addressed. It is addressed in the scriptures of the Holy Bible. There are no more prophets after AD 70. Prophecy and vision have been sealed.

> Seventy weeks are determined upon thy people and upon thy holy city, to finish the transgression, and to make an end of sins, and to make reconciliation for iniquity, and to bring in everlasting righteousness, and to seal up the vision and prophecy, and to anoint the most Holy. (Daniel 9:24, KJV)

There is much confusion that could be caused by Daniel's statement above if one is not familiar with all of scripture. As I have stated elsewhere in this compilation, even after the new heaven and earth have come, people are still committing sin, dying, and being consigned to the lake of fire: *"But the cowardly, the unbelieving, the vile, the murderers, the sexually immoral, those who practice magic arts, the idolaters and all liars— they will be consigned to the fiery lake of burning sulfur. This is the second death"* (Revelation 21:8, NIV). This verse in Revelation is after the new heaven and earth have come. People believe that there will be a day on this earth when no one commits sin or dies anymore. That is not what the scriptures state. Man will never experience heaven on earth. His kingdom is not of this world. It is in heaven. This scripture contains a list of those who shall not enter the realm of His kingdom. I encourage you again to go to the Blue Letter Bible and look at this verse in all fourteen English translations. Make sure that you are not among the crowd listed here in this verse. Nowhere in the scripture does it state that this behavior is excused because you have made a confession of faith. It does not state that the repentant sexually immoral will make it into heaven. If you are repentant, you are no longer sexually immoral. Jesus told the woman that was about to be stoned for sexual immorality to go and sin no more. He did not say "You are covered. Go and do as you please." To repent means to do a 180-degree turn. If there is no repentance there is no salvation.

"Love never ends. As for prophecies, they will pass away; as for tongues, they will cease; as for knowledge, it will pass away" (1 Corinthians 13:8, ESV). Daniel addresses prophecy and vision in the second scripture above this one stating "and to seal up the vision and prophecy, and to anoint the most Holy." Paul stated that once AD 70, the destruction of the temple and the city of Jerusalem took place, that prophecies would pass away and that tongues would cease. If prophecies would pass away, then that means that there are no more prophets. Also, tongues would cease. This is a whole other subject for another work. If you say that I am wrong, then you are saying that the Bible is wrong. It is in scripture. Look it up on the Blue Letter Bible online and do a "Bibles" comparison under "Tools." Look at each of the fourteen English versions, not just the KJV. The other versions render a better understanding of what is being communicated here. The HCSB gives the best interpretation. If prophecy has come to an end, and men understood that, there would be several sects, religions, and denominations that would not exist today. Denominations are of man and not of God. His will is that His people be of one mind. Ignorance is what brought about denominationalism. Denomination is division. God is into math. He is into addition and multiplication, not division (denomination) and subtraction.

"Yet she multiplied her whoredoms, in calling to remembrance the days of her youth, wherein she had played the harlot in the land of Egypt" (Ezekiel 23:19, KJV). When Israel entered Egypt, she consisted only of the immediate family of Jacob. This would be him, his sons and daughter-in-law's, and their children. Exodus informs us that seventy people entered Egypt, which was the family of Joseph, who was already in Egypt. They were there for several centuries and multiplied greatly. Egypt was into nature worship. She was much into carved images of creatures that God created. There were many false gods that were born out of the pagan Egyptian system. Evidently, the family of Jacob had participated in the worship of the false gods of Egypt. Recollect that the Jews longed to return to Egypt when they felt that things were tough on their sojourn to the Promised Land. They wanted to return to slavery under the pagan system, rather than to be true to God and create real character by going through the fires of life and staying true to God. Experience has always proven that this is the correct path. There are many today whom God views in the same light as the nation of Israel. Do not play the harlot with man's evil systems. The ways of God lead to peace and joy. The ways of man lead to death and destruction.

"Though thou, Israel, play the harlot, yet let not Judah offend; and come not ye unto Gilgal, neither go ye up to Bethaven, nor swear, The LORD liveth" (Hosea 4:15, KJV). Hosea was a prophet to Israel before the Assyrian captivity. He prophesied the destruction of the kingdom of the ten tribes and warned their sister kingdom, Judah, against such heresy and antagonism toward their Creator. The northern kingdom of Israel had played the harlot. God denounced them as His children, and they became known as the lost tribes of Israel when He issued them the divorce decree. The southern kingdom of Judah, which consisted of the tribes of Benjamin and Judah, would go on another seven hundred and ninety years, approximately, before God would issue His divorce decree to them in AD 70. Please, do not pass from this life without bowing the knee to Jesus and accepting Him as Messiah. Get on board and learn of His ways and His laws. Your life will not be hindered. It will be enhanced; I promise. "Experience keeps a dear school, but fools will learn in no other." Man does not have to participate in sin. Man chooses to lie. Man chooses to steal. Sexual immorality is a choice. Anger gets a lot of people into trouble. With the word of God burning in the heart and the Holy Spirit abiding in a believer, sin can be overcome. There are many out there today who think they can just go and live their lives as they did before salvation. They think all is forgiven. They think they can lie, cheat, steal, gossip, commit sexual immorality, and do all manner of sin and that there is no price to be paid. Those may just find that when they take their last breath in this life that they descend to the pit of perdition and not to heaven. Self-control is a fruit of the spirit. If you have no self-control you have a spiritual problem. Israel had a spiritual problem. They thought they could play the harlot with no consequences. Well, AD 70 proves that the prophets, John the Revelator, and Jesus were correct when they insisted that this "generation of vipers" repent. Vipers, harlots—what difference does it make? It is just language that describes behavior that God hates.

"And all the graven images thereof shall be beaten to pieces, and all the hires thereof shall be burned with the fire, and all the idols thereof will I lay desolate: for she gathered it of the hire of an harlot, and they shall return to the hire of an harlot" (Micah 1:7, KJV). Micah was a prophet to Israel prior to the Assyrian captivity and was co-prophet with Isaiah in his latter years. Graven images are man-made gods. As the children of Jacob had melted their gold and formed an image of a calf in the wilderness, so had this generation. Israel was also making gods out of other nations. They were allowing other nations to become their protection and

their shield. This would not work out very well for them. The people of God are not to be a harlot, nor are they to play with harlots. It is either God's way or the highway. Even after God allowed the children of Israel to wander in the wilderness for forty years, and these people knew that history, they were bound to offend their Creator and suffer judgment for it. Nations will rise, and nations will fall. Wake up, world!

"Thou hast played the whore also with the Assyrians, because thou wast unsatiable; yea, thou hast played the harlot with them, and yet couldest not be satisfied" (Ezekiel 16:28, KJV). Ezekiel is admonishing the southern kingdom of Judah here. It appears that this is before they were taken into exile. The verses that follow this one are very strong words against a nation that had played a harlot with other nations that were pagan in nature. Of course, the Assyrians had taken the ten tribes of Israel into captivity, and they lost their identity as a nation and a people. Obviously the southern kingdom of Judah had also flirted with the Assyrians. Ezekiel likens Judah to a harlot. We know that God ordained marriage in the beginning as between a man and a woman. God also ordained a relationship with mankind, between Himself and man. Our relationship with God is not for procreation or feelings of ecstasy. We are to glorify God, and He will give us a sense of joy and peace that we have never known before. We can learn much from the verses that precede this verse in Ezekiel of how God views and ordained the relationship of husband and wife. How many will open their Bible to this chapter? Read and receive.

> And the light of a candle shall shine no more at all in thee; and the voice of the bridegroom and of the bride shall be heard no more at all in thee: for thy merchants were the great men of the earth; for by thy sorceries were all nations deceived. And in her was found the blood of prophets, and of saints, and of all that were slain upon the earth. (Revelation 18:23–24, KJV)

There is a great number within the church who believes that God would never divorce or abandon Israel. We have shown elsewhere that God issued a divorce decree to the northern kingdom in the 700s BC. If the bridegroom has abandoned the house, a divorce has occurred. The bride has also abandoned the house. This is prophecy of the coming divorce decree for Judah. This complies with the history documented by Josephus where he states that not a single known Christian was found among all the dead bodies in Jerusalem after the Roman forces stormed the city and the temple. The southern kingdom of Judah was about to be abandoned by God, the Father, Son, and Holy Spirit, as well as the church. All that was good was about to be gone. There are many scripturally illiterates that preach Old Testament prophecies about the Babylonian exile and restoration as a future event, yet it was fulfilled in the latter years of the 500s BC. Of course they do not perceive that they are preaching/ teaching a past event. Well, Jesus stated that "all would be fulfilled" within the last generation of the covenant people of God. AD 70 is in our past. All prophecy was fulfilled with the destruction, the judgment, of the southern kingdom of Judah.

I just got through reading an online devotional that I read every day. There was reference to "Mystery, Babylon the Great . . ." The subject matter was not about end-times, but how the Bible is historically correct, as well as archeologically correct. It was obvious to me, though, that it attributed this character of Revelation to the nation of Iraq. It is obvious that the writer of this daily devotional needs to get educated to truth and not a lie. I am sure he is so caught up in science, though, that he misses what is available in Bible 101. He speaks of how the Bible confirms science, yet He misses that the Bible also confirms that the consummation of the OC occurred in AD 70 and that we now live in the new heaven and earth. I agree with his science, but obviously, science has taken the driver's seat, and the Bible has taken the back seat.

Tell me this. Who is the bridegroom and the bride? The term "bridegroom" is used fifteen times in twelve verses of the KJV of the New Testament. It is used to describe Messiah, Jesus, in every instance except one time. That was when Jesus turned water into wine, and the governor called the bridegroom and asked him why he waited to serve the best wine last (John 2:9–10). We know that "bride" is used to describe the children of God, the church, those who have bowed the knee to Jesus. The children of God, those who heeded Jesus warnings, fled the city of Jerusalem for the safety of the mountains. This scripture is written in Old Testament apocalyptic language. Did it actually mean that there would never be candlelight seen in it for all eternity? Did it actually mean that not a single Christian would ever step foot on this once-hallowed ground forevermore? No, it did not. It was communicating to the contemporaries of John's day that the end was at hand. Sadly, we have those today who are yelling this to the bride, and the bride has lost all sense of reality due to a lack of true knowledge of the AD 70 *wipe out, consummation, divorce decree*. It was all of the preceding.

> The same day there came certain of the Pharisees, saying unto him, Get thee out, and depart hence: for Herod will kill thee. And he said unto them, Go ye, and tell that fox, Behold, I cast out devils, and I do cures today and tomorrow, and the third day I shall be perfected. Nevertheless I must walk to day, and tomorrow, and the day following: for it cannot be that a prophet perish out of Jerusalem. O Jerusalem, Jerusalem, which killest the prophets, and stonest them that are sent unto thee; how often would I have gathered thy children together, as a hen doth gather her brood under her wings, and ye would not. Behold, your house is left unto you desolate: and verily I say unto you, ye shall not see me, until the time come when ye shall say, blessed is he that cometh in the name of the Lord. (Luke 13:31–35, KJV)

Jesus appears to be mocking the Pharisees here. His statement of "for it cannot be that a prophet perish out of Jerusalem" is a forthtelling of His soon-to-come demise. The prophets of God were killed by the children of Israel. Not a single one of the Old Testament prophets was killed in the streets of Rome. Jerusalem was founded in the fourth millennium BC. The Israelite history of Jerusalem began circa 1000 BC. The city of Rome was not founded until 753 BC. When Jesus made the statement "your house is left unto you desolate," was He referring to the temple or the city of Jerusalem? I dare say that He was referencing both. The presence of the Holy Spirit would depart the temple upon Jesus' death. This would certainly leave that house desolate, whether the Jews knew it or not. They would have forty years to repent. Many who did were either martyred in the streets of Jerusalem prior to the Neronian persecution, as was Stephen, or they fled to the mountains to Pella, after the abomination of desolation was set up in the temple. Things would get so bad that the Christians would long for the day when it would all end. It would take total chaos and the destruction of *the mother of harlots* to end their grief. There is no consensus on the last verse here. Who is the "he" that comes in the name of the Lord? Look at all fourteen English versions, and you will see that only a couple capitalizes "He." This would be the "coming on clouds" event. The one who would actually be coming, though, was the one who God had selected to pour out His wrath on the *mother of harlots*. This would be the Roman Empire, which consisted of many nations and provinces. This was all about AD 70 and the consummation of the OC. Once this event occurred, it ended the Jewish persecution of the first-century believers. The scattered believers would take the Gospel throughout the nations.

There are many today that say Babylon, current-day Iraq, is what is being referred to in Revelation. Well, if "Babylon" is the mystery, why is it mentioned in the title? If it was truly Babylon, then it would surely not have been a mystery since it was in the title. No, it is not Babylon, or current-day Iraq. Judah had played the whore with other nations. She had worshipped other gods and was practicing idolatry. She was guilty of killing the prophets that told truth and honoring those who tickled her ears. She had killed the very son of God, her Messiah. I believe that the true mystery here is: how could a people be so ignorant as to keep on repeating history? To keep on denying the truth of God always led to destruction for the children of Jacob. The arrogance and pride of the people, the obstinacy of the leaders, and the rejection of Messiah is what led to the destruction of Jerusalem and the temple in AD 70. The Tower of Babel is believed by many to have been destroyed by God. That is not what the scripture states. It states the following: *"So the LORD scattered them abroad from thence upon the face of all the earth: and they left off to build the city"* (Genesis 11:8, KJV). The people left the tower and city as it was and scattered from there. God was about to scatter His remnant across the Roman Empire and eventually the world with the Gospel message. Because Judah rejected Messiah and played the harlot, God would take His promises from Judah and give it to the Gentiles. Did Jesus not make a parable about this very subject? Yes.

I may have taken a bit longer with this particular character, but I pray that it was worthwhile to all. I hope that it has opened the eyes to the discerning soul and to those who have, or had, other views of "MYSTERY, BABYLON THE GREAT, THE MOTHER OF HARLOTS AND ABOMINATIONS OF THE EARTH." It is obvious that this character is none other than the remaining nation of Jews, the rebellious children of God. If it were Babylon, current-day Iraq, John surely would not have stated "Mystery, Babylon the Great, The Mother of Harlots." It was not meant to be a mystery, and it surely was no mystery to the first-century believers. If Babylon was the key, John would not have put it in the statement. I believe that this would also be a great place to reflect back to the Tower of Babel. The people had become so arrogant that they believed they could make their own way to heaven by building a tower that would reach heaven. How foolish was that? They would still be building it today and probably would not have reached the moon yet. God has only one Way for man to reach heaven. The key is

Jesus. Those who bow the knee to Jesus will rise, and those who reject Him will fall.

The Beast

The beast is a character that has garnered much attention in certain circles. Many people today are curious about who this character is because they are deceived into believing that he is in our near future. Many people also believe that the antichrist and the beast are one and the same, as we mentioned earlier. Nowhere in scripture are these two entities identified as each other, nor would anyone garner that from reading the scripture. If you were just reading the Bible for the very first time and had no preconceived ideas about it whatsoever, there is no way that you could link these two together as one entity or person. Antichrist is only mentioned in four places in the Bible, in the epistles of John, and never mentioned in the book of Revelation, nor is the beast ever mentioned in the epistles of John. Many today associate the number 666 with the antichrist, but that is not correct. The beast and the antichrist are not one and the same, as we have shown in the antichrist section. We will look at some verses in Revelation and parse through them.

> The revelation of Jesus Christ, which God gave him to show to his servants the things that must soon take place. He made it known by sending his angel to his servant John, who bore witness to the word of God and to the testimony of Jesus Christ, even to all that he saw. Blessed is the one who reads aloud the words of this prophecy, and blessed are those who hear, and who keep what is written in it, for the time is near.

> John to the seven churches that are in Asia: Grace to you and peace from him who is and who was and who is to come, and from the seven spirits who are before his throne, and from Jesus Christ the faithful witness, the firstborn of the dead, and the ruler of kings on earth.

> To him who loves us and has freed us from our sins by his blood and made us a kingdom, priests to his God and Father, to him be glory and dominion forever and ever.

Amen. Behold, he is coming with the clouds, and every
eye will see him, even those who pierced him, and all
tribes of the earth will wail on account of him. Even so.
Amen. (Revelation 1:1–7, ESV)

The time element is present in this sequence. The time is "near."
The KJV uses "at hand." John sets up the timeframe for his contemporaries right off the bat. Since knowledge has passed or decreased about
this once-in-an-eternity event, we shall never know the exact year that
John passed this writing out among the seven churches in the Roman
province of Asia, which is in modern-day western Turkey, which would
place the seven churches northwest of Israel and likely all were over 650
miles from Jerusalem. Think about traveling that on a donkey or a camel.
Knowledge of history of the area certainly determines that Revelation
was written prior to AD 64 when the Roman persecution began after the
burning of the city of Rome. It could have been any time after AD 54.
Now, we must reveal why I have set this date as the earliest possible
point for the writing of Revelation. Who was in charge of the "beast" at
this time? Who was caesar at this time? John describes who the beast is
in the following verses:

The Seven Heads

"And here is the mind which hath wisdom. The seven heads are seven
mountains, on which the woman sitteth" (Revelation 17:9, KJV). The
City of Seven Hills is the city of Rome. That is the moniker that she was
known by in that area of the world at that specific time. The "woman" can
be considered to be the city of Jerusalem, the nation of Israel or Judea.
Jerusalem was in a strategic location for trade at that time. She was the
link that connected Africa to India, Asia, Europe, and all the other entities
of the Middle East. She was in a great location to reap the rewards from
worldwide trade. The merchants of the world would certainly mourn the
loss of this precious resource. The Jews were not barbaric like the other
nations were at that time. She was a safe haven to bring your goods to
trade. No one would have brought their goods to the likes of the surrounding barbarian pagan nations. They would have been murdered and
robbed. It is amazing that the GREAT MOTHER OF HARLOTS would play the
harlot for financial gain with the nations of the world but would kill the
innocent Messiah. Yet, it had to be done for the salvation of mankind. It
was appointed before time began. We need to quit bemoaning it and rise

up to be what He would have us to be, salt and light, as well as peace-makers; *"and the leaves of the tree were for the healing of the nations"* (Revelation 22:2c, KJV). Blessed are the peacemakers, not the pot stirrers and war mongers.

The Seven Kings

"And there are seven kings: five are fallen, and one is, and the other is not yet come; and when he cometh, he must continue a short space" (Revelation 17:10, KJV). I used to ponder this when I was much younger. When I came back to the Father in 1998 after fleeing from Him for over half my life, the book of Revelation was always a stumbling block to me, as it is to most people. Once you have been educated to the history of that area and epoch of time, it all begins to come together. The only way you can know the history of that era is to read the writings of the historians of that era. Josephus was a contemporary of John, Peter, and Paul. They may not have known each other, but they lived at the same time.

The kings in this verse are Roman caesars. Some would state today that caesars are not kings. Well, the Jews shouted "We have no king, but Caesar." when confronted with what to do with Jesus, King of kings. They considered caesars kings, regardless of what we think today. It is documented in His word. John is not attempting to be totally concise here, up to the nth degree. He is pointing out the beginning point of the great tribulation and the ruler that would initiate it. The first five caesars were Julius, Augustus, Tiberius, Caligula, and Claudius. Since John states that "five are fallen" we know that the sixth, Nero, was on the throne and that the others were dead. Nero ascended the throne in AD 54. He is the "one who is" at the time John handed out his prophetic Revelation to the seven churches in Asia Minor. The Jews had been at peace in the Roman Empire up until that time. The skirmishes between the Christians, the Jews, the Zealots, and other factions that had popped up among the Jews at that time are what drew the attention of the Roman Empire. Paul had gone to Rome to be tried before Caesar. Israel was within the Roman Empire, and their skirmishes were drawing much attention. The Roman forces would rise up in due time and destroy the city, the temple, and the nation of Israel.

The one who was *"the other is not yet come; and when he cometh, he must continue a short space"* was Galba. Nero began his persecution after the city of Rome burned. His persecution began late in the year AD 64. He accused the Christians of starting the fire and began to target them for persecution. The believers were thrown into the arenas with wild beast, burnt alive, mutilated, etc. Nowhere in scripture is a seven-year tribulation mentioned. It does speak of a three and a half year time of persecution. Nero's persecution, or tribulation, would last for three and a half years, from late AD 64 to June of AD 68, when he committed suicide. This began what became known as the year of four caesars. The Roman Empire almost fell at this time due to infighting and the nature of man.

Paul even gives the Thessalonians a glimpse of things to come concerning this character of the end times in the following verses:

> For the mystery of lawlessness is already at work; only he who now restrains it will do so until he is out of the way. And then the lawless one will be revealed, and the Lord Jesus will slay him with the breath of his mouth and destroy him by his appearing and his coming.
>
> (2 Thessalonians 2:7–8, RSV)

The one "who now restrains" has been relegated to Claudius, the caesar who preceded Nero. He was the great uncle of Nero. It is thought that he was poisoned to death, possibly by his wife, or others. Nero ascended the throne upon Claudius's death. After Nero's three and half year persecution of the Jews and Christians that began after the city of Rome burned in AD 64 and ceased in June 68 AD, Nero committed suicide. Hmmm—it sounds like the Lord Jesus slayed Nero with the breath of His mouth.

"And there are seven kings: five are fallen, and one is, and the other is not yet come; and when he cometh, he must continue a short space" (Revelation 17:10, KJV). Galba succeeded Nero. He was on the throne only seven months. In January of 69, he was assassinated. There was much derision going on within the Roman Empire at this time. People of the empire thought that she was on the very edge of falling off of a cliff. Galba's seven month reign was the shortest for a caesar at that time. Caligula's reign expanded over four years. Galba was the first caesar that was not of the Julio-Claudian dynasty. He would be the second caesar of the year of four caesars.

"And the beast that was, and is not, even he is the eighth, and is of the seven, and goeth into perdition" (Revelation 17:11, KJV). John states here that the eighth is also the beast, but also that the seventh was, too. So, it is obvious that the beast is the Roman Empire with caesars as representatives. Otho was next to become caesar, the eighth. His reign would be even shorter than Galba's. He lasted three months before committing suicide.

His successor was Vitellius, who was the last of the year of four caesars. Vitellius would reign for only eight months and would be killed in a battle that was going on within the Roman Empire at that time. The Roman Empire appeared about ready to fall. The next to rise to the throne would be Vespasian, the first of the Flavian Dynasty, which would last from AD 69 to AD 96. The Flavian Dynasty would include the rule of three caesars, Vespasian, who ruled from AD 69–79, and his two sons. They would revive the Roman Empire, the beast that destroyed Israel. The city of Jerusalem and the temple were destroyed under the rule of Vespasian.

Paul's statement about the decrease of knowledge certainly applies here. Many commentators state that a resurrection of the beast took place here. Well, the beast was actually the Roman Empire, but it had representatives that were the caesars. Satan has never had power to perform a resurrection. The Roman Empire was about to fall at this time. There were battles going on within the Empire. This is why they experienced the year of four caesars. They were not killed from without. They were killed from within or took their own lives due to the wretched times they were experiencing within the Roman Empire. Many even thought that Nero was still alive at this time and hiding. John is using imagery here to describe what is going to happen. You would have to have been there to experience it to truly get a feel for the details that John gave. I am not even sure that John understood all of the details that he was warning the first-century believers of. He obviously knew that Nero would begin the persecution as a representative of the beast, the Roman Empire. Nero is even reported to have taken Jews, soaked them in oil, put them on poles along the streets of Rome, and set them on fire to light the streets. It appears that Nero's persecution of the first-century believers could have been mainly Christians within close proximity of Rome, the city. Jerusalem was not attacked until after Nero's reign. All the Roman caesars from Nero through Vespasian would have been representatives of the "beast."

Mark of the Beast

> And that no man might buy or sell, save he that had the mark, or the name of the beast, or the number of his name. Here is wisdom. Let him that hath understanding count the number of the beast: for it is the number of a man; and his number is Six hundred threescore and six.
> (Revelation 13:17–18, KJV)

313

Was this to be a literal mark? Many today claim that this is future for the world and it will involve the forced placement of computer chips into the hands of people. A reading of Josephus would expose this myth. John was speaking to his contemporaries and not us today. He had sense enough to know that it was his generation, the one who killed Jesus, which would experience all of this mayhem. Josephus even speaks of how the Christians were not allowed to trade and carry on commerce within the Roman Empire. They were barred from trading because they had no king but Jesus. The Bible speaks many times in the Old Testament about being marked, but it is never meant as a literal mark. I have the mark of Christ on me. Where is it at? It is on my heart. Can you see it? No, because it is not literal. It is symbolic language.

John told his contemporaries that they would know him by his number. The Hebrew language of that era was tied to gematria, which is a numerological system. Their alphabet had numerical values. The English alphabet has never had numerical values assigned to it. How could the Jews of John's day possibly look ahead one thousand, nine hundred, and fifty-plus years to calculate a man's number?

Nero was truly a beast. He did atrocious things. During his caesarship, he murdered his mother and his first wife and was alleged to have murdered his second wife. It was rumored that he had burnt the city so that he could rebuild the center of the city to his preferences. He even considered himself as deity, as did many if not all the caesars. There are even records that report that he would put Christians in the arena in Rome and would disguise himself in animal skins and attack their private parts, male and female, in front of the crowds. There are also records that state that he was a pedophile. He sure sounded like a beast. Actually, he was just another representative of the beast that was the Roman Empire.

Over my years of research, I have looked at many sources and could not even document all the sources that I have looked at. I do recollect that I ran across some information where the "666" number in Hebrew totaled out to be 616 in some early manuscripts of the scriptures. I thought this was an error. Well, Caesar Nero could have two different ways of spelling it in the ancient tongue: Nrwn Qsr and NRW Qsr. The first version gives a total of 666, and the other gives 616. There is much about this on the Internet. There are also many lies out there on the Internet, as well as in the pulpits. Is it out of ignorance or evil? I say mostly out of ignorance of historical facts of the waning days of the Old Covenant. Regardless, ignorance or evil, the results are the same—defeat and failure.

I encourage all to do an online search of "gematria," "the beast of Revelation," and "666." I will state this as fact. Any source that states that the beast is in our future has been deceived. Jesus stated that "this generation" shall not pass until all these things come to fruition. He even states that some of those who pierced Him would live to see it. Anyone who states that Jesus was ignorant of the generation who would experience His prophecies, John's prophecies, as well as the Old Testament prophets' prophecies, is calling Jesus a liar. He certainly knew the generation that would experience the *consummation, the end of the Old Covenant era*.

I will note this very briefly. Daniel speaks of four beasts in his prophetic book. These beasts represented empires that ruled over the southern kingdom of Judah, beginning with Nebuchadnezzar, king of the Babylonian Empire. Hmmm—did he not get to spend seven years as a beast of the field as a punishment from God? God gave Nebuchadnezzar the heart of a beast; *"Let his heart be changed from man's, and let a beast's heart be given unto him; and let seven times pass over him"* (Daniel 4:16, KJV). He ruled over Judah as a beast. He was actually the representative of the Babylonian Empire. All the beasts are empires but are represented by kings. Kings of the Babylonian Empire would have been representatives of the first beast, the Babylonian Empire. The Babylonians were defeated by the Medes and Persians. Cyrus was the king over this empire. The Greeks rose up as a world power during this epoch of time under Alexander the Great. This was the third beast. When he died, four of his generals divided his kingdom and the Alexandrian Empire was splintered. The fourth beast is the Roman Empire that overtook the southern kingdom of Judah in 63 BC. The beast is representative of world powers from the Babylonian exile to the destruction of the temple and city of Jerusalem and the consummation of the OC in AD 70. Jerusalem had much experience dealing with beasts by the time Nero took the throne in AD 54. His persecution began in AD 64. Irenaeus and Hippolytus began the heresy of combining antichrist and the beast as one character. I will state this here. There will be no revival of the Roman Empire. God achieved His objective with them when they destroyed the temple and not a stone was left unturned. This was the consummation of the ages, once for all time. There are those who are ignorant of scripture and historical facts that confirm fulfilled prophecy. These have stolen Nero's fiddle and are fiddling with the minds of the church. Wake up!!

Abomination of Desolation

> And arms shall stand on his part, and they shall pol-
> lute the sanctuary of strength, and shall take away the
> daily sacrifice, and they shall place the abomination that
> maketh desolate. (Daniel 11:31, KJV)

> And from the time that the daily sacrifice shall be taken
> away, and the abomination that maketh desolate set up,
> there shall be a thousand two hundred and ninety days.
> (Daniel 12:11, KJV)

In the KJV of the Bible Jesus is the only one who states "abomination
of desolation." Daniel states "abomination that maketh desolate" in two
places. These are two separate prophecies that occurred at different times,
separated by about two hundred and forty years. Daniel's first account of
"abomination that maketh desolate," listed in Daniel 11:31, was attributed
to Antiochus IV Epiphanes, who reigned as king of Syria between 175 and
164 BC. During this time he had an image of likely Zeus or Baal set up in
the Jewish temple. This account is documented in the book of Maccabees.
It is obvious, though, from Jesus' statement that is recorded in Matthew
and Mark, that Daniel 12:11 is the prophecy Jesus was speaking about that
was still in His contemporaries' future. The books of Maccabees, which
reports events prior to Jesus birth, heavily around 165 BC, are not considered canonical in the Protestant Church, nor are the writings of Josephus,
but they are a great testament to fulfilled prophecy. The Catholic Church
canonized I Maccabees. Keep in mind that footnotes and comments documented within both compilations are from people hundreds, and even over
fifteen hundred-plus years removed from the events documented in these
writings. Josephus was an eye witness, and the writer, or writers, of the
book of Maccabees was either contemporary with the generation that he
documented or just one generation later, but more likely a contemporary.

> When ye therefore shall see the abomination of desola-
> tion, spoken of by Daniel the prophet, stand in the holy
> place, (whoso readeth, let him understand).
> (Matthew 24:15, KJV)

> But when ye shall see the abomination of desolation,
> spoken of by Daniel the prophet, standing where it ought

not, (let him that readeth understand,) then let them that
be in Judaea flee to the mountains. (Mark 13:14, KJV)

In the writings of Josephus is documented an instance when Galba
took an image of Nero and had it set up in the Jewish temple. Galba
reigned from June 68 to January 69. This symbolic resurrection event
of the "one who was" could also be the resurrection that John spoke of
about the beast. This event was very close to the end that the prophets
and Jesus had foretold. We do not know the exact timing of Galba's setting the image of Nero in the temple, but obviously it was between June
of 68 and January 69 AD. This would have been nineteen to twenty-six
months prior to the destruction of the temple.

Temple rituals and sacrifices were still being carried out when Jesus
was walking the earth, as well as during the span of time between Jesus'
death and the deaths of his apostles. Temple sacrifices and rituals continued on until a time in the latter days when they were halted. I do not
have an exact date for the abomination of desolation, the image of Nero,
being set up in the temple, but we must allow scripture to interpret scrip
ture. When looking at a particular subject, we must look at all scripture
that is associated with that event or subject. That is a very difficult, if not
impossible, task to perform because we are about 1,950 years away from
the "latter days" and about 2,500 years from Daniel's prophecy. Well,
for this particular event the answer is glaring at us. We may not be able
to whittle it down to an exact day and time, but we can whittle it down
to . . . well, let's just see how close. Daniel states that it would be 1,290
days from the time daily sacrifices would be halted until the abomination that "maketh desolate" would be set up in the temple. The image of
Nero was an image, or representative, of the Roman Empire. We know
from the writings of Josephus that Galba set an image of Nero up in the
Jewish temple after his death. This would be an image that represented
the empire that would make the temple, the city, and the Jewish nation
desolate. Since Galba reigned only seven months, we can whittle the date
of the halting of temple sacrifices and rituals to about November of AD
64 to about June of 65. This would allow time for Galba's seven-month
reign as caesar. He could have set up the image of Nero in June when he
took office, or any time up until his death in January of 69.

It becomes obvious that the Roman Empire, under Nero, had made an
edict that the Jewish rituals in the temple were to be halted. What could
have caused such an edict? Well, I think that the burning of the city of
Rome was surely enough to cause such an aggressive move against the

317

Jews. We shall never know who was truly responsible for the burning of the city of Rome in our earthly lifetimes. It could have been an edict from Jesus Himself to bring the Jews to their knees. God did not recognize temple sacrifices or rituals at this time, anyway. When Jesus stated "It is finished" from the cross, it was also an announcement from the King of kings that animal sacrifices and temple rituals would no longer be accepted by the Father.

Jesus' contemporaries would certainly understand when the abomination of desolation took place about thirty-eight years after his death. I imagine that many had forgotten the statement until they witnessed the event, or heard about it as news traveled from the city of Jerusalem to the mountains. I imagine that many of them had a revival of memory. This verse is also a time warning for those living in the "last days." Jesus warned the first-century believers to flee to the mountains in the following; *"But when ye shall see the abomination of desolation, spoken of by Daniel the prophet, standing where it ought not, (let him that readeth understand,) then let them that be in Judaea flee to the mountains:"* (Mark 13:14b, KJV). Judaea was the southern kingdom of Judah. I see no one today selling their assets and moving to the mountains. I guess they will have to wait for the third temple to be built, which is never mentioned in all of scripture. Jesus foretold the destruction of the second temple, and it was for all time. Man just may build a third temple, but the Spirit of God shall never inhabit it. I believe that an attempt today to rebuild the temple for a third time will be an abomination to God. What need do we have for a temple? The body of the believer is the temple of the Holy Spirit today. For those who want to rebuild that temple, God just may leave their temple desolate.

I want to make mention of this here. The heresies of Irenaeus and Hippolytus link the abomination of desolation to the beast and antichrist, too. They actually state that the abomination of desolation is an individual that is Satan. Therefore, they are stating that antichrist, the beast, and the abomination of desolation are all one and the same individual, Satan. That is not at all what John taught. This teaching conflicts with what John taught. It also conflicts with John's timeframe. By the time these men were born, all of this was in the past, about fifty years for Irenaeus and a hundred years for Hippolytus. It is about one thousand, nine hundred, and forty-six years in our past. The church is waiting on God to rapture them out of this world, and God is waiting on man to bring about the healing of the nations. Will He have to wait forever?

The Ten Horns

> And there appeared another wonder in heaven; and
> behold a great red dragon, having seven heads and ten
> horns, and seven crowns upon his heads.
> (Revelation 12:3, KJV)

> And the ten horns which thou sawest are ten kings, which
> have received no kingdom as yet; but receive power as
> kings one hour with the beast. (Revelation 17:12, KJV)

I used to attribute these ten kings as the ten caesars that existed up until the destruction of AD 70. Vespasian was the tenth caesar. I was wrong. These ten kings are highly likely leaders of other provinces within the Roman Empire. The Roman Empire was made up of many more nations than just ten. We will never be able to truly state as fact who these ten kings were. I imagine that after much more study of the "ten horns" that I could probably list a few of the nations, or provinces of the Roman Empire, that this is in reference to. The issue is that the ten horns are in consolidation with the Roman Empire and that they come to hate the harlot that is Judaea, the Jews. There are those who probably attempt to negate what I have stated in this section, but I will take one last stab to solidify my stance on the characters of the "end times." We will use the best source that is available to interpret the scriptures. We will allow scripture to interpret scripture. Let's go back to the Old Testament and take a look at who Daniel defined the beast to be.

> After this I saw in the night visions, and behold a fourth
> beast, dreadful and terrible, and strong exceedingly; and
> it had great iron teeth: it devoured and brake in pieces,
> and stamped the residue with the feet of it: and it was
> diverse from all the beasts that were before it; and it had
> ten horns. (Daniel 7:7, KJV)

The only way that anyone in our day and age could interpret the meaning of this scripture is to have knowledge of the epoch of time between the latter days of the 600s BC up until 64 BC. That is an epoch of time that is a bit over twice as long as the United States has been a sovereign nation. The first beast would be the one who Judah was exiled to for seventy years. This would be the Babylonian Empire. The next to rise was the Medo-Persians. After them was the Alexandrian or Grecian Empire. All of these empires antagonized the children of Jacob, but none of these were as brutal as the last beast was, the Roman Empire, that conquered Judah in 63 BC. After the initial conquest, Judah settled into the empire and experienced great peace for many years from outside forces. After the skirmishes began after the death of Jesus between the Christians, the Judaizers, the Zealots, and so on, the beast that was the Roman Empire would wipe the temple and the city of Jerusalem off the face of the earth. This was the divorce decree that was akin to the one which God issued to the Northern Tribes when they were lost to the Assyrians.

"And of the ten horns that were in his head, and of the other which came up, and before whom three fell; even of that horn that had eyes, and a mouth that spake very great things, whose look was more stout than his fellows" (Daniel 7:20, KJV). In this verse, the word *head* is used as a symbolic figure for the Roman Empire. The ten horns are ten kings as is defined in the following verse:

"And the ten horns out of this kingdom are ten kings that shall arise: and another shall rise after them; and he shall be diverse from the first, and he shall subdue three kings" (Daniel 7:24, KJV). The ten horns are defined as ten kings, and the beast is defined as ruling over these ten kings. We now know that the final beast, the fourth beast as mentioned in Daniel, and the beast that John prophesies, is defined as the leaders of the Roman Empire, which ruled over the ten horns, which were kings within the Roman Empire. King Herod was king over Judah, yet Judah was within the Roman Empire. The beast was the forces of the Roman Empire, which consisted of many provinces and nations, under the rule of the caesars. That fulfills Jesus revelation to John that is documented in the book of Revelation. The beast is not the antichrist, as many teach and preach today on television, the radio, and pulpits across the globe. Knowledge and wisdom conquer the beast.

The 144,000

There is much confusion today as to whom this one hundred and forty-four thousand represents. It was no mystery to the first-century faithful. It was the first-century faithful. These are the ones who fled the cities of Israel and heeded Jesus' warnings. These were those whom were spared death because they were obedient. The language is symbolic. This in no way represents only males. This was symbolic language for all who had not played the whore to the pharisaical religious system and those who did not bow the knee to caesar. Remember, "We have no king but caesar." These are the ones who had no King but Jesus.

> And they sung as it were a new song before the throne, and before the four beasts, and the elders: and no man could learn that song but the hundred and forty and four thousand, which were redeemed from the earth. These are they which were not defiled with women; for they are virgins. These are they which follow the Lamb whithersoever he goeth. These were redeemed from among men, being the firstfruits unto God and to the Lamb.
>
> (Revelation 14:3–4, KJV)

These were the first generation, those who lived through the consummation of the Old Covenant. We also know that John was among this group. The language here is symbolic. They were not in heaven at the time, but they are now in their glorified bodies.

The false prophet mentioned in Revelation could be attached to several individuals. Of course, there were many false prophets at that time. The leader of the antichrist temple system at that time was certainly considered a false prophet by the Christians. The leader of the Zealots could also have been the false prophet. Eleazar ben Simon was the leader of the Zealots. John of Giscala was a man of reputation amongst the Jewish nation at that time, as was Simon bar Giora. Each of these men had a following; they had split the nation of Jews into factions. Obviously, the people chose whom they deemed to be a man of God to side with. This schism is attributed as the number one reason that Jerusalem and the temple fell. If the nation had been united at that time many believe that she likely could have withstood the forces of the Roman Empire. Men sided up with the side that was most convincing to them instead of the One that was Messiah. Therefore, they were destroyed by the beast of the Roman Empire. These men, as well as others, could have been the false prophet, but still there were many false prophets at that time. A deeper study into this could produce an individual. The main point is that the false prophet is past and not future.

We mentioned Gog and Magog elsewhere, but I do want to reiterate here that there are legends of Alexander the Great having dealings with these. Magog was a territory within modern-day Turkey. The Battle of Armageddon may not have even been a literal battle. It could have been symbolic of the whole timeframe of the destruction of the nation of Israel

FOR SUCH A TIME AS THIS: LET MY PEOPLE Go

that truly began with the burning of Rome in AD 64 and the beginning of the Roman persecution against the first-century Christians and the pagan system of Judaism that removed God and Messiah from their midst. The bottom line, however, is that it is all in our past. Not one jot or tittle was left unfulfilled. "This generation" experienced all the prophecy that Daniel, John, and Jesus had foretold. Jesus stated that *"This generation shall not pass until all these things be fulfilled."* That would be the generation of vipers that Jesus lived among and the very one who crucified Him. This is my standard. Now, if my standard is a lie, then what parts are truth and what parts are a lie? You either believe it or you reject it. I am a "jot and tittle" man. I believe my Lord and Savior. Either you do, or you do not. If you do not, then you are saying that He is a liar and a false prophet.

Is there any doubt now as to who the characters of the "end times" are? We may not know the identity of the ten kings, but we do know that they were likely kings or emperors within the Roman Empire. We know that the beast was the Roman Empire and that 666 was representative of Nero. Antichrist is just a spirit of denial that Jesus was Messiah, the very Son of God, and Deity. It was prevalent in the first century, and it is present in the twenty-first century. Mystery, Babylon the Great, Mother of Harlots is none other than the first-century Jews who denied that Jesus was their Messiah, but as caesar was the representative of the beast, Jerusalem was representative of the harlot. The abomination of desolation was not a person, but an act that was carried out by Galba when he ordered an image of Nero to be put in the Jewish temple. The seven heads were seven hills, which was just symbolic language for the City of Seven Hills, Rome. Using scripture to interpret scripture is key here, but also extra-biblical historical knowledge of the peoples and nations that comprised the Roman Empire is paramount. This is history, but it is also His story. Until man mandates this history into our education system, we shall continue to repeat history. Nations will rise, and nations will fall. People will rise, and people will fall. What direction are you heading? You can do an about-face any time before you take your last breath, but the sooner the better.

It has taken me eighteen years, from 1998 to 2016, to arrive at the point I am today with my beliefs. I will not go into all of that, but my point is the sooner you get onboard, the greater your experience shall be. We have to deal with life on this earth. We have to be humble and meek with others. We have hope for a better day, but until man understands His story, which is contained in history, we will continue to repeat ourselves. It is like a child getting shocked by putting a paper clip in an electrical socket and getting knocked to their face in unconsciousness and then getting up and repeating themselves for all eternity—expecting different results each time. Keep rejecting Jesus as Messiah, which is the Way, the Truth, and the Life, and you will keep falling into perdition. Pride, arrogance, and obstinacy, will keep many out of the Kingdom of God, which is not of this world nor ever shall be. Study His story and saturate your life with His ways, and you will be well on your way to Thy Kingdom Come. It came in AD 70. It is not of this world, nor shall it ever be. His Kingdom was not accessible until the key came, yet there was still a forty-year timeframe for the evil generation to repent before they experienced the wrath of God.

CONCLUSION

Conclusion

This has been quite the endeavor, probably for you, the reader, and certainly for me. It has taken me many years to evolve to the point of understanding that I have now of the scriptures. It has taken unfathomable hours of research and study of the scriptures and extra-biblical sources. As I stated elsewhere, just because it is not in the scriptures does not mean it is not fact. The founding of the United States is not scriptural, nor is the nation of China, Russia, Mexico, Canada, Brazil, Bolivia, and so on. None of our wars are documented in the scriptures, but you can be assured of their reality because of historical facts documented in the past. I believe that Flavius Josephus is as good a historian of that epoch of time as there is. He documented the facts of the timeframe of the latter days of the Old Covenant. He makes mention that the destruction of the temple and city of Jerusalem is the fulfilling of prophecy. He even stated that the Jews on the wall were shouting "The Son cometh. The Son cometh." Josephus was an eyewitness to this event. This was not hearsay. He saw it with his own two eyes and heard it with his own two ears. I will trust his view of what happened at that time above any modern-day commentators. He actually had a real-life view of the events. Much of what is out there today is just hearsay and heresy. Any views being propagated today are about two millennia away from the occurrence of the prophesied judgment on the southern kingdom of Judah. If you are attuned to the facts of the age, you will not fall for this garbage. I recommend the writings of Josephus. The one that I used for study and research is *The Works of Josephus Complete and Unabridged*. It is a 926-page hardcover book that has all of Josephus's writings that are relevant to the prophesied end times. *The Wars of the Jews* is within this book and is where I gleaned most of the historical events for that epoch of time.

A very important issue that man has with the scriptures today is that he thinks that it was written for us in the here and now. That is just a symptom of false teaching and the self-centeredness of man. The scriptures, and particularly the portions written by prophets, were written to the Jews and only the Jews. It was about their future and not our future. What man needs to glean from this is that if we live Godless lives and in ways that dishonor Him, then we can expect judgment on our culture. The judgment will not necessarily be the pouring out of God's wrath, but likely civil unrest and misery from dealing with those who do not believe as others believe. God's people are to be of one mind. God's people cannot even come together in the church because of different beliefs. Isaiah prophesied that God's people would be given a new name in the future. He did not say that God would have two peoples. The new name is Christian and not Jew. Until the church figures this out, there will not be peace in this world. Now, it is a two-way street. Others in the Middle East need to realize that there are no prophets since the destruction of the temple in AD 70. Prophecy has been sealed; therefore, there are no more prophets. The Jewish issue and the false prophet issue will have to be addressed before the healing of the nations can take place. I am doing my part in bringing it to the forefront. It may not be popular with those on either side, but it has to be addressed. It is time for men to man-up and admit that he was fooled with false teachings for generations now. It is time to reprogram our hearts and our minds before this world crashes. The thing about the crash, though, is it will not be the "end." The end has already been. Where are the peacemakers today?

One of the things that I stressed in this writing is the standard that man chooses. What is your standard? Is it the teachings of man or the word of God? I have heard radio preachers quote the writings of Hal Lindsey as if they are superior to scripture, when in fact they contradict the scriptures. I have also seen where the writings of Irenaeus and Hippolytus are documented as if what they wrote is scripture, yet they also contradict the facts of scripture and history. If man's teaching contradicts the word of God, then who is right? I believe by now that you know whom I will choose and what my source will be. Sadly, most people are not familiar enough with the word of God, and particularly not with extra-biblical sources that affirm fulfilled prophecy that took place within a generation of the death of Jesus. This is critical to the church today, but it appears that most men in the pulpit are not even aware of the historical events, prophesied events, that took place in AD 70. It also appears that the majority of the ones who are aware of the destruction of AD 70 do not realize that this was the fulfillment of the prophecies going back to what Moses prophesied concerning the final judgment on this culture of anti-Christ people. This judgment is in our past. Book it. Not one jot or tittle has been left unfulfilled.

Man has elevated the teachings of man as superior to the scriptures. All that we have today is the revelation from God that was handed down through His servants. The apostles lived in the last generation that was under the Old Covenant. It is obvious from the writings of John and Paul that the "end" was near. Jesus even told them that they would not have gone through the streets of Israel before He came back, which was His "coming on clouds." Paul stated that once the "end" had come and gone, then prophecy would be sealed. Man today has elevated the early church fathers' teachings as if they are par for the course with what Jesus and His apostles taught, when in fact they contradict the teachings of Messiah and His "elect." I shall continue my research and studying the teachings of others to see how they compare with what the actual Teacher taught. It appears that the motivating factor behind all of the false teaching that began just a generation or two after the apostles was likely fame, fortune, and prestige. I am still working on this one, but if Jesus stated that salvation would be free after the consummation of the Old Covenant, then why is it not free? I am neither a seminary student nor a paid preacher. I am under the tutelage of the Holy Spirit. The Spirit has revealed to me that the average individual has made the teachings of man their messiah. Now, some of this comes out of the church, but much comes out of the antichrist education system that denies that there is a God. Both are at odds with what Messiah taught. The destruction of the Jewish temple was the revelation of Jesus the Christ. It was proof positive that He was who He claimed to be. Do you not realize that the ones who were left of the Jews, after the AD 70 event, were wailing and experiencing the gnashing of teeth when His promises occurred?

As I have stated elsewhere, eschatology (end-times view) may not be an essential for salvation, but it sure enhances one's life. Actually, that is not my view. I do believe that it is essential if man is to accomplish what God has mandated, the healing of the nations. Otherwise, we are saying that Jesus and the prophets are false prophets because what they prophesied did not come to fruition within "this generation." Eyesight is not essential for life, nor or arms and legs or both feet. I see people on occasion that are blind, missing an arm or leg, or even lacking the use of both legs. Even the absence of a foot or hand hinders life. A wrong end-times view may be even more crippling. If two plus two is five to you, or one plus one is three to you, then you are considered a failure in math. If you said that World War I occurred in 1700, World War II occurred in 1800, the Korean

Conflict happened in 1860, and the Civil War occurred in 1602, you would be a failure at history. Why do some think that we can have a false view on biblical history and not be a failure? Is knowledge of God, Jesus, and His story not more relevant or important as other things in life? Maybe not to most, but to me it is paramount, and I believe that is the way our Lord and Savior would have it to be. He would not have the church to be ignorant. If this history was taught in the schools of all nations, the world would be a better place today and on its way to the healing of the nations. I will make this statement here because it is an observation that I have made. Only those with a false, or heretical, end-times view make the statement that your "eschatology (end-times view) is not an essential for salvation." I believe that Satan would have attempted to state likewise, except He has been crushed and destroyed. Such lies come out of a sense of superiority, when in fact inferiority is where such views come from. When knowledge increases, these heresies will be destroyed.

We have covered much territory between these covers. We have used the word of God, the Bible, as well as extra-biblical sources such as the works of Josephus, Wikipedia, and much that is in my memory from years of study. I have studied and read countless sources that I cannot even recall. One thing you should notice about the writings of Josephus is that he was a contemporary with the ones who walked the earth with Jesus. Jesus' apostles documented the Holy Spirit-inspired New Testament, which was really the latter days of the Old Covenant. This work has touched on the fact that the Resurrection was for the Old Covenant dwellers only, and not for those under the New Covenant, which is us in the here and now that began after the destruction of the temple and city of Jerusalem in AD 70. The first generation of New Covenant believers was the 144,000 in Revelation. There are no living involved in the great white throne judgment. They are absent because it was not for the living. The Marriage Supper of the Lamb was the Old Covenant believers being married into the New Covenant, which does away with death for the repentant believers. This was not for those who lived through the consummation or for us today. We are under the new and better covenant that allows entry into heaven upon death of the flesh for the repentant.

I hope that our look at symbolic language and numerical figures has been an eye-opener for you. We have shown that "thousand year" or "thousand years" is used to show completeness or fullness of time, as is "seven seventies." If Daniel meant to give a timeframe of 490 years, he would have just stated, "490 years." Seven is a number of completeness. Seventy is a number of immense completeness. Completeness times immense completeness gives you fullness of time. Perfection was born out of that which is new and superior to that which passed away in AD 70. There is no future millennial reign. It is in our past, and it was never intended that man would interpret it as a literal thousand-year binding of Satan and a thousand-year reign with Jesus on the throne. "Thousand" had a very symbolic meaning to that culture, as it also does to ours. I hope that most will comprehend this, but there are some that will not get it once in a thousand years.

We have people today that are literally awaiting a new heaven and earth. They believe that this will be the perfection that will go on into eternity. We have shown where this is just not the case using scriptures as our standard and not the teachings of man. We have revealed that the scripture even states that there are still sinners walking and talking in this new heaven and earth. The scripture uses dogs as symbolic for the sinner and states that such will never enter the holy city. Holy city is used here as symbolism for the Kingdom of God—heaven. When Jesus demonstrated to His apostles how to pray, He stated *"Our Father which art in heaven. Hallowed be thy name. Thy kingdom come."* Jesus would not have asked them to pray for something that they could not expect during their lifetimes. His kingdom has come. It is just not of this earth. If His kingdom has not come yet, then all that have ever died are still in the earth experiencing "soul sleep." His kingdom has always been there, but it was not accessible until the key to the gate came: Messiah, Jesus the Christ.

Due to the lapse in time from the consummation of the Old Covenant to today, which is fast approaching two millennia, we will likely never figure out all the "who's, what's, and where's," but we looked at a portion that revealed many of the end-times characters. We know that "666" is Nero who was representative of the Roman Empire. The Roman Empire was actually the beast, but caesars were representative of the Empire. Daniel speaks of four beasts that we attributed to the Babylonians, the Medo-Persians, the Alexandrian Empire, and the most fearsome and ferocious fourth beast, the Roman Empire. Mystery Babylon, Mother of Harlots is no longer a mystery. This entity is none other than apostate Israel, the southern kingdom of Judah. If it was meant to be a mystery and is current-day Iraq, I do not believe that John would have put the answer in the moniker. Actually, it was no mystery to the ones who received John's Revelation, the seven churches in Asia Minor. They knew that it was the Jews.

The antichrist is a character that gets too much attention today. We can thank the heretical teachings of Irenaeus and Hippolytus for this mockery of the prophecies of John. If a man professed today that Jesus was fifty-something years old when He was crucified, I believe that man would either be voted out of the pulpit of that church or many would abandon that church because of the ignorance of one who would state obvious mistruths about Jesus. Yet, that is exactly what Irenaeus claims.

I hear of people today speaking of a new world order and a single one-world currency. I am sorry. As long as there are greedy men in control of the financial markets, there will be no one-world currency. Currencies are being manipulated for the benefit of the wicked and greedy. There are fortunes made on currency exchange deals every year at the demise of the nation's people of the chosen manipulated currency. It is of no advantage of the powers that be to attempt to create a one-world currency. This system has perpetuated the loss of jobs in America. There is also no mention of a one-world currency in the scriptures. There is no one-world government. This was not about the world. It was about the Roman Empire, and particularly the apostate nation of Israel. There is also no mention of antichrist being an individual that walks, talks, and breathes. John explains that antichrist is a spirit of denial that is among the apostate nation of Jews during his lifetime. He even states that the "antichrists" are the ones who departed the first-century church when the persecution heated up. There were many and not one. We have antichrists today. They abound. It was not a person but a state of denial that Jesus was Messiah. Can you think of anyone who fits this description today? There are gazillions out there. Ooops! I hope no one reads this a thousand years from now and believes that there was a gazillion people in this earth a thousand years in their past. It could cause a panic attack. They will be pondering and wondering what in the world happened with all of those people.

We have shown that there are those who have escalated the teachings of Irenaeus and Hippolytus above the scriptures that were written by the apostles and particularly the teachings of John. The teachings of these men conflict with what John taught, yet men have raised them to the status of "early church fathers." There is no consensus on this, though. There are also many that call them heretics. These are the ones who see the truth that what they taught does not align with what the apostles taught. Paul gives a great description of such as these in his day that would still apply to many today in the following statement:

> And I will keep on doing what I am doing in order to cut
> the ground from under those who want an opportunity

to be considered equal with us in the things they boast about. For such people are false apostles, deceitful workers, masquerading as apostles of Christ.

(2 Corinthians 11:12–13, NIV)

Beware of any that have a teaching that contradicts or conflicts with the teachings of the apostles. Flee from such. Jesus is the Church Father, and Paul, Peter, John, James, Stephen, and others are the "early church fathers," not someone who came along a generation-plus after the apostles. Scripture says that anyone who teaches anything that contradicts anything that they taught is a false, deceitful, masquerading liar.

I have demonstrated that the world was not the focus on the end-times timeframe, but the Roman Empire and particularly the part comprised of the descendants of Abraham. The term oikoumenē is the term used by the original transcripts, which means a localized area and not the world. *Kosmos* is world and not oikoumenē, yet the King James, as well as other versions, give a false interpretation. This was not about the destruction of the world but of the consummation of the Old Covenant with Israel and the destruction of the temple and city of Jerusalem. The mistranslation of this term and of *kosmos* has been very detrimental to the true understanding of the scriptures since the King James Bible hit the world. I am sorry, but all of the King James-only advocates should do a 180 on this issue. Truth is truth. I have revealed truth through very simple means of getting the proper definition of the original language of the scriptures. It does not matter what the King James says. What matters is what the original manuscript stated that the King James was translated from. The King James is not the only version that gets it wrong, but concerning "end of the age" and "end of the world," the King James Version gets it wrong 100 percent of the time. There are no versions that are perfect, but the ESV and NASB are as good as any. All scripture is inspired of God, but all the translators were not. There are no prophets today, but there are those seeking profit.

The seven heads mentioned in Revelation are seven mountains, as revealed by John. We know that the City of Seven Hills is a moniker for the city of Rome. The seven kings were the caesars. The "and one is" was none other than Nero, the beast of Revelation, which fit the *gematria* numerical code of 666. The ten horns we know to be representatives of those allied with the Roman soldiers that destroyed the city of Jerusalem and the temple. It was likely nations within the Roman Empire, but there could have been some that were outside allies of Rome involved in this battle, too. The abomination of desolation that Jesus and Daniel

333

prophesied was the image of Nero that was put in the temple of the Jews by Galba after Nero committed suicide in AD 68.

Jesus stated, along with the apostles, that the events they prophesied would take place shortly. It was near, at hand. Jesus even stated that "not one jot or tittle" would be left unfulfilled. Peter states to his audience that the events the prophets spoke of were for their generation, that they were living in the days that were foretold. "This generation" was the one who would experience the wrath of God, the Day of the Lord, and the consummation of the Old Covenant. This was an elect generation. This was the very elect of God. I hope that this has opened the eyes of those who believe in predestination, or the elect. Jesus died once for all, not once for some. If predestination were a fact, then all missionaries should pack it in and come back home. It is all for naught. If man is predestined, then sharing your faith is useless. This is another schizophrenic symptom of false teaching. If you are predestined to be in, then you are in with no need for a witness. I thank God that I was not of that elect generation. It was truly hell on earth, the likes of which the Jews had never experienced before. Jesus as Messiah is a fact. Whether you choose Him as your Savior or not is a choice. He stands at the door and knocks. If He is coming in anyway, why would He need to knock? Knock-knock!

Prophecy has been sealed, along with visions. Paul and Daniel state this in the scriptures. When the end of the old covenant took place, prophecy ended. When that which is perfect came, prophecy was done away with.

> Charity never faileth: but whether there be prophecies, they shall fail; whether there be tongues, they shall cease; whether there be knowledge, it shall vanish away. For we know in part, and we prophesy in part. But when that which is perfect is come, then that which is in part shall be done away. (1 Corinthians 13:8–10, KJV)

> Seventy weeks have been decreed for your people and your holy city, to finish the transgression, to make an end of sin, to make atonement for iniquity, to bring in everlasting righteousness, to seal up vision and prophecy and to anoint the most holy place. (Daniel 9:24, NASB)

Paul and Daniel are both speaking of the same event here, the consummation of the Old Covenant. We know that all prophets from that time until today all have one thing in common. They always fail, yet the sheep continue to finance them. Flee from such as these before you are deceived beyond repair. That which is perfect has come, the New Covenant, which allows all nations of people's access to the throne upon repentance. Tongues have ceased. Again, if you think that this was about the end of the world, then you shall be deceived. It was not about the end of the world, but about the end of the Old Covenant. That is not my opinion. That is the fact of the scriptures. Ignorance of the law is no excuse in the courts of the world, nor shall it be before the throne of God.

Based on the word of God, there have been no prophets since AD 70. John the Revelator was among the last prophets. After the consummation of the Old Covenant, none ever had a prophetic word from God since. I am not saying that God does not speak to His children today. I am agreeing with the scriptures that any that profess to be prophets since AD 70 are liars and dogs. Actually, I believe that a dog would be in higher standing with God than one such as this. John was the only apostle to pass from the Old Covenant era to the New Covenant era. He never experienced what all the other apostles experienced: "soul sleep" or death. His flesh died, but his soul did not sleep. All that have prophesied since that time are false prophets. This eliminates Mormonism, Jehovah's Witnesses, and the Muslim religion. It also weakens certain sects within the Christian church. Prophecy was not all that ceased. Tongues also ceased, so says Paul. My standard is the word of God, and no man that states other than what the scriptures state is a standard that any professing Christian should be paying homage to. Hate me if you must, but the scriptures are my standard and not babbling tongues.

I made mention of the leaves on the tree of life many times throughout this study. The leaves on the Tree of Life are for the healing of the nations. I have checked commentaries to see what others' opinions are on this verse. I have shown where there is much symbolism in the scriptures. I read one commentary that literally states that this Tree of Life is in the heavenly paradise and is literally used to nourish the bodies of the saints in the afterlife. That is not at all what this verse states. This is another instance where symbolism is used. The leaves on the Tree of Life are the Christians. There will be no division by nation in heaven. Unity will be just one of the reasons that it will be a paradise. There will be no need for healing in heaven. It is perfection. It may be a hundred times the size of earth, or even larger. I have not been there yet, nor has anyone else that has claimed to have been there. No man shall ever enter heaven and then come back into this life. It is unbiblical heresy. This scripture is totally symbolic. Our Father who is in heaven and the repentant dead are in heaven, along with Jesus. We, the leaves on the Tree of Life, have access to the throne of our Father in the here and now. If we had the love in our hearts that He intended, then the healing of the nations would have been a reality by now. As I have stated elsewhere, in this new heaven and earth that we live in today, there is neither Jew nor Greek (Gentile). This is scripture and not my opinion. It was also not just Paul's opinion. He stated it as fact. Now, if the greatest of apostles is wrong on this issue, then we may as well just set fire to our Bibles and have a weenie roast. No, this is not about just being in heaven.

We have access to heaven today upon death. The Father abides with us in the here and now. Our bodies are the temple of the Holy Spirit. We, the leaves on the Tree of Life, are for the healing of the nations. This is for the here and now. The writer of Hebrews states the following, which relegates to man the role of peacemaker and overseer of this world: *"For unto the angels hath he not put in subjection the world to come, whereof we speak"* (Hebrews 2:5, KJV). God expects man to bring about the healing of the nations, not the angels. This world is in subjection to man, not angels, so says God's word. Racism and bigotry will not be allowed into heaven. He sent His Son to die for our sins and to give the repentant believer ever-lasting life. He cut life off on this earth due to sin. Racism and bigotry are not material. God does not cast adultery, fornication, thievery, lies, and so forth into sheol. What is cast into eternal perdition is the perpetrator, not the sin. Those who foster racism and division in this world shall never enter the Pearly Gates. Now, I am not talking about only racism in America, yet it is a reality. It is also a two-way street. I am talking about nationalism and racial division in the worldly sense. Actually, there is only one race of man, the human race. God gave the differences in appearance. What God has put asunder, let no man put back together. Ooops! We are too late for this one. It will have to be dealt with in a proper fashion as God would deal with it. What we all need to do is to be sons of God in word and deed. This will require diligence and responsible individuals. God created man in His image. No, we cannot create something out of nothing, and no, man did not have access to heaven before the Key arrived. This scripture is in the last book and chapter of the Bible:

> In the midst of the street of it, and on either side of the river, was there the tree of life, which bare twelve manner of fruits, and yielded her fruit every month: and the leaves of the tree were for the healing of the nations.
> (Revelation 22:2, KJV)

Finally, be strong in the Lord and in the strength of His might. Put on the full armor of God, so that you will be able to stand firm against the schemes of the devil. For our struggle is not against flesh and blood, but against the rulers, against the powers, against the world forces of this darkness, against the spiritual forces of wickedness in the heavenly places. Therefore, take up the full armor of God, so that you will be able to resist in the evil day, and having done everything, to stand firm. Stand firm therefore, HAVING GIRDED YOUR LOINS WITH TRUTH, and HAVING PUT ON THE BREASTPLATE OF RIGHTEOUSNESS, and having shod YOUR FEET WITH THE PREPARATION OF THE GOSPEL OF PEACE; in addition to all, taking up the shield of faith with which you will be able to extinguish all the flaming arrows of the evil one. And take THE HELMET OF SALVATION, and the sword of the Spirit, which is the word of God. (Ephesians 6:10–17, KJV)

Anyone who believes that the prophets spoke about the end of the world and not the end of the Old Testament Covenant era shall misinterpret the scriptures in every way. This river is the fountain of life flowing from the throne of God. Man has access in the here and now, on Planet Earth, to His throne. This is the H_2O that Jesus offered the woman at the well. Eternal life is just part of what it brings. It was also meant to bring discernment and a passion for His creation. We are to have compassion toward others. We are not to favor people groups based on ethnicity. Abraham was from current-day Iraq. Are we to despise his ancestors forevermore? We, the leaves on the Tree of Life, are to bring unity through the healing of nations. This is also a two-way street. It takes a strong man to admit that he has been deceived by false teachings. The obstinate, the small-minded, will likely never admit that he was deceived. Well, I was deceived from my childhood, but after a time of fleeing from God and then repenting, the Holy Spirit placed a fire in my heart for His word. After many years of study and research, it appears that I was misled by false teachers in my childhood. Trinity Broadcasting Network also fostered such falsehood in my early years as an adult babe in Christ. I have manned up, and I confess that I was misled and wrong. What I have put before you is far more truthful than what the average person has been fed. I may need to tweak my understanding on certain characters of the end-times, but the main thing is that it is in the past. Our future, the future of this world, is not documented anywhere. Do you want it to be about peace and compassion or about racism and division? The choice is man's to make. The choice we make on this issue will reveal what is truly in our hearts. It is not what is on the outside that will determine our eternal destination. God judges the heart, what can't be seen by man. Your fruit will bare you out. Again, this is a two-way street. This is for the lost and the saint.

God is still tweaking my life. I am evolving as a Christian. My views on some things may be enhanced as I study the word of God and research extra-biblical sources of history. Paul stated that knowledge would decrease after the consummation. Certainly that has happened, but I do not believe that he thought there would be total ignorance of the event. I may discover who the ten kings were in the end-times, but most of the characters are a surety. One thing that shall not ever change, though, is the fact that the prophecies, all of them, have been fulfilled. Not one jot or tittle has been left unfulfilled. The issue now is that the believer is not fulfilling his role as a healer of the nations. Quit living in the past and let the healing begin.

Paul was speaking to the Ephesians about how to handle the end that faced that generation. We know from scripture that Satan was crushed at the end spoken of in the Bible. It is past, not future. The Gospel message is a message of peace and not racism and bigotry. Until all come to the realization that God does not favor peoples or nations, there will not be peace on this earth. "Blessed are the peacemakers" is a statement made by Messiah, Jesus the Christ. Because God is not a God of double standards, we can read into this the following: Cursed are the war-mongers. Those who are preaching a gospel of hate and division shall never harken the Pearly Gates of heaven. There is right and wrong in the world. You do not have a "wrong" that is my "right" and I do not have a "right" that is your "wrong." If man chooses the ways of man as his standard, he will quickly learn that man's ways are schizophrenic. What man means is that "my ways" are superior to "your ways," unless both believe the same way. Well, there is only one Way. He is the Way, the Truth, and the Light. Only His way leads to everlasting life in His kingdom, which is in heaven. To know His way, man must eat His word. Are you hungry yet?

It has been about one thousand, nine hundred, and fifty years since Paul penned Ephesians. Most of the churches today are preaching racism and bigotry, whether they realize it or not. Zionism is racism and bigotry. If you hate the people of Iraq today, do you realize that you hate the people group that Abraham came from? Still, this is a two way street. Do they realize that they hate the ones who profess the prophesied One, Jesus, as Messiah? The sign of the divorce decree to the southern kingdom of Judah was when the city of Jerusalem was defeated by the forces of the beast, the Roman Empire, and the walls of the temple fell and not a stone was left unturned. Doom and gloom is in our past. We need to be about the mandate given in Revelation, bringing about the healing of the nations. Paul states in his letter to the Ephesians the following: *"and having shod your feet with the preparation of the gospel of peace."* Is it a gospel of peace? It surely was meant to be. Those who profess otherwise shall have a sheol of a price to pay at the end (the end of their life). If you are attending a church that teaches racism and bigotry, *leave*. If you do not leave such, then you are not a leaf on the Tree of Life. The leaves will leave.

I know for a fact that there is at least one black preacher in my hometown who has preached hatred against the whites. A black woman who was attending that church told a relative of mine about it. She stated that she could not go back to that church. Obviously, she is a leaf on the Tree of Life. There is racism in the white churches, too. Racism is a two-way street, whether you are in the majority or in the minority. In God's eyes both are in the "lostority."

One thing that I hope all have observed within this compilation is the fact that the views stated within these pages are biblically correct and are scripturally accurate. In no way has the scripture been bowed, warped, or twisted to mean something that it absolutely does not state. "This generation" was the generation that walked the earth with Messiah. It was not the generation that was to see the nation of Israel become a reality again in 1948. False teachers were responsible for this abomination to God Almighty.

Doom and gloom are big sellers. Drama, drama, drama, draws the sheep to the slaughter. Facts do not tickle the ears. Well, I am not here to tickle your ears. I hope that your heart has been tickled, for what you have read here is truth. Other views that do not stack up with the facts of biblical prophecy and extra-biblical facts must twist the scriptures beyond this world to come up with their heretical views. A doom-and-gloom view is not the view that God painted for all ages. This was for the antichrist Jews who rejected their Messiah. Is it heretical to think that God and Jesus desire the healing of the nations? He has not left this to the angels. He has left this responsibility to the leaves on the Tree of Life. The believer has fallen away from the Tree. We need to spring into action, if you catch my drift. The "fall" has been. Spring is coming!

I recently saw where a missionary posted on social media that "Your theology is not important . . ." Well, theology is the study of the nature of God and religious truth. Based on that statement, then the study of God's word is irrelevant. One who would make such a statement must believe that the Bible is not worthy of study. I know this is not what he meant, but that is what he stated. What he meant to state was that one's eschatology is not essential to salvation. Well, I take issue with such. If you are ignorant of a subject in grade school, high school, or college, you receive a failing grade in that class. I suppose you just may be allowed into heaven with the status as a failure, but you will get in only by the hairs of your chinny-chin- chin. Eternity is a mighty long time to be considered "least in the kingdom of heaven." The "end" is in our past. It is up to man to make the future brighter. A true understanding of God and His ways is the only way that this shall come to reality. Do we want it sooner, or later? Eventually a generation will man up, wise up, and get it right. It is time to start the healing of the nations.

Denomination has separated the church. This schism has weakened the church greatly. When Isaiah prophesied that the people of God would be given a new name, he did not consider the following as the name he had in mind: Baptist, Methodist, Presbyterian, Lutheran, Pentecostal, Protestant, Catholic, Muslim, Hindu, Buddhist, Atheist, and so forth. His people are the Christians. There will be many Baptists, Methodists, Pentecostals, Catholics, Hindus, Atheists, and Muslims banished to perdition, to hades. There will not be a single Christian there. That is a surety.

I revealed within this book the fact that Elijah, nor Enoch, had gone to Heaven prior to 70 AD. Elijah wrote a letter to a king that was years away from becoming king when Elijah had his fiery chariot experience. The letter was hand delivered to the king. Obviously, Elijah was still on planet earth. God had likely sent him to the mountains so he could have peace. Many that are not familiar with all of scripture believe that Enoch went to heaven. Hebrews 11:5 states the following: *"By faith Enoch was translated that he should not see death; and was not found, because God had translated him: for before his translation he had this testimony, that he pleased God"* (KJV). The NLT is the only version that states that Enoch was taken to heaven. The NIV gives the best translation: *"By faith Enoch was taken from this life, so that he did not experience death: "He could not be found, because God had taken him away." For before he was taken, he was commended as one who pleased God"* (NIV). Sermons have been preached on this using the Genesis 5:24 scripture along with the Hebrews scripture to declare that man had gone to heaven prior to the consummation. They fail to add the following scripture, which shows otherwise: *"These all died in faith, not having received the promises, but having seen them afar off, and were persuaded of them, and embraced them, and confessed that they were strangers and pilgrims on the earth"* (Hebrews 11:13, KJV). Based on this scripture it becomes obvious that Enoch was translated from life to death without having to experience the agony of death. He was not translated to heaven, as per Jesus statement in the following: *"No one has ascended into heaven except the One who descended from heaven — the Son of Man"* (John 3:13, HCSB). No man had ever gone to Heaven when Jesus made this statement. So, man has had a false understanding of this scripture because he fails to look at all the scriptures concerning the matter at hand. If man misses such as this, what else has man missed? If one missed this, then could he also have a false view on much meatier issues? This alone should be a revelation to many that they do not know as much as they claim to know. This is a minor issue compared to the "end" that the scriptures prophecy. I hope this writing will be a revelation to many that their eschatology(end-times view) needs adjusting. The "end" ain't near!

As a young child, I was deprived of peaceful night rest due to false end-times theology. False teachings have consequences, as I can attest to. Many parents today are subjecting their children to heretical teachings that are not scripturally sound nor historically correct. The experience I had as a child left me with insomnia that lasted fourteen to sixteen years. I believe that everything happens in a life for benefit. Hopefully, many will choose to do a 180 on their end-times views because they have been exposed to truth. Many people seem to thrive on drama and are drawn to it. Well, the drama was over in AD 70. What is happening today is to the demise of future generations. Those who perpetuate such heresies shall have a sheol of a price to pay one day. I am not sovereign, nor am I a prophet. There are no prophets today. The price to be paid shall either be eternal condemnation to perdition or to be considered least in the kingdom of God forevermore. Open your eyes my people. I have come along for such a time as this. Let my people go, you end-times doomsday sayers—*and let the healing begin.* The end is nowhere in sight!

Recommended Reading Material

The Apocalypse Code by Hank Hanegraaff

Last Days Madness: Obsession of the Modern Church by Gary DeMar

The Last Days According to Jesus by R. C. Sproul

Matthew 24 Fulfilled by John L. Bray

Three Views on the Millennium and Beyond by Craig A. Blaising, Kenneth L. Gentry, and Robert B. Strimple

Identifying the Real Last Days Scoffers by Gary DeMar

The Parousia by J. Stuart Russell

Christian Hope through Fulfilled Prophecy by Charles S. Meek

The Works of Josephus: Updated Edition, Complete and Unabridged Edited by William Whiston

Eusebius' Ecclesiastical History by Eusebius Translated by C.F. Cruse

The Case for Christ by Lee Strobel

The Case for a Creator by Lee Strobel

These are just a few books that I have read over the years that have helped to open the eyes of my heart. However, if the words of man contradict the word of God, we need to trash the words of that man. The key with reading this material is that it reveals that there are other, more biblical views available that most people in the pulpits are not even aware of. If a view does not align with what the scriptures state, then it is coming from the likes of what Jesus warned His apostles and contemporary first-century audience to avoid. Is it out of evil or out of ignorance? I believe that the majority of it is out of ignorance, but certainly some of it is out of evil motivations. I cannot judge the heart. Only God can do that. Even if it is out of ignorance, that is no excuse to God. I have done my own biblical studies for this book. Reading these books will begin an evolutionary process in your thinking if you have been steeped in the current end-times doomsday madness theology that is being taught in many churches today, if not the majority, and even in the seminaries. *The Works of Josephus* is a long read, but it really helps one to understand what that elect generation, the very elect of God, had to go through in order to establish the first-century church that is still going today. Most of the books listed here demonstrate a partial preterist's view. I am a jot and tittle man. I advise you to do your own studies. The Blue Letter Bible is a great online study tool that will allow you to do word searches, as well as comparing the many different versions of the Bible. As I have stated, no version is perfect. All versions of the Bible are translations that have been done by men. The scripture is infallible. The men that interpreted and translated them are not. The King James Version is as far from perfect as any version when it comes to the end-times prophecies in the New Testament. From personal experience, the ESV and the NASB are as good as any, but still far from perfect. The end of the age is not the end of the world. The destruction of Jerusalem is also not the destruction of the world. This is critical to any logical thinking person. I pray that this has been made obvious throughout this book. If you are a leaf on the Tree of Life, then the healing of the nations should be your priority. If you have a false end-times view, then you have a false view of this scripture. Who is the Tree of Life? The original scriptural language did not have capital letters or lowercase letters. They were all the same case. Without Jesus, you have no access to heaven. He is the Tree of Life, and the believers are the leaves. We have a mighty task before us. God is not a racist. There will be no racist in heaven. I hope to see you there.

CPSIA information can be obtained
at www.ICGtesting.com
Printed in the USA
FSHW010219060219
55484FS

9 781545 610442